The ISLE Reader

The ISLE Reader

ECOCRITICISM, 1993–2003

Edited by Michael P. Branch and Scott Slovic

The University of Georgia Press   *Athens & London*

© 2003 by the University of Georgia Press
Athens, Georgia 30602
All rights reserved

Set in Palatino by Bookcomp
Printed and bound by Maple-Vail
The paper in this book meets the guidelines for permanence and
durability of the Committee on Production Guidelines for Book Longevity
of the Council on Library Resources.

Printed in the United States of America
07 06 05 04 03 C 5 4 3 2 1
07 06 05 04 03 P 5 4 3 2 1

Library of Congress Cataloging-in-Publication Data

The ISLE reader : ecocriticism, 1993–2003 / edited by Michael P. Branch and Scott Slovic.
p. cm.
Includes bibliographical references and index.
ISBN 0-8203-2516-3 (hardcover : alk. paper) — ISBN 0-8203-2517-1
(pbk. : alk. paper)
1. Ecocriticism.   I. Title: Ecocriticism, 1993–2003.   II. Title: Interdisciplinary Studies in
Literature and the Environment reader.   III. Branch, Michael P.   IV. Slovic, Scott, 1960–
PN98.E36 I85 2003
809'.93355—dc21   2002156531

British Library Cataloging-in-Publication Data available

Contents

Part 2: Reaching Out to Other Disciplines

Part 3: New Theoretical and Practical Paradigms

Foreword

TEN YEARS GONE in the blink of an eye, but the first years were like running dunes in a high head wind. When Scott and Mike contacted me I could hardly believe we were approaching the ten-year anniversary of *ISLE: Interdisciplinary Studies in Literature and Environment*. Sometimes that beginning seems so recent and vivid; after all, I don't feel more like fifty than forty—well, not most days—although I may look it. At other times, however, the beginnings of *ISLE* seem so distant from the state of ecocritical scholarship today. I have to remind myself that part of that distance has come about precisely as the result of the founding of *ISLE*, the providing of a scholarly forum for a new kind of literary and rhetorical study that was still struggling for academic recognition and public acceptance of its critical validity.

I remember my own excitement when I received an issue of *The American Nature Writing Newsletter* because somebody somewhere had recognized the importance of a way of writing about literature into which I had been stumbling since writing my M.A. thesis on Wendell Berry and Gary Snyder. But even in the flush of excitement at this sense of recognition, I also felt some disappointment. "Too narrow," I thought. After all, I was interested in these two writers mainly as poets, not essayists, not "nonfiction" writers, and the term "nature writing" seemed insufficient to me; not inadequate but more like those math problems we studied in high school where the answer about the data would come up "necessary but insufficient to answer the problem." When getting *ISLE* up and running, I hoped that most of the readers would be able to feel a similar initial flush of excitement without any sense of insufficiency, without any sense that their emphasis had been omitted or underrated. The current range of articles in this anniversary volume attests to the success of *ISLE* in encouraging that extensiveness and inclusiveness.

ISLE has helped ecocritics in this country demonstrate the validity and value of their critical activities, which have been recognized in an amazing range of already established academic and not-so-academic journals and magazines, a wide venue of conferences, and a significant number of presses eager to publish ecocritical scholarship and, alongside it, an increasing array of nature-oriented literature. *ISLE* and the Association for the Study of Literature and Environment (ASLE) have taken that effort at range and diversity literally to the far corners of the world, even including Antarctica through time spent there by several ASLE members. And this international dimension of the growth of ecocriticism strikes me as the second great achievement of these past ten years. From the beginning I wanted to include essays by writers and about works from beyond American shores. I had limited success in my few years as editor, so I have been gratified to see that not only has Scott continued to pursue this objective, but he has done so with far greater success than I had. The pages of *ISLE*, however, rightfully do not represent the true international development of ecocriticism because journals and other ASLE affiliates have sprung up in several other countries and are producing their own journals, anthologies, and conferences. At the same time, other ecocritics, whose numbers do not yet provide a critical mass for establishing an ASLE or its equivalent, educate and inform their colleagues through presentations and publications in non-ecocritical venues. These critics beyond our borders have an important role to play in continuously encouraging American critics to question our own assumptions and to review what we might take as a universality that is really a particularity of one national literature, one national perspective.

Getting the journal started was not an easy enterprise. Four years passed, I think, from when I first convened a meeting in California to talk about the concept of this journal to when the first issue appeared. Funding from Indiana University of Pennsylvania, my previous employer, resulted from a combination of coincidence and cunning, but unfortunately reflected a lack of vision on the part of administrators there. But vision did show when Cheryll Glotfelty arranged a meeting with Ann Ronald to secure support from the University of Nevada, Reno, to fund a journal whose first issue had not appeared and which would be housed at another academic institution. Another vision sustained me through the initial two years or so it took to get out the first issue, the vision of the first 275 subscribers who paid out their money on the promise, and only the promise, that *ISLE* would appear. *ISLE* continues today to reflect the vision of ecocritics around the world, a vision that includes but extends far beyond literary and linguistic analyses, and to spur that vision forward in additional fruitful directions.

While basking in the elation of success and the joy of celebration of the achievement of a decade of *ISLE* publication, I must remind myself that we remain very much at the beginning. Not being a fad, but a fundamental orientation toward the world and the literature produced by beings in that world, ecocriticism has to be perceived and practiced as a sustainable and rejuvenative method of criticism that always includes recognition that many questions remain unasked, much less unanswered, and that the answers given so far, such as those in the articles contained in this book, must remain in our own minds provisional and open to correction. Part of an ongoing dialogue, which many of us believe must contribute to different ways of living in the world, ecocriticism requires humility on the part of its practitioners. With this volume, I must remind myself that "we realize we know only a little," as the Alcoholics Anonymous "A Vision for You" states so clearly; at the same time, thanks to Scott and Mike, I can celebrate, consolidate, and share what we do know.

Patrick D. Murphy
ISLE Founding Editor
University of Central Florida

Acknowledgments

At the University of Georgia Press we want to thank former executive editor Barbara Ras, a friend and colleague who has long encouraged and supported the work of scholars in our field. And we appreciate the good work of the Press's Emily Montjoy, who came on board to see this project through to completion. Deep thanks go to Patrick Barron, from the University of Nevada, Reno's Graduate Program in Literature and Environment, for substantial assistance in preparing this volume for press. For additional help with manuscript preparation, thanks also to Crystal Koch and Kate Hoagland. And for carefully proofreading the full manuscript, we extend our gratitude to Madison Furrh.

For their continued financial support of the journal *ISLE*, we wish to thank the Association for the Study of Literature and Environment (ASLE) and the University of Nevada, Reno. And for their patient work in evaluating and commenting on the hundreds of manuscripts we receive each year, thanks to all the members of the *ISLE* Editorial Board. We all owe a debt of gratitude to Patrick Murphy, Cheryll Glotfelty, and editorial assistant Michelle Campbell Toohey for their labors in bringing *ISLE* into existence and shepherding the journal through its early issues. And thanks also to Cam Sutherland, Margaret Dalrymple, Carrie House, and the other University of Nevada Press staff who helped to get *ISLE* on its feet during the mid-1990s.

The production of *ISLE* here at the University of Nevada, Reno has been a community effort that has, over the years, depended upon the talent, goodwill, and generous volunteerism of many people. Nearly every faculty member and student in the UNR Graduate Program in Literature and Environment has contributed to this effort in some way—perhaps by offering to do photocopying, filing, proofing, or by attending the biannual "mailing party" that allows us to get the journal to its readers at minimum cost. We wish to take a moment to thank all of these people, among whom we want especially to acknowledge the following: Patrick Barron, Mike Colpo, Janean Curnutt, Jennifer Dawes, Peggy Drake, Elaine Egbert, Todd Fisher,

Ayano Ginoza, Ed Gray, Kerry Grimm, Jimmy Guignard, Lilace Guignard, Tom Hillard, Richard Hunt, Matt Kaplan, Crystal Koch, Janet Kolsky, Tere Linde, Jennifer Love, Brad Lucas, Susan Lucas, Laura Mack, Massey Mayo, Barney Nelson, Lynette Padilla, Amy Patrick, Anna Marie Randolph, Chris Robertson, Colin Robertson, Terre Ryan, Tracy Sangster, Michelle Satterlee, Susan Sink, Amy Staniforth, Bill Stobb, Chris Wolak, Gioia Woods, Shin Yamashiro, and Masami Yuki. Special thanks to George Hart for serving as guest editor of *ISLE* while Scott Slovic was on sabbatical during 2001–02.

Finally, thanks to all our ASLE friends and colleagues around the country and around the world. We feel fortunate that this work has brought us together. As a gesture of appreciation, we dedicate this volume to our ASLE compatriots, and we will contribute all royalties from its sale directly to *ISLE*.

MICHAEL P. BRANCH AND SCOTT SLOVIC

Introduction

Surveying the Emergence of Ecocriticism

THE WEEK we drafted this introduction, Scott Slovic received an e-mail out of the blue from the other side of the planet, from Brazil. At the time Scott was in Australia, familiarizing himself with the lively contemporary work of Australian environmental artists and scholars, when he received the message from a Brazilian student asking for assistance with an ecocritical graduate thesis on Walt Whitman's *Leaves of Grass*. The same week Mike Branch sat in the Nevada desert and opened a letter from a Swedish graduate student asking for advice regarding ongoing scholarship on Henry Thoreau's attitudes toward nineteenth-century technology. "Which aspects are very important and should I point out in order to read *Leaves of Grass* from a 'green' perspective?" asked Maria in her e-mail. "I thought to be so bold as to send you copies of my Thoreau texts, being interested to hear your reactions," wrote Henrik in his letter. These are not unusual experiences for us, and for many of our colleagues—one week the message comes from Brazil or Sweden, the next week from Taiwan, Poland, Germany, or Estonia, from China, Turkey, Finland, or India. And though the questions come from different parts of the world, they tend to be quite similar: What exactly is an ecocritical approach? Which texts should I read to support my own green reading? How does ecocriticism interact with other disciplines and with other modes of literary criticism? What are some of the new directions in ecocriticism?

Often these sorts of queries—sent by plane and ship, or directed into the stars and then back to Earth via satellite—are sent to us because of the journal *ISLE: Interdisciplinary Studies in Literature and Environment*. When Patrick D. Murphy and Cheryll [Burgess] Glotfelty began working together in the early 1990s to develop a journal devoted to scholarship and teaching in the field of environmental literature, they were working out of a sense of fascination with this writing and a devotion to both the physical world and human culture. But in those early days of this discipline, a mere decade ago, few had any idea how vast this scholarly movement might be-come. If there were graduate students in Brazil and Sweden—or in Taiwan, Poland, Germany, Estonia, China, Turkey, Finland, and India—pondering the ecocritical nuances of *Leaves of Grass, Walden,* or the environmental liter-ary works emerging from their own cultures, they had no particular place to turn in order to seek guidance or share ideas. And those of us teaching and writing about environmental literature in the United States had little idea there was such deep interest in this work in so many far-flung parts of the globe.

IN OCTOBER 1992, the Western Literature Association (WLA) held its an-nual conference in Reno, Nevada. Scott Slovic, Cheryll Glotfelty, and Mike Branch asked the conference organizers to announce a special planning meeting for a new organization to support the study of "nature writing." This auspicious meeting occurred at the end of the conference and was attended by fifty-four scholars and writers, who squeezed together in a cramped meeting room at the Sands Regency Casino Hotel—just two blocks from where the Truckee River carries Lake Tahoe water through the city and out to its spectacular desert terminus in Pyramid Lake. Outside the meeting room, slot machines flashed and clanged. Inside it, we spent nearly an hour discussing the name for the proposed organization. All agreed that the time was right to start a new organization to promote environmentally oriented work in the humanities, but what should the group be called? Although the journal *ISLE* had yet to produce its first issue, Cheryll proposed that we adopt a version of the journal's name and refer to the new community of scholars as the "Association for the Study of Literature and Environment." We would abbreviate the name as "ASLE" (pronounced "AZ-lee").

"Ecocriticism," the term now widely used to describe scholarship that is concerned with the environmental implications of literary texts (or other forms of artistic expression), was almost unknown in the early 1990s, even when we launched ASLE. Although the term is credited to William Rueck-ert, attributed to his 1978 essay "Literature and Ecology: An Experiment in Ecocriticism," most green literary critics squirmed and balked at the use of the term. In 1994, Mike Branch and Sean O'Grady coordinated a roundtable session at the WLA conference in Salt Lake City, asking ap-proximately twenty scholars, ranging from graduate students to senior crit-ics, to offer one-page definitional statements about "ecocriticism" (these statements can be viewed on the ASLE Web site: www.asle.umn.edu [last checked 03 August 2002]). There was little precise consensus, except for the understanding that ecocriticism was a scholarly perspective attuned to the place of the more-than-human world in particular works of art. A number of the participating scholars felt uncomfortable with the word itself— "ecocriticism." It felt somehow too trendy, too vague. To some the term implied too much familiarity with the science of ecology—more familiarity than their own work could reasonably demonstrate. To others the term implied an unintended activist agenda.

A year later, Scott Slovic and Ian Marshall organized a follow-up WLA roundtable session, this time focusing on "Ecocriticism and Narrative"— that is, on the use of storytelling in ecocritical studies. Many of the same critics present the year before also participated in this conference session (position papers from the session can be viewed on the ASLE Web site). There was considerable debate about what constituted effective "narrative scholarship" and about who had the prerogative to include stories amid formal literary critical analysis. And yet by this time resistance to the term "ecocriticism" was already subsiding, at least within this particular group of scholars. That was 1995.

Eight years later, ASLE has now hosted five major conferences (each attracting between four and five hundred participants) and four special symposia on topics ranging from Japanese and American environmental literature to the literature of farming, from desert literature to the literature of the American South. ASLE has thriving branches not only in the United States but in Japan and the United Kingdom. A new ASLE-Korea was launched in late 2001, and we are hopeful that branches (or affiliates) of ASLE will emerge in Australia and in the Nordic-Baltic region in the coming year. Numerous academic publishers in the United States and elsewhere are now routinely publishing scholarly books in the field of ecocriticism: for instance, the University of Georgia Press, the University of Virginia Press, the University of Utah Press, the University of Arizona Press, Harvard University Press, MIT Press, Oregon State University Press, the State University of New York Press, the University of Iowa Press, the University of Nevada Press, University Press of New England, Milkweed Editions, and Island Press. *ISLE* has now gone to press with the first issue of volume 10 and will complete its tenth anniversary volume in summer 2003.

There have now been several well-received collections of ecocriticism published, both in the United States and abroad. Each of the first two ASLE conferences resulted in such a volume: *Reading the Earth: New Directions in the Study of Literature and the Environment,* coedited by Michael P. Branch, Rochelle Johnson, Daniel Patterson, and Scott Slovic, was published by the University of Idaho Press in 1998; and *Reading under the Sign of Nature*, coedited by Henry R. Harrington and John Tallmadge, was issued by the University of Utah Press in 2000. Ken-ichi Noda and Scott Slovic coedited the first collection of Japanese ecocriticism: *Environmental Approaches to American Literature: Toward the World of Nature* appeared from Minerva Press in 1996. The first major ecocritical reference work, John Elder's *American Nature Writers*, was published by Scribner's in 1996, and the first major ecocritical study with a multinational focus, Patrick Murphy's *The Literature of Nature: An International Sourcebook*, came out from Fitzroy Dearborn in 1998. Richard Kerridge and Neil Sammells published *Writing the Environment: Ecocriticism and Literature* with Zed Books in the United Kingdom in 1998. More recently, Karla Armbruster and Kathleen Wallace have edited *Beyond Nature Writing*, published by the University of Virginia Press in 2001, and David Mazel's *A Century of Early Ecocriticism*, out from the University of Georgia Press the same year, offers a useful backward glance at where ecocriticism came from. Steven Rosendale's *The Greening of Literary Scholarship: Literature, Theory, and the Environment*, which features various theoretical approaches to ecocritical studies, was recently released by the University of Iowa Press, while Joni Adamson, Mei-Mei Evans, and Rachel Stein have collaborated on the volume *The Environmental Justice Reader: Politics, Poetics, and Pedagogy*, published in late 2002 by the University of Arizona Press.

At the foundation of this burgeoning field, however, is Cheryll Glotfelty and Harold Fromm's *The Ecocriticism Reader: Landmarks in Literary Ecology*, published by the University of Georgia Press in 1996. Cheryll Glotfelty's introduction to that volume, in which she defines ecocriticism as "the study of the relationship between literature and the physical environment," may be the most quoted essay in the field. But many other scholars have now joined the chorus seeking to describe, define, challenge, and extend ecocriticism—a dozen such statements appeared in the special forum on "Literatures of the Environment" in the October 1999 issue of *PMLA*, while others have been included in the publications of ASLE-UK, ASLE-Japan, and, more recently, the Australasian Universities Language and Literature Association. Individual scholars such as Lawrence Buell (in *The Environmental Imagination* [Harvard University Press, 1995] and *Writing for an Endangered World* [Harvard University Press, 2001]), Patrick Murphy (in *Farther Afield in the Study of Nature-Oriented Literature* [University of Virginia Press, 2000]), and Joni Adamson (in *American Indian Literature, Environmental Justice, and Ecocriticism* [University of Arizona Press, 2001]) have also attempted magisterial descriptions of ecocriticism and the canon of environmental literature. Nevertheless, Glotfelty's early statement remains the closest thing we have to a general definition of the field.

In addition to the numerous books now appearing in the field of eco-criticism and environmental literature, many scholars have been writing fine articles that extend the theoretical reaches of ecocriticism and refine our knowledge of specific traditions and texts. Environmental writers such as Barry Lopez and David James Duncan have joined the critical fray with interesting essays on nature writing and environmental narrative in such publications as *Orion* and *Northern Lights*. David Rothenberg, an innovative environmental philosopher, musician, and writer, has reprinted and com-missioned anew an eclectic assortment of literary and critical writings for the journal *Terra Nova*, which evolved into a book series from MIT Press in 1999.

OUR ASSOCIATION with the journal *ISLE* began in 1995. Supported by Indiana University of Pennsylvania (IUP), Patrick Murphy had published three issues of the journal by the summer of 1994 and had collected material for an additional three issues. Scott came to the University of Nevada, Reno, from Southwest Texas State University in 1995, and Mike came the same year from Florida International University—at Nevada we joined Cheryll Glotfelty and Ann Ronald, forming the nucleus of the university's new Graduate Program in Literature and Environment. Aware that IUP could offer only limited future support for *ISLE*, Patrick approached the Associa-tion for the Study of Literature and Environment and proposed that ASLE "adopt" *ISLE* as its official journal, which would mean choosing a new edi-tor who could offer funding from his or her institution. With Scott's term as ASLE's founding president coming to an end, he applied and was selected to serve as the editor of *ISLE* upon his arrival at Nevada; at the same time, Mike agreed to serve as the journal's book review editor.

When we helped found ASLE in 1992, it was our hope to create a sup-portive network of scholars, teachers, and writers—a diverse but friendly community of people devoted to exploring and demonstrating the implica-tions of environmental thought in the arts and humanities. We have often said that the creation of the ASLE Directory—the simple list of names and contact information for members of the organization—has been a crucial achievement in ASLE's history, for it is a material manifestation of the size and breadth of this group of scholars and a means of enabling interactions among them. In helping to guide the journal *ISLE*, we have had a differ-ent kind of opportunity to contribute to this field. Because a journal is a substantial written record of the progress of a community of thinkers, *ISLE* has served not only as a rich meeting place of ideas but also as a dynamic, longitudinal study in the emergence of ecocriticism. And there has been, from the very beginning, a close relationship between *ISLE*, the journal, and ASLE, the community it represents. ASLE was born in the autumn of 1992, while *ISLE* issue 1.1 was published in spring 1993. As we mark the ten-year anniversaries of the association and the journal, it occurs to us that environmental literary scholars, like environmental philosophers and activists, often do well to take the long view. It is our hope that someday, perhaps a century from now, scholars interested in the advent of a new environmental movement during the late twentieth century will access printed or electronic issues of *ISLE* in university libraries around the world and through these journals will find it possible to better understand how scholars, teachers, and writers in our time sought to use literature, criticism, and theory to explore the intricate relationship between nature and culture.

The early issues of *ISLE*, compiled under Patrick Murphy's aegis, contained primarily critical and theoretical articles, statements about pedagogical practice, and a limited number of book reviews. Since that time, we have introduced substantial changes in the journal's format. Thanks to steady financial support from both ASLE and the University of Nevada, Reno, we have been able to maintain a reasonably regular winter/summer publication schedule. As the quantity of excellent submissions increased, we have also increased the size of each issue, eventually reaching a length of approximately three hundred pages. Perhaps our major editorial change was to begin recruiting creative writing—fiction, nonfiction, and poetry, in English and sometimes in both English and other languages (so far Spanish, Maltese, and Italian, with a number of other translation projects currently in progress)—in addition to scholarly writing. Our book review team devised a comprehensive, streamlined system for collecting new books in the general field of environmental humanities, arranging to have them reviewed or included in the annotated booklist, and contributing thousands of fresh entries to the ASLE Bibliography of Recent Scholarship in Literature and Environment. Each new issue of *ISLE* typically contains ten to twelve scholarly articles, several literary essays and short stories, and poems by as many as half a dozen authors; each issue also contains between fifteen and thirty reviews of recent books, plus annotations of up to one hundred additional recent publications. Although about 80 percent of submissions to *ISLE* come from American writers and scholars, we are receiving an increasing number of manuscripts from international contributors. In addition to the material actually published in *ISLE*, the process of gathering helpful commentary on manuscripts *not* ultimately published in the journal and sharing these evaluations and suggestions with prospective contributors is also an important means by which the journal supports and strengthens the field.

ALTHOUGH, as mentioned above, there are quite a few fine recent volumes of collected ecocriticism, there exists no single book representing the general range of ecocritical studies reflected in *ISLE*, the central scholarly journal in the field; equally important, there is none that provides a dynamic sense of the evolution of ecocritical theory and practice during the field's dramatic emergence over the past decade. Although an interested reader might gain a snapshot of the current state of the field of ecocriticism by examining recent issues of the journal, until now there has been no easily accessible means by which to gain a full view of the various new directions that ecocriticism has explored during this rich decade of expansion and experimentation. Over the years, the pages of *ISLE* have contained some of the earliest and most penetrating forays in new ecocritical directions, such as urban studies, field studies, bioregionalism, literary activism, narrative scholarship, green film studies and cultural studies, and postcolonialist and ecofeminist critiques. By offering a range of distinguished scholarly essays chosen from a variety of theoretical and methodological approaches, we aim in this book to provide an overarching view of the fertile ground ecocriticism has covered so far, to help assess what kind of scholarly practice it has become, and, perhaps, to suggest some of the important new directions the field is likely to take.

Cheryll Glotfelty's well-known definition of ecocriticism as "the study of the relationship between literature and the physical environment" certainly describes many of the articles included here. However, we prefer to operate under an even more encompassing definition of the field. In his contribution to the 1999 *PMLA* forum on "Literatures of the Environment," for example, Scott suggests that the ecocritical bailiwick includes not only the study of the explicit treatment of human-nonhuman relationships in literature, but also the reading of any work of literature (in any genre) in an effort to discern its environmental implications. We believe that every literary work can be read from a "green" perspective, and that linguistic, conceptual, and analytical frameworks developed in any nonliterary discipline may be incorporated into an ecocritical reading. Such an expansive conception of the field is borne out by the substantial and growing body of scholarly essays, many of which were initially published in *ISLE*, that seek to chart the methodological, critical, and disciplinary edges of nature writing, environmental cultural studies, and ecocritical theory and practice. Nineteen of those essays are included here.

WHEN WE DECIDED to mark the tenth anniversary of *ISLE* with a book-length selection of articles from the journal's decade-long run, we had to make several early decisions about what sorts of material could be most fruitfully included. Although creative work and book reviews are crucial parts of the journal itself, many of the poems and literary essays have been (or will soon be) incorporated into books by the individual authors, thus making these texts available elsewhere; and book reviews, although significant immediately after new books are published, lose currency after a few years. In order to make available work that has not been easily accessible elsewhere, we also decided to omit scholarly studies that have been (or will soon be) incorporated into other collections or single-author volumes. This editorial criterion meant, for example, that we could not include any of the fine articles published in *ISLE* 3.1, the special issue later reprinted by the University of Illinois Press as the book *Ecofeminist Literary Criticism* (1998). Nor could we use any number of other excellent essays that, after debuting in *ISLE,* went on to become important parts of single-author monographs. Even after adopting these editorial criteria, however, we were left with an embarrassment of riches from which to select: several hundred scholarly articles that have, for ten years now, formed high points along which the emerging trajectory of ecocriticism may be traced.

In scanning the issues of the journal published so far, and the material planned for the issue currently in press, we observed three general tendencies defining what the ecocritical articles in *ISLE* have sought to accomplish. We have used these tendencies, or directions, as the section headings in this book: Re-evaluations, Reaching Out to Other Disciplines, and New Theoretical and Practical Paradigms.

The essays in part 1, Re-evaluations, provide new (sometimes revolutionary) readings of familiar environmental writers or, conversely, newly environmental perspectives on authors or literary traditions not usually considered from a green perspective. Few would dispute that Aldo Leopold and Gary Snyder are major figures in the American tradition of environmental literature. However, Harold Fromm's focus on Leopold's anthropocentrism offers a challenging new twist on the progenitor of the "land ethic." Meanwhile, Katsunori Yamazato's detailed explanation of Snyder's poetics of "reinhabitation"—and the architectural forms it manifested—

offers a crucial lens through which to read all of the poet's place-based, homeward-tending writings. The work of Gretel Ehrlich, another much-studied American environmental writer, provides Gretchen Legler the opportunity to link contemporary environmental literature with an avant-garde "postmodern pastoral"—a hybrid of postmodern narrative and pas-toralism that few had identified until the 1990s. While Legler focuses on the postmodern, Carol H. Cantrell takes us back to the early twentieth century and Virginia Woolf's modernist vision of place; Cantrell's study demon-strates the value of rereading work that is not explicitly "environmental" from an environmental perspective. Gordon M. Sayre's article on Thomas Jefferson and the wilderness sublime pushes even further back in literary history: this treatment of eighteenth-century aesthetic discourse is an excel-lent example of the important ecocritical trend to "read the roots," as Mike Branch puts it in the title of his forthcoming anthology of early American environmental literature (*Reading the Roots: American Nature Writing before Walden*, University of Georgia Press). Although their explicit topics may appear divergent, Andrew Furman, Ursula K. Heise, and Niall Binns all demonstrate the same kind of broad re-evaluative process in their articles: Furman contends that Jewish American literature, often stereotyped as ur-ban and disinterested in nature, is replete with natural emblems and ideas; Heise shows how the genre of science fiction often functions as an important mode of ecological expression (through its frequent focus on such topics as "overpopulation, space, and speciesism"); and Binns, in his environmental survey of Latin American poetry, suggests another crucial direction for ec-ocriticism by helping to lift the sights of United States–centered ecocritics beyond our national and linguistic borders.

The acronym *ISLE* stands for "interdisciplinary studies in literature and environment." From its inception, the journal has aspired to reach beyond the limitations of traditional modes of literary analysis to promote cross-pollination among various disciplines and methodologies in the environ-mental arts and humanities. In part 2, Reaching Out to Other Disciplines, we have sought to represent the strong current of interdisciplinarity in the eco-critical scholarship published in *ISLE*. Lisa Lebduska's article, published in the very first issue of the journal, offers a textual analysis of the discourse of green advertising, demonstrating the value of cultural studies methodology applied in the context of marketing. Nandita Batra's study, which explores zoological discourse of the Romantic era for evidence of gendered and an-thropocentric language, is an important contribution to the larger project of ecofeminism. The theories of language, technology, and "metabiology" that Randall Roorda derives from the work of Kenneth Burke represent a daring exploration of proto-postmodern thought, a scholarly effort that demonstrates surprising continuities between Burke's ecological perspective and the views of Foucault, Derrida, Rorty, and other thinkers seldom read as environmentalists. Moving from the philosophy of language to the anthropological analysis of hunting brings us to Ian Marshall's lively braiding of first-person storytelling and critical commentary on environmental texts (both oral and written); the use of anthropology is an important part of Marshall's reaching beyond traditional literary criticism, but his practice of "narrative scholarship" also demonstrates the increasingly effective ways in which ecocritics are reaching beyond traditional literary analyses to infuse scholarly discourse with the discourse of story. Although recent issues of *ISLE* no longer contain a section dedicated to pedagogy, articles on teaching continue to appear regularly in the journal; for example, R. Edward Grumbine's piece on the future of wilderness field studies suggests a significant role for environmental literature in using experiential education to teach new generations of students to value and understand wild places. Scott MacDonald recently published a monumental book, *The Garden in the Machine* (University of California Press, 2001), examining the treatment of nature in alternative films and videos; his contribution to the current collection focuses specifically on the representation of urban places in the medium of experimental film and thus provides a useful model for ecocritics seeking to discuss literature and film (or other aesthetic media) together.

The final section of this book is devoted to New Theoretical and Practical Paradigms. Of course, many of the articles in the preceding sections also offer theoretical and practical paradigms that stretch the boundaries of ecocriticism. However, the essays collected in part 3 are especially significant for the conceptual and methodological terrain they map. One of the productive debates within ASLE, and within academia in general, is between those who believe teaching and scholarship should be ways of militating for social reform and those who believe academic work should transcend political and social agendas. Paul Lindholdt's article challenges readers to respond to the social context of the literature they study and teach—and to consider the potential of advocacy-based ecocritical studies to revivify the teaching of literature and writing. In his essay, Robert Kern closely examines the assumption that all literary texts may be read fruitfully from an ecocritical point of view—a theoretical and practical stance that is essential to several of the studies included in the first section of this book. The value of introducing insights gleaned from lived experience to scholarly writing is the focus of John Tallmadge's meditation on "a natural history of reading"—indeed, this study could be read as a theoretical foundation for the approaches to scholarship and teaching demonstrated in the Marshall and Grumbine pieces in part 2. Increasingly, ecocritics and environmental writers are thinking more carefully about the meaning of nature in the urban places where many of us live—one of the focal issues of Lawrence Buell's recent book, *Writing for an Endangered World*, is the notion of "reinhabiting the city." Michael Bennett's "urban challenge to ecocriticism" considers the special difficulties and significance of performing ecocriticism with traffic and birdsong simultaneously in our ears. And although some literary scholars focus on issues of gender and ethnicity to the exclusion of environmental awareness, Cheryl Lousley's essay shows that feminist and postcolonial theoretical constructs can contribute effectively to the ecocritical reading of particular literary texts.

Although we hope that readers of this volume will enjoy the range and diversity of contemporary ecocriticism included here, we recognize that some may fret about what has been left out. Contained here is but a representative sample of the diverse perspectives available in the actual pages of *ISLE*—a mere nineteen essays out of the two hundred or so scholarly statements that have appeared during the first decade of the journal. The larger momentum of the field is further suggested by the fact that this 1:10 ratio also describes the number of essays published each year from among the hundreds submitted for consideration. For those who wish to see, at a glance, the entire body of work published in *ISLE* (excluding book reviews and annotations), the tables of contents for every issue of *ISLE* (along with subscription and back issue ordering information) are available on the journal's website, at www.unr.edu/artsci/engl/isle (last checked 3 August 2002).

We hope that readers of this book will be able to discern in its pages a larger pattern—to gain a richer sense of how this field has grown and developed, to gather an impression of some of the major currents of ecocritical thought, and to discover some of the helpful strategies for analysis and communication being produced within this vibrant and rapidly growing community of scholars.

When future correspondence arrives from students in Brazil or Sweden seeking advice, reading lists, and innovative examples of ecocritical theory and practice, this will be one of the books we point them to. This is *ISLE* in a nutshell—this is a decade-long window onto the emergence and current state of the fertile, weedy field of ecocriticism.

PART 1

Re-evaluations

Aldo Leopold

Aesthetic "Anthropocentrist"

ALL LIFE continues in existence by feeding on other life, favoring itself at the expense of everything else. Though crude, depressing, insane, no way has yet been found to circumvent this enabling murderousness—except by means of upbeat redescriptions, like "image of God," "realm of freedom," "new world order." Thus, mice, rats, cockroaches, and the AIDS virus look to their own survival at all costs, and people are necessarily anthropocentric. Biocentrism, a recent invention that one might call "cosmic pro-lifeism," entails the redescribed alter-egos of certain types of well-fed, bourgeois anthropocentrists, more or less freed from the struggle for survival, and now with time on their hands for romancing the wild from which they have been emancipated by the technology that keeps them alive with little effort, but which they frequently profess to hate. Indeed, Aldo Leopold, a pretty straight talker, in his introduction to *A Sand County Almanac* says of "wild things": "These wild things, I admit, had little human value until mechanization assured us of a good breakfast" (vii). But do real biocentrists eat breakfast, or anything at all? For the authentic inaugurating act of a would-be biocentrist should properly consist of suicide, since by staying alive he uses up another creature's resources—even its very life. To be alive, it would seem, is to be against life, or at least everyone else's life except one's own. But nobody appears to be doing themselves in out of biocentric remorse. On the contrary, "biocentrists" consume paper, electricity, computer products, as well as food (and jet fuel to attend conferences) just like ordinary people (and jet fuel could be said to have been made available not just by the ancient deaths of fossils but by the recent deaths of hundreds of thousands of Iraqis). Biocentrism begins to look a lot like one more redescription of the anthropocentric will-to-power, with an agenda whose worldly underpinnings are conveniently muffled by transcendental neologisms. In a word, a lot like conventional religiosity. Instead of the "will of God," one invokes the "will of the biota."

Still, even Roderick Nash in *The Rights of Nature* is ready to concede that "no environmentalist seeks literal equality for the subjects of his or her concern" (205), but such a concession (that one may perhaps be a little bit anthropocentric) is tantamount to admitting that one may be only a little bit pregnant. Because once a "biocentrist" is free to pick and choose, there is little to distinguish him from vulgar anthropocentrists, who also pick and choose, since very few people are total monsters of depravity. Though I myself sometimes step on ants and take antibiotics to murder bodily invaders, I certainly don't ever step on dogs and cats. What must I *really* not step on to qualify as a bona fide biocentrist? The toes of other biocentrists? But I shouldn't say "other biocentrists" because, like Aldo Leopold, I'm just an anthropocentrist.

Why then did I put ironic quotation marks around "anthropocentrist" in referring to Leopold in the title of this essay? Not because Leopold is not really an anthropocentrist. But because everybody is an anthropocentrist, except corpses pushing up daisies: *they* are the real biocentrists, giving their all so others can live. When John Muir talks about "thinking like a glacier," or when Leopold talks about "thinking like a mountain," they are engaging in quintessentially anthropocentric appropriations of reality, for to think like glaciers or mountains is already to have nothing to do with those things and everything to do with people. Only a person can think like a mountain, and that thinker is inevitably someone whose genetic inheritance is to think like an anthropos, never more thoroughly than when "thinking like a mountain." Biocentric terms like "ecological egalitarianism," "inherent value," "a sense of place," "bioregionalism," "ecosystem," "sacred space," "aesthetic experience of the wilderness," "caring about nature" (all of which I've taken from Devall and Sessions's *Deep Ecology*), are saturated through and through with the anthropocentrism of creatures constructed like us. To attempt to think "biocentrically" is to try to sneak a look through the back door of the universe so quickly that one's observations would escape the indeterminacy principle, and one would see things as they really are in their unseen selves. But things as they really are in their unseen selves are presumably not perceptions or thoughts. No matter how empathetically we try to apprehend noumena on the sly, the act of knowing in itself transforms them into phenomena, that is, into humanized interests. If it is therefore impossible for human beings to know the intrinsic interests of animals and trees (because knowing is the quintessential anthropocentric act of appropriation), perhaps when we talk about the interests of trees we are really talking about our own interests, as when we used to talk about the will of God. This is not to say that there is no difference between selfishness and unselfishness, between inhumaneness and humaneness. Rather, even unselfishness (call it "biocentrism" if you wish) derives its force from a context of human interests in which neither trees nor animals participate. Yet despite this interestedness, only human beings have displayed the faculty of empathy with the rest of creation, an empathy entertained by no other species, however much it is a projection of human pathos upon unknowable "others."

The paternity behind much of today's rights-based and deep ecological ethics is Aldo Leopold's pioneering work *A Sand County Almanac*, written during the course of many years before being published posthumously in 1949. Since this book has now achieved almost scriptural status, a brief but revisionary glance at its purported biocentrism is needed in order to correct what has latterly become an out-of-context misappropriation of a few germinal sentences from the section called "The Land Ethic."

In this by now excessively quoted chapter, Leopold introduces (or reintroduces) for his contemporaries the idea that the use of the Earth solely as an economic resource will eventually destroy both it and us. Ethics, therefore, must be extended to include "soils, waters, plants, and animals," and humans must change their role from "conqueror of the land-community to plain member and citizen of it" (204). His most cited statement is that "A thing is right when it tends to preserve the integrity, stability, and beauty of the biotic community. It is wrong when it tends otherwise" (224–25). These remarks, which are made in the course of a rich and well-considered account of contemporary ecological deterioration (and things were much less dire when Leopold wrote than they are now), have been taken up as part of a new set of doctrinal imperatives by a number of recent biocentric ecologists. Leopold's aim, however, was to show the extent to which society's response to nature had been determined almost exclusively by economic considerations throughout the colonial and postcolonial periods of United States history. To redress this imbalance, therefore, he warns us "1) That land is not merely soil. 2) That the native plants and animals kept the energy circuit open; others may or may not. 3) That man-made changes are of a different order than evolutionary changes, and have effects more comprehensive than is intended or foreseen" (218). After outlining the character of "the land pyramid" and the operation of its food chain in order to suggest this comprehensiveness, he concludes with a summary: "A land ethic, then, reflects the existence of an ecological conscience, and this in turn reflects a conviction of individual [as opposed to purely governmental] responsibility for the health of the land. Health is the capacity of the land for self-renewal. Conservation is our effort to understand and preserve this capacity" (221). At the time he makes his famous remark about "integrity, stability, and beauty," he has been urging his readers to take into account not just economics (which he concedes will always be foremost) but "what is ethically and aesthetically right" as well. In other words, trying to counterbalance the overwhelming force of almost universal ecological shortsightedness in the 1930s and 1940s, he allows himself a moment of dogmatic insistence on the longer perspective.

But Leopold's now almost Mosaic criteria, far from being inscribed on sacred tablets derived from the biota itself, are rooted in ultimately anthropocentric concepts that have been newly refurbished by environmental proselytes to serve as "revelatory" foundations for a contemporary ecotheology. Taken as absolutes lifted from the needs of Leopold's rhetorical context, however, these criteria pose serious problems. The notion of "wholeness" or "integrity," for example, has come in for a good deal of poststructuralist criticism, particularly in connection with the old "New Criticism's" touchstone of "organic unity," but it is also generally dismissed in other fields besides the literary. Understood to exist in the mind of the beholder, who selects a number of qualities and data to stand for the whole while ignoring everything else, integrity or wholeness are nowadays seen as purely conventional moments of understanding, not aspects of "reality." Could anyone ever expect to enumerate all the possible qualities and data that might be said to inhere in any given entity or system? Indeed, to name them is in large measure to create them, since colors, textures, relationships, and so forth are mind-dependent. And if an entity's essential characteristics cannot be finitely identified, how can anything be proclaimed to be a system or whole? ("O chestnut tree, great rooted blossomer," asked Yeats, "Are you the leaf, the blossom or the bole?" And what about the chemical transactions of symbiotic micro-organisms?) Thus, the qualities and data involved in describing a system would appear to have little to do with "nature" and a lot to do with the cultural history and teleological interests of the describer. As for "stability," the belief that ecosystems are stable is no longer generally supportable. Daniel Botkin, having devoted an entire book (*Discordant Harmonies*) to demonstrating the falsity of this idea, explains how stability, in a case like that of ecosystems, is attuned to human perceptions of what is relatively enduring (from a short-term perspective) in a constantly changing material universe. "Wherever we seek to find constancy we discover change" (62), a phenomenon that Botkin illustrates over and over again in his discussions of forests, predators and prey, winds, fire, elephant preserves, and birds. By the end of his book, the idea of "nature undisturbed" seems like an incomprehensible contradiction in terms. As for "beauty," it is too obviously culturally determined and consciousness-generated to require comment. (John Passmore points out that wild alpine landscapes were regarded as junk vegetation before the late eighteenth century and owe their aesthetic appeal to the cultural program of the Romantics.) Perhaps speaking in a figurative way one could say Leopold's outlook is "biocentric" as compared with the traditional attitudes that he criticizes, but when his entire book is taken into account, Leopold's preoccupations look simply like another set of *human* interests, different from those of General Motors and Exxon, and almost certainly better *for the world of human beings* in the long run, but anthropocentric nonetheless.

Benign as *A Sand County Almanac* may be overall in its aim of preserving a usable and beautiful world, it has a regressive side as well. Leopold can at times appear to extol the preservation of "systems" at the cost of the individual members, with all of the transcendental religious implications that are present in such viewpoints. Although at first glance such positions may seem "biocentric" and "disinterested" in their apparent put-down of people, they can also be seen as a form of elitist, gnostic transcendentalism, related to Leopold's powerful response to natural phenomena, which he wants to preserve for aesthetic contemplation and defend from the invading, democratized rabble, with their motorcars, high-tech sports equipment, and sports columnists who tell them where the fish are biting. (It's not for nothing that the essays recently collected as *The River of the Mother of God* keep referring to "Mr. Babbitt," Sinclair Lewis's arch philistine, or to the mass mind, or to Ortega y Gassett's *The Revolt of the Masses*. Leopold, if alive today, would never pass muster as a spokesman for political correctness.) Indeed, despite his precursorship of today's "biocentrism," with its pretensions to cosmic egalitarianism, Leopold has no objection to killing for sport and can talk, just like you or me, about "worthless" grasses and vegetation. His "thinking like a mountain" is actually an expression of concern for the destruction of mountain vegetation by a deer population allowed to grow because human beings have killed their natural predators, the wolves. Because this denuding of mountains is in the long run harmful to various *human* interests, the aesthetic as well as the ecological, he believes that predators must be allowed to flourish. Although most of Leopold's strictures would, in fact, benefit the human race at large, his own interest in them often betrays the concerns of an elite, high-toned sportsman with exquisite aesthetic tastes verging on mysticism, though a mysticism sorely compromised by a powerfully atavistic (to use his own word) attachment to hunting that begins to trouble him only late in his life. (In his essay "Goose Music," from the collection *Round River,* he rhapsodizes over the flights and sounds of geese while simultaneously extolling the pleasures of shooting them, a paradox he doesn't attempt to iron out.) In sum, there is more ideological complexity and affective strife in Leopold's many-faceted book than is suggested by the handful of ecological imperatives that have been abstracted from it in the interests of postmodern biocentric politics. Indeed, the need to appropriate Leopold for what they prefer to call "non-instrumental" values drives even such philosophers as Eugene Hargrove and J. B. Callicott to criticize some readers of "The Land Ethic" for describing Leopold as anthropocentric, even though they concede such a reading is easily possible. Recently, they have jointly remarked that Leopold's program there and elsewhere was "primarily motivated by aesthetic concerns, rather than concerns about human welfare. Thus [reading these writings] as grounded in instrumental rather than the intrinsic value of wild nature does not correctly represent Leopold's views as they historically developed" (336). But aesthetic response is the most powerfully anthropocentric interest of all, produced as it is by the very nature and operation of our bodies and psyches: our metabolism, sense mechanisms, heart rate, sexuality, brain cells, and enculturation in temporal human societies. The "beauty of nature," strictly a "human interest" (however *indirectly* instrumental), leaves geese and bats quite cold.

Drawn to evolutionary biology to satisfy his frustrated religious longings, viewing the universe through aesthetic glasses and thus disdainful of capitalism's cash nexus while at the same time acknowledging its inevitability (and its attractive side as well), caught somewhere between a down-home concern for the future of human life and a type of intellectualist snobbery, Leopold would very likely have a few wry words for today's Luddite, misanthropic biocentrists. Call him what you will, it is Leopold's highbrow anthropocentrism, with all its unresolved contradictions, that finally makes him so ambiguously attractive.

REFERENCES

Botkin, Daniel B. *Discordant Harmonies: A New Ecology for the Twenty-first Century.* New York: Oxford UP, 1990.

Devall, Bill, and George Sessions. *Deep Ecology: Living As If Nature Mattered.* Salt Lake City: Gibbs Smith, 1985.

Hargrove, Eugene C., and J. Baird Callicott. "Leopold's 'Means and Ends in Wild Life Management.'" *Environmental Ethics* 12 (Winter 1990): 333–37.

Leopold, Aldo. *A Sand County Almanac.* New York: Oxford UP, 1987.

———. *The River of the Mother of God and Other Essays.* Madison: U of Wisconsin P, 1991.

———. *Round River: From the Journals of Aldo Leopold.* New York: Oxford UP, 1953.

Nash, Roderick Frazier. *The Rights of Nature.* Madison: U of Wisconsin P, 1989.

Passmore, John. *Man's Responsibility for Nature.* New York: Scribner's, 1974.

Kitkitdizze, Zendo, and Place

Gary Snyder as a Reinhabitory Poet

SINCE THE 1970s, Gary Snyder has increasingly used the terms "reinhabitory" or "reinhabitation." In his own words, "reinhabitation" means "moving back into a terrain that has been abused and half-forgotten—and then replanting trees, dechannelizing streambeds, breaking up asphalt" (*Practice* 178). Moving into the Sierra foothills of northern California in the 1970s, into an area that had been devastated by hydraulic gold mining, he built a house, planted trees, raised children, and explored the terrain. His departure from industrial society and turning back to the land was "a moral and spiritual choice," a seeking for a life committed to a place (Snyder, *Old Ways* 65). Snyder, by beginning to live in the back country, in an abandoned rural area in California, chose to explore how to live in a place, to become "placed" or "re-placed," an act that would lead him to a new, alternative culture and eventually to a new sense of "what it means to be human," which is the central thesis of his recent collection of essays, *The Practice of the Wild* (178). In such a life, the house where a reinhabitory person lives and the buildings that surround it play a significant role in creating a new life and a new culture.

In resisting industrial civilization and trying to understand "what it would mean to live carefully and wisely, delicately in a place" (Snyder, *Real Work* 86), Snyder built a house that he named "Kitkitdizze" in 1970.[1] The name was taken from the Wintu Indian word for *Chamaebatia foliolosa*, a low-growing, spicy-odored shrub, "The ubiquitous Sierra Western slopes understory perennial . . . Of the family of Rose" (Snyder, "Brief Account, I" 9). The plant is also known as mountain misery, bear clover, and tarweed. Choosing a Native American name for the house clearly indicates Snyder's vision of the significance of the house and the life in and around it. It is to be a place-based, environmentally integrated life, and the house is meant to be a model for leading a reinhabitory life. As Snyder delineates in "What Happened Here Before," included in *Turtle Island*, the actual land parcel on which he built the house was first occupied by Native Americans who "came with basket hats and nets / winter-houses underground / yew bows painted green" 40,000 years ago. The poem then tells of what happened 125 years ago:

> Then came the white man: tossed up trees and
> boulders with big hoses,
> going after that old gravel and the gold.
> horses, apple-orchards, card-games,
> pistol-shooting, churches, county jail. (79)

As Patrick D. Murphy points out, "the 'white man' did not come to inhabit, to adapt himself to the land and the creatures already there, human and nonhuman, but to make all else adapt to him. And therein began the trouble" (126). The land was ruined after this exploitation, and when the poet and his family moved in in 1970, it remained abandoned.

Kitkitdizze is a house that combines elements from different traditions. First, it takes its basic structure from the traditional Japanese farmhouse. The Japanese magazine *Eureka* printed both the floor and frame plans of Kitkitdizze in the November 1973 issue (25, contents page), and the plans show that the Snyder house shares certain characteristics with the traditional Japanese farmhouse. According to Hirotaro Ota, the typical Japanese farmhouse gradually came to be divided basically into three sections: a dirt floor (called *niwa*), the living room (called variously *dei, oie, oue, oie,* or *joi*) where the hearth is placed, and the bedroom (variously called *nema, heya, nando,* or *chodai*). Social and public activities such as entertaining guests and visitors were conducted in the *dei*, and the *niwa* contained space for kitchen, work, and dining (9–10). The floor plan of the Kitkitdizze house shows that it too is divided basically into three sections: a kitchen floor (dirt floor), a living room with a firepit, and three rooms (children's room, a study, and a six-*tatami*-mat room).

The second outstanding feature of the house is that it also employs a Native American architectural tradition. The frame plan printed in *Eureka* suggests that the Snyder house, with its high inner poles and short outer poles (taken from local ponderosa pines) topped by a smoke hole, shares the basic structure of the earthlodge of the Mandan of the upper Missouri River.[2] Snyder has emphasized the importance of "the sense of 'nativeness,' of belonging to the place," and this is an attitude and wisdom that a reinhabitory person can learn from Native Americans (*Real Work* 86). Thus the Native American elements in the structure of Kitkitdizze help integrate the house and its residents with the landscape and suggest that it is a house for new "Native Americans," who hope to be truly "at home on this continent . . . properly called Turtle Island" (Snyder, *Practice* 40).

The house also contains a pantry and is surrounded by a workshop, a woodshed, a sauna bath, a barn, and an outdoor kitchen used mainly in summer. These outbuildings indicate that Snyder and the building crew designed and built a house that could naturally adapt to the climate of the foothills of the Sierra Nevada with hot, dry summers and cold, wet winters. The building crew made up of "friends and workers" camped out in an adjacent meadow during the construction of the house in the summer and fall of 1970 (Snyder, "Brief Account, I" 8). They knew the place and the climate, and thus Kitkitdizze inherited features of place-based California buildings.

The Kitkitdizze house thus shares its basic structures with three traditions and adopts from these traditions forms and wisdom characteristic of an inhabitory life. In his essay "Blue Mountains Constantly Walking," included in *The Practice of the Wild,* Snyder writes: "Houses are made up, heaped together, of pine boards, clay tiles, cedar battens, river boulder piers, windows scrounged from wrecking yards, knobs from K-Mart, mats from Cost Plus, kitchen floor of sandstone from some mountain ridge, doormat from Longs" (105). The Kitkitdizze house is certainly one of these houses, combining and incorporating local materials and thus rendering itself interrelated and integrated with the place that it is located. It is a house based on a cultural vision that resists communal, ecological irresponsibility. It is, moreover, a house capable of sustaining a culture of rootedness and as such shows possibilities of transcending the twentieth-century alienation that arises from homelessness and placelessness.

Kitkitdizze now has a photovoltaic electric system for lighting and other electric equipment such as a computer and a refrigerator. When the family moved into the house in 1970, however, kerosene and propane gas lamps were used for light, and wood was used for cooking and heating. Incorporating solar energy for daily use in November 1981, the house began to embody "the possibilities of energy decentralization." As Snyder states in a 1979 interview, photovoltaic solar cells provide decentralized energy, and this energy can set the user free from the centralized energy sources (*Real Work* 147). Kitkitdizze has thus evolved into a model household for living in a place "gently and easily and with a maximal annual efficiency" (28). By fusing basic forms and wisdom of various inhabitory traditions, exploring at the same time the possibilities of renewable, decentralized energy sources, the Kitkitdizze house shows how humans and their homes can be self-sufficient and integrated with the bioregion in which they are placed.

IN *The Practice of the Wild,* Snyder describes himself as "foremost a person of the Yuba River country in the Sierra Nevada of northern California" (ix). His location, in his own words, is "on the western slope of the northern Sierra Nevada, in the Yuba River watershed, north of the south fork at the three-thousand-foot elevation, in a community of Black Oak, Incense Cedar, Madrone, Douglas Fir, and Ponderosa Pine" (41). Snyder reached this place after many years of wandering and searching. Prior to establishing his life in the foothills, among oaks and pines, he had lived in "hermitages." They were not, however, places to retire or, put in Buddhist terms, to withdraw from "the dusty world," as the traditional image of a hermitage would imply. Like Thoreau's cabin at Walden, which Hawthorne calls a "hermitage" (23), they were temporary homes that supported Snyder's tireless, vigorous search for a place to ground his vision. In Berkeley, California, in the early 1950s, for example, he lived in a cabin that he compared to that of the thirteenth-century Japanese writer-recluse Kamo no Chomei. In Kyoto during his first sojourn in Japan (1956–57), he lived at Rinko-in in Shoko-ku-ji, an aggregate of temples. In Marin County, California, during his brief return from Japan to Turtle Island in 1958–59, Snyder lived in the woods, in "the hermitage of Marin," abandoning it when he returned to Japan. And in Japan in 1959, he found a house to rent in Yase, Kyoto, which he named "Jinchu-an," meaning a "hermitage in the dust," that is, a hermitage in this world (Yamazato 74–75). In 1968, after leaving Japan permanently, Snyder and his family first lived in San Francisco and then moved into the Kitkitdizze house in 1970.

These turns and returns, a search for a permanent house beginning in the 1950s and coming full circle in 1970 with the completion of the Kitkitdizze house, are based on two important experiences that the poet has had while on his "path":

> I first stumbled a bit off the trail in the mountains of the Pacific Northwest, at twenty-two, while a fire lookout in the North Cascades. I then determined that I would study Zen in Japan. I had a glimpse of it again looking down the aisle of a library in a Zen temple at age thirty and it helped me realize that I should not live as a monk. I moved near the monastery and participated in the meditation, the ceremonies, and the farmwork as a layperson. (Snyder, *Practice* 151–52)

These stumblings "off the trail" refer to the *kensho,* or *satori,* the moments of enlightenment that Snyder has had while disciplining himself in Zen. The first moment is depicted in *Earth House Hold* when Snyder had the vision of "no identity": "One thinks, 'I emerged from some general, non-differentiated thing, I return to it.' One has in reality never left it; there is no return" (10). It was a vision that points up the interconnectedness of all things in this universe, and this led him to his decade's sojourn in Japan. The second moment took place on June 11, 1960, when he was working in the library of Ryosen-an, a temple in Daitoku-ji, an aggregate of Zen temples in Kyoto. This was also a kensho that deeply influenced the direction of Snyder's ideas and poetry, and it led to his permanent return to Turtle Island to test and put into practice what he gained in Japan (Yamazato 30, 89–90). The Kitkitdizze house thus was built after a long search for a vision, and it reflects Snyder's decision to be regional, to lead a life committed to a place and the community of all beings.

The construction of the Kitkitdizze house was followed by another important project, that is, building a *zendo*, a Zen meditation hall, and forming a *sangha*. While the house was being completed in 1970, the autumn rains started in the foothills, and some of the construction crew who had joined Snyder in his daily practice of *zazen* (sitting in meditation) in a grove of pines moved into the central room of the house. As Snyder states, they started zazen around the firepit and set up an informal zendo inside the semi-finished house ("Brief Account, I" 8). The formal dedication of the central room of Kitkitdizze as a zendo took place in May 1974, and it was named the "Ring of Bone Zendo" after an untitled poem by Lew Welch (1926–71), a fellow poet from Reed College:

> I saw myself
> a ring of bone
> in the clear stream
> of all of it
>
> and vowed,
> always to be open to it
> that all of it
> might flow through
>
> and then heard
> "ring of bone" where
> ring is what a
>
> bell does.
>
>   (Welch 77)

In "A Brief Account of the Ring of Bone Zendo, I" Snyder explains the character and function of the zendo around the firepit in terms of its relation to the place:

> It was not so much Zen as it was Chan. By that I mean not so narrowly monastic and Japanese, but more "Chinese"—earlier, less codified, more ecumenical, ecological, and playful. Still, I gave it the forms I had learned in the Daitoku-ji monastery zendo where I had studied six years. Although I lectured in the early days on such texts as the *Hannya Shingyo,* the *LinJi-Lu* (Record of Rinzai) and the *Platform Sutra,* we also read and discussed Maidu mythology, Tibetan songs, ecology articles. We acknowledged the need to harmonize with the wind and water of Turtle Island. We found singing, hiking, sweating, and working together, and spontaneous gathas of praise or apology to rattlesnakes, deer, babies, or tools, part of our play. I mention this because those creative commitments to women- men- babies- houses- soil- and All Beings—being together spirit has been central to the inspiration of this Sangha for years. (8)

Although Snyder's Japanese discipline in Zen is reflected in his application of the "forms" learned at the Daitoku-ji Meditation Hall, the Ring of Bone Zendo also attests to his skepticism of a "narrowly monastic" form that arises from the institutionalization of a tradition. Moreover, Snyder's conception of a zendo beyond a Japanese model is reflected in the subjects of discussion in the zendo inside the house: Maidu mythology, Tibetan songs, and ecology articles. These and the attitude of the members of the sangha toward the place that it is located—"the wind and water of Turtle Island"— clearly point to the character of an American zendo in its embryonic stage.

The zendo and the Kitkitdizze house in which it is contained played an important role in the new community and in forming a communal attitude toward the place. As Snyder states in his account of the zendo, "new neighbors were steadily arriving and some came to join our sessions. Construction, childraising, local politics, and forming the bonds of a larger community took a lot of our time. . . . Diverse as these new settlers were, they could all get together and agree on their commitment to the place and its future" ("Brief Account, I" 9). The zendo was not only a place of religious disciplining but also a center of various activities aimed at creation of a new culture, that is, a culture of place by a group of people committed to the land where they live. After the formal dedication, more people from San Juan Ridge joined the house zendo, making it too small for general practices. By moving into the barn (which Snyder later coined the "barndo"), the range of topics discussed in the new zendo enlarged. As Snyder explains in "A Brief Account of the Ring of Bone Zendo, II," the sangha held seminars with poet-priest Philip Whalen, discussed Deep Ecology with philosopher George Sessions, sang songs of the Amami Islands of Japan, and started celebrating Shakyamuni's birthday on April 8 (7).

The forms of the zendo were still basically Japanese, and yet the language used in the Ring of Bone Zendo reflected the place where it was located. Snyder, for instance, notes the special terms used by the sangha for whom the zendo is central in their pursuit of a new culture of place: "Our seasonal language comes from the terminology of the southern Maidu, or Nisenan, who lived in this area. They called winter 'Snow,' spring 'Flower,' summer 'Dust,' and autumn 'Seeds'" ("Brief Account, II" 7). By the time a new, formal zendo was finally built in 1982 in the meadow adjoining the Kitkitdizze house, the Ring of Bone Zendo had evolved into an American zendo, departing gradually from Asian models and adapting to and increasingly reflecting the spirit of the place. As Snyder writes in *The Practice of the Wild*, "The heart of a place is the home, and the heart of the home is the firepit, the hearth. All tentative explorations go outward from there" (26). The Kitkitdizze house has thus played a central role in starting a regional culture, and from the zendo, first placed around the firepit at the heart of Kitkitdizze, started an exploration that seeks a spiritual and ecological interrelation with the land.

THE POEMS that Snyder wrote and included in *Turtle Island* (1974) and *Axe Handles* (1983) reflect his life as a reinhabitory person. The poems in *Turtle Island*, written after Snyder and the family moved into the foothills, are notable for the intensity of exploration. The poet wants to know accurately where he is and how to be in place. Thus with his family he explores the forest and wilderness surrounding Kitkitdizze. Such exploratory poems as "The Wild Mushroom" and "Ethnobotany," for instance, show the poet exploring the forest around Kitkitdizze. And the exploration sometimes involves the possibilities of a deadly mistake when, for example, the poet attempts to learn the nature of an unknown mushroom in the woods—"only I got just so slightly sick" (51). The book as a whole shows how the residents at Kitkitdizze explore the land and create their sense of place out of direct contact with the land.

In *Axe Handles*, the intensity of exploration wanes somewhat, and the poet is now relaxed, confident, and comfortable with his life in the terrain that he has chosen. Instead of an intense exploration, a deepening sense of place becomes the outstanding characteristic of the book, as revealed in such poems as "Among" and "All in the Family," which show the detailed knowledge of the land that the poet has gained during the past decade. In short, the poems are deeply grounded in the inhabitory life at Kitkitdizze, and many poems depict activities around the house—"changing diapers," "fencing a part of the forest," or "screwing nuts down on bolts"—a round of chores that are nevertheless an inescapable part of "practice." Reading *Axe Handles*, the reader realizes that Kitkitdizze has become the home of an established reinhabitory person that can be rightly called "the heart of the place."

"Building," a recent poem collected in Snyder's new book, *No Nature*, depicts the construction of the house and the zendo and the significance of the two buildings for the poet and the place:

> We started our house midway through the Cultural Revolution,
> The Vietnam war, Cambodia, in our ears,
>   tear gas in Berkeley,
> Boys in overalls with frightened eyes, long matted hair, ran
>   from the police.
> We peeled trees, drilled boulders, dug sumps, took sweat baths
>   together.
> That house finished we went on
> Built a schoolhouse, with a hundred wheelbarrows,
>   held seminars on California paleo-indians during lunch.
> We brazed the Chou dynasty form of the character "Mu"
>   on the blacksmithed brackets of the ceiling of the lodge,
> Buried a five-prong vajra between the schoolbuildings
>   while praying and offering tobacco.
> Those buildings were destroyed by a fire, a pale copy rebuilt
>   by insurance. (366)

In the first stanza quoted above, the house building is contrasted with the seemingly more important affairs of the world politics on which the decade focused its attention. Despite the seeming urgency of these political affairs, the carpenters—men and women—do not divert their attention from what is to be done, that is, the building of a house and a culture of place. They peel the trees that they felled in the woods, drill the boulders that they gathered from the Yuba River, and sit together in meditation. Not that they are uninterested in politics, but rather they focus their attention on what is fundamental and lasting, the creation of a culture, "a network of neighborhoods or communities that is rooted and tended" (Snyder, *Practice* 179).[3]

Building a house is fundamental for the creation of a culture of place, and a newly built public building, a schoolhouse, for instance, becomes imbued with the same spirit. As in building the house, work in building the schoolhouse is done slowly, by hand with "a hundred wheelbarrows," and the spiritual traditions that are studied and discussed around the firepit of the Kitkitdizze house—Native American, Zen Buddhist, and Shingon traditions—now help shape the schoolhouse and the community that builds it.

The schoolhouse is built for reinhabitory persons and their descendents who, following Native Americans, learn from the land, and Buddhism and ecology teach them the spiritual, scientific relations of interdependence in this universe. The *vajra* that the workers bury is a bar with five prongs on each end used by priests in the Shingon sect. Hisao Inagaki explains that the five points in the vajra "represent various series of five, especially the five wisdoms" (75). These wisdoms are: (1) "the wisdom of knowing the quintessence of all existences," (2) "the wisdom which reflects all phenomenal things as they are, like a clear mirror," (3) "the wisdom of observing the ultimate sameness (of all things)," (4) "the wisdom of discerning the distinctive features of all phenomena," and (5) "the wisdom of accomplishing what is to be done (to benefit sentient beings)" (67). Burying "a five-pronged vajra" between the schoolbuildings, then, is indeed an appropriate act and points up the kind of ontological wisdom that the reinhabitory community endorses and hopes to attain.

The second and third stanzas depict the building of the zendo in the 1980s and the ceremony held after its completion. The stanzas again focus on the communal efforts that go on amid changes and fads:

> Ten years later we gathered at the edge of a meadow.
> The cultural revolution is over, hair is short,
>   the industry calls the shots in the Peoples Forests
> Single mothers go back to college to become lawyers.
>
> Blowing conch, shaking the staff-rings
>   we opened work on a Hall.
> Forty people, women carpenters, child labor, pounding nails,
> Screw down the corten roofing and shape the beams
>   with a planer,

The building is done in three weeks.
We fill it with flowers and friends and open it up. (366)

The poem then focuses on the 1990s and discusses the significance of the buildings that the poet and his neighbors built in the past two decades:

Now in the year of the Persian Gulf,
Of Lies and Crimes in the Government held up as Virtues,
   this dance with Matter
Goes on: our buildings are solid, to live, to teach, to sit,
To sit, to know for sure the sound of a bell—

This is history. This is outside of history.
Buildings are built in the moment,
   they are constantly wet from the pool
      that renews all things
   naked and gleaming.

The moon moves
Through her twenty-eight nights.
Wet years and dry years pass;
Sharp tools, good design. (366–67)

The buildings outlive political events and accompanying styles and fashion. These are passing phenomena that belong to "history" and are partly engendered by "Lies and Crimes" in the government "held up as Virtues." The reinhabitory buildings in which living, teaching, and sitting take place cannot help but belong to this history, although, contrasted with passing events, the buildings remain solid and unchanging. In these buildings reinhabitory persons shape a culture of place, transmit knowledge gained in the land, and continue to sit in meditation, "to know for sure the sound of a bell" coming through "history" that is full of things that are liable to change. The bell teaches how to be, how to live in place.

The buildings, environmentally integrated into the place and inheriting various inhabitory traditions, possess another dimension as well. They are certainly temporal, for they are "built in the moment," but, like the Greek goddess Artemis, or the Roman goddess Diana, the protectresses of wildlife who bathe and refresh themselves in "the pool" in the woods, the buildings now deeply rooted in the place are able constantly to refresh and "renew" themselves. Built solid with "sharp tools" and "good design" that endures, the buildings are like the goddess of the moon, "naked and gleaming," who "moves" through mythic time—"Through her twenty-eight nights," through "Wet years and dry years"—an existence that is "outside of history."

Gary Snyder's recent works focus on the perennial questions of how to be and what it means to be human. As he states in "Tawny Grammar," an essay collected in *The Practice of the Wild*, "the 'proper study of mankind' is what it means to be human," and he chose to make philosophy "a place-based exercise" (68, 64). Seen in this context, building Kitkitdizze and the Ring of Bone Zendo in the Sierra foothills of northern California has been part of a larger attempt at "self-rediscovery" (Snyder, *Practice* 28). Snyder believes that "the dialogue to open next would be among all beings, toward a rhetoric of ecological relationships" (68), and this dialogue is eventually to change the anthropocentrism of the dominant worldview. It will be an attempt to go beyond the paradigm formed by modern industrial civilization, and Snyder proposes in his poetry and prose ways to solve existential problems born of modern civilization. To become "reinhabitory," to build a house and a zendo in an abandoned rural area in America, meant to reclaim the home and the place that humans had lost in modern industrial civilization. The dialogue among all beings will continue in Snyder's writing, and Kitkitdizze and the Ring of Bone Zendo will certainly help the poet deepen his meditation on place and what it means to be human.

NOTES

1. Snyder bought the land jointly with Richard Baker roshi, Allen Ginsberg, and Swami Kriyananda ("Brief Account, I" 8).

2. See Walker, *American Shelter* (23). I am indebted to my colleague, Dr. Nobuyuki Ogura, for drawing my attention to this book.

3. For a poem that reflects Snyder's reaction to the political events in the 1970s, see "The Great Mother" (*Turtle Island* 20). It expresses his anger at political savageries in the decade, specifically the killing of four students at Kent State University.

REFERENCES

Eureka (Tokyo: Seidosha) 20 Nov. 1973.

Hawthorne, Nathaniel. *The Scarlet Letter*. 2nd ed. New York: Norton, 1978.

Inagaki, Hisao. *A Dictionary of Japanese Buddhist Terms*. 2nd ed. Kyoto: Nagata Bun-shodo, 1985.

Murphy, Patrick D. *Understanding Gary Snyder*. Columbia: U of South Carolina P, 1992.

Ōta, Hirotarō. *Nihon no jutaku [The Japanese home]*. 9th ed. Tokyo: Shōkokusha, 1976.

Snyder, Gary. *Axe Handles*. San Francisco: North Point, 1983.

————. "A Brief Account of the Ring of Bone Zendo, I." *Ring of Bone Zendo Newsletter* 15 Oct. 1986: 8–9.

————. "A Brief Account of the Ring of Bone Zendo, II." *Ring of Bone Zendo Newsletter* 10 March 1987: 6–7.

————. *Earth House Hold*. New York: New Directions, 1969.

————. *No Nature: New and Selected Poems*. New York: Pantheon, 1992.

————. *The Old Ways*. San Francisco: City Lights Books, 1977.

————. *The Practice of the Wild*. San Francisco: North Point, 1990.

————. *The Real Work: Interviews and Talks, 1964–1979*. Ed. Scott McLean. New York: New Directions, 1980.

————. *Turtle Island*. New York: New Directions, 1974.

Walker, Lester. *American Shelter: An Illustrated Encyclopedia of the American Home*. Woodstock, N.Y.: Overlook, 1981.

Welch, Lew. *Ring of Bone, Collected Poems 1950–1971*. Ed. Donald Allen. Bolinas, Calif.: Grey Fox, 1973.

Yamazato, Katsunori. "Seeking a Fulcrum: Gary Snyder and Japan (1956–1975)." Diss., U of California, Davis, 1987.

Toward a Postmodern Pastoral

The Erotic Landscape in the Work of Gretel Ehrlich

What is this wild embrace? This slipping away of heat from air at daybreak,
these clothes made of bird cries being peeled from my body? *Who is
holding me?* Why do your arms keep sliding down my back and hips,
then start again at my face? What is in my throat, what have I said
or swallowed? Is it foam from the river where it collides with
pointbars and cutbanks, or the rolling r's of sandhill cranes?

GRETEL EHRLICH, "The Fasting Heart"

THE WRITING of Wyoming essayist and poet Gretel Ehrlich offers some of
the most exciting and challenging representations of landscape and human
relationships with nature in contemporary American literature. In her essays in *Wyoming Stories, The Solace of Open Spaces*, and, most recently, *Islands,
the Universe, Home,* Ehrlich offers a new vision of human-nature relations, a
postmodern pastoral, that challenges the "pornographic" vision of human
relationships with nature that is articulated in much of traditional American
nature writing.[1]

The tradition in American nature literature that Ehrlich is writing against
has been Romantic and androcentric. In such texts the land has almost
always been constituted as an "other," a "thing-for-us," not as a "thing-
in-itself."[2] Even in the Romantic tradition of John Muir and Henry David
Thoreau, the widely acknowledged "fathers" of American nature writing,
the land has been rendered an object for the construction and maintenance
of the "self" of the writer; not as an agent, but as a mute mirror of the explorer's self, the naturalist's self, the discoverer's self, the adventurer's self.
As Annette Kolodny points out in *The Lay of the Land,* the American pastoral
impulse, as revealed in the works of early literary naturalists such as Muir
and Thoreau and in the journals, diaries, and other writings that came out
of the period of westward expansion and exploration in the nineteenth century, has been to project upon the land an image of land-as-woman, either
virgin or mother, agentless female object; a move which has encouraged a

way of dealing with the land (in literature and in life) through regression or willful violation. It is in this sense that human-nature relationships have been rendered in American nature literature as pornographic.

I wish to show that in her essays Ehrlich has constructed a startlingly clear and articulate challenge to this pornographic relationship. Her vision is a posthumanist vision of landscape that, instead of imaging the land as agentless female object, emphasizes erotic conversation between humans and the land; a reinvention that constitutes the land as an agent, a "speaker" with erotic autonomy.

I also wish to suggest that Ehrlich's "nature writing" is part of an overall postmodern critique and reformulation of modernist concepts that is reshaping ideas about self, knowledge, language, desire, and, not least of all, landscape in disciplines as diverse as anthropology, physics, and literature, to name only a few.

Postmodern theory helps illuminate Ehrlich's work, and vice versa. Postmodern theory helps us better understand Ehrlich's constructions and helps place her in the context of other scholars, critics, theorists, and activists who are looking for ways not only to reformulate our relationship to language but, through language, to revise our relationships with the land. Like Ehrlich, postmodern theorists insist on challenging modernist, humanistic formulations of the coherent, self-contained individual; critique traditional hierarchies and dualisms; challenge the myth of objectivity; and reject the notion of an authoritative center of value or meaning. Like Ehrlich, postmodern theorists also insist on the notion of networks, of pivots, rather than centers. Like postmodern theorists, Ehrlich is also deeply concerned with language. Brenda Marshall argues that "Postmodernism is about how 'we' are defined within that language, and within specific historical, social, cultural matrices. It's about race, class, gender, erotic identity and practice, nationality, age, ethnicity. It's about difference" (4).

Ehrlich's work also has a feminist dimension. Just as she strives to establish an erotic relationship with land, she strives to name desire, her own and nature's, in and through landscape. Crucial to understanding the relationship of language and desire is the notion posited by American and French feminists that the self is constituted in language and that the binary and limiting language of Western culture has determined and named all desire, women's desire especially, only within a phallocentric context. In other words, within "male language" there has been no way for women to creatively shape their own erotic identity; woman's desire is always defined in relation to male desire. There has also been no room in "male language" to imagine nature as a thing in itself and as a subject or agent that "desires." It is in Ehrlich's challenging of modernist ideas and ideals and in her bending and breaking through language that she is able to converse erotically with the land, to let it "speak" its own desires.

Ehrlich's essays work toward weaving a network of connections across the borders between mind, body, nature, culture, between self and land, animals and humans, throwing traditional systems of value into chaos and offering a critique of Cartesian philosophy, which has influenced all modern relationships with landscape, self, and body in Western culture.

In addition, I want to show how Ehrlich challenges what some theorists have suggested is a fundamentally pornographic relationship between humans and nature, a relationship bred out of Cartesian philosophy. Susan Bordo describes the Cartesian era as an era in which the separate self and the idea of "objectivity" or "psychic distance" were born as a strategy for dealing with the awesome and utterly changed modern world; a world where the Earth was not the center of the universe, where the naked senses had to give way to the authority of the telescope, where there was no longer one true church. What Descartes offered as a solution was "a program of purification and training—for the liberation of *res cogitans* from the confusion and obscurity of its bodily swamp" (92).

This "liberation" of reason from "its bodily swamp" is what Susan Griffin in *Pornography and Silence* defines as the pornographic impulse in modern culture. Griffin suggests that since they are located in the same mythical space in modern philosophy, woman, nature, the "other," all are silenced and objectified by this separation. Griffin argues that pornography is an expression of fear of bodily knowledge and a desire to silence eros. For Griffin, Cartesian objectivity is pornographic because it falsely separates the mind from the body. The opposite of the pornographic for Griffin is eros, what she describes as "the capacity for speech and meaning, for culture, for memory, for imagination, the capacity for touch and expression and sensation and joy" (254).

In the American literary tradition and cultural imagination the land has been treated as, represented as, woman—silent, receptive, passive; a nonspeaking agent. Restoring agency in the land, and with that agency restoring an independent sense of eroticism, humor, anger, and desire in the land, is what Ehrlich's work is all about. An investigation of her work shows that she establishes "contact" with the land by discarding the "modern" or "pornographic" lens through which other writers have seen natural terrain, instead adopting a precarious postmodern position that allows her a different vision; a fragmented, multiple, subjective, and ever-shifting view; the only position that offers the opportunity for erotic conversation.[3]

What the construction of a postmodern pastoral has to do with eros and the language of desire is partly explained by French feminist Luce Irigaray. Irigaray relates the exploitation of the body of women in Western culture with the body of nature and suggests that the breakdown of that dominance requires a breakdown of language, or sign systems. Irigaray writes that in phallocentric language, "Woman is never anything but the locus of a more or less competitive exchange between two men, including the competition for the possession of mother earth" (31–32). She also asks, posing a potentially terrifying result, what would happen to the symbolic processes of Western culture if both women and nature got to be speaking subjects? (85). Ehrlich asks a very similar question in her work. When women "cause trouble" with the language system, as I argue that Ehrlich does, we see the "turbulence" and "whirlwinds" that Irigaray writes about; a "transgression and confusion of boundaries," a challenge to what is "real" (106).

In "A Storm, the Cornfield and Elk" from *The Solace of Open Spaces* we can see Ehrlich "causing trouble" with language in this way; she challenges "what is real," challenges the language that has typically been used to image human-nature relationships, challenges the silencing of women's desire. She writes of watching elk mate, adding, "In the fall, my life, too, is timbered, an unaccountably libidinous place: damp, overripe, and fading. . . . Now I want to lie down in the muddy furrows, under the frictional sawing of stalks, under corncobs which look like erections, and out of whose husks sprays of bronze silk dangle down" (130).

In "Architecture" from *Islands, the Universe, Home* Ehrlich weaves her musings on space with her profound insight into the relationship of body to land, of desire to space, of language to body. Implicitly, she is also critiquing the hierarchical foundation of Western thought and language with her suggestion that one can EAT or DRINK space; a chaos-making transgression of boundaries if ever there was one. She writes: "I want to break down the dichotomy between inside and outside, interior and exterior, beauty and ugliness, form and function, because they are all the same" (156). Space itself becomes a sensual thing, a thing to hold, eat or drink: "Space . . . starts right here at my lips. I gulp it in, and it oxygenates my blood" (157).

Patricia Yaeger claims, like Irigaray, that "patriarchal obsessions are structured into the very fabric of communication" (84), and that women have been limited in their power as speakers, in their power to construct themselves in language. But, she argues, within masculine language women have always been speaking their desire in "terroristic" ways. In expressing an erotic relationship with land Ehrlich engages in a kind of excess, which Yaeger suggests is a "form of textual violation that exceeds the sociolect, that overgoes social norms by doubling them, by making them visible" (117). In these ways Ehrlich has constructed an "emancipatory relation to a dominant literary tradition" (87), that tradition being the Romantic, androcentric tradition in American nature writing.

Ehrlich's excessiveness is most evident when she eats the earth; handfuls of miners lettuce, dirt, wild strawberries, ash from the Yellowstone fire; when she licks the faces of rocks, lets milk from a pigeon's crop drip into her throat, when she gulps space itself into her mouth. This is a kind of breaching of sign systems, a kind of madness, what Yaeger calls "honeymadness"; the equivalent of going language mad, which is an act that contests the boundaries between the natural and the cultural, the raw and the cooked (27). The honey-mad woman's excess throws the dominant ideological classification systems into chaos. And for Ehrlich, this eating of the earth is clearly part of establishing an erotic relationship with land. The eating is "not about gluttony but about unconditional love, an acceptance of whatever taste comes across my tongue" (*Islands* 29). Like the honey-mad woman Yaeger writes about, Ehrlich is crossing boundaries in her effort to "find wildness," to cross over the artificial line between culture and nature. Ehrlich's feasting is a way of breaching subject and object worlds.[4]

The breaching of subject and object worlds is at the heart of what ecofeminist philosopher Jim Cheney says is necessary for the construction of a postmodern environmental ethic. Cheney argues that phallocentric language and philosophy have privileged a way of thinking and seeing that is incompatible with the kind of relationship making that needs to happen between humans and the land, especially at this crucial juncture in our world. He argues for a contextualist ethic to replace our androcentric land ethic; an ethic voiced through a language that bridges subject and object worlds. He writes that "for a genuinely contextualist ethic to include the land, the land must speak to us; we must stand in relation to it; it must define us, and we it" (129). The knowledge of how to do this, how to speak with the land, is conveyed through "mythic thinking" (123). He suggests that in Western culture the predominant myth has been that reality can be defined outside the self, and that we need a new myth that insists on the opposite. He cites tribal cultures as places where this contextualized discourse takes place. Drawing on Native American theorist Paula Gunn Allen's ideas in *The Sacred Hoop,* he defines myth as a kind of story making, or the making of narratives.

The making of such narratives begins with "the inscribing of the nervous system *in* the landscape" (130). In this way, he suggests, "the body is the instrument of our knowledge in the world" (130).

As I have already shown, Ehrlich's representations of land are inextricably bound up with her own body. In "This Autumn Morning" she writes, "I can't help wondering how many ways water shapes the body, how the body shapes desire, how desire moves water, how water stirs color, how thought rises from land, how wind polishes thought, how spirit shapes matter, how a stream that carves through rock is shaped by rock" (*Islands* 81). She locates desire not in self but, as Cheney suggests, in place, IN the world, not outside of and independent of it.

We also can see how Ehrlich inscribes her nervous system in the land and vice versa in her first short collection of writing, *Wyoming Stories,* published in 1986, which is the seed of what later becomes her novel *Heart Mountain.* These are stories set during World War II that detail the lives of the lonely rancher McKay, the Japanese cook Bobby Korematsu, and Pinky, an eccentric, alcoholic cowboy. The stories take place on and near the Heart Ranch and a Japanese internment camp near Luster, Wyoming. In these stories Ehrlich writes about the land as if it were a body, and she infuses/confuses human interactions with other humans and the land with a certain animalness and eroticism. In "Pinky," Pinky looks up one morning to see a cloud shaped like a human penis that reminds him of his solitary state and somehow blesses his nuisance morning erection (11). Later, Pinky looks again and sees that "yesterday's phallic cloud has softened and drained and come apart like cooked meat into the white smithereens falling on him as snow" (11). Still later there is a cloud shaped like an appendix, which bursts, "dropping its white cargo like poison" (42).

Later in the story "Pinky," McKay rides out to open the pasture gates to let the cattle drift in. Ehrlich writes: "As he rode, Heart Mountain disappeared from sight. The cloud that took it did so quickly, like a hunger, McKay thought. Now the peak broke the skin of the cloud. Nothing about it resembled a heart. It was, instead, a broken horn or a cubist breast" (15). McKay's mother had told him how the mountain had formed, breaking off from the Rockies, skidding down. "So that's how love works, he thought and chuckled out loud. He reduced his mother's geology lesson to a list of words: detachment, skidding, breast, horn, heart" (16).

Again in "Just Married," from *The Solace of Open Spaces,* Ehrlich focuses on using her body or *a* body as an instrument of knowledge and as a tool for connecting with the natural world. She writes: "Mowing hayfields feels like mowing myself. I wake up mornings expecting to find my hair shorn. The pastures bend into me; the water I ushered over hard ground becomes one drink of grass" (90). In these passages we can see Ehrlich's success at creating what Cheney has called "storied residence" through her "inscribing of the nervous system *in* the landscape." We also see how the expression of desire is interwoven with geography; again she locates desire not simply in self, but in a chaotic conflation of self and place, which is part of what Cheney argues is essential to forming a postmodern environmental ethic.

Ehrlich's challenge is also a challenge to revise our modernist concepts of what it means to know, how knowledge is produced, and what constitutes knowledge. Donna Haraway's concept of "situated knowledges" defines an embodied objectivity that challenges both relativism and totalization (183–201). What we need to seek, she writes, are those knowledges "ruled by partial sight and limited voice. We do not seek partiality for its own sake, but for the sake of connections and unexpected openings situated knowledges make possible. The only way to find a larger vision is to be somewhere in particular" (196). Being situated, "accounts of a 'real' world do not, then, depend on a logic of 'discovery' but on a power-charged social relation of 'conversation'" (198). Haraway argues for "the view from a body, always a complex, contradictory, structuring and structured body, versus the view from above, from nowhere, from simplicity" (195).

Ehrlich takes up a situated knowledge and uses it to challenge the knowledge claims of traditional nature writing. In "Spring," from *Islands, the Universe, Home*, Ehrlich argues a similar position to Haraway's, insisting on understanding and relating to the land and to her "self as a text in flux, not as order and stillness, not as "time-bound determinacy," but instead as "a mirage suspended above chaos" (13). Ehrlich frequently uses quantum physics to illustrate how she sees the relationship between land, language, and desire, and in doing so, she echoes Haraway's insistence on an embodied objectivity. Her whole notion of human relationships with the land is framed through this lens. She writes: "If I dice life into atoms, the trajectories I find are so wild, so random, anything could happen: life or nonlife. But once we have a body, who can give it up easily? Our own or others? We check our clocks and build our beautiful narratives, under which indeterminacy seethes" (23). Ultimately, she writes that spring teaches her what space and time teach her, "that I am a random multiple; that many fit together; that my swell is a collision of particles" (24).

In "Island," a small island in a pond on Ehrlich's ranch becomes a kind of symbol for her ideas of the world as a system of networks where there is no "objectivity," no single place to stand from which to gain a "truthful" perspective (*Islands* 63–66). The island becomes a kind of pivot, not a center. In this piece, Ehrlich illuminates Cheney's notion that we must look for our new myths to "the mindscape/landscape which emerges from our narrative and mythical embedment in some particular place" (Cheney 130). Ehrlich writes that "Islands beget islands: a terrestrial island is surrounded by an island of water, which is surrounded by an island of air, all of which makes up our island universe. . . . To sit on an island, then, is not a way of disconnecting ourselves, but rather, a way we can understand relatedness" (64). Ehrlich's critique of Western rationalism is clear when she writes: "To separate out thought into islands is the peculiar way we humans have of knowing something, of locating ourselves on the planet and in society. We string events into temporal arrangements like pearls or archipelagos. While waiting out winter, I listen to my mind switch from logic to intuition, from tree to net, the one unbalancing the other so no dictatorships can stay" (60).

Key to seeing the postmodern possibilities in Ehrlich's work is understanding the importance of the ways she lets the land speak through her. Patrick Murphy writes that in order to work toward the contextualist ethic Cheney insists upon, nature or the land needs to be constituted as a speaking subject, and to achieve this we need to acknowledge the nonhuman "anotherness" of the world, which also articulates itself by means of various dialects (see "Ground, Pivot, Motion").

It is in "The Fasting Heart" in *Islands, the Universe, Home* that Ehrlich's erotic conversations with a "speaking" land take full shape. The fasting heart, she writes, is the heart that is so empty that it is full, open to all possibilities. Only with such a heart, with what Haraway has called "situated knowledge," Ehrlich suggests, can we hear the land talk to us. What is most remarkable about this essay is the way in which Ehrlich establishes the land not only as a "speaker" but also as a "lover." She writes: "In December I watched the sun lower itself to the horizon and saw how snowbanks rose up to it like a wave far out to sea, growing bigger as it pushed for shore. . . . Above me mountains walk in clouds, are made of clouds. Beneath, hidden lake ice moans: *Oh darling, what are you saying to me?*" (163). Ehrlich in this essay writes that she has had to struggle to redefine knowledge in her world, and it is only through such redefining that she allows her body to name its own desire and the land to name its desire as well. Again and again, the land speaks to Ehrlich and Ehrlich speaks with the land through rich, erotic encounters. She writes, "The end of March, Where is spring? . . . Snow on the lake curdles, and underneath, the ice cover has grayed like bruised skin. . . . Wind deepens: winter is so difficult to dislodge. I hear it groan as it leaves: *Oh darling, why are you doing this to me?"* (168). These italicized lines suggest that for Ehrlich the land itself is speaking, calling her "darling," asking her to be accountable to it somehow. Later, Ehrlich is camped with friends in Yellowstone Meadows, not far from the scenes of the recent great fires. She writes: "Early every morning I go for a walk, bear bell banging against my thigh. A stand of trees to my left is all black trunks crowned with the gray hair of charred needles and branches. On the ground, where willow burned hot, circles of tall grass have appeared, their inflorescence like lace between my legs as I walk. . . . *Who is embracing me?"* (191). Whether it is Ehrlich here who asks the land this question, or the land that asks Ehrlich, seems unclear, but part of her strategy is to confuse and in confusing to enlighten, to suggest that the land *can* speak, can be spoken to, can be engaged with as a body.

At the end of "The Fasting Heart" Ehrlich walks to a place near her ranch where monolithic limestone tablets rise three hundred feet from a mountain slope. In this fantastic finale, she engages with the land both as a text and as a body, refusing merely to "read" it, but instead engaging with the monolith by licking it, by "feeling" its "hands" on her (196).

In her essays and novel Ehrlich offers us a stunning postmodern pastoral, a vision that rattles everything from our idea of nature to our idea of what nature writing is or should be. Ehrlich's work is some of the most challenging American nature writing today precisely because of the way it forces readers to question assumptions about the interrelationship of Western constructions of gender, knowledge, power, sexuality, the erotic, and nature. Most importantly, Ehrlich challenges what I have called a pornographic construction of human-nature relationships, a construction that often forms the foundation of much "traditional" nature writing. As Brenda Marshall remarks regarding postmodern theory, "This is not chaos, this is not anarchy, this is not entropy, although it may be chaotic, anarchic, entropic. There is sense here, but not safe sense. Sense made here is limited, local, provisional. . . . That is the postmodern" (2). There *is* sense in Ehrlich's vision; not safe sense. Ehrlich's revision of human relationships with land is remarkable and dangerous because it asks us not only to see land itself as erotically autonomous, but to see ourselves through an entirely different lens. She asks us to reject the pornographic mindset that has dominated our relationship with the land and our relationship to our own bodies. She asks us to embrace nature itself as a speaking subject; she asks us to embrace the erotic.

NOTES

1. By traditional American nature writing I mean a specific form that privileges a style of writing largely practiced in Western culture by white men, that is, non-fictional literary prose that emphasizes observation, an almost scientific attention to physical detail, and assumes as its founding premise that there is a definable boundary between "nature" and "culture" and that "man" is alienated from the natural world.

2. Patrick Murphy suggests in "Prolegomenon for an Ecofeminist Dialogics" that ecology is the study of interrelationships, and that one of its fundamental assumptions is that there is a distinction between things that exist "for us" and things that exist "in themselves."

3. The way nature has been constructed in nature narratives is intricately related to the textual construction of identity. The dichotomy between nature and culture, the city and the wilderness, the urban and the rural, *manage* the construction of identity by establishing clear spatial and psychological boundaries between self and other (me and not me, culture and nature). The authentic, autonomous self that emerged from the Cartesian era is broken down, fragmented, when the boundaries between nature and culture (me and not me) are broken down or challenged.

4. See Mikhail Bakhtin, *Rabelais and His World* (278–302), for a discussion of the role of feasting in bridging the space between the body and the world.

REFERENCES

Allen, Paula Gunn. *The Sacred Hoop: Recovering the Feminine in American Indian Traditions*. Boston: Beacon, 1986.

Bakhtin, Mikhail. *Rabelais and His World*. Trans. Helene Iswolsky. Bloomington: Indiana UP, 1984.

Bordo, Susan. *The Flight to Objectivity: Essays on Cartesianism and Culture*. Albany: State U of New York P, 1987.

Cheney, Jim. "Postmodern Environmental Ethics: Ethics as Bioregional Narrative." *Environmental Ethics* 2 (1989): 117–34.

Ehrlich, Gretel. *Heart Mountain*. New York: Viking, 1988.

———. *Islands, the Universe, Home*. New York: Viking, 1991.

———. *The Solace of Open Spaces*. New York: Penguin, 1985.

———. *Wyoming Stories*. Santa Barbara, Calif.: Capra, 1986.

Griffin, Susan. *Pornography and Silence: Culture's Revenge against Nature*. New York: Harper and Row, 1981.

Haraway, Donna. *Simians, Cyborgs and Women: The Reinvention of Nature*. New York: Routledge, 1991.

Irigaray, Luce. *This Sex Which Is Not One*. Trans. Catherine Porter. Ithaca: Cornell UP, 1985.

Kolodny, Annette. *The Lay of the Land: Metaphor as Experience and History in American Life and Letters*. Chapel Hill: U of North Carolina P, 1985.

Marshall, Brenda. *Teaching the Postmodern: Fiction and Theory.* New York: Routledge, 1992.

Murphy, Patrick D. "Ground, Pivot, Motion: Ecofeminist Theory, Dialogics and Literary Practice." *Hypatia* 6.1 (1991): 146–61.

———. "Prolegomenon for an Ecofeminist Dialogics." *Feminism, Bakhtin, and the Dialogic Voice.* Ed. Dale Bauer and Susan Jaret McKinstry. New York: State U of New York P, 1991. 39–56.

Yaeger, Patricia. *Honey-Mad Women: Emancipatory Strategies in Women's Writing.* New York: Columbia UP, 1988.

"The Locus of Compossibility"

Virginia Woolf, Modernism, and Place

MODERNIST ART, including modern literature, would seem to be hostile territory for a student of literature and the natural environment. Oscar Wilde's insistence that "Life imitates Art," that "Life in fact is the mirror, and Art the reality" (307), echoes through modernism, a body of art which has taught us to privilege the formal and the abstract over the referential. Moreover, modern writers are famously expatriates, wanderers, exiles; they seem to be rooted in the shifting ground of the twentieth century rather than in local and national traditions. The elusive nature of "the real world" in much modernist art and thought is memorably captured by the title of Marshall Berman's book on modernism, *All That Is Solid Melts into Air*.

Yet modern writers were uniquely situated as witnesses to the profound changes in human relations with the planet which have become visible in this century. Modernism, at least as the term is used in relation to painting and literature, is located between the turn of the century and the beginning of World War II, a period which saw a flourishing of innovation in all the arts fed by dialogue between the arts. Modernist art was produced by artists who were born in one century, most commonly in the 1880s, and came to maturity in another. For them, World War I was the most visible evidence of a fault line of catastrophe which utterly reshaped reality and their sense of reality. The profundity of this change is suggested by Virginia Woolf's witty phrase "On or about December 1910 human character changed" (*Essays* 70). One measure of the shift in the human experience of the world registered by modern art is its insistent expression of a deep distrust in the foundations and institutions of Western culture.

This distrust is part of a more elusive sense of things, a sense virtually all modern artists shared, that they had experienced a revolutionary change in "the given," including "the given" we call nature. Such foundational changes had been felt before in human history, but what was unique about this experience is that the changes in "the given" were manifestly a function of human culture. For the moderns, this sense of things was simultaneously devastating and exhilarating. Standing as they did on the relatively firm footing of what Perry Anderson has called the archaeology of "a still usable classical past" and the shifting sands of a "still indeterminate technical present" and "a still unpredictable political future" (qtd. in DeKoven 19), it seemed not only possible but necessary to create or invent new ways of seeing, new ways of registering the perceptual shock of change, new ways of being readers and viewers, and to respond with a new urgency to questions about the consequences of human creativity.

Implicit in the modernist aesthetic project is a critique of Western understanding of reason, particularly as it is based on the separation of perceiving mind from the perceived world. Much of the infamous difficulty of modern art is inherent in its attempt to explore alternative conceptions of perception, to dramatize the involvement of the perceiver within what is perceived. Elements of the experience of the world which our culture conventionally treats as background—issues of perspective, framing, and medium, for example—become for modernists the foreground and even the subject of much of their work. Related projects for many modernists involve the exploration and representation of various kinds of otherness, particularly non-Western cultures, and the multiple territories which lie outside of language, and the converse project of exploring the self-referentiality of language and perception. Key elements of modernism—the attack on dualistic thinking, the foregrounding of backgrounds, the exploration of the relation of language to alterity, and the self-referential nature of symbol making— are vital areas of inquiry for those of us who are interested in the relationship between literature and the natural environment.

My entry into the subject of modernism and the natural environment is through the notion of "place." Unlike "landscape" or "wilderness," "place" necessarily includes the human presence and in fact is centered around it. At the same time, "place" is where our embodied selves experience the world, and through which we receive the sources of energy and nurturance which keep us alive and in which our activities make themselves felt most immediately. It is where, in David Abram's words, "the sensing body is not a programmed machine but an active and open form, continually improvising its relation to things and to the world" (49). Yet "place," like women's traditional work, is usually backgrounded in Western thought, in part because both are intimately connected with the body, the mundane, the ephemeral. Without bodies, without places in which bodies live, none of the human achievements that erase their own conditions of creation would be possible. My conception of place rests on the insight that just as we cannot talk about mind without body, we cannot talk about body without place.

In developing the notion of "place" I am using in this essay, I am drawing on work ranging from geography to perceptual psychology growing out of the work of the phenomenological philosopher Merleau-Ponty. Merleau-Ponty's emphasis on bodily situation and his exploration of "the perceptual faith" that it engenders are useful tools for ecocritical analysis because their beginning point is the continuity between human and world. "We grasp external space through our bodily situation," he writes. "Our body is not in space like things; it inhabits or haunts space" (*Visible* 369). The "living" body or the "phenomenological body," in Carol Bigwood's paraphrase, "is not a separate physical entity in a world external to it but is of the same stuff as its environs" (50). Moreover, like the rest of the physical world, the phenomenological body is not fixed but "continually emerges anew of an ever-changing weave of relations to earth and sky, things, tasks, and other bodies" (51). For the phenomenologist as for the ecologist, the weave of relations which we know as "reality" is in fact neither fixed nor stable; not only do living things change in themselves, but constitutive relations constantly change as well.

What Merleau-Ponty does that much ecological thought does not do is to put the human perceiver in the picture; indeed, for phenomenology, the experience of the human observer is the starting point, not an irrelevance or nuisance. At the same time, Merleau-Ponty rejects the notion that the human is all that there is, or all that we can know. His assumption as a philosopher is the same assumption we make in everyday life: that our perceptions are based in a continuity between our bodies and the world. In his words, "my body is made of the same flesh as the world (it is a per-ceived), and moreover . . . this flesh of my body is shared by the world" (*Visible* 248). Furthermore, we share perceptions with other perceivers, who "have the power to decenter me, to oppose [their] centering to my own" (82). Objective knowledge rests on a costly omission of interactions between perceivers: "High places attract those who wish to look over the world with an eagle-eye view. Vision ceases to be solipsist only up close, when the other turns back upon me the luminous rays in which I had caught him" (78).

Merleau-Ponty's double stress on reciprocality and ongoing process gives us a way to describe and understand the interactive nature of human relations with the natural world no less (or more) than with human cul-ture. Indeed, Merleau-Ponty's work offers the possibility of a connection between the dialogics of language use and the interaction we have with the world. Merleau-Ponty uses the metaphor of conversation to describe the way in which interactions with the world around us lead us to new knowledge, and suggests that this is not only an analogy: "it is the same world that contains our bodies and our minds, provided that we understand by world not only the sum of things that fall or could fall under our eyes, but also the locus of their compossibility, the invariable style they observe, which connects our perspectives . . . and . . . makes us feel we are two witnesses capable of hovering over the same true object, or at least of exchanging our situations relative to it, as we can exchange our standpoints in the visible world in the strict sense" (*Visible* 13).

Because Merleau-Ponty insists on the possibility of exchange between multiple centers of perception, his work has affinities with the ecofeminist dialogics developed by Patrick Murphy: "The dialogic method is a way to incorporate that decentering recognition of a permanent *in media res* of human life and a constantly widening context for human interaction and interanimation within the biosphere and beyond" (Murphy 17).

It may be useful to pause at this point and clarify where a phenomenological understanding of "place" differs from concepts of "place" we are used to using, especially in relation to literature. First, this notion of place is emphatically not about regionalism, the effects of place on writing, or the effects of specific places on identity. Not only do all these definitions of place assume a foreground/background relation between person and world, they also do not provide much help in thinking about what the geographer E. Relph has called the "flatscape" of much twentieth-century reality. Within the notion of place I am using, "place" is not something we have more or less of, but a condition of being alive; even a bulldozed placelessness is a kind of place within which and out of which many human beings make their lives. A related understanding of "place" which I resist is an identification of place with stability, with permanence. Instead, the emphasis on moment-by-moment interaction in the work of Merleau-Ponty, Abram, Bigwood, Gibson, and others suggests that place is as unstable as the horizon. Not only does place change with our orientation, even nonbiological entities are in flux. This is perhaps most obvious from the air, where the fractalline patterns of desert and mountain, of rivers converging and meandering, record the inscriptions of wind and water. Indeed, once place is acknowledged as being as much in process as any living being, though the rates of change vary dramatically, it is easier to think of time as an essential component of any place, of the interdependence of "here" with the "now." In this sense, the clouds and weather which comprise most of what we see of the "places" described in Wallace Stevens's poetry are exemplary representatives of place.

The notion of "place" I am suggesting here might be useful in thinking about virtually any kind of writing, for the phenomenological perspective implies that any writing—any product of human creativity—will bear the imprint of interactions between human and world. At the same time, a phenomenological understanding of place seems especially relevant to the study of modernist texts. In modern literature, "place" is a problematic, not a given. Its difficulty and significance is suggested by the array of ways in which modern writers represent place. Kafka's mazes, Hemingway's reliance on place-names when words have lost meaning, Rilke's angels, and Joyce's Dublin are just a few instances of the rich variety of ways in which modern writers have struggled with representations and understandings of place. For these and other modern writers the relation of human self to world, or, more accurately, the terms of the dialogic between the "sensing, improvising" human maker and a world full of places potentially "unselved" (to use Hopkins's word) by human technology must be imagined in new ways. Much of the task of re-imagining for modern writers involves jarring themselves and their viewers or readers not just out of conventional thought but out of routine habits of perception, and specifically out of the habit of thinking of place as "landscape," "out there," "objective," and thus without relation to the self.

For both moderns and phenomenologists, self-referentiality is an essential aspect of human relations with the world. Modern art is famous for its preoccupation with the self-referentiality of language: modernist paintings no less than poems demonstrate that to name something is to refer back to the one naming. Merleau-Ponty's emphasis is on the reciprocality of perceiver and perceived: "my hand, while it is felt from within, is also accessible from without, itself tangible. . . . Through this criss-crossing within it of the touching and the tangible, its own movements incorporate themselves into the universe they interrogate" (*Visible* 133). Merleau-Ponty's concept of the "flesh," a concept developed in his last writings, names the folding back of perception upon the perceiver which makes relationality the ground of experience. "The flesh we are speaking of is not matter," he writes. "It is the coiling over of the visible upon the seeing body, of the tangible upon the touching body, which is attested in particular when the body sees itself, touches itself seeing and touching. . . . these two mirror arrangements of the seeing and visible, the touching and the touched, form a close-bound system" (146).

Though the "flesh" makes a "close-bound system" possible, it is anything but a closed or solipsistic system. Merleau-Ponty's concept of the
"flesh" depends upon difference as much as connectedness, for we are connected with what we perceive as we are being interrogated by it. We are,
in Cataldi's words, "*simultaneously* open to and closed off from others; simultaneously intermingled with *and* distanced from them" (28). If Merleau-Ponty provides a way of resisting the dualistic separations which have
sanctioned the treatment of animals as mere mechanisms and some human
beings as animals, he does not substitute identity for separation. And this
is an issue important to anti-dualist thought, whether it be modernist, ecological, or feminist. The alternative to the detached, egotistical self is not, as
Val Plumwood has pointed out, the collapse of difference between selves;
rather, "the resolution of dualism requires . . . recognition of a complex, in-
teracting pattern of both continuity *and* difference" (67). Thinking about
place dramatizes the usefulness of Merleau-Ponty's shuttling between continuity and difference, for within a given place there are multiple reciprocal
and dialogical relationships, ranging from those studied by the geographer,
for whom "physical setting, activities, and meanings are always interrelated" (Relph 48), to more nebulous and shifting boundaries between "inside" and "outside"—which are "always ready to be reversed, to exchange
their hostility" (Bachelard 217–218).

Finally, before turning to the example of Virginia Woolf, I want to explore the dimension of "place," which is probably most comfortable in modernism and least comfortable in an ecocritical literary environment—that
is, the dimension of human making or creativity which I think is implicit
in what I have been saying about "place." The first of the numerous entries
under "place" in the OED is "An open space in a city; square, market-place,"
and virtually all the uses of the term suggest human activity—humans living together, making a "place together," with connotations of fittingness
and locatedness. These meanings accord well with the thought of the ecological psychologist James Gibson, whose work explicitly explores the experience of place. Place, he points out, precedes "space" in our experience,
for space is an abstraction derived from place which establishes coordinates
separate from the perceiving subject. Place, for Gibson, is defined by the perceiving subject, for whom horizons and occluded objects shift and change
as the perceiver walks or turns her head. Thus the perceiver is literally the
center of her world. At the same time this perceiver looks and walks in
the direction she does because the environment prompts these responses
in what Gibson calls *affordances*, a word he made up to describe what an

environment *"offers* to the animal, what it *provides or furnishes,* whether for good or ill" (33). Different species within the same environment—and different members of the same species as well—will be drawn to different affordances within it.

Thinking of "place" as interdependent with a perceiver of place may seem to undercut environmental thinking, particularly thinking about wilderness areas and other places we want to spare from human presence. I would contend, however, that the discipline of thinking about "places" rather than "spaces" is at the very least a useful corrective to ways of thinking in which humans are either all or nothing in relation to their environments. And there are several features of "places" which cut humans down to size. One is that the human (or other animal) perceiver is conceived of as being within something that surpasses her—that is, place—not the other way around. Another is that we are not authorized to generalize about place on the basis of one center of perception, as we are with space. Finally, and most important, the relation with place I have been describing is dialogic. A "place" has an open-ended identity negotiated by multiple voices, not just one, and not just by human voices.

At the same time, thinking of human relations to environments as inevitably participatory clarifies and complicates the role of human creativity. From the phenomenological standpoint, the "radical intentionality of human consciousness is fundamental," joining perception and creativity on a single continuum. "The world is both revealed and shaped by the acts of perception in which it is grasped"; thus, perception is not passive "but an active taking hold and a molding of one's own world" (Fisher 10). Indeed, for Merleau-Ponty—and for Gibson following him—intentionality is inherently a part of human perception, as our orientation to affordances in the environment suggests. Human creativity, that is, an active, shaping response to place, is inherent in virtually everything we see and do, for we are constantly improvising our relation to the world around us, responding to affordances, making sense of things. Indeed, "For Merleau-Ponty, all of the creativity and free-ranging mobility that we have come to associate with the human intellect is, in truth, an elaboration, or recapitulation, of a profound creativity already underway at the most immediate level of sensory perception" (Abram 53). This creativity invents and reinvents the world we see as given and authorizes the changes we make in the given. Particularly in this century, we have learned to enforce meaning and unity on large parts of the world by turning them into abstract spaces, which are "understood to be empty and undifferentiated and objectively manipulable" (Relph 23).

Yet even an extreme rationalist relationship with an environment is a relationship, though it is not seen as such, and it proceeds from and leads
to further relationships, many of them unintended. The question Merleau-
Ponty invites us to ask is not what kinds of relationships can be imagined
with the places in which we live and with the wild places in which we do
not live, and what kinds of human construction and creativity possible relationships set in motion. Modern writers saw that the disastrous world
they came to inhabit was the result of choices made at very deep levels of
creativity—including the level of perception—and their work gives us the
chance to explore some of the unexamined ways in which we are making
and unmaking the world at every moment.

At this point, I want to use some of these ideas to talk about one modern
writer, Virginia Woolf. Woolf is emphatically an experimental writer; each of
her books explores different issues of craft and aesthetics, and even among
feminists, who have shown how seriously she took women's issues—and
thus addressed real-world issues—she is sometimes seen as an aesthete creating what Elaine Showalter called "uterine environments" (Kaivola 17).
My contention, however, is that her writing career can better be described
as a series of efforts to find more satisfactory ways of representing human
relationships with the real than were available to her in the conventional
novel in the realist tradition. My focus is on her last novel, *Between the Acts,*
which I believe is a remarkable culmination to this long process, and which
I believe embodies many of the issues I have tried to explore in the first
part of this essay. Indeed, I want to argue that *Between the Acts* can usefully
be seen as a detailed and instructive representation of what Merleau-Ponty
called "the flesh of the world." To provide some sense of the distance Woolf
traveled as a novelist, I note some points of contrast with her first novel, *The
Voyage Out.*

Woolf was, as we know from her essays, dissatisfied with the conventions available to her as a novelist. Her most explicit objection to the conventional realistic novel was to its lifeless materialism, but she has other
concerns as well. In her famous essay "Mr. Bennett and Mrs. Brown," she
explores the reasons why the realistic novel as written by Mr. Bennett is incapable of representing a woman she observes on a train whom she names
"Mrs. Brown." Woolf makes it clear that the patriarchal eye is incapable of
seeing Mrs. Brown because she can never be more than mere background;
but there is something else about her that escapes as well—that is, the sense
that she announces something to Woolf by her very presence; she evokes a
response. "The impression she made was overwhelming," Woolf writes. "It

came pouring out like a draught, like a smell of burning" (*Woman's* 74). This imagery, which Woolf uses again later in the essay, joins the issue of backgrounding with the issue of affordances, with the sense of being hailed by something, and the combination of otherness and continuity between lives this connection implies.

Woolf's first novel, written in the decade before she wrote "Mr. Bennett and Mrs. Brown," suggests the difficulty of her struggle to escape the world of Mr. Bennett. Woolf's choice of setting ensures that the novel will be unrealistic at the least: most of the novel takes place in a town in Brazil, and its crisis takes place in an excursion up the Amazon. These settings are no more than backdrops. This landscape is remarkable for having virtually no affordances, foreign though it is. Instead, its noticeable elements of setting are symbolic: the separate rooms which house the British tourists clearly symbolize their separated but joined lives, for example, and the dangerous trip up the river which gives the protagonist the fever which kills her is clearly transgressive. This is very much a novel with a background and a foreground: the foreground is exclusively composed of human activity, and the background, like a Greek chorus, comments on this activity.

That setting can be a presence, one interactive with its human inhabitants, is suggested by the way descriptions of "the shrinking island" of England rip through Woolf's more conventional description of the voyage to Brazil.

> Great tracts of the earth lay now beneath the autumn sun, and the whole of England, from the bald moors to the Cornish rocks, was lit up from dawn to sunset, and showed in stretches of yellow, green, and purple. Under that illumination even the roofs of the great towns glittered. In thousands of small gardens, millions of dark-red flowers were blooming, until the old ladies who had tended them so carefully came down the paths with their scissors, snipped through their juicy stalks, and laid them upon cold stone ledges in the village church. (*Voyage* 23; see also 24–25; 78)

Woolf's career as a novelist can be seen as a search for ways of writing a whole novel that does what this passage does, one which has as its subject the interactions among multiple lives and life processes—that is, about place as I have been redefining it.

When Woolf wrote *The Voyage Out*, she was beginning her own journey through and beyond the conventions of realistic character and setting. As the novel's title suggests, it is about a journey into the unknown for its protagonist, a young woman named Rachel. She falls in love, becomes engaged, and dies from a tropical fever before she and Terence can return home, much less marry. Woolf's challenge to realism in this novel is its depiction of Rachel's voyage inward, for by far the most powerful section of the novel is the depiction of the hallucinatory state which precedes Rachel's death. In this state, Rachel's feverish delusions become her whole environment—and the reader's as well—and this environment is intensely detailed, present, and arresting. Though the delusional environment is frighteningly full of affordances which demand attention—sights like the "peaked shadow on the ceiling" which demands that "all her energy was concentrated upon the desire that this shadow should move" (*Voyage* 323)—this is neither a shared environment nor one which allows for intentionality, much less creativity; indeed, in the course of her illness "Rachel ceased to have any will of her own" (327). Though her experience of illness has some of the features of the phenomenological environment, it lacks the crucial element of reciprocity and its complement, intentionality. In the sense that Rachel's journey into love, illness, and death is a journey through worlds she is less and less able to share or affect, it is a voyage out away from "place," the site of reciprocal relations with human and nonhuman others, a site for which marriage is both metaphoric and metonymic.

In contrast, Woolf's last novel, *Between the Acts*, is both open-ended and "thick," woven of multiple layers of life processes, including the human but not restricted to it. The setting of this novel is not merely background but a complex presence—a "place" in the phenomenological sense. *Between the Acts* takes place on a single day, midsummer 1939, and follows the activities of the three generations of the Oliver family of Pointz Hall which is—as it is every year—the site of a pageant in which the whole community participates. Though the house is not "rank[ed] among the houses that are mentioned in guide books," there is something about it which makes people ask about it as they drive by. It is an affordance, a place which speaks to people, despite its "lying unfortunately low on the meadow" (*Between* 7). In fact, it seems to be a place composed of layers and layers of kinds of speech, only some of which are composed of human language. Human history, geological process, the ongoing present life of the biosphere—all are articulate presences lightly felt as part of ordinary life.

The novel opens with talk: "It was a summer's night and they were talking"; the silences in the human conversation are filled by sounds coming through the open windows: "a cow coughed" and "A bird chuckled outside." To human ears, this chuckle is expressive of place, if nothing else; the bird is not a nightingale because "nightingales didn't come so far north."

The humans' discussion about a cesspool is in its own ordinary way expressive of place as well; the site is inscribed by history—just as an ordinary human body wears its own life history:

> The old man in the arm-chair—Mr. Oliver, of the Indian Civil Service, retired— said that the site they had chosen for the cesspool was, if he had heard aright, on the Roman road. From an aeroplane, he said, you could still see, plainly marked, the scars made by the Britons; by the Romans; by the Elizabethan manor house; and by the plough, when they ploughed the hill to grow wheat in the Napoleonic wars. (*Between* 5)

Geological, biological, and human historical processes are foregrounded as part of the weave of "the present" in which the novel takes place. Bart Oliver's sister, Lucy, taking her tea in the barn set up for refreshments at the pageant's intermission, watches the swallows:

> Excited by the company they were flitting from rafter to rafter. Across Africa, across France they had come to nest here. Year after year they came. Before there was a channel, when the earth, upon which the Windsor chair was planted, was a riot of rhododendrons, and humming birds quivered at the mouths of scarlet trumpets, as she had read that morning in her Outline of History. (66)

The inscriptions in the earth, the swallows in the barn, are more than setting and more than symbol; they are affordances acting as a kind of language, providing a weave of information in which the multiple modes of human language participate. In Merleau-Ponty's terms, this is a weave of the visible and the invisible, the literal world registered by the senses as one "side" of the Möbius strip whose other "side" simultaneously holds the multiple "invisible" meanings inhering in the sensible world seen by the human perceiver.[1]

Just as the natural world is foregrounded as a participant capable of generating meaning rather than being relegated to mere setting, human language is also foregrounded as a process in itself rather than a mere vehicle for transporting thought or meaning. The reader is constantly made aware of the life of language which exists between people, in large groups and small, a life which exists beyond the intent of any speaker or listener. Woolf's depiction of collective language is so central to this book that I want to provide two examples. The first is the audience discussing the play they've seen:

> I thought it brilliantly clever. . . . O my dear, I though it utter bosh. Did *you* understand the meaning? Well, he said she meant we all act a part. . . . He

said, too, if I caught his meaning, Nature takes part. . . . Then there was the
idiot. . . . Also, why leave out the Army, as my husband was saying, if it's
history? And if one spirit animates the whole, what about the aeroplanes?
(*Between* 117)

The nurses after breakfast were trundling the perambulator up and down the
terrace; as they trundled they were talking—not shaping pellets of information or handing ideas from one to another, but rolling words, like sweets on
their tongues. . . . This morning that sweetness was: "How cook had told 'im
off about the asparagus; how when she rang I said: . . ." (9)

As the comparison of the maids' chitchat to sweets suggests, language acts
in and of themselves are for humans preeminent affordances in the environment. Isa Oliver, the young woman married to Bart Oliver's son, finds
her attention caught and then betrayed by a newspaper item about a "A
horse with a green tail" and, like the woman in the report, finds that she
has been tricked by fanciful language. For the story goes on to read, " 'And
they dragged her up to the barrack room where she was thrown upon a
bed. . . .' That was real" (15).

If the focus of *The Voyage Out* is on the unsharable experience of a fevered
illness, the focus of *Between the Acts* is on the collective experience of a community event. It is one of the meanings of the title: meaning making occurs
between language acts between participants, and no language act is final.
The newspaper account, for example, does not have the last word:

in the barrack room the bed [Isa reads], and on the bed the girl was screaming
and hitting him about the face, when the door (for in fact it was a door) opened
and in came Mrs. Swithin carrying a hammer. . . . Not a word passed between
them as she went to the cupboard in the corner and replaced the hammer,
which she had taken without asking leave. (15)

Gestures and actions are part of the dialogics of the novel; so is the silence
of the painting the visitors look at—all are part of the ongoing collective activity of making meaning. But Woolf's dialogic melody is triple, not limited
to the human:

The view repeated in its own way what the tune was saying. . . . The cows,
making a step forward, then standing still, were saying the same thing to perfection. Folded in this triple melody, the audience sat gazing. (81)

The pageant ends with "the present time," represented by mirrors paraded
through the audience—who doesn't get it. "This is death," thinks the director, "when illusion fails." Then rain pours down, leaving "a fresh earthy

smell" and leaving as well a sense of meaningfulness: "The tune was as simple as could be. But now that the shower had fallen, it was the other voice speaking, the voice that was no one's voice" (107).

The dialogics of this novel preclude both the privileged point of view and the finality of closure. The Rev. Streatfield tries to provide a summary of what the pageant meant, and his failure to leave the audience with his stamp of interpretation is part of a general pattern in the novel of "scraps and orts" of partial or thwarted understanding, interruption, dispersion. Miss LaTrobe's production does indeed satirize, as one critic has put it, "traits of money-getting, disdain for people seen as inferior . . . and blindness to the waste of young men regarded as expendable" (Phillips 202–3), but the audience reaction is diffuse and obtuse. In the pageant, in responses to the pageant, in conversation at lunch, it is always the same: "But before they had come to any common conclusion, a voice asserted itself" (*Between* 111). Indeed, interruptions are signs that the world (with its human and nonhuman elements) is in fact not just looking back, but answering back.

In contrast to the ebb and flow of language and the living landscape, the characters in the novel are virtually caricatures, crammed into the husks of their given roles (Dick 75). To a greater or lesser extent, all these roles (both on and off stage) are defined in relation to the patriarchy governing the human world. Those closest to patriarchal power are most rigidly constrained, but no one escapes. Even "the wild child of nature," as Mrs. Manresa characterizes herself, is playing a role governed by the task of flaunting propriety. Her stylized performance offers the men of the Oliver household a delightful counterpoint to their own insistence on order and reason. The patriarchal inheritance being passed from father to son to grandson is at least as much an attitude toward property as it is property itself: one of its chief features is that the give-and-take which Merleau-Ponty characterizes as inherent in our relations with the rest of the world is reduced to the mechanics of possession and control. The Oliver men have learned to respond to affordances in the environment by immediately asserting their right— their duty—to claim possession and maintain order. The importance of this generational pattern is indicated by key passages in the novel which are as disturbing as they are opaque.

In the first of these anti-epiphanies, the youngest Oliver, Isa's young son George, is startled by a flower:

> The flower blazed between the angles of the roots. Membrane after membrane was torn. It blazed a soft yellow, a lambent light under a film of velvet; it filled the caverns behind the eyes with light. All that inner darkness became a hall,

leaf smelling, earth smelling, of yellow light. And the tree was beyond the
flower; the grass, the flower and the tree were entire. (*Between* 9–10)

George's response to the flower is to pull it up. His paradoxical action—
uniting desire with destruction, comprehension with blindness—is emblematic of a response to an affordance which lacks a sense of the autonomous life of the other, which does not see itself as part of the ongoing life
it observes. George's well-meaning destruction bears a family relationship
to the grandfatherly prank which destroys his reverie. For when his grandfather Bart sees George with the flower, he terrifies him with a booming
"Good morning, sir" from behind a beak he makes of his newspaper, and
then complains that George is a crybaby.

The other landmark anti-epiphany in the novel takes place later in the
day when George's father, Giles, also registers the disturbance of an undis-
ciplined natural presence. This time the experience is of revulsion rather
than attraction; he sees

a snake? Dead? No, choked with a toad in its mouth. The snake was unable to
swallow; the toad was unable to die. A spasm made the ribs contract; blood
oozed. It was birth the wrong way round—a monstrous inversion. So, raising
his foot, he stamped on them. (61)

Like his son, Giles finds himself presented with something in the environment that is unspeakable, and like his son, he can't just leave it alone. Instead, he finds a satisfaction in action, in the illusion of control through destruction. Giles is the sole member of the family who is worried about what
is happening in Europe, yet the satisfaction he feels in action for the sake of
asserting authority is itself ominously akin to the fascism he fears.

This common generational response suggests how vulnerable a place
is to the humans who own it. Cultures, histories, and places may be destroyed by the very efforts undertaken to defend them, as Virginia Woolf's
delineation of the "connection between militarism and masculine education" (Beer 180) made clear in *Three Guineas*. Indeed, as Gillian Beer has
shown, "[*Between the Acts*] holds the knowledge that cultures and histories
are obliterated, that things may not endure." At the same time, the response
of the Oliver males to affordances in the environment is part of a much
larger pattern of "call and response"—that is, of dialogics—which goes on
between all the participants, between acts, between people, between human
and nonhuman.

Between the Acts ends with parallel images linking inherently dialogical institutions, the theater and marriage. Putting the pageant behind her, Miss LaTrobe glimpses the possibilities of a new play, a play dominated by the image of "two figures, half concealed by a rock. The curtain would rise. What would the first words be?" (124). In Pointz Hall, the old and the young go to bed, leaving Giles and Isa alone to say the first words to each other they have spoken all day. The last two paragraphs of the novel read:

> Isa let her sewing drop. The great hooded chairs had become enormous. And Giles too. And Isa too against the window. The window was all sky without colour. The house had lost its shelter. It was night before roads were made, or houses. It was the night that dwellers in caves had watched from some high place among rocks.
>
> Then the curtain rose. They spoke. (130–31)

Both of these moments are poised on the edge of what Merleau-Ponty calls an "emergent order"; both, significantly, are dialogical. Miss LaTrobe must reach her audience; Giles and Isa must reach each other. Both will participate in the making and remaking of their world as part of a project that is beyond their control. And either or both may fail. Woolf leaves open the possibility of catastrophe, even extinction. But she also leaves open the possibility of making a new life, inventing a new script, a different plot, perhaps one which will make use of the "unacted parts" each of the characters has, perhaps parts of themselves to which the pageant has spoken. Against the bullying force of fascism, Woolf pits the dialogic process; against the threat of extinction, she pits the making and remaking of possibility that constitutes the fragility and strength of place.

NOTE

1. I am borrowing the metaphor of the Möbius strip from Elizabeth Grosz, who uses it to express a phenomenological understanding of mind/body relationships.

REFERENCES

Abram, David. *The Spell of the Sensuous: Perception and Language in a More-Than-Human World.* New York: Pantheon, 1996.

Bachelard, Gaston. *The Poetics of Space.* 1958. Trans. Maria Jolas. Boston: Beacon, 1964.

Beer, Gillian. *Arguing with the Past: Essays in Narrative from Woolf to Sidney.* London: Routledge, 1989.

Bigwood, Carol. *Earth Muse: Feminism, Nature, and Art.* Philadelphia: Temple UP, 1993.

Cataldi, Sue L. *Emotion, Depth, and Flesh: A Study of Sensitive Space. Reflections on Merleau-Ponty's Philosophy of Embodiment.* Albany: State U of New York P, 1993.

DeKoven, Marianne. *Rich and Strange: Gender, History, Modernism*. Princeton: Princeton UP, 1991.

Dick, Susan. *Virginia Woolf*. London: Edward Arnold, 1989.

Fisher, Alden L. Introduction. *The Essential Writings of Merleau-Ponty*. San Diego: Harcourt, Brace, 1969.

Gibson, James. *The Ecological Approach to Visual Perception*. Hillsdale, N.J.: Lawrence Erlbaum, 1986.

Grosz, Elizabeth. *Volatile Bodies: Toward a Corporeal Feminism*. Bloomington: Indiana UP, 1994.

Josipovici, Gabriel. *Touch*. New Haven: Yale UP, 1996.

Kaivola, Karen. *All Contraries Confounded: The Lyrical Fiction of Virginia Woolf, Djuna Barnes, and Marguerite Duras*. Iowa City: U of Iowa P, 1991.

Merleau-Ponty, Maurice. *The Essential Writings of Merleau-Ponty*. Ed. Alden L. Fisher. San Diego: Harcourt, Brace, 1969.

———. *The Visible and the Invisible*. Ed. Claude Lefort. Trans. Alphonso Lingis. Evanston, Ill.: Northwestern UP, 1968.

Murphy, Patrick. *Literature, Nature, and Other: Ecofeminist Critiques*. Albany: State U of New York P, 1995.

Phillips, Kathy J. *Virginia Woolf against Empire*. Knoxville: U of Tennessee P, 1994.

Plumwood, Val. *Feminism and the Mastery of Nature*. London: Routledge, 1993.

Relph, E. *Place and Placelessness*. London: Pion, 1976.

Wilde, Oscar. "The Decay of Lying." *The Artist as Critic: Critical Writings of Oscar Wilde*. Ed. Richard Ellmann. New York: Vintage, 1968.

Woolf, Virginia. *Between the Acts*. Ed. Stella McNichol. London: Penguin, 1992.

———. *A Woman's Essays*. Ed. Rachel Bowlby. London: Penguin, 1992.

———. *The Voyage Out*. Ed. Jane Wheare. London: Penguin, 1992.

No Trees Please, We're Jewish

ONE'S LEISURE TIME often provides a much needed respite from one's professional occupation. This is all to the good. Chafing against the pressures of article deadlines and uncorrected stacks of undergraduate papers, I have often found comfort in Henry David Thoreau's bold take on the issue of work versus leisure. We should only work "about six weeks in a year," according to Thoreau (57). Leisure, in fact, *is* Thoreau's "business" at Walden Pond and scarcely resembles the work he eschewed at his father's pencil-manufacturing plant.

Still, a distinction exists between the leisure activity that offers relief from one's occupation (even for the lucky soul who need only work the Thoreauvian six weeks per year) and the leisure activity that wrestles against the very soul of one's occupation. As a critic and teacher of Jewish American literature in my professional life, and an avid birder and would-be naturalist in my leisure life, it seems to me increasingly that I have crossed that line—that my avocation downright undermines my vocation, and vice-versa.

Early on in my career as a professor of literature, I pledged my allegiances to Malamud rather than Melville, to Bellow rather than Balzac, to Rebecca Goldstein rather than Cristina Garcia. I hardly regret my decision, nor do I seek to renounce it here. All the same, as my passion and concern for the environment increases, I find that reading and teaching Jewish American literature has become more and more problematic. For Jewish American fiction writers in this century have, by and large, created a literature that either ignores, misrepresents, or, at its most extreme, vilifies the natural world.

IT SHOULD BE of little surprise, of course, that the natural world rarely muscles its way into the margins of the Jewish-American imagination. Writers, the most successful ones anyway, tend to write about what they know, and Jewish Americans in this century, to put it simply, know cities. Immigrant populations, generally, flock toward locales and specific occupations

based upon the demands of the economic marketplace. I am not the first
to point out, for example, that there were no Chinese laundries in China
when the first Chinese immigrants carved out this occupational niche for
their community in urban centers like San Francisco and New York; likewise, the current abundance of Jewish Americans in the *shmatteh* business
largely reflects the marketplace demands of New York at the turn of the century. While there has never been much of an economic demand for Jewish
American writing, its overwhelmingly urban focus, at the most essential
level, merely betrays the sociological realities that have defined the Jewish American experience. Jews in this country generally do not know the
dense thickets of Thoreau's Concord or the fragrant honeysuckle and ver-
bena of Faulkner's Yoknapatawpha; they know the gritty streets of New
York and Chicago and, thus, have primarily contributed "city scriptures"
to the rich and diverse canon of American literature, to borrow the title of
Murray Baumgarten's influential study of Jewish American writing.

To my mind, Alfred Kazin's powerfully elegiac *A Walker in the City* (1951)
brings us as close as the Jewish American literary voice has come to what
we might properly call nature writing:

> At Highland Boulevard the last of the factories vanished below the hill, and
> the park emerged in its summer sweetness. At every corner along the boule-
> vard there were great trees; as we stopped at the top to catch our breaths, the
> traffic lights turned red and green on the trees and each leaf flushed separately
> in the colored light. . . . and as the light poured on the leaves, green and red,
> green and red, with a moment's pause between them, I seemed to see some
> force weary of custom, aroused against the monotony of day and night, play-
> ing violently with color in the freedom of the summer evening. (174)

Kazin's memoir bursts at the seams with such vivid evocations of the
marriage between the natural and urban environment. Here, Kazin
glimpses the transcendent in the play of a New York traffic light against
the leaves of a great tree. Still, it must be said that the "*Beyond!*" of Kazin's
memoir—the great physical and spiritual locus toward which Kazin's soul
aspires—is not to be found amid the verdant upstate woods; rather, "Beyond was 'the city,' connected only by interminable subway lines and some
old Brooklyn-Manhattan trolley car rattling across Manhattan Bridge" (88).
Between traffic light and tree, Kazin casts his lot with the traffic light.

Crossing Brooklyn Ferry to Manhattan, of course, represented something
entirely different for Kazin than it did for Whitman before him. In moving beyond the provincial Brownsville (pronounced *Brunzvil* by Kazin's

contemporaries) to the cosmopolitan Manhattan, Kazin achieved the immigrant dreams of his parents, and he would write eloquently about New York throughout his long and illustrious life. He, interestingly, would write just as eloquently as a critic on the work of Whitman, Emerson, Thoreau, and Dickinson, but he could not adopt their more pastoral literary turf as his own.

In an aptly entitled essay, "Strangers," Irving Howe poignantly described "the barriers of sensibility that separated Concord, Massachusetts from the immigrant streets of New York," barriers that alienated first-generation Jewish American writers, like Kazin and himself, from one of the core principles of the American literary tradition, the celebration of nature (14). To Howe and his cohorts, Emerson, for example,

> seemed frigid and bland, distant in his New England village—and how could we, of all generations, give our hearts to a writer who had lived all his life "in the country"? . . . Nature was something about which poets wrote and therefore it merited esteem, but we could not really suppose it was as estimable as reality—the reality which we knew to be social. Americans were said to love Nature, though there wasn't much evidence of this that our eyes could take in. Our own tradition, long rutted in *shtetl* mud and urban smoke, made little allowance for nature as presence or refreshment. (16)

THE SHEER PAUCITY of Yiddish terms when it comes to specific varieties of trees, flowers, and birds further illustrates Howe's point. One of my Jewish colleagues, in fact, has expressed his bemusement concerning my enthusiasm for bird-watching by teasing me with the chant, "A bird is a bird is a bird. A *faigeleh*." Yet if nature seemed altogether "unnatural" to early Jewish American writers, as it still does to my colleague above, it was not merely because of their shtetl and urban environs. Howe cannily recognized that more substantive socio-religious stuff was at play, impelling Jewish American writers to pay short shrift to the natural world. For "Nothing in our upbringing," Howe continued, "could prepare us to take seriously the view that God made his home in the woods. By now we rather doubted that He was to be found anywhere, but we felt pretty certain that wherever He might keep himself, it was not in a tree, or even leaves of grass. . . . What linked man and God in our tradition was not nature but the commandment" (16).

Howe alludes here to the Jewish rationalist, or *Mitnagged*, tradition from whence most of our Ashkenazic Jewish American writers come. Reaching its zenith in eighteenth-century Lithuania and Russia under their leader, the Vilna Gaon, *Mitnaggedism* embraces the rigorously text-centered mode of Jewish life. The *Mitnagdim*, in fact, boasted that the Vilna Gaon studied Jewish texts for eighteen hours a day (the number, incidentally, that symbolizes the Hebrew word *chai*, or life). Jonathan Rosen instructively traces the origin of Jewish "text-centeredness" to the story in the Talmud of Yochanan ben Zakkai, who manages resourcefully to found a yeshiva outside Jerusalem in Yavneh after the Romans destroy the Jewish Temple. Here, in Yavneh, during the first centuries of the Common Era, the Oral Law begins to take shape as a written document, the *Mishnah*, the first sixty-three tractates of the Talmud. "Jews," Rosen writes, "died as a people of the body, of the land, of the Temple service of fire and blood, and then, in one of the greatest acts of translation in human history, they were reborn as the people of the book" (53). This book, the Torah, has enabled Jews to survive as a distinct people for two thousand years in exile, living amid (and expelled from) various hostile nations. Indeed, Jews have *outlived* most of these hostile nations by privileging Torah over terrain. As George Steiner has famously noted, "the text *is* the homeland" (24).

While practicing text-centeredness has ensured the survival of the Jewish people, it has also bolstered a Jewish ethos wary, if not downright hostile, to the natural world. Writing squarely in the *Mitnagged* tradition, the eminent Rabbi Joseph Soloveitchik argued in this century that "[w]hen halakhic man approaches reality, he comes with his Torah, given to him from Sinai, in hand" (19). The halakhic man, according to Soloveitchik, does not seek inspiration in the natural world and must not even be "overly curious"; rather, he views the natural world only through the prism of the Law (20). In the "fading rays of the setting sun," the halakhic man sees the religious obligations attendant to that particular sunset: "he knows that this sunset or sunrise imposes upon him anew obligations and commandments" (20). In culling especially breathtaking examples from the natural world to make his point (e.g., the setting sun, mighty mountains, a spring bubbling quietly), Soloveitchik betrays his prescience that the natural world's splendor threatens ever to lead the less than "halakhic man" toward pantheism. (Importantly, both the rationalist and mystical Jewish traditions insist upon the separation between God and the physical world.) Girded with the "rules, judgments, and fundamental principles" of the Law, a Jew stands little chance of confusing the created with the Creator—of, in short, idolizing nature (19).

Rabbis steeped in the rationalist tradition, then, wary of paganism, have mainly posited an antagonistic relationship between Judaism and nature, and a consequent Jewish hostility toward nature has long pervaded Jewish life in the Diaspora. The great Russian Jewish writer Isaac Babel poignantly engaged this hostility in a 1930 story, "Awakening." To become a writer, the autobiographical narrator of the story (an adult looking back upon his childhood) must rebel against the acceptable text-centered mode of Jewish life, a cloistered existence that stunts the physical and spiritual growth of Jewish children, turning them into "starvelings with blue, swollen heads" (Babel 60). He chooses the harbor and the sea over violin lessons and Torah study, realizing that his flirtation with the natural realm rips him away from the acceptable Jewish realm: "the heavy waves by the sea wall distanced me further and further from our house, which was steeped in the smell of onions and Jewish destiny" (62). Unable to swim like the Christian boys, the narrator laments that he has yet to learn the "essential things!" (63). He continues, "In my childhood, nailed to the Gemara [a section of Talmud], I led the life of a sage" (63). An elderly Christian mentor affirms the narrator's growing conviction that he will never be a writer until he learns the names of the trees, bushes, and birds—until he cultivates a "feeling for nature" (64). Toward the end of the story, the tension between Torah and trees comes to a head, and the narrator flees his father's home in the middle of the night. "The moonlight," he reflects, "froze on unknown bushes, on trees that had no name. An invisible bird gave a peep and was silent—perhaps it had fallen asleep. What kind of bird was it?" (67). We know that this artist as a young man will learn the names of those bushes, trees, and that "invisible bird." He will become a writer. He will *not* return to his father's Jewish hearth in Odessa.

This seems a harsh fate. But one can readily appreciate, in pragmatic terms, the trepidation with which Jews living in Babel's Odessa, and elsewhere in the Diaspora, have long regarded the awesome environment teeming just outside the yeshiva walls. The mountains, the sea, the forest—Jews at any given moment might be ripped from their presence. All it took was the evil capriciousness of mufti, king, or czar. It made pragmatic sense, then, to spurn any emotional or spiritual investment in the natural world, because Jews could never really count upon it. They were constantly reminded that the physical world did not belong to them, but to their host country. What Jews *could rely* upon, what would always be theirs, was the Torah and their status as the "Covenanted." The principal condition that has accounted for Jewish survival in the Diasopora, the French philosopher Emmanuel Levinas has noted, is that Jews are a "nation united by ideas" (257). All of which is to say that a host of influences, from the deeply theological to the pragmatic, have compelled Jews from the Talmudic era to the present to regard the natural world as a dangerous threat to the Law that has sustained them.

SMALL WONDER, then, that the natural world often occupies a malevolent role in the work of Jewish American writers. The fiction of Cynthia Ozick, perhaps most significantly, embodies this Judaic hostility toward the natural realm. "The Pagan Rabbi," one of her most famous stories, opens with the following epigram from the tractate of Talmud called the *Pirkei Avot: "Rabbi Jacob said: 'He who is walking along and studying,' but then breaks off to remark, 'How lovely is that tree!' or 'How beautiful is that fallow field!'—Scripture regards such a one as having hurt his own being"* (Ozick 3). Here, before we even read the first paragraph of the story, Ozick evokes the dichotomy between the natural world and the Judaic. In the story that follows, Ozick continues to insist upon this dichotomy as her narrator struggles to discover what drove his childhood friend, the brilliant Rabbi Isaac Kornfeld, to commit suicide. After consulting with Kornfeld's widow and reading Kornfeld's journal, it becomes clear to the narrator that the natural realm vied against the Jewish realm for Kornfeld's soul. (The very name, Isaac Kornfeld, evokes this central tension.) Kornfeld strays from Torah by studying horticulture, hiking, writing fairy tales, taking his family on far too many mosquito-infested picnics (as his embittered widow reveals), and even nuzzling up shamefully against a tree. In short, Pan defeats Moses. "Great Pan lives," Kornfeld writes in his diary, thereby renouncing the Judaic for the pagan realm (17).

The story might best be understood as a meditation upon the incongruity between these two realms and the tragic consequences that ensue once they are forced into contact with one another. Kornfeld realizes only too late that he has expelled his Jewish soul through his paganism. "In your grave beside you I would have sung you David's songs," his Jewish soul admonishes him (36). "The sound of the Law," his soul continues, "is more beautiful than the crickets. The smell of the Law is more radiant than the moss. The taste of the Law exceeds clear water" (36). Seeing no hope for redemption, Kornfeld hangs himself on a tree limb by his prayer shawl. It is a wonderfully evocative image, one that suggests that the natural world is altogether *treif*, unkosher, for the Jew. Prayer shawl and tree do not mix any better than *milchik* and *flaishik,* milk and meat. In this image, and in the story's epigram, title, and central character's name, Ozick yokes the natural world with the pagan, pitting it foursquare against the Judaic. Put simply, a Jew, according to Ozick, has no business with trees.

I have taught Ozick's story several times to undergraduates in my "Jewish-American Literature" course but find it an increasingly uncomfortable exercise. Students these days, for better or for worse, read literature as vehicles of access to whatever particular race, culture, or religion they feel is being described. So just as I often find myself explaining to an "American Novel" class that Zora Neale Hurston's African Americans of Eatonville do not represent all African American voices, experiences, and perspectives, I find myself somewhat defensively making a similar claim when students in my "Jewish-American Literature" class read Ozick's "The Pagan Rabbi" and sheepishly wonder, what gives? I try to explain that the natural world and paganism are not nearly so inextricably bound as Ozick suggests, that a Jewish space does exist for Jews concerned about the environment.

Like any good Jewish rationalist worth his salt, I turn first to the Torah itself and an oft-quoted passage from Deuteronomy: "When thou shalt besiege a city a long time, in making war against it to take it, thou shalt not destroy the trees thereof by wielding an axe against them; for thou mayest eat of them, but thou shalt not cut them down; for is the tree of the field man, that it should be besieged of thee?" (Deuteronomy 20:19) The rabbis have interpreted this passage to exemplify the Jewish principle of Baal Tashkhit, the preservation of nature, which applies even during times of war. The Talmud even records that scholars were instructed to pray for the health of sick trees (*Shabbat* 67a). This discussion usually leads me to mention the Jewish holiday of Tu B'shvat, the new year for trees, observed each year on the fifteenth day of the Jewish month of Shvat, during which Jews customarily plant trees and partake of their fruit. (Given the confluence of such examples, is it any wonder that students are bewildered upon coming across one of Ozick's more lubricious characters in her more recent work, *The Shawl* (1989), named James W. Tree, Ph.D.?) It strikes me as nothing less than staggering that the rabbis who forged the Talmud expressed ecological concerns ranging from city planning to air, water, and even noise pollution. In a more secular vein (but, no doubt, related to Judaic values), I occasionally cite the inordinate number of Jewish Americans who occupy leadership positions in environmental organizations, and I have noted that—owing to widespread hunting practices and illegal poaching in the Arab states—Israel's Hula Nature Reserve is practically the only safe place in the Middle

East for a migratory bird to land. I turn to various places, then, to complicate and interrogate the specific Jewish perspective toward the natural world that Ozick powerfully affirms in her story.

Where I find I cannot turn, however, is to a significant body of Jewish American literature that asserts a greater appreciation for the environment. Whereas I usually introduce students to Richard Wright's militant Bigger Thomas to counterbalance Zora Neale Hurston's more felicitous African American characters, nearly unbesmirched by the stain of racism, I still search in vain for Jewish American fictionists who imagine a harmonious Jewish space amid the natural world.

So briefly: the only novels by Saul Bellow and Bernard Malamud in which nature figures prominently are *Henderson the Rain King* (1959) and *Dubin's Lives* (1979), respectively. Rather than mere exceptions that prove the rule, these works, set miles outside Bellow's and Malamud's familiar urban terrain, go a long way toward asserting the incompatibility between Jews and nature. In Eugene Henderson, Bellow creates one of his few gentile protagonists, which perhaps suggests how un-Jewish the natural realm strikes Bellow from the start. Dogged by a ceaseless inner voice, "*I want, I want!*" Bellow's Henderson pulls up the stakes and travels to the wilds of Africa in search of his soul (14). While Bellow affirms his protagonist's desire to burst his spirit's sleep, he does not endorse the strategy Henderson adopts. The novel, instead, parodies such Hemingwayesque—note Eugene Henderson's initials—forays into the rugged, natural realm. (Bellow, revealingly, never even felt the need to take a research trip to Africa before writing the novel.) Emerson's famous passage from "Self-Reliance"—"traveling is a fool's paradise. We owe to our first journeys the discovery that place is nothing. . . . My giant goes with me wherever I go"—represents the most significant Emersonian precept that Bellow affirms (149). "[T]he world is a mind," Henderson comes to understand. "[T]ravel is mental travel. I had always suspected this" (*Henderson* 167). Indeed, Bellow does not allow his protagonist to receive illumination, real illumination, through his journey deep into the African interior. Henderson "bursts his spirit's sleep" not through his misguided adventures in Africa, but through reflecting upon his childhood job at an Ontario amusement park, riding the roller coaster with an aged, bedraggled bear for the perverse entertainment of onlookers:

> This poor broken ruined creature and I, alone, took the high rides twice a
> day. . . . By a common bond of despair we embraced, cheek to cheek, as all
> support seemed to leave us and we started down the perpendicular drop. I

was pressed into his long-suffering, age-worn, tragic, and discolored coat as he grunted and cried to me. . . . Whatever gains I ever made were always due to love and nothing else. (338)

In *Dubin's Lives*, Malamud depicts rural Vermont far less satirically than Bellow depicts Africa's remote interior. But it is just as true that Malamud's lush New England countryside nearly precludes rather than precipitates the gains that William Dubin achieves by the end of the novel. Malamud makes it clear at the outset that Dubin's relationship with nature, overbrimming on every side of him, is a tentative one: "In sum, William Dubin, visitor to nature, had introduced himself along the way but did not intrude. He gazed from the road, kept his distance even when nature hallooed" (14). This Jewish man, reared in Newark and Bronx tenements, does not quite belong in nature. A professional biographer of Thoreau and others, Dubin seems to thrive as a writer tucked away in the reclusive Vermont woods; he founders, however, as a human being. His isolation from the social world obfuscates his attendant social obligations, namely toward his wife, Kitty. The sensual world of nature encourages him to adopt D. H. Lawrence's "religion of sexuality" as he pursues licentious affairs with both the nubile Fanny Bick and Flora Greenfeld, the middle-aged wife of one of his few Vermont friends (243).

Pastoral imagery, revealingly, suffuses Malamud's description of Dubin's illicit sexual affairs. While Flora Greenfeld's name speaks for itself, Malamud invokes pastoral imagery even more pervasively when it comes to Dubin's affair with Fanny. "With this girl," Dubin reflects in one of his more ridiculously ebullient moments, "I know the flowering pleasure, heathen innocence, of the natural life. I live in her sun-strong garden" (243). Clearly, Malamud suggests, this is no way for a Jew to behave. Dubin triumphs, finally, through reflecting upon the social attachments and the concomitant responsibilities that defined his Jewish upbringing, through embracing these values that Malamud so volubly affirms here and elsewhere in his oeuvre, and through renouncing the libidinous realm so strongly linked in the novel with Vermont's verdant woods.

Philip Roth's work proves even more instructive than Bellow's or Malamud's. Despite the many permutations that have defined Roth's career, he has consistently cast a skeptical eye toward the natural world. In one of his earliest stories, "Eli, the Fanatic," a precipitous moral decline accompanies the Jews' postwar migration to the pastoral New York suburb of Woodenton. These affluent Jews of Woodenton manage to live "in amity" with

their gentile neighbors, they believe, through eschewing their "more extreme practices" ("Eli" 189). They live in "comfort, beauty and serenity" and
enjoy their "long lawns" (189, 202). To this assimilated cohort, the newly
established Orthodox yeshiva in town represents a threat to their bucolic
existence. Through enlisting the help of Eli Peck, the lawyer among them
and the story's protagonist, they seek rather ruthlessly to evict the yeshiva
students and their Hasidic teacher, all of whom are Holocaust survivors. "If
I want to live in Brownsville, Eli, I'll live in Brownsville," a minor character
bemoans (184). Eli demurs but nonetheless descends to a moral nadir of
his own as he offers the Hasidic teacher one of his own business suits in
an attempt to erase his Jewishness. It is no accident, I would argue, that
this business suit happens to be green. Whatever the material and aesthetic
delights of wooded "Wood"-enton, the Jewish soul, Roth implies through
his pensive protagonist (who manages to redeem himself by the end of the
story), enjoyed far better health along Brownsville's asphalt and cement.

   Roth has reaffirmed his skeptical vision toward the pastoral only in his
more recent work. For example, in two recent award-winning novels, *The
Counterlife* (1987) and *American Pastoral* (1997), the natural realm continues to emerge as antithetical to the Jewish realm. Maria Freshfield, Nathan
Zuckerman's lover in *The Counterlife*, embodies the pastoral. She lives in
Gloucestershire, nestled deep in the English countryside, "where the grass
couldn't be greener," and writes self-described "fluffy ephemera . . . about
the mists, the meadows, the decaying gentlefolk I grew up with" (*The Counterlife* 222, 215). As lovely and tempting as both Maria and the English countryside seem, they emerge finally as altogether *treif* for Zuckerman. (Roth's
"Fresh"-field, to put it another way, is no more compatible with the Jew than
Ozick's "Korn"-field or Malamud's "Green"-field.) The pastoral might be
said to reject Zuckerman as he repeatedly encounters an insidious brand
of anti-Semitism in Gloucestershire. All the same, *he* rejects the pastoral
when he excoriates its naive, asocial aspect. To Maria's horror, for example, he would insist upon having their son circumcised because this Jewish
ritual, according to Zuckerman, "gives the lie to the womb-dream of life
in the beautiful state of innocent prehistory, the appealing idyll of living
'naturally,' unencumbered by man-made ritual" (370). To live with Maria
in Gloucestershire would be to cower from the social realm—the realm, according to Howe above, that has long defined the Jewish reality, and that
clearly consumes Zuckerman's energies as a Jewish writer (albeit a secular one) living in the tumultuous twentieth century. His relationship with
Maria dissolves as he recognizes that "the pastoral is not my genre" (369).

Roth further scrutinizes the pastoral possibilities in the sardonically entitled *American Pastoral*. Nathan Zuckerman, Roth's familiar alter-ego, here reconstructs the story of his childhood hero, Seymour "the Swede" Levov, and discovers that tragedy accompanied Levov's embrace of the ostensibly idyllic, pastoral existence. Through his apparently effortless embrace of an "all-American" ethos, Levov achieves a nearly mythic reputation in Newark. A brilliant athlete in high school and college, Levov proceeds to serve honorably in the Marine Corps, marry an Irish Catholic beauty queen, and move, physically and symbolically, far far away from the immigrant Jewish streets, "some thirty-odd miles west of Newark, out past the suburbs, a short-range pioneer living on a hundred-acre farm on a back road in the sparsely habitated hills beyond Morristown, in wealthy, rural Old Rimrock, New Jersey, a long way from the tannery floor where Grandfather Levov had begun in America" (*American Pastoral* 14). As Zuckerman reflects, the Swede leapfrogs the Jewish suburbs—like, say, Woodenton—when he acquires "A hundred acres of America" (307). Zuckerman further projects himself into Levov's passion for the pastoral, embodied in Old Rimrock: "I want to see the *land*. I want to see the streams running everywhere. I want to see the cows and the horses. You drive down the road, there's a *falls* there" (308).

Roth, however, cannot allow Levov to partake of the utterly uncomplicated, pastoral existence. And so he creates Merry Levov, the Swede's daughter, who kills an innocent civilian when she plants a bomb in Old Rimrock's post office to protest America's involvement in the Vietnam War. Her act of violence "transports him out of the longed-for American pastoral and into everything that is its antithesis and its enemy, into the fury, the violence, and the desperation of the counterpastoral—into the indigenous American berserk" (86). But it is not simply that Merry's act of violence precludes the pastoral existence for Levov. Roth implies that the reclusive, asocial existence that Levov adopts and imposes upon Merry contributes to her despondency as a child and, at least in part, provokes her destructive and self-destructive actions. Roth depicts Levov's reclusive life in the country in all its fatuousness (he and his wife, for example, raise cattle) to suggest how far he has removed himself and his family from his immigrant Jewish past in Newark. Merry's headlong immersion in radical social causes represents, at least on one level, her revolt against her father's asocial, amoral, and downright anti-Jewish existence in Old Rimrock. "You can't keep hiding out here in the woods," she admonishes him. She continues later, stammeringly, "All you can deal with is c-cows. C-cows and trees. Well, there's something besides c-c-c-c-cows and trees. There are people. People with real pain" (109). While Roth hardly endorses Merry's violent brand of social protest, the narrative clearly affirms her views here. Roth, to be sure, couches his hostility toward the pastoral realm in ethnic rather than overtly Judaic terms. (The same might be said of Bellow and Malamud.) But Jews and trees make every bit as incongruous a match through Roth's artistic vision as through Ozick's. "You'll never heat it," Levov's father immediately reacts upon seeing the Old Rimrock farmhouse that his son imprudently purchases (308). The line resonates long after one has put the novel down.

But here I feel, as I so often do, that I must return to Bellow, and to *Herzog* (1964), specifically. For in Moses Herzog's misguided decision to move himself and his family to the most remote fringes of the Berkshires, Bellow in many ways anticipated Roth's more extended meditation upon the American pastoral. Bellow names the Berkshire town in which Herzog buys property "Ludeyville" to evoke the sheer lunacy of his Chicago Jew living in the woods. As Herzog draws nearer and nearer to his Jewish soul, to his Herzog heart, he recognizes his purchase of rural real estate for what it is: "Herzog's folly! . . . symbol of his Jewish struggle for a solid footing in White Anglo-Saxon Protestant America" (309). A life of solitude and privacy in the rural woods, while central to the ethos of White Anglo-Saxon Protestant America, is anathema to the Jewish soul, Bellow suggests. Herzog amusingly, while poignantly, refers to his wooded environs as a "remote green hole" and readily infers what his brother thinks of his Ludeyville home: "*In drerd aufn deck. The edge of nowhere. Out on the lid of Hell*" (322, 329). He finally dismisses Robert Frost's famous passage that he intoned at John F. Kennedy's presidential inauguration—"the land was ours before we were the land's"—as the sententious declaration of an old man (309). So much for the trees, vines, bushes, and blossoms.

WHAT OF our younger Jewish American novelists? They, somewhat surprisingly, have yet to create a literature more receptive to the natural world. A brief look at two recent novels by two of our most celebrated younger Jewish American writers, Rebecca Goldstein and Allegra Goodman, will suffice to make my point. In *Mazel* (1995), which won the National Jewish Book Award and the Edward Lewis Wallant Prize (awarded annually to the finest work of Jewish American fiction), Goldstein offers a distinctively feminist vision of Jewish life in three essential Jewish milieux—a prewar shtetl, cosmopolitan Warsaw, and suburban New Jersey—but does not essentially depart from Ozick's hostile vision of nature. To wit: Goldstein depicts unfettered nature as a realm decidedly beyond the perimeter of her mythical shtetl, Shluftchev, and inextricably bound to the pagan realm of the Gypsies. When the sisters Sorel and Fraydel dare to visit this realm,

> It was as if the two sisters had crossed foreign seas and faraway lands to come to this place that Sorel had never before seen, far more frightening and more beautiful than the little spot beside the river where she went each autumn to cast off her year's worth of sins. The evening was falling into the forest with a bluish tint to it that seemed to Sorel a Gypsy color. The smell of the earth rose up all around her, heavy and rich as after a rain, and the trees whispered so insistently above their heads that she felt she could almost make out distinct words here and there, spoken in the Gypsy tongue. (106)

The Jews of Shluftchev make their foray into nature, then, only once a year to observe the Rosh ha-Shana ritual of *Tashlikh*. Otherwise, nature is for, and of, the Gypsies. Even the color of a forest's atmosphere seems to Sorel a Gypsy, rather than Jewish, color. The natural world is intoxicating, to be sure. On their way home from the Gypsy camp, Fraydel and Sorel find it difficult to trade this sensuous realm of the Gypsies for the Judaic realm of their shtetl. They plunge into the "farmer's field instead of taking the longer road back," ostensibly to save time and make it home before nightfall; all the same, they take the time to soak in the sensuous delights: "the throbbing of the crickets . . . sounded loudly in their ears. The air itself was heavy and sweet with the smell of the ripening grains and melons, apples and pears, and the insects were making themselves crazy in the tall singing grass. . . . And the stars!" (113). Goldstein, however, stops far short of embracing the natural realm of the Gypsies as a viable option for her Jewish characters, or even as a desirable one. That Sorel and Fraydel must endure the fierce welts from relentless insects that somehow penetrate the fabric of their long, Judaically modest, skirts betrays the trepidation with which Goldstein regards nature in the novel.

Raw nature emerges, finally, as a force equally seductive and destructive as it lures Fraydel irrevocably away from the secure, albeit constrictive, Judaic realm. Faced with the prospect of an arranged marriage, Fraydel chooses nature instead, flouting the rules of the Sabbath by picking and carrying flowers (see the *Mishnah Shabbat* 7:2). As Sorel observes at the time, Fraydel, flowers in hand, eschews the Judaic for the libidinous codes of the pagan: "Fraydel wasn't walking like Fraydel either, not like any Jewish girl or woman walked. She was barefoot—where were her shoes?—and was rolling her hips in the loose and easy motions of the Gypsy women" (148).

One can almost hear the collective groan, enough is enough, emanate from Shluftchev's shanties. The shtetl will simply not tolerate Fraydel's paganism, and her fiancé's family predictably calls off the wedding. Since Fraydel, for her part, cannot embrace Shluftchev's piety, she sews rocks into the bottom of her skirt and—à la Shakespeare's Ophelia—drowns herself. Of course, through Fraydel's tragic story, Goldstein offers an incisive critique of the repressive patriarchal mores of Shluftchev. Fraydel's sheer individuality dooms her in the pious shtetl, where, as Sasha reflects, "the girls were all supposed to be pressed out from the same cookie cutter, anything extra trimmed away" (18). Yet the natural realm—embodied by the brook in which Fraydel drowns herself—hardly emerges as a viable option for Goldstein's Jewish girls. Goldstein unsurprisingly cannot bring herself to imagine Fraydel actually running off with the Gypsies. But further, Goldstein does not allow Fraydel or Sorel to glimpse any sort of integration between the natural realm and a revised, Jewish (rather than pagan) feminist identity.

This is not to say that Goldstein fails to envision more hopeful alternatives for the Jewish woman in the twentieth century. However, one discovers her corrective for Shluftchev in Warsaw rather than the woods. Sorel, who changes her name to Sasha, flourishes only once her family moves to the cosmopolitan city. What, in fact, provokes Sasha's euphoria upon first setting her sights on Warsaw is its stark contrast to the natural realm:

> No crookedly leaning homes of unwhitewashed wood sinking half buried in the mud. Where was there even a patch of naked earth to be turned into mud? Not a tree, not a blade of grass dared to show itself here. Everything was forged of massive pale stone and great slabs of concrete. . . . Serious buildings, which took *themselves* seriously too. . . . How remarkable to have so transformed the naked earth that nothing of its original state remained! (159–60)

LIVING AS I DO in south Florida, where countless stuccoed developments and strip malls have so completely erased the "original state" of the "naked earth" as to render it irretrievable—and nearly unfathomable to my nonnative eyes—Sasha's initial impressions of Warsaw send shivers up my spine. For Sasha admires the way in which the people of Warsaw have managed to subdue, even erase, the natural world. That nary a blade of grass dares show itself in Warsaw bothers Sasha not a whit. She, somewhat ironically, only flowers as an individual once Goldstein removes her from the realm of flowers.

While I would not claim that Goldstein speaks through Sasha, Sasha does emerge as the most winning character in *Mazel*. So it strikes me as significant that Goldstein's most fully realized and indomitable female character cannot bring herself, even later in life while visiting her granddaughter's New Jersey suburb, to say one kind word about a tree. Upon seeing the magnolias in Lipton, she opines, "What *senseless* trees. They flower for all of two minutes, then they rot. What's the *point*?" (15).

What is more, Goldstein does not suggest elsewhere in the novel a more receptive Jewish vision toward the natural world. Granted, Goldstein is not glibly dismissive of Phoebe's embrace of Orthodoxy in the tree-lined suburb of Lipton, New Jersey. Phoebe, Sasha's granddaughter, thrives in Lipton. Still, in choosing to live there, Phoebe embraces a *less* pastoral community than the genteel Princeton, where she works as a mathematics professor. Despite its magnolia trees, Sasha associates Lipton not so much with nature but with dreary Shluftchev, given the constrictive Orthodox gender mores that hold sway. Goldstein's new Jewish women, then, realize viable identities either amid the secular urban milieu, antithetical to the natural environment, or amid a re-energized *Mitnagged* community, dutifully obedient to the Law and oblivious to nature.

In *Kaaterskill Falls* (1998), a finalist for the National Book Award and winner of the Edward Lewis Wallant Prize, Allegra Goodman ups Goldstein's ante, in a sense, through creating a more rigorously Orthodox community than Goldstein's Lipton Jews, and through situating them in a far more rural setting than Lipton. The members of the Kirshner sect spend their summers in the tiny upstate New York town of Kaaterskill Falls, where Rav Kirshner and his followers seek relief from the sweltering heat of Washington Heights, New York, amid the lakes and forested mountains of the Catskills. As the Anglo-Dutch name of the town suggests, Goodman defines the Judaic realm of the Kirshners against the rural ethos of Kaaterskill Falls. Evoking the *Mitnagged* tradition, Goodman writes that the Kirshners "array themselves with gorgeous words"; by contrast, they have little regard for gorgeous woods (4). Indeed, the rugged landscape painting emblazoned on the front cover, Thomas Cole's "The Falls of Kaaterskill," smacks of the sardonic touch to roughly the same degree as the title of Roth's recent novel, *American Pastoral*. Similarly, the epigrams to most of the novel's seven sections, passages of refulgent nature writings by the likes of John Keats and Thoreau, evoke the tension at the center of this novel between Judaic Law (which Goodman scrutinizes, but volubly affirms) and the Romantic, pagan impulse (which Goodman also explores, and rejects).

Goodman engages this tension most pointedly through Andras Melish, who undergoes a crisis of faith and begins to look outside the Judaic realm. An elderly female recluse, Una, who lives in the woods outside Kaaterskill, serves as a model of an alternative existence for Andras, an existence unbound by the rigors of filial and religious commitment. Una, whose very name evokes the pagan pages of Edmund Spenser's *The Faerie Queene*, embodies the natural realm: "Una has removed herself from the company of other people; she chooses animals and trees as her companions" (124). Such an existence initially appeals to Andras, which explains his frequent visits to Una's remote cabin. "Una lives in luxury, living alone," Andras reflects (133). "She does not have people to her house," he continues, "does not invite them to dinner or worry about what they think of the food. She has no garden. *All her trees grow wild*" (133; emphasis added). But this misanthropic existence, ultimately, seems a shabby one. Perhaps Goodman's least convincingly drawn character, Una emerges as little more than a model of how a Jew should not live. She dies alone as a stone, and it is Andras who discovers her decomposing body in her cabin. After notifying the proper authorities, he speeds back to his Jewish home and hearth in the city. He, ultimately, manages to realize a meaningful existence, not in the remote woods, but in the relationships he has forged with his wife and his two doting older sisters.

This is not to say that Goodman repudiates nature altogether in her novel. Her authorial vision, like Goldstein's, strikes me as far less strident than Ozick's in "The Pagan Rabbi." In several richly drawn passages through which she describes the change of seasons in the upstate woods, Goodman allows herself to luxuriate for some precious prose moments in the beauty of the natural world. That the Kirshners spend the summers in the Catskills, in the first place, suggests a certain tolerance toward nature. And more. Rav Kirshner's wife convinced her husband that they should spend their summers in the bucolic Kaaterskill because it was "[n]ot good to have only one thing and not another" (110). It is this balance between the secular and the sacred that Goodman seems to advocate. Could Goodman, who clearly treasures the sacred but writes creative fiction rather than *Responsa*, come to any other conclusion?

Still, Goodman, like Goldstein, does not essentially depart from Ozick's vision. Nature remains a dangerous realm that ever threatens to lure Jews from Judaism. What becomes clear by the end of *Kaaterskill Falls* is that the natural world, in Goodman's view, poses a far greater threat toward upsetting the balance between the secular and the sacred than, say, German poetry or Shakespeare. A closing vision of Jewish continuity—the dead Rav's books being returned to his library by his wayward son—implicitly illustrates Goodman's fervent desire to hold the natural realm in check. "A river of books," Goodman writes, "flowing back smoothly into the Rav's shadowy apartment" (313). It is not enough, finally, for Goodman to insist upon a dichotomy between the natural realm and the Judaic. She must assiduously prune back the pagan leaves, subdue the pagan influence. She tames this realm most tersely above through appropriating the language of nature to affirm the text-centeredness of the Kirshners.

Lest I strike a strident chord of my own, I should explain that I find the Jewish American writers above, Ozick included, guilty of no real transgression, either in the literary or Jewish sense. Through their fiction, they have embraced a particular, even prevalent, post-exilic Jewish vision toward the natural world. But, as I hope I have shown, it is not the *only* Jewish vision toward the natural world. And it is not a vision I embrace.

That I grew up in the northern stretches of the San Fernando Valley in Los Angeles rather than in New York City (where I was born) has much to do, I believe, with my more ecologically receptive ethos. While cities do a good job, too good a job, of keeping the natural world at bay, the inexorable force of nature occupied the foreground of my childhood in Northridge. Vicious droughts, after all, often required that we conserve water by limiting our baths and even the number of times that we flushed the toilet; in the same year, torrential downpours could transform streets into veritable rivers, the valley's intricate web of concrete runoff canals into drowning pools for unwary children my age; brushfires in the chaparral hills surrounding the valley routinely glowed against the night sky, sending cautious home owners onto their vulnerable wood-shake roofs with garden hoses to discourage that single stray ember; the violent rumblings and occasional smooth waves of subterranean tremors often woke me from my sleep.

While the natural world could seem impervious, it could also seem terribly vulnerable, especially during my bicycle riding adventures with friends along the treacherous rock and dirt trails in the valley's foothills. Vast as the untainted stretches of chaparral, dirt, and oak seemed to me, the neighborhoods just to the south and east were even more expansive and were scarcely a few years old. The forces of S&S homes had amassed on the east side of Tampa Avenue, a street aptly named after a city conquered by invaders from the east; it was only a matter of time, I knew, before this human force would gather the will to cross to the west side of Tampa and transform my treasured backyard of dust and oak into, well, just another neighborhood of asphalt, cement, stucco, and flourescent lights to blot out the night sky. Of course, this is exactly what happened in the northern stretches of the San Fernando Valley, where people have supplanted, once and for all, the rattlesnakes, coyotes, and red-tailed hawks. During a recent visit, I cringed upon driving into these neighborhoods I had glimpsed on the horizon some twenty years ago. Only a blink of an eye ago, the terrain upon which these houses now sit was accessible only to rugged shoes or puncture-proof bicycle inner tubes.

Meanwhile, my recent move to south Florida has started me thinking once again about what has happened to the land of the red-tailed hawks in Southern California. While my birding "life list" has nearly doubled after two years of living in the semi-tropics, the birds here are in great peril as residential, commercial, and agricultural developers (read: Big Sugar) set their sights further and further west into the embattled Everglades. A strong sense of déjà vu overtook me as I recently drove to a favorite birding spot—a dry prairie usually teeming with swallows, northern harriers, kestrels, and meadowlarks—to find it utterly destroyed. The saw palmetto, wax myrtle, and wire grass had been plowed under, the slash pine and live oak felled and removed. A flourishing ecosystem was suddenly a vast stretch of nothingness. Not a single bird was in sight or sound.

And my thoughts drifted to the extinct passenger pigeon. Most in the know agree that in the early nineteenth century the passenger pigeon outnumbered every other North American bird species, combined. *Combined!* Consider John James Audubon's early-nineteenth-century account of the incredibly prolific flocks of passenger pigeons and the ruthless manner in which these flocks, taking roost for the night, were decimated by hunters who awaited their arrival:

> The air was literally filled with Pigeons; the light of noon-day was obscured as by an eclipse; the dung fell in spots, not unlike melting flakes of snow; and the continued buzz of wings had a tendency to lull my senses to repose. . . . As the period of their arrival approached, their foes anxiously prepared to receive them. Some were furnished with iron-pots containing sulphur, others with torches of pine-knots, many with poles, and the rest with guns. . . . The Pigeons were picked up and piled in heaps, until each had as many as he could possibly dispose of, when the hogs were let loose to feed on the remainder. (554, 556)

The most haunting passage of Audubon's account? Not by a long shot. The most haunting passage follows as he seeks to allay his readers' fears: "Persons unacquainted with these birds might naturally conclude that such dreadful havoc would soon put an end to the species. But I have satisfied myself, by long observation, that nothing but the gradual diminution of our forests can accomplish their decrease" (557). The passage, no doubt, comforted Audubon's original readers in the mid–nineteenth century. It now strikes us as darkly ironic, tragically prophetic.

The case of the passenger pigeon illustrates how irrevocably we have damaged the natural environment in North America. While the Jewish principle of Baal Tashkhit, the preservation of nature, seeks to preclude the very behavior that led to the passenger pigeon's extinction (the decimation of the forest), Jewish American writers have yet to broach in a serious or sustained way any such ecological quandaries in their work. Thus, while I continue to read and write about Jewish American literature, I find myself increasingly drawn to our non-Jewish writers who were fortunate enough to live in an America still crisp and new. It saddens me that there are fewer and fewer wild spaces to inspire the ardor of discovery that bursts through the prose of, say, William Bartram's *Travels* (1791). Consider, for example, his encounter with Georgia's Alatamaha River: "How gently flow thy peaceful floods, O Alatamaha! How sublimely rise to view, on thy elevated shores, yon Magnolia groves, from whose tops the surrounding expanse is perfumed, by clouds of incense, blended with the exhaling balm of the Liquidamber, and odors continually arising from circumambient aromatic groves of Illicium, Myrica, Laurus, and Bignonia" (31).

Ralph Waldo Emerson, Henry David Thoreau, Margaret Fuller, Walt Whitman, Emily Dickinson, and others would succeed Bartram and, adding intellect to his exuberance, tap into nature's transcendental potential. But what all of these writers shared was a reverence toward the ineffable beauty and majesty of the natural world. Moreover, they leaned an attentive ear to heed its instruction. Mourning the death of President Lincoln, Walt Whitman hears the chant of his own soul in the warbling of that gray-brown bird:

> sing on there in the swamp,
> O singer bashful and tender,
> I hear your Notes, I hear your call,
> I hear, I come presently, I understand you. (235)

Whitman was reared in a freethinking household and felt no qualms about absorbing a veritable potpourri of cultural and religious principles and incorporating them into his own passionately democratic artistic vision. That he flirts with paganism above—where, after all, is the Creator here?—would hardly have troubled him. What does it mean, however, that a self-consciously Jewish literary type like me frets little over the arguable paganism of Whitman's vision? Worse, that I respond to it. That amid the din of our increasingly urbanized society (heralded by the locomotives that Thoreau heard rumble threateningly off in the distance from his cabin aside Walden Pond), the voice of the natural world resounds for me. Have I, like Ozick's pagan Rabbi Kornfeld, been lured astray by the natural world?

To be sure, there are several who would be inclined to reply in the affirmative and take my case as a textbook example of the tragic waning of Judaism in America. Like, say, the spokesperson for the Conservative Jewish group Toward Tradition, who responded to a recent article in the *Forward* on the Jewish environmental movement by excoriating the movement in a letter to the Jewish newspaper. "We believe," David Friedman wrote, "that the newfound concern for resource 'deprivation,' the trees in the forest and global warming is more distortion than fact and more pagan than Jewish" (6). Unlike Friedman, I do not believe that the phrase "Jewish environmentalism" is an oxymoron. Rather, it seems to me that America's pluralist ethos and the creation of a Jewish state in this century has simply allowed for less rigidly defined modes of Jewish existence and expression than people like Friedman, and organizations like Toward Tradition, have in mind.

Living a precarious life of exile for centuries inspired an acute Jewish wariness toward the pagan realm and necessitated the implacable text-centeredness of the *Mitnagged* tradition which, ironically enough, continues to subordinate the ecological precepts writ large in the Torah. But exile no longer quite defines Jewish existence, at least not in Israel, or even in America, for that matter. As Martin Peretz, editor-in-chief of *The New Republic*, recently articulated in a speech at the 92nd Street Y, America is a unique locus in the history of the Jewish people, having emerged as "the very first diaspora which is not exile" (4). The Jews will always be people of the book; I do not expect or hope for this to change. All the same, living in a "home," rather than merely "host," country, and living increasingly in areas outside the city, Jewish Americans might finally lift their eyes from the book for a moment to examine their environment and bring their Jewish soul to bear upon the natural realm.

Such a literature, I believe, would hardly reject the Jewish social realm for a solipsistic existence in nature. What it would implicitly reject is the notion that this imperfect dichotomy—which has long enjoyed an immutable and exasperating currency in the realm of Jewish letters—sufficiently expresses all that Jewish writers need say about the natural world. I see hope for the burgeoning of such a literature in a poem by the National Book Award–winning poet Gerald Stern in which the poet spots a dead opossum on a country road and refuses to dismiss it as roadkill:

> I am going to be unappeased at the opossum's death.
> I am going to behave like a Jew
> and touch his face, and stare into his eyes,
> and pull him off the road. (15–18)

In this poem, instructively titled "Behaving Like a Jew," Stern brings his Jewish soul to bear upon a rather commonplace scene of country life; and, if only implicitly, he challenges human encroachment upon the opossum's land, exemplified by the "bloodstained bumpers" and "slimy highways" (7–8, 9). He addresses the natural world as a writer *and* a Jew. It is an option that Isaac Babel, living at an especially precarious moment in modern Jewish history, could never have fathomed. A new wave of Jewish writers might take Stern's lead and further explore the integration between the Judaic and natural realm, the ways in which the Jewish social vision, codified in the Talmud, informs even the most contemporary and secular Jewish responses to the environment. As Judith Plaskow argues in her influential study, *Standing Again at Sinai: Judaism from a Feminist Perspective* (1990), "the reexamination of Jewish attitudes toward sexuality and nature . . . will not 'paganize' Judaism so much as restore to it values disparaged and lost in the process of defining itself over against another religion" (154).

THAT I COULD not claim the urban ethos of my Jewish American predecessors, literary and otherwise, had for a long while left me feeling disenfranchised—robbed of a birthright, if you will. (After all, the ABA to which I belong is the American Birding Association of Colorado Springs, not the American Bar Association of New York, the legal profession being the secular deployment in modern times of Jewish text-centeredness.) But perhaps there has always been something delimiting about such a rigidly defined Jewish American identity. And as impressive as the literature that has emerged from this ethos continues to be, perhaps it too begins to show signs of, well, wear and tear. A new creative outpost, one actively engaged with the natural realm, awaits the imagination of the Jewish American writer. While I am hardly convinced that I am the one best qualified to stake out this artistic territory, I am thoroughly convinced that it is a territory, a Jewish territory, of untapped potential and unforeseeable rewards.

NOTE

This essay is based on an essay that originally appeared in *Tikkun,* Nov./Dec. 1999, 73–77.

REFERENCES

Audubon, John James. "The Passenger Pigeon." *Selected Journals and Other Writings.* Ed. Ben Forkner. New York: Penguin, 1996. 552–60.

Babel, Isaac. *Collected Stories.* Trans. David McDuff. New York: Penguin, 1994.

Bartram, William. *The Travels of William Bartram: Naturalist's Edition.* Ed. Francis Harper. Athens: U of Georgia P, 1998.

Bellow, Saul. *Henderson the Rain King.* 1959. New York: Penguin, 1986.

———. *Herzog.* 1964. New York: Penguin, 1988.

Emerson, Ralph Waldo. "Self-Reliance." *Selected Writings of Emerson.* Ed. Donald McQuade. New York: Modern Library, 1981. 129–53.

Friedman, David. "Environmentalism More Pagan Than Jewish." Letter. *Forward* 26 Feb. 1999: 6.

Goldstein, Rebecca. *Mazel.* New York: Penguin, 1995.

Goodman, Allegra. *Kaaterskill Falls.* New York: Bantam Doubleday Dell, 1998.

Howe, Irving. "Strangers." *Celebrations and Attacks: Thirty Years of Literary and Cultural Commentary.* New York: Harcourt Brace Jovanovich, 1979. 11–26.

Kazin, Alfred. *A Walker in the City.* 1951. New York: Harcourt Brace Jovanovich, 1979.

Levinas, Emmanuel. *Difficult Freedom: Essays on Judaism.* 1963. Baltimore: Johns Hopkins UP, 1990.

Malamud, Bernard. *Dubin's Lives.* New York: Penguin, 1979.

Ozick, Cynthia. "The Pagan Rabbi." *The Pagan Rabbi and Other Stories.* 1971. Syracuse: Syracuse UP, 1995. 1–37.

Peretz, Martin. "Diaspora but Not Exile: American Jewry and the Triumph of Zionism." Text of an Address in the Annual "State of the World Jewry" Series at the 92nd Street Y. New York, 20 Jan. 1994. 1–15.

Plaskow, Judith. *Standing Again at Sinai: Judaism from a Feminist Perspective.* 1990. New York: HarperCollins, 1991.

Rosen, Jonathan. "The Talmud and the Internet." *American Scholar* 67.2 (Spring 1998): 47–54.

Roth, Philip. *American Pastoral.* New York: Houghton Mifflin, 1997.

———. *The Counterlife.* New York: Farrar, Straus and Giroux, 1986.

———. "Eli, the Fanatic." *Goodbye, Columbus.* 1959. New York: Bantam, 1970.

Soloveitchik, Rabbi Joseph B. *Halakhic Man.* 1944. Trans. Lawrence Kaplan. Philadelphia: Jewish Publication Society of America, 1983.

Steiner, George. "Our Homeland, the Text." *Salmagundi* 66 (1985): 4–25.

Stern, Gerald. "Behaving Like a Jew." *This Time: New and Selected Poems.* New York: Norton, 1999. 31.

Thoreau, Henry David. *Walden, or Life in the Woods.* 1854. New York: Vintage, 1991.

Whitman, Walt. "When Lilacs Last in the Dooryard Bloom'd." *Walt Whitman: Complete Poetry and Selected Prose.* Ed. James E. Miller Jr. Boston: Houghton Mifflin, 1959. 233–39.

The Virtual Crowd

Overpopulation, Space, and Speciesism

POPULATION EXPLOSION Unique in human experience, an event which happened yesterday but which everyone swears won't happen until tomorrow.
JOHN BRUNNER, *Stand on Zanzibar* (1968)

OVERPOPULATION has lost its terror for the Western imagination. Even though the world population reached six billion in October of 1999—double the number of 1960—population growth is no longer associated, in the West, with the images of nightmarishly overcrowded cities it conjured up in the 1960s and 1970s. In part, this is no doubt due to changed growth projections for the future; although the world population will, according to the most recent U.N. projections, continue to grow until approximately the middle of the twenty-first century and will add at least another 20 percent and perhaps more than 50 percent to the current figure (the forecast for 2050 ranges from a low of 7.3 billion to a high of 10.7, with a median projection of 8.9 billion), it is now clear that this increase will affect particular regions in very different ways.[1] Whereas a number of industrialized nations, from Italy and Spain to Japan, will actually face shrinking populations (to the point where some demographers are beginning to worry about the sociological consequences of a society in which few people will have siblings any longer), other regions such as sub-Saharan Africa and the Middle East will continue to undergo explosive population growth, with the attendant challenges of providing education, jobs, and medical care to an ever-growing number of people.[2] As far as population figures are concerned, then, the future will be a divided one, with industrialized countries significantly less affected by problems of continued population growth than in the past; this may be part of the reason why so many of the Western overpopulation dystopias of the 1960s and 1970s seem dated by now.

Yet overpopulation re-emerged as a topic in both popular and high-literary texts of the late 1980s and the 1990s, although it was approached with a very different perspective and represented by means of quite different literary strategies. This essay traces the evolution of population growth as a literary topic in Western texts from the 1960s to the 1990s. In the first half of this period, overpopulation was envisioned as an essentially urban condition that manifests itself in nightmarish crowding and the erosion of individual privacy, with serious social, psychological, and economic consequences. Quite often, it was associated with totalitarian political structures, although much of this earlier fiction relied on conventional and rather simplistic notions of both individual identity and social control mechanisms. The nature and impact of overpopulation outside urban space or in relation to other species and environments were only rarely considered. As a consequence of such quite class-specific paranoias about the city experience and the fate of the individual in mass society, the tone of most of the texts remained bleakly dystopian. But the most interesting novel in this earlier set, British novelist John Brunner's *Stand on Zanzibar*, develops a different perspective of human identity on an overcrowded planet by foregrounding the transforming impact of emergent media technologies; as a consequence, the outline of an alternative conceptualization of the relationship between communities and space, on one hand, and between human and nonhuman forms of consciousness, on the other, begins to emerge.

More recent texts tend to adopt a much less millennial tone; more explicitly than the earlier novels, some of them attempt to envision a reconciliation of humans with other species or, more abstractly, with nature. This reunion is quite often enabled by advanced technology, whether it be genetic engineering or digital computer networks. Texts such as Sheri Tepper's *The Family Tree*, David Brin's *Earth*, and John Cage's "Overpopulation and Art" are a good deal less ideologically invested in the integrity and hegemony of the human subject; they present human (and in Tepper's work, nonhuman) individuals and communities as irreversibly altered by technologies in such a way that conventional definitions of subjectivity no longer hold. Concurrently, Brin and Cage envision such individuals and communities as inhabiting a global space that is partly natural and partly created by technology; the physical crowds of earlier overpopulation novels, under these circumstances, begin to transmute into virtual crowds of electronic voices that end up relating back to nature in different and unexpected ways. All of these texts contribute to the reflection on how human identity and the literary forms through which it is usually articulated need to be rethought in the context of systemic and global ecological concerns.

Mr. and Mrs. Everywhere

CONCERN over global human population growth is not new: at least since Thomas Malthus's *Essay on the Principle of Population* (1798), the rapid growth of humankind has periodically given rise to deep worries and dire predictions about the future. In the twentieth century, concerns over population growth came to a head in the 1960s and 1970s with the publication of such books as Paul Ehrlich's *The Population Bomb* (1968), the Club of Rome's report on *The Limits to Growth* (1972), and Lester Brown's *The Twenty-ninth Day* (1978), all of which predicted horrendous consequences for the environment as well as global society if population growth were not brought under control.[3] At the same time, Garrett Hardin's seminal essay, "The Tragedy of the Commons" (1968), which is today mainly remembered for its discussion of the collective use of public resources, really was most centrally concerned with population increase and how it affects such usage over time; that this central issue is often not even mentioned in more recent discussions of Hardin's argument shows the extent to which the focus of socio-ecological concern has shifted.

As a literary topic, overpopulation had begun to make occasional appearances in the 1950s but remained limited to isolated short stories such as Kurt Vonnegut's "Tomorrow and Tomorrow and Tomorrow" (1953), Frederik Pohl's "The Census Takers" (1955), and Cyril Kornbluth's "Shark Ship" (1958). It only became a major theme in science fiction in the 1960s, inspiring a whole series of novels such as Anthony Burgess's *The Wanting Seed* (1962), Lester Del Rey's *The Eleventh Commandment* (1962; revised edition 1970), Brian Aldiss's *Earthworks* (1965), Harry Harrison's *Make Room! Make Room!* (1966)—the model for the much inferior film *Soylent Green* (1973)— Lee Tung's *The Wind Obeys Lama Toru* (1967), James Blish and Norman L. Knight's *A Torrent of Faces* (1967), and John Brunner's *Stand on Zanzibar* (1968). Short stories such as J. G. Ballard's "The Concentration City" (1960; first published as "Build-up" in 1957) and "Billennium" (1961), Brian W. Aldiss's "Total Environment" (1968), Kurt Vonnegut's "Welcome to the Monkey House" (1968), Keith Roberts's "Therapy 2000" (1969), James Blish's "Statistician's Day" (1970), and Keith Laumer's "The Lawgiver" (1970) also focused on population growth and its consequences, as did the Star Trek episode *The Mark of Gideon*, which first aired in early 1969.[4]

In 1971, Ballantine Books co-published a collection of short stories with Zero Population Growth (an organization dedicated to the promotion of population control) under the title *Voyages: Scenarios for a Spaceship Called*

Earth (Sauer, 1971), and more novels and short stories followed until the mid-1970s: Robert Silverberg's *The World Inside* (1971), Maggie Nadler's "The Secret" (1971), Thomas Disch's *334* (1972), Larry Niven and Jerry E. Pournelle's *The Mote in God's Eye* (1974), and John Hersey's *My Petition for More Space* (1974).[5] Michael Campus's film *Zero Population Growth* (1971) also focused on an overpopulated future society. At the same time, reflections on population increase appeared in literary texts whose main concerns lay elsewhere: thus, Gary Snyder's volume of poetry *Turtle Island* (1974) ends with a prose section entitled "Four Changes," which addresses central environmental problems and how they might be mitigated, with "Population" as the first one (91–93); Italo Calvino includes, among the imaginary cities described in his *Le città invisibili* [*Invisible Cities*] (1974), the city of Procopia, whose population grows so precipitously over the years that by the time of the narrator's last visit, the twenty-six inhabitants of his hotel room turn any movement into an obstacle race (146–47).

Between the early 1960s and the mid-1970s, then, a considerable body of scientific as well as literary works emerged that addressed questions of human population growth and its consequences. Indeed, the two types of approach were not completely separate at the time: Paul Ehrlich illustrated his statistical predictions with three science fiction scenarios in *The Population Bomb*, and he wrote prefaces to Harry Harrison's novel *Make Room! Make Room!*, Rob Sauer's *Voyages* anthology, and another collection of ecologically oriented short stories, Frederik Pohl's *Nightmare Age* (1970); on the other hand, Harrison's novel and the short stories in *Voyages* are followed by bibliographical references that include not only literary but also scientific and sociological works on ecological and demographic problems.

The issue was conceptually framed in somewhat different ways in the two genres, however. Scientists and demographers were primarily concerned with what persistent population growth implies for humankind's relationship to its planetary environment, and explored the ecological and social consequences of growth beyond "carrying capacity."[6] They therefore often focused on those Third World countries where population growth rates were highest (even as they emphasized the depletion of natural resources due to Western populations' higher standard of living and levels of consumption). Novelists and short story writers, by contrast, tended to set their overpopulation scenarios in Western cities and to examine the fate of individuals and communities under conditions of extreme crowding.[7] Burgess's *The Wanting Seed*, Harrison's *Make Room! Make Room!*, Blish and Knight's *A Torrent of Faces*, Brunner's *Stand on Zanzibar*, and Hersey's *My*

Petition for More Space all prominently feature descriptions of crowd behavior, while other texts—Vonnegut's "Tomorrow and Tomorrow and Tomorrow," Ballard's "Billennium," Aldiss's "Total Environment," Silverberg's *The World Inside*, and Disch's 334—comment on the social and psychological transformations that occur in densely populated cities. Literary texts, then, tend to articulate problems of population increase in terms of concerns over the availability and distribution of space.

This anxiety about space occasionally also surfaces in the scientific texts. Paul Ehrlich, for example, begins the first chapter of his classic *The Population Bomb* with the following anecdote:

> I have understood the population explosion intellectually for a long time. I came to understand it emotionally one stinking hot night in Delhi a few years ago. My wife and daughter and I were returning to our hotel in an ancient taxi. The seats were hopping with fleas. The only functional gear was third. As we crawled through the city, we entered a crowded slum area. The temperature was well over 100, and the air was a haze of dust and smoke. The streets seemed alive with people. People eating, people washing, people sleeping. People visiting, arguing, and screaming. People thrusting their hands through the taxi window, begging. People defecating and urinating. People clinging to buses. People herding animals. People, people, people, people. As we moved slowly through the mob, hand horn squawking, the dust, noise, heat, and cooking fires gave the scene a hellish aspect. Would we ever get to our hotel? All three of us were, frankly, frightened. It seemed that anything could happen—but, of course, nothing did. Old India hands will laugh at our reaction. We were just some overprivileged tourists, unaccustomed to the sights and sounds of India. Perhaps, but the problems of Delhi and Calcutta are our problems too. (1)

The scenario that Ehrlich here describes is meant to prepare the reader for the ensuing argument about demographic statistics by conveying a moment not of rational comprehension but of emotional confrontation. It is intended to give the "feel" rather than the facts of overpopulation, the visceral experience of what are otherwise abstract mathematical figures. Yet most of the details that give the scene its emotional force have little to do with population growth: certainly the heat, a crucial component of the city's "hellish" feel, has no causal relation to it at all, and the fleas, the technical malfunctioning of the cab, the pollution of the air, and the lack of plumbing all seem to have more to do with poverty and underdevelopment than with overpopulation. Not even the sense of a looming threat from dense masses of humans surrounding the individual that culminates in his outcry, "People, people, people, people," is exempt from this ambiguity. Is this an experience of overpopulation, or is it the sense of suffocation that can overcome one in the midst of big city crowds even in countries that are not at all considered overpopulated? Do we see such masses of people in this scene because there are really "too many" of them by some standard, or because poverty has kept them out of the kind of housing that would hide more affluent but no less numerous crowds from public view?[8]

Pointing out the dubious logic that underlies this anecdote does not, of course, imply any challenge to Ehrlich's general argument that the perpetuation of 1960s population growth rates into the future would lead to dire environmental and social consequences. But it does foreground an associative connection that is also typical of many of the neo-Malthusian literary texts of the period: they link the abstract demographic concept of overpopulation to experiences of intense anxiety in urban environments that are described as consisting principally of human bodies, as if physical crowding were the most immediate or the most significant consequence of excessive population growth. From a demographic perspective, of course, "overpopulation" is a far more elusive phenomenon—one that might lead to shortages of water, food, or heating materials, insufficient resources for education and medical treatment, or the destruction of natural ecosystems (to name just a few), rather than to accumulations of human bodies in one place; conversely, shortages of living space and crowded conditions can have a wide variety of causes that are unrelated to population growth rates. Nevertheless, the association of overpopulation with urban crowding is persistent in novels and short stories of the 1960s and 1970s.

Typically, the situation such texts focus on and describe with dread is the erasure of individuality under the double pressure of immense human crowds and crushingly anonymous bureaucratic institutions. Sam Poynter, the protagonist of Hersey's *My Petition for More Space*, perhaps best exemplifies this predicament: the entire novel describes a morning he spends waiting in lines so as to reach a counter where he can submit a petition to have his living space in a communal residence increased from 7 × 11 to 8 × 12 feet. The waiting experience is one of unbearable physical and mental claustrophobia as his body, wedged in between those of others, is constantly scanned by the controlling eyes of strangers ready to denounce him for the slightest misdemeanor. At the same time, he is periodically overcome by a sense of dissolution and vertigo when he envisions the crowd beyond the people with whom he is in actual physical touch:

> My own circle . . . leaps out to include all those who touch the four who touch
> me. I must not let myself consider the touchers of those touchers of my touch-
> ers, for like flash-fire the sense of contact, of being not a separate entity but a
> fused line-unit, will carry my selfhood out to the sides of the waitline and
> crackling along it forward and backward until my perception of myself is
> wholly lost in crowd-transcendence. In that lost state I will be nothing but
> an indistinguishable ohm in this vast current of dissatisfaction. (11)

His actual encounter with authority at the end of his wait stands in stark
contrast to this sense of fusion, since Poynter cannot even see the official
behind the counter but only hears a voice that urges him to present his petition clearly and concisely. His request for more space ends up being denied
as his faltering sense of individuality prevents him from articulating any
coherent justification for it.

This portrait of an individual quashed as much by the crushing physical
presence of multiple bodies as by oppressive and all-powerful bureaucracies repeats itself in novels such as *Make Room! Make Room!* or *The World
Inside*. Harrison's novel describes a policeman in turn-of-the-millennium
New York who is personally and professionally destroyed by the contradictory demands of his superiors to solve a difficult murder case, on one hand,
and to be available for crowd control during food riots, on the other. Silverberg's characters live in twenty-fifth-century "urban monads," gigantic
skyscrapers inhabited by 800,000 humans each, and are allowed complete
reproductive freedom; but they are brainwashed or exterminated without
ado if they exhibit any behavior that is considered a threat to social cohe-
sion—for example, a desire to leave the building for a walk in the surrounding landscape. As works of literature, these and quite a few other novels and
short stories about overpopulation from the 1960s and 1970s are of limited
interest; often, their vision of cultures to come is heavily indebted to earlier descriptions of totalitarian societies such as Aldous Huxley's *Brave New
World* or George Orwell's *1984* but ignores more contemporary and complex treatments of the individual under authoritarian control as they appear
in the novels of, for example, William Burroughs or Thomas Pynchon.[9] Even
as they draw on concerns about the fate of the individual in mass society
that were widespread in the 1960s,[10] their paranoia about living space is
rooted in middle-class fears about the urban experience, as Fredric Jameson
has pointed out:

> [In] the crowded conurbations of the immediate future . . . the fear is that of
> proletarianization, of slipping down the ladder, of losing a comfort and a set

of privileges which we tend increasingly to think of in spatial terms: privacy, empty rooms, silence, walling other people out, protection against crowds and other bodies. (286)

Overcrowded urban living conditions, in other words, can function as a dystopian image of the future only for a readership that is privileged enough not to have to cope with such conditions in the present.

If literary texts in the 1960s and 1970s translate ecological concerns about humans' impact on nature into social fears about the fate of the individual in urban society, this transfer is no doubt in part due to the fact that twentieth-century narrative provides much more obvious literary models for presenting the individual in the mass than for examining ecological issues. Both the modernist urban novel of the 1920s and totalitarian dystopias in the tradition of Huxley and Orwell offer narrative paradigms that can easily be deployed in the fictionalization of overpopulation. This shift from an ecological to a sociocultural emphasis has important consequences: compared with the scientific literature, which discusses a variety of social and environmental impacts of population growth, narrative texts tend to focus on urban environments and scarcity of personal space with its psychological, social, and cultural implications as the most important dimension. Due to this focus, population growth turns into an issue that by and large concerns the human species alone: it is perceived as problematic when it raises physical and social problems for humans themselves, but not when it exerts intense pressure on natural ecosystems and the survival of other species.[11] This anthropocentrism in the treatment of space and species is transcended in only one major novel, which, ironically, does not focus on the survival of nature but the emergence of new technologies: Brunner's *Stand on Zanzibar* (1968).

Stand on Zanzibar, which has by now become a classic of science fiction, breaks with the genre convention of linear narrative with clearly defined protagonists. Instead, Brunner presents his future world through a multitude of narrative fragments—party conversations, advertisements, news bulletins, television images, legal texts, quotations from books—that confront the reader with a wide range of characters from diverse national, social, racial, ethnic, and religious backgrounds. Through this mosaic of perspectives and discourses, the reader gradually comes to know the world in 2010, first in New York and subsequently in a number of other locations around the globe. To the extent that this novel can be said to have protagonists, they are Donald Hogan and Norman House, two men who are sent on political and economic missions to Asia and Africa, respectively. But their individual experiences are subordinated to the more global image that emerges of an overpopulated world characterized by densely crowded cities, sudden outbreaks of violence, savage social inequalities, and eugenic laws that, varying by region and nation, impose more or less severe restrictions on the reproductive rights of individuals who carry the genes for certain disabilities and diseases. As Brunner himself points out, his narrative technique is adapted from the modernist urban novels of John Dos Passos such as *Manhattan Transfer*, the *USA* trilogy, and especially *Midcentury*, which Brunner refers to as the most immediate model for *Stand on Zanzibar* ("Genesis" 36).

That a novelist aiming to acquaint his readers with as multifaceted an image of future society as possible would fall back on techniques that were first developed to describe the bewildering variety of the modern metropolis is not in itself surprising.[12] But it is significant that Brunner chose Dos Passos as his model rather than other varieties of the modernist urban novel such as James Joyce's *Ulysses*, Virginia Woolf's *Mrs. Dalloway*, Alfred Döblin's *Berlin Alexanderplatz* (itself influenced by *Manhattan Transfer*), or Robert Musil's *Der Mann ohne Eigenschaften* [*The Man without Qualities*]. All of these novels, even as they paint a comprehensive panorama of the big city, simultaneously affirm the uniqueness of the individual; and all of them, even though they feature a plethora of characters, have clearly identifiable protagonists whose movements through the metropolis the reader is invited to follow. Dos Passos's *Manhattan Transfer*, by contrast, persistently refuses to focus on any one of its several dozen characters in New York City from the 1890s to the 1920s: each character is foregrounded in a short narrative segment, then abandoned for other characters, and appears again in another story segment further along. Even though Brunner allows two of his characters, Donald Hogan and Norman House, to dominate more of his story than any of the others, they do not compare to Leopold Bloom and Stephen Dedalus, let alone Franz Biberkopf or Mrs. Dalloway, in narrative centrality. The narrative structure itself, in other words, is designed in such a way as to turn the reader's attention away from the individual and toward the more general social, economic, and cultural patterns of Brunner's crowded twenty-first-century world. As a consequence, the reader is left with the sense that the main threat to the individual in the age of overpopulation does not come from eugenics legislation or random outbreaks of violence, but from the sheer overwhelming multitude of individualities that constantly surround each one.

In the world of *Stand on Zanzibar,* these multitudes are dealt with by means of standardization. One of the advanced technologies that most clearly foregrounds this process is the customized TV set which, in 2010, allows viewers to insert themselves into the images on the screen, rather than watching other characters perform. Gradually, the novel conveys that this technology is available at different levels of individualization. On TV screens in public places, the characters representing the viewer are standardized by gender, age, and racial group: for example, when Donald Hogan boards an airplane, the flight attendant immediately switches his TV to the " 'white stocky young mature' version of the man" (333), represented in an interior resembling that of the plane. The cheaper TV sets for home use allow the viewer a similar choice: Norman House, for example, has chosen an African American male to represent himself and a Scandinavian woman to stand in for his rapidly changing lovers. But the more expensive sets are able to represent an actual viewer in completely individualized fashion. This technology, which allows viewers to project themselves into the virtual world of the screen and to watch *themselves* visiting exotic locations and participating in extraordinary events at varying levels of abstraction from their actual selves, is referred to in the novel as "Mr. and Mrs. Everywhere," the standard personae who are everywhere and form a part of everything.

Norman House comments on the experience of this new technology when he observes,

> [I]t's eerie. There's something absolutely unique and indescribable about seeing your own face and hearing your own voice, matted into the basic signal. There you are wearing clothes you've never owned, doing things you've never done in places you've never been, and it has the immediacy of real life because nowadays television *is* the real world. . . . We're aware of the scale of the planet, so we don't accept that our own circumscribed horizons constitute reality. (314; original emphasis)[13]

This confusion between images and the real world carries over into the routine conversations in the novel, in which Mr. and Mrs. Everywhere are mentioned frequently. At a party, for example, one person mentions that "We were going to spend [our vacation] under the Caribbean, but Mr. and Mrs. Everywhere go there such a lot we're afraid it'll be dreadfully crowded," and another comments on a trip to Antarctica by saying, "I hate the snow but whereinole else is there that Mr. and Mrs. Everywhere haven't been recently? I can't stand all these interchangeable people!" (234). In conversations such as these, Mr. and Mrs. Everywhere are not so much figures on a television screen as a way of referring to the ubiquitous masses in an overcrowded world. The technology that was designed to individualize standard programming ends up standardizing the real world and amalgamating individuals into "interchangeable people." But Brunner does not roundly criticize or reject this technology as other overpopulation novelists no doubt would have; on the contrary, what seems to interest him is the ambiguous status of Mr. and Mrs. Everywhere as at the same time specific individuals, abstract types, and virtual reality constructs: the distinction between embodied identities and technologically generated images of the self begins to blur.

Brunner's consideration of visual and electronic technologies and the way in which they may come to alter notions of the human subject is decisive not only because it eerily prefigures current developments in virtual reality software. It also begins to destabilize the integrity and autonomy of the individual that in other overpopulation novels of the period function as touchstones for any dignified human existence. By suggesting, both through the narrative structure and the motif of interactive TV technology, that the future of humankind may incorporate a wide variety of coexisting spheres of reality and types of—sometimes technologically hybridized— identity, Brunner opens the way for a less speciesist world in which other kinds of subjectivity might emerge. This possibility is concretely realized in the novel through the figure of the corporate-owned supercomputer Shalmaneser, who apparently achieves a humanlike consciousness by the end— at least if a sense of humor and the capacity for self-deception are indicators of such consciousness. Even though this vision of the future does not include any sustained consideration of species displaced by human population growth, Brunner thereby begins to question the primacy of the human over all other kinds of identity. This altered sense of human selfhood contributes to the optimistic tone of the novel's ending, which offers prospects for diminished violence but not decreased population growth in the future: the problem of the individual in the masses remains, but the terms of the relationship have subtly changed.[14]

The Virtual Crowds

BY THE LATE 1970s, overpopulation receded from literary texts as a prominent topic, even as environmental problems slowly began to establish themselves as a concern not only in science fiction but across a wide variety of genres from nature poetry to mainstream novels.[15] When it resurfaces in the literature of the late 1980s and early 1990s, it is no longer addressed in the apocalyptic mode of earlier decades. This change in tone is not limited to literary texts: popular scientific approaches to population issues in the 1990s also combine more cautious and complex forecasts with a greater emphasis on how population growth is related to such factors as economic conditions, social inequality, and women's health and access to education. Donella and Dennis Meadows's *Beyond the Limits* (1992), a follow-up to their 1972 report, emphasizes that current levels of growth and development are excessive, but at the same time gives grounds for cautious optimism. Some of the possible future scenarios they develop by means of computer modeling do not include economic collapse and social decline: therefore, if population growth as well as levels of affluence and consumption are brought under control, they argue, there is still room for hope. Paul and Anne Ehrlich's two books on population issues, *The Population Explosion* (1990) and *The Stork and the Plow: The Equity Answer to the Human Dilemma* (1995), while reaffirming the Ehrlichs' earlier predictions of dire consequences in the absence of comprehensive population planning, present a more complex view of the problem than Paul Ehrlich's book from 1968: both emphasize the importance of equitable social structures and improved conditions, especially for women, in any attempt to come to terms with population growth. Both books also stress that in the authors' view it is not too late to solve the problem. Similarly, one of the most recent demographic analyses of the population problem, Joel Cohen's *How Many People Can the Earth Support?* (1995), gives a much more nuanced and complex assessment of the difficulties in forecasting reproductive behavior and estimating the carrying capacity of different regions than earlier discussions and thereby makes it more difficult to sustain any simple apocalyptic rhetoric. Bill McKibben's *Maybe One* (1998), at the same time, approaches the problem from a more personal perspective, exploring the implications of population growth and consumption for affluent Westerners' reproductive decisions.

Literary texts generally share this more cautious approach and tend to approach overpopulation not so much as the dominant theme it was in earlier fiction but as one important dimension among others that shape the world of the future. Novels such as Philip José Farmer's *Dayworld* (1985), Australian writer George Turner's *The Sea and Summer* (1987; published in the United States under the title *Drowning Towers*), German author Carl Amery's *Das Geheimnis der Krypta* [The mystery of the crypt] (1990), Sheri S. Tepper's *The Family Tree* (1998), David Brin's *Earth* (1991), Kim Stanley

Robinson's trilogy *Red Mars* (1992), *Green Mars* (1994), and *Blue Mars* (1996),
as well as John Cage's poem "Overpopulation and Art" (1994), all consider population growth as one factor in a whole complex of environmental, social, and political problems such as pollution, climate change, social
inequality, uneven access to power, and international competition and conflict. The mode in which the topic is broached differs fundamentally from
texts written twenty or thirty years earlier: even though bleak background
scenarios are taken for granted in much science fiction of the 1980s and
1990s, these circumstances are no longer addressed in the millennial mode
that characterized comparable works from the 1960s. Indeed, quite a few
of these texts have utopian endings, though this utopianism is by no means
unqualified: a sense of horror or apocalypse is still present in many of them,
but it is often displaced from the main plot or the narrative present into a
subplot or the narrative past.

In the literary texts, overpopulation is approached through a wide range
of perspectives and techniques, not all of which can be discussed here.
The three texts I examine in some detail—Sheri S. Tepper's *The Family Tree*,
David Brin's *Earth,* and John Cage's "Overpopulation and Art"—all reflect,
in their thematic emphases as well as their literary strategies, an altered
sense of human subjectivity. Brin and Cage, in their more experimental
texts, point in addition to the connection between reconceptualizations of
human identity and the emergence of a new kind of spatial experience created by global networks of communication and information. Beyond the
specific problem of population growth, Brin and Cage thereby address a
more general literary, cultural, and philosophical problem: the question of
how global ecological and technological systems can be represented, and
what implications such representations have for our vision of human identity, both individual and collective.

Sheri S. Tepper's *The Family Tree* aims centrally at developing a nonanthropocentric vision of Earth's long-term future. Her novel describes how
toward the beginning of the twenty-first century, a quasi-religious ecological group, the Koresans, deliberately sets off a plague that kills all of humankind except for a small group. This mass extinction allows animals that
had attained human-grade intelligence through genetic engineering to gain
the evolutionary upper hand, and in the far future of A.D. 5000 it is various
intelligent animal species such as bears, pigs, and macaques that have built
up a new civilization. Humans, now called "umminhi," are not considered
intelligent and serve as beasts of burden much as horses or camels had under human rule. As several of these intelligent animals time-travel back to

the twenty-first century and upon their return bring two humans with them into the future, the encounter of humans and umminhi reveals the latter to be the Koresans' far-future offspring: as an atonement for their genocide as well as for humans' wanton destruction of nature, their ancestors took an oath to no longer use language publicly and to submit voluntarily to the newly emerging intelligent species. The arrival of humans from the past signals the end of this period of atonement, and the umminhi are allowed to co-exist with the dominant animal species. Ultimately, then, Tepper's vision of the far future presents a humankind whose population growth no longer exerts a lethal pressure on other living species but has achieved a balance with them.

Resistance to this pressure first manifests itself in the early twenty-first-century world of the protagonist, Dora Henry, in a rather unexpected fashion: a conspiracy of trees. In her city, as well as subsequently in others across the nation and the globe, plants and trees grow up practically overnight in spaces that had been used by humans for transportation and residence. This supernatural growth inhibits car traffic and forces humans to resort to alternative means of transport; soon, trees also invade empty buildings at the edges of cities and then proceed to reclaim human living space more aggressively. Dora Henry summarizes the surreal invasion: "There are these trees, suddenly growing everywhere. At the edges of the town, any houses that're left vacant disappear. The trees eat them. Occupied houses, the trees eat any room that isn't used. In some occupied houses, where there are a lot of children, the trees eat all the bedrooms except three, one for boys, one for girls, one for the adults. [. . .] where there are large numbers of children, babies disappear" (265–66). Once again, the problem of population growth is here figured in terms of space; yet, in contrast to the emphasis on human crowding in earlier novels, Tepper's sentient trees foreground a struggle for living space that no longer takes place between differently privileged classes of humans, but between humans and other types of living beings. The reconfiguration of the urban landscape through an uprising of the most easily domesticated and exterminated components of nature—Henry's husband's well-groomed garden and weed killer use are foregrounded early on—signals a narrative that, half humorously and half seriously, plays with the inversion of anthropocentric assumptions about nonhuman forms of life. Only through such an inversion, Tepper suggests, can humankind achieve any kind of balance with the natural.

That this utopian harmony will be purchased at the price of an almost universal genocide is not revealed until the end of the novel. The narrative of *The Family Tree* shuttles back and forth between the time before this extinction and a much later age, so that the reader is never directly confronted with the details of global death. It hardly needs to be mentioned that this elision is extremely problematic from a moral and ideological perspective; yet one could argue that detailed accounts of human suffering from overcrowding, disease, hunger, and violence all the way to planned exterminations had already been supplied in abundance by the overpopulation novels of earlier decades. Tepper's goal seems to be precisely not to ignore such suffering, but to put it into the comparative perspective of other species' misery and extinction. She achieves this comparison by means of a specific narrative strategy: for several hundreds of pages, the novel goes back and forth between a third-person narrative that presents events at the beginning of the twenty-first century from the viewpoint of Dora Henry and a first-person account by a female narrator, Nassif, at a time period which by the end of the novel turns out to be the fifty-first century. Only when Nassif and her companions travel back to the twenty-first century and are seen through the eyes of humans is it revealed that they belong to other species: Nassif herself is a Japanese macaque, and some of her companions are pigs, dogs, raccoons, and parrots. Or at least this is what humans would call them, whereas Nassif calls her own people "ponjic" and refers to other species as "scuinic" (pigs), "kastoric" (beavers), or "armakfatidian" (raccoons). While Tepper plants subtle clues as to her protagonists' identity throughout the novel, these remain difficult to interpret until the crucial journey back in time: for most of the narrative, the reader is made to see the world through the eyes of evolved animals whose perspective is not easily distinguishable from that of geographically or historically remote humans.[16] This strategy, it is true, still leaves a humanlike way of looking at the world in place as a standard of intelligence, but it marks a first step toward granting nonhuman characters narrative agency. "We have so long rejoiced in being intelligent, in pointing to the poor beasts who are not and comparing ourselves to them, that it is hard for us to relinquish our position of superiority," says one of the protagonists in summing up the difficulties of such an inverted perspective—not, as it happens, one of the humans, but a pig (331).[17]

David Brin's novel *Earth* (1990) also envisions fundamental changes in humans' relationship to the environment, though it focuses on a future that is much closer to the turn of the twenty-first century. Set in 2038, *Earth* develops a panoramic vision of world society that pays close attention to social, ecological, and technological developments: among these, the abolition of privacy as a positive cultural value no doubt stands out as one of the most striking consequences of electronic technologies and international legislation (Brin's characters associate privacy with governmental misdeeds rather than with personal rights); but increasingly aged populations and their conflict with the young in industrial nations, the risks associated with advanced weapons technologies, global warming, rising sea levels, pollution, population pressure, and rampant species extinction equally form part of the picture. It is worth emphasizing, however, that Brin's vision, for all its ecological bleakness, is by no means apocalyptic: rather, the novel again and again stresses how humans continuously struggle with these problems and always seem to find new solutions, though few of them turn out to be long-lasting or definitive. Following Brunner's model in *Stand on Zanzibar*, Brin presents this panoramic vision through a large number of characters and a wide range of narrative episodes as well as "quotations" from the various media and institutions of the day: news announcements, letters, legal texts, excerpts from electronic books, and on-line newsgroup discussions establish a complex mosaic of life in the global society of the mid-twenty-first century.

The novel's plot, briefly, revolves around a minuscule black hole that scientists discover deep in the crust of the Earth, whose gradual absorption of more and more mass threatens the existence of the planet. Since the artificial creation of small black holes is one of the more recent branches of science, scientists at first assume that this lethal threat was created by a state, a group of nations, or a corporation that has lost control over its experiment; they therefore design strategies to remove the hole in the utmost secrecy. But in the course of their investigations, they soon discover that this particular singularity is much older than the human science of "cavitronics" and might be of alien origin. Their attempt to remove it by means of "gravity lasers" causes earthquakes and disasters all over the globe, however, and soon governments, military organizations, and secret services lock in battle with them over control of the black hole. Inevitably, some information about this struggle leaks into the Net, where a particularly gifted hacker-environmentalist, Daisy McClennon, has long fought a guerrilla war against those she perceives to be polluters and destroyers of nature. Through her extraordinary abilities to seek out and correlate electronically transmitted information, she discovers and appropriates gravity laser technology, whose destructive power she first turns against its inventors and then diverts to a more gruesome purpose: the systematic extermination of practically all of humankind, whom she, not unlike the Koresans in Tepper's novel, has come to consider an ultimately destructive species.

Her plan is to leave only ten or twenty thousand hunter-gatherers alive who would pose no threat to natural ecosystems.

But McClennon's genocidal rampage across the globe leads to an unexpected outcome. Due to the constant firing of gravity laser beams through the Earth's core from many different locations, more and more electronic currents are activated within the Earth itself. When McClennon attacks a station where a Nobel Prize–winning biologist, Jennifer Wolling, is in the process of building a complex model of human cognition on the Net, Wolling's consciousness fuses with the electronic currents that kill her and triggers a spontaneous, quasi-natural expansion of the Net into the currents that crisscross the Earth's core. As McClennon is defeated by one of the natural disasters she herself had helped to trigger, this innovative kind of artificial intelligence, an electronic Gaia of sorts, gradually asserts its power to impose a new, more ecologically conscious mode of existence. Excess populations are moved into the areas that McClennon had depopulated, and extraction of minerals is shifted from the Earth to asteroids. The planetary artificial intelligence, which Brin describes as a collective consciousness that encompasses almost all human voices and minds, does not intervene in ordinary political matters but sets limits to the exploitation of natural resources that no human government will any longer be able to transcend.

What this utopian ending seeks to portray is nothing less than an existential convergence between the most advanced human technologies and the planet Earth in its most basic materiality. Unlike Tepper, who articulates her vision of humans' reconciliation with nature through biology, Brin chooses geology as the medium of this fusion. Not only are all of the novel's twelve epic chapters preceded by brief sections that chronologically describe the physical evolution of Earth from its cosmological beginnings to the present, but Brin also subdivides these chapters into subsections called "spheres," each of which is associated with a particular set of characters. Most of the names of these spheres, such as "core," "crust," "lithosphere," "ionosphere," or "exosphere," designate parts of the Earth's geological and atmospheric structure. Some do not: the term "noosphere," associated with the events surrounding Wolling's transformation into the template for the new Gaian consciousness, is derived from the vocabulary of French theologian and paleontologist Pierre Teilhard de Chardin, who used it to refer to what he saw as a collective human consciousness that would arise from increasing technological connectedness. [18] Even in the terms that outline the architecture of the novel, then, Brin indicates the connection between Earth's physical spatiality and the virtual space created by the most recent technologies. Like Brin's central mythological metaphor, the fusion of Gaia and the Net, the structure of the narrative welds Earth as a physical place and material object together with the abstract, immaterial space of the digital cybermatrix.

The literary figuration of an overpopulated planet, then, begins to take a very different form in *Earth* from either the nightmare cities of the 1960s or Tepper's animal civilization. Population growth is no longer the only central issue, but one among many social, economic, environmental, and technological problems that never quite get solved but never lead to the apocalypses that they were predicted to trigger, either: "As for starvation, we surely have seen some appalling local episodes. Half the world's cropland has been lost, and more is threatened. Still, the 'great die-back' everyone talks about always seems to lie a decade or so in the future, perpetually deferred. Innovations [. . .] help us scrape by each near-catastrophe just in the nick of time," one of the on-line books in the novel observes (48). One of *Earth*'s scientists similarly reflects on how mass death as a consequence of overpopulation has so far been avoided, in spite of dire predictions: "Malthusian calamity and the so-called S-curve. On the one hand, utter collapse. And on the other, a chain of last-minute reprieves . . . like self-fertilizing corn, room-temperature superconductors, and gene-spliced catfish . . . each arriving just in time for mankind to muddle through another year, eking out a living from one brilliant innovation to the next" (531; original ellipses). While Brin foregrounds the serious implications of human population growth for the ecological structure of the planet, therefore, he deliberately avoids apocalyptic scenarios of the kind that characterized earlier environmentalist texts.

Scenes of physical crowding, accordingly, while they do occasionally occur, are relatively rare in *Earth*. To the extent that the novel does convey a sense of crowding, it is of a very different kind: the density and detail of information about the society of the future that Brin communicates to his readers through a multitude of textual and media sources (statistical surveys, legal documents, newscasts, formal and informal on-line discussion groups, personal letters) create the impression of an extremely crowded information space in which billions of voices compete for attention. It is in this context that Brin's vision of a "post-privacy society" in which secrecy in most forms has become illegal assumes part of its significance: if all (or almost all) information is freely shared among ten billion people via advanced global communication technologies, a densely "populated" realm of information exchanges emerges in which competing bits of facts, factoids, details, stories, images, and sounds jostle each other as masses of human bodies did in earlier visions of an overcrowded future.

This does not mean that the problem of large numbers of human bodies simply disappears in the novel. Accumulations of bodies and the concomitant anxieties over space remain a part of the picture, and one can reproach Brin with a double moral in his treatment of this topic: while the character who carries out large-scale exterminations, Daisy McClennon, is vigorously condemned, her atrocities actually become the basis for an at least temporary solution to the population problem in that they free up space for the relocation of people who were formerly confined to boat settlements on the oceans. Even while he rejects it, Brin is apparently not able to envision a less violent remedy to the problem.[19] Yet the central image of a fusion between Earth and the Net does in fact respond to the concern over space in a very different fashion: the crowds that dominate his text are not really the physical ones of human bodies, but the virtual ones of human voices communicating incessantly by means of electronics. Wolling's metamorphosis from an embodied being to an electronic presence is only the most dramatic instance of a process that in more mundane form has become commonplace even for many of the underprivileged in Brin's world. In this transformation, the space anxieties disappear: if the lack of privacy was precisely what made Ballard's billennial city, Harrison's New York, Hersey's New Haven, and Silverberg's urban monad so horrific, the citizens of Brin's global society rejoice in the disappearance of an informational privacy that they have come to regard as nothing more than a protection for the privileges of the affluent (e.g., Swiss bank accounts) or a cloak for the unlawful maneuvers of governmental and corporate institutions. The central narrative response of Brin's novel to overpopulation lies in this metamorphosis of physical into virtual crowds.

It would be easy to argue that such a transformation is nothing more than a metaphor that evades more practical solutions. But the point of Brin's fusion of Earth and Net lies precisely in its metaphoricity: it is an attempt to envision in narrative form a global, utopian space in which fundamental questions of scarce resources, wealth, social class, and place can be reconsidered on the basis of new premises. Brin is at pains to emphasize that even though new artificial intelligence speaks with the voice of Jennifer Wolling, it is not one entity, but really a metaphor for the global multiplicity of human voices: it is, in other words, a more condensed version of the multifarious world society that the entire novel describes. Representing global humanity as both multiple *and* connected in narrative form is no easy task, and Brin is not entirely successful in either his combination of ancient epic with the modernist urban novel or in his choice of a single character as a provisional ordering shape for the global meeting of minds.[20] But these shortcomings weigh perhaps less heavily when one considers the ambitious scope of Brin's project: finding a narrative form to articulate a new concept of space that links the ecological and the technological, and a utopian kind of human identity that would erase neither the individual nor the small community but nevertheless link both to a global ecological self-awareness. If there is a narrative correlative to the environmentalist slogan "Think globally, act locally," Brin's novel is certainly one of the most daring attempts to envision what such a form might look like.

The attempt to articulate in literary form how human consciousness might be reconceived in its relation to global ecosystems also underlies John Cage's "Overpopulation and Art" (1994), a long poem that, like many of Cage's earlier poetic works, is a hybrid between a lecture of sorts and avant-garde poetry. Cage sees overpopulation as the force for change that will propel humanity into the future by forcing it to break with outdated forms of social organization and communication. The first stanza immediately establishes this link between population growth and communication:

> abOut 1948 or 50 the number of people
> liVing
> all at oncE
> equaled the numbeR who had ever lived at any time all added together
> the Present as far as numbers
> gO
> became equal to the Past
> we are now in the fUture
> it is something eLse
> hAs
> iT doubled
> has It quadrupled
> all we nOw
> kNow for sure is
> the deAd
> are iN in the minority
> they are outnumbereD by us who're living
> whAt does this do to
> ouR
> way of communicaTing   (II. 1–20)

This initial poetic conceit presents the relationship between present and past as a mathematical equation based on population figures and defines the future as a numerical excess of the present over the accumulated past. It thereby provides an amusing algebraic shorthand for Cage's overarching claim that humanity has undergone a fundamental historical break: the future cannot be symmetrical to the past because economic, demographic, and ecological conditions have changed in such a way that radical new forms of social organization are required. In this context, "ouR / way of communicaTing" refers not only to means of exchanging information such as mail, e-mail, phone, or fax, all of which Cage mentions, but also in a broader sense to forms of organizing community. In the age of overpopulation, increased crowding and scarcity of resources force human communities to break up petrified organizational hierarchies and create "new foRms of living together" (I. 306) so as to confront its principal challenge:

> . . . the wOrld's prime
> Vital
> problEm is how
> to multiply by thRee swiftly safely and satisfyingly
> Per
> pOund kilowatt and workhour the overall
> Performance realizations of the world's
> comprehensive resoUrces this
> wiLl render those resources
> Able
> To support
> 100% of humanIty's
> increasing pOpulace at levels
> of physical liviNg
> fAr above whatever
> has beeN known
> or imagineD   (II. 483–98)

Just how the anarchist society of the future Cage portrays will accomplish this enormous leap without the dire environmental consequences he deplores elsewhere in the poem is, of course, not clear and could not possibly be in a text of this sort, which spells out a hope for the future rather than a full political program.

The concrete suggestions Cage's outline of an anarchist utopia does include—emphasis on creative unemployment and self-education, the privileging of use over ownership and profit, the rejection of centralized bureaucracies and nation states—are not new to his work; many of these ideas already appeared in his serial poem "Diary: How to Improve the World (You Will Only Make Matters Worse)" from the 1960s and have recurred in many other works of his since. Much of "Overpopulation and Dystopia" reformulates Cage's anarchist politics and avant-garde aesthetics in the context of rapid population increase. What is particularly interesting about this reformulation is the role Cage attributes to different communication media (another long-standing interest of Cage's, who was one of the first to work Marshall McLuhan's media theory into literature and music in the 1960s). Even as he hails new media such as the Internet for their capacity to create a world in which connectedness is more important than conceptual or political borders, he expresses reservations about an unlimited accessibility that makes creative solitude almost impossible:

enDless

interpenetrAtion

togetheR

wiTh

nOnobstruction

of what aVail

thEn the use

of answeRing service

attemPt

tO free oneself from

interruPtion

solitUde for just a moment regained

is utterLy

finAlly

losT

fInding 19th

nOt 21st

iN 20th century

Are you

iN to fax

anD

                    electronic mAil
                         aRe you
                    in Touch hce   (I. 57–80)

"Being in touch" anytime and anyplace is the obligation the new media impose, creating on one hand a tight web of connected individuals and communities, but also eliminating times and spaces for silence and solitude, two
cornerstones of Cage's aesthetic as well as existential philosophy. His half-
resigned and half-amused invocation of a character from Joyce's *Finnegans
Wake*, H. C. Earwicker, at the end of the last line of verse above—a character
who makes appearances in many of Cage's works—is doubly ironic in this
respect, since "hce" also at times stands in for "here comes everybody" in
Joyce's text: not only does this reference invite a comparison between the
artist and the work of art in the early and late twentieth century and their
altered position in the media landscape; it also evokes a character whose initials make him merge with an inescapable collectivity. Yet Cage, even as he
mourns the loss of solitude, never expresses the kind of paranoia about the
lack of privacy we saw in 1960s texts on overpopulation. On the contrary,
the very next stanza celebrates the merging of private space with a global
landscape of images: "we live in glass hOuses / our Vitric surroundings /
transparEnt / Reflective / Putting images / Outside / in sPace of what's
inside / oUr homes / everything's as muLtiplied / As we are" (I. 82–91).
As in Brin, the multiplication of people here begins to shade into the multiplication of signs and images, in a scenario that inspires joy rather than
fear: "each momenT / Is magic" (II. 92–93), Cage exclaims. The vision of a
world without conventional boundaries enabled by the new media finally
outweighs Cage's fear of constant intrusions on creative silence.

  In analogy to the unhierarchical and decentralized social order Cage envisions, he calls for "wOrks of art / in which no Place / is mOre / imPortant
than another / beaUty / at aLl points" (II. 105–10), and whose principal
objective is not artistic self-expression but the experimentation with new
forms of aesthetic organization (II. 122–37). This principle echoes precisely
the decentralizing tendency of Brunner's and Brin's novels, which, as we
saw earlier, present the interlaced stories of a whole series of characters,
none of whom is allowed to monopolize the reader's attention. Cage's own
poem is structured in terms of a numerical principle that is derived from
the title: the twenty letters of the phrase "overpopulation and art" form
the backbone for "mesostics," a kind of acrostic in which the letters to be

read vertically are not placed at the beginning but in the middle of each line of verse.[21] On the basis of this principle, stanzas of twenty lines each are created, which are in addition set off by a capitalized bold letter that precedes the first line of each stanza on the left margin: these bold letters once again spell "overpopulation and art" twice over through the total of forty stanzas. Visually, the capitalized mesostic letters in each line of verse do give the poem a center, a backbone of what are otherwise lines of widely varying lengths. But in oral delivery, the mesostic letter is indistinguishable from the rest, and a second look at the typographic layout immediately reveals that if the mesostic runs down the center of the page, it is not situated at the center of each line: the mesostic letter is sometimes located near the middle of a line, but it can also appear at the very beginning or the end. Perhaps more importantly, however, the double mesostic within and across stanzas does not spell out any hidden or additional dimension of meaning to be read along with and against the meaning of the horizontal lines. Instead, by repeating the words of the title and dispersing them over the entire poem, it serves as a visual reminder that, at least in the poet's intention, no one line is more important than any other; at the same time, the numerical structure these words yield emphasizes that the poem is not formally designed to reflect the poet's subjective experience or perceptions, but as a game that coaxes alternative ordering principles out of the typographical arrangement of printed language.

Cage certainly did not design these formal strategies specifically to deal with the topic of overpopulation in poetic form—he had used them before in many other poems dealing with quite different topics—but it is easy to see how they work to reinforce the sense that in a world characterized by physical overcrowding and manifold new "virtual" modes of connection, the individual is no longer the hub of social or aesthetic forms of organization. Cage celebrates this development with an optimism that has often been criticized as naive, and certainly the social, political, and cultural outline he sketches in "Overpopulation and Art" is open to this charge. But the least one would have to say in his defense is that this optimism is programmatic, based on the firm conviction that pessimism and the unwillingness to imagine utopias merely help to perpetuate outdated sociopolitical structures: "we begin by belieVing / it can bE done / getting Rid / of Pessimism / blindly clinging tO / oPtimism / in no sense doUbting / the possibiLity of / utopiA" (II. 566–72).

None of the more recent texts I have discussed here can be understood to propose practical solutions to the demographic and environmental prob-

lems of the early twenty-first century. Rather, they offer metaphors and narrative patterns that might contribute to a reconceptualization of the partly
natural, partly socio-technological space that we share with nonhuman
species, and to a reconsideration of our own identity in this space. As I
have shown, these texts differ quite significantly from most earlier literary
approaches to the issue of human population growth. Unlike overpopulation novels of the 1960s and 1970s, which focused almost exclusively on
the consequences of increasing populations for humans themselves, more
recent texts such as Tepper's, Brin's, and Cage's tend to adopt a less anthropocentric perspective by taking humans' impact on other species and
natural environments into account. Some of them also transform the earlier class-coded paranoia about the consequences of omnipresent crowds of
humans for the individual into a celebration of physical crowds that merge
with or metamorphose into virtual ones and thereby gain access to a different category of space that is not envisioned as a scarce and unevenly
distributed resource. While this transformation opens up new avenues of
communication with nature, nature itself is portrayed as irreversibly altered
in the process, whether by means of genetic engineering (as in Tepper) or by
electronic and media technologies (as in Brunner, Brin, and Cage). But part
of what this change metaphorizes is really humans' altered understanding
of their own identity and place in a global ecological network: if advanced
technologies have enabled humans' exploitation of nature, they are here
also envisioned as a means of remapping global space. It is this reconfig-
ured spatiality that becomes the medium for a different kind of encounter
between humans, nonhumans, and the natural environment. This is, to be
sure, a utopian vision of the future—but not, I would argue, so naively optimistic that it cannot contribute to our own rethinking of human identity
as it evolves in the context of increasingly global ecological networks.

NOTES

1. United Nations Population Division, *World Population Prospects: The 1998 Revi-*
sion, 1–5. The U.S. Census Bureau, which uses different forecasting procedures from
the U.N., predicts a population of 9.3 billion for 2050 (*World Population Profile: 1998*),
higher than the U.N.'s 1998 median projection of 8.9 billion but almost identical to its
1996 median projection of 9.37 billion (*World Population Prospects: The 1996 Revision*
6–7).

2. On the divergent population developments in different regions, see Haub. Cultural concerns over the consequences of shrinking populations in some industrialized societies were expressed after the U.N.'s *1996 Revision* in Crossette's *New York*

Times article "How to Fix a Crowded World: Add People," Eberstadt's "The Population Implosion" in the *Wall Street Journal* and "World Population Implosion?" in *The Public Interest,* Laing's "Baby Bust Ahead" in *Barron's,* and Wattenberg's essay "The Population Explosion Is Over" in the *New York Times Magazine.* For critiques of these views, see Gelbard and Haub's "Population 'Explosion' Not Over for Half the World" and the responses to Wattenberg's article in the *New York Times Magazine* 14 Dec. 1997: 20–24.

3. See Laing (38) for a brief summary of U.S. concerns over population growth prior to the 1960s.

4. I am grateful to Deborah White for pointing me to this episode.

5. It would have been impossible for me to trace many of these texts without Brian Stableford's excellent survey article on overpopulation in science fiction in the *Grolier Science Fiction* encyclopedia.

6. Carrying capacity is a more elusive term than appears at first sight: for an excellent discussion, see Cohen, pt. 4 (159–364).

7. Aldiss's *Earthworks* is an interesting exception to this rule in that it focuses on the toxic agricultural hinterlands of big cities.

8. Quoted in isolation, this passage also appears tinged by racism in its juxtaposition of the affluent Western family and the poverty-stricken Eastern masses, as well as by Ehrlich's distinction between "our" problems and those of India, which excludes an Indian reader from the circle of those whom the author is addressing. I am hesitant to accuse Ehrlich of any such racism, however, given the persistent emphasis in many of his books that population growth, due to the West's disproportionate use of world resources, is as much a problem of the First World as it is of the Third World: this is precisely the core of much of his argument, which he deliberately addresses to a mainly Western audience.

9. For a comparison of Disch's *334* with *1984,* see Swirski (170).

10. For two studies of the individual in mass society that were influential in the 1960s, see David Riesman's *The Lonely Crowd* (originally published in 1950, but republished in 1961 and 1969 in a slightly abridged version due to its extreme popularity) and Herbert Marcuse's *One-Dimensional Man* (1964). Riesman's claim that in advanced societies, "[i]ncreasingly, *other people* are the problem, not the material environment" (18; original emphasis), is spelled out quite literally in overpopulation novels.

11. This is not to say that the scientific literature is exempt from the charge of anthropocentrism: as long as "carrying capacity" is discussed only in terms of the resources a region can provide for its human population and not simultaneously in terms of what cost this channeling of resources toward humans has for natural ecosystems and other species, the perspective remains human-centered. Literary texts in the 1960s, however, take this perspective a good deal further than scientific ones.

12. This was not the opinion of the novel's first reviewers, however, who either

criticized Brunner's technique or credited him with having invented an entirely new form of science fiction novel. Brunner scoffed at both: "Since . . . sf is a notoriously conservative field in the stylistic sense, it didn't surprise me that a lot of people felt something that was actually a couple of generations old was too much of the *avant garde* to be tolerated" ("Genesis" 36).

13. This remark prefigures a very similar one uttered by one of the characters in Don DeLillo's *White Noise* (1985): "For most people there are only two places in the world. Where they live and their TV set" (66).

14. For a more detailed analysis of Brunner's narrative strategy and the figure of Shalmaneser, see Heise (246–49). On Shalmaneser, see also Lamie and De Bolt, "The Computer and Man."

15. The anthology *No Room for Man: Population and the Future through Science Fiction* (Clem, Greenberg, and Olander), published in 1979, consists in large part of reprints of earlier short stories.

16. The world of the future is presented by Tepper in premodern and vaguely orientalizing terms: it consists of small political territories ruled by sultans and countesses who are subordinate to an emperor. While little advanced technology is in evidence, magic is occasionally practiced (albeit with the help of such "futuristic" substances as "Sorc-a-Powr" and "Jorush's All-Purpose Ampli-fire").

17. While the novel provides what by the standards of fantasy literature is a reasonably plausible account of how the animals acquired intelligence and the use of language (experiments in gene transplantation), a similar type of reasoning is not supplied for the man-eating trees: how some plants came to possess the limited sentience and ability to communicate that they display in the narrative is never explained. In Nassif's far future, sentient trees are as unusual as they are in the early twenty-first century and are assumed to be of magical origin (see chapter 13).

18. As early as 1947, Teilhard saw computers as part of this network of the future: see his essay "Une interprétation plausible de l'Histoire Humaine: La formation de la 'Noosphère.'"

19. See Amery's *Das Geheimnis der Krypta* for a much more sophisticated narrative confrontation with the question of overpopulation and genocide.

20. I have examined Brin's strategies and shortcomings in *Earth* in more detail in "Science Fiction zwischen Öko-Angst und Informationsutopie" (253–259).

21. The following interpretation of Cage's mesostics is based on Perloff's reading of this technique in her article on *Roaratorio*, "Music for Words Perhaps."

REFERENCES

Aldiss, Brian. *Earthworks*. Holborn: Four Square, 1967.
———. "Total Environment." *No Room for Man: Population and the Future through Science Fiction*. Ed. Ralph S. Clem, Martin Harry Greenberg, and Joseph D. Olander. Totowa, N.J.: Rowman and Littlefield, 1979. 24–65.
Amery, Carl. *Das Geheimnis der Krypta*. Munich: List, 1990.

Ballard, J. G. "Billennium." *The Best Short Stories of J. G. Ballard.* New York: Henry Holt, 1995. 125–40.

———. "The Concentration City." *The Best Short Stories of J. G. Ballard.* New York: Henry Holt, 1995. 1–20.

Blish, James. "Statistician's Day." *No Room for Man: Population and the Future through Science Fiction.* Ed. Ralph S. Clem, Martin Harry Greenberg, and Joseph D. Olander. Totowa, N.J.: Rowman and Littlefield, 1979. 212–22.

Blish, James, and Norman L. Knight. *A Torrent of Faces.* Garden City, N.Y.: Doubleday, 1967.

Brin, David. *Earth.* New York: Bantam, 1991.

Brown, Lester R. *The Twenty-ninth Day: Accommodating Human Needs and Numbers to the Earth's Resources.* New York: Norton, 1978.

Brunner, John. "The Genesis of 'Stand on Zanzibar' and Digressions." *Extrapolation* 11.2 (1970): 34–43.

———. *Stand on Zanzibar.* New York: Ballantine, 1969.

Burgess, Anthony. *The Wanting Seed.* London: Heinemann, 1962.

Cage, John. "Overpopulation and Art." *John Cage: Composed in America.* Ed. Marjorie Perloff and Charles Junkerman. Chicago: U of Chicago P, 1994. 14–38.

Calvino, Italo. *Invisible Cities.* Trans. William Weaver. San Diego: Harcourt Brace Jovanovich, 1974.

Clem, Ralph S., Martin Harry Greenberg, and Joseph D. Olander, eds. *No Room for Man: Population and the Future through Science Fiction.* Totowa, N.J.: Rowman and Littlefield, 1979.

Cohen, Joel E. *How Many People Can the Earth Support?* New York: Norton, 1995.

Crossette, Barbara. "How to Fix a Crowded World: Add People." *New York Times* 2 Nov. 1997, sec. 4: 1+.

DeLillo, Don. *White Noise.* New York: Penguin, 1986.

Del Rey, Lester. *The Eleventh Commandment.* Evanston, Ill.: Regency, 1962.

———. *The Eleventh Commandment.* Rev. ed. New York: Ballantine, 1970.

Disch, Thomas. *334.* New York: Avon, 1974.

Eberstadt, Nicholas. "The Population Implosion." *Wall Street Journal* 16 Oct. 1997: A22.

———. "World Population Implosion?" *Public Interest* 129 (Fall 1997): 3–22.

Ehrlich, Paul R. *The Population Bomb.* Cutchogue, N.Y.: Buccaneer, 1971.

Ehrlich, Paul R., and Anne H. Ehrlich. *The Population Explosion.* New York: Simon and Schuster, 1990.

Ehrlich, Paul R., Anne H. Ehrlich, and Gretchen C. Daily. *The Stork and the Plow: The Equity Answer to the Human Dilemma.* New Haven: Yale UP, 1995.

Farmer, Philip José. *Dayworld.* New York: Putnam, 1985.

Gelbard, Alene, and Carl Haub. "Population 'Explosion' Not Over for Half the World." *Population Today* Mar. 1998: 1–2.

Hardin, Garrett. "The Tragedy of the Commons." *Science* 162 (1968): 1243–48.

Harrison, Harry. *Make Room! Make Room!* New York: Berkley, 1967.

Haub, Carl. "New UN Projections Depict a Variety of Demographic Futures." *Population Today* Apr. 1997: 1–3.

Heise, Ursula K. "Netzphantasien: Science Fiction zwischen Öko-Angst und Informationsutopie." *Klassiker und Strömungen des englischen Romans im 20. Jahrhundert: Festschrift zum 65. Geburtstag von Gerhard Haefner.* Ed. Vera and Ansgar Nünning. Trier: Wissenschaftlicher Verlag Trier, 2000. 243–61.

Hersey, John. *My Petition for More Space.* New York: Knopf, 1974.

Jameson, Fredric. *Postmodernism; or, The Cultural Logic of Late Capitalism.* Durham: Duke UP, 1991.

Killingsworth, M. Jimmie, and Jacqueline S. Palmer. "Millennial Ecology: The Apocalyptic Narrative from *Silent Spring* to *Global Warming.*" *Green Culture: Environmental Rhetoric in Contemporary America.* Ed. Carl G. Herndl and Stuart C. Brown. Madison: U of Wisconsin P, 1996. 21–45.

Kornbluth, Cyril. "Shark Ship." *Voyages: Scenarios for a Spaceship Called Earth.* Ed. Rob Sauer. New York: Zero Population Growth/Ballantine, 1971. 268–305.

Laing, Jonathan R. "Baby Bust Ahead." *Barron's* 8 Dec. 1997: 37–42.

Lamie, Edward L., and Joe De Bolt. "The Computer and Man: The Human Use of Non-Human Beings in the Works of John Brunner." *The Happening Worlds of John Brunner: Critical Explorations in Science Fiction.* Ed. Joe De Bolt. Port Washington, N.Y.: Kennikat P, 1975. 167–76.

Laumer, Keith. "The Lawgiver." *The Year 2000.* Ed. Harry Harrison. Garden City, N.Y.: Doubleday, 1970. 213–26.

Malthus, Thomas. *Essay on the Principle of Population.* London: J. Johnson, 1798.

Marcuse, Herbert. *One-Dimensional Man: Studies in the Ideology of Advanced Industrial Society.* Boston: Beacon P, 1964.

The Mark of Gideon. Dir. Jud Taylor. Perf. William Shatner, Leonard Nimoy, Sharon Acker, David Hurst. Paramount Pictures, 1969.

McKibben, Bill. *Maybe One: A Personal and Environmental Argument for Single-Child Families.* New York: Simon and Schuster, 1998.

Meadows, Donella, Dennis L. Meadows, and Jørgen Randers. *Beyond the Limits: Confronting Global Collapse, Envisioning a Sustainable Future.* Post Mills, Vt.: Chelsea Green, 1992.

Meadows, Donella, Dennis L. Meadows, Jørgen Randers, and William W. Behrens III. *The Limits to Growth: A Report for the Club of Rome's Project on the Predicament of Mankind.* New York: Universe, 1972.

Nadler, Maggie. "The Secret." *No Room for Man: Population and the Future through Science Fiction.* Ed. Ralph S. Clem, Martin Harry Greenberg, and Joseph D. Olander. Totowa, N.J.: Rowman and Littlefield, 1979. 194–204.

Niven, Larry, and Jerry E. Pournelle. *The Mote in God's Eye.* New York: Simon and Schuster, 1974.

Perloff, Marjorie. "Music for Words Perhaps: Reading/Hearing/Seeing John Cage's

Roaratorio." *Postmodern Genres.* Ed. Marjorie Perloff. Norman: U of Oklahoma P, 1989. 193–228.

Pohl, Frederik. "The Census Takers." *Nightmare Age.* Ed. Frederik Pohl. New York: Ballantine, 1970. 39–46.

Riesman, David, with Nathan Glazer and Reuel Dennehy. *The Lonely Crowd: A Study of the Changing American Character.* Abr. ed. New Haven: Yale UP, 1969.

Roberts, Keith. "Therapy 2000." *The Passing of the Dragons.* New York: Berkley, 1977.

Robinson, Kim Stanley. *Blue Mars.* London: HarperCollins, 1996.

———. *Green Mars.* London: HarperCollins, 1994.

———. *Red Mars.* London: HarperCollins, 1992.

Sauer, Rob, ed. *Voyages: Scenarios for a Spaceship Called Earth.* New York: Zero Population Growth–Ballantine, 1971.

Silverberg, Robert. *The World Inside.* Toronto: Bantam, 1983.

Snyder, Gary. *Turtle Island.* New York: New Directions, 1974.

Soylent Green. Dir. Richard Fleischer. Perf. Charlton Heston, Edward G. Robinson, Leigh Taylor-Young, Chuck Connors, Joseph Cotten, Paula Kelly. MGM, 1973.

Stableford, Brian. "Overpopulation." *Grolier Science Fiction: The Multimedia Encyclopedia of Science Fiction.* CD-ROM. Danbury, Conn.: Grolier, 1995.

Swirski, Peter. "Dystopia or Dischtopia? The Science-Fiction Paradigms of Thomas M. Disch." *Science-Fiction Studies* 18 (1991): 161–79.

Teilhard de Chardin, Pierre. "Une interprétation plausible de l'Histoire Humaine: La formation de la 'Noosphère.'" *Revue des questions scientifiques* 118 (1947): 7–37.

Tepper, Sheri S. *The Family Tree.* New York: Avon, 1998.

Tung, Lee. *The Wind Obeys Lama Toru.* Bombay: Kutub-Popular, 1967.

Turner, George. *Drowning Towers.* New York: Avon, 1996. [U.S. ed. of *The Sea and Summer.* London: Faber and Faber, 1987].

United Nations Department of Economic and Social Affairs, Population Division. *World Population Prospects: The 1996 Revision.* New York: United Nations, 1998.

———. *World Population Prospects: The 1998 Revision.* New York: United Nations, 1999.

U.S. Bureau of the Census. *World Population Profile: 1998.* Washington: U.S. Department of Commerce, Bureau of the Census, 1999.

Vonnegut, Kurt. "Tomorrow and Tomorrow and Tomorrow." *Welcome to the Monkey House.* New York: Delacorte, 1968. 284–98.

———. "Welcome to the Monkey House." *Welcome to the Monkey House.* New York: Delacorte, 1968. 27–45.

Wattenberg, Ben J. "The Population Explosion Is Over." *New York Times Magazine* 23 Nov. 1997: 60–63.

Weinkauf, Mary. "Aesthetics and Overpopulation." *Extrapolation* 13 (1972): 152–64.

Zero Population Growth (Z.P.G.). Dir. Michael Campus. Perf. Geraldine Chaplin, Diane Cilento, Don Gordon, Oliver Reed, Sheila Reid. Sagittarius, 1971.

GORDON M. SAYRE

If Thomas Jefferson Had Visited Niagara Falls

The Sublime Wilderness Spectacle in America, 1775–1825

It would be vain presumption on my part, to attempt a minute
description of this "most sublime of nature's works;" a distinction
which Mr. Jefferson would not have conferred on the Natural Bridge
across Cedar creek, in Virginia, if he had seen this stupendous cataract.

CHARLES JOHNSTON, on seeing Niagara Falls during his voyage
eastward in 1790 after being ransomed from Indian captivity

HOW DID AMERICANS regard sublime nature in the eighteenth century?
Johnston's comment suggests that just a few years after the founding of
the United States, its citizens were seeking out the land's scenic marvels,
measuring their sublime effects in language, and even staging an informal
competition for which site would claim preeminence as a scenic emblem of
the young nation. Johnston was a lawyer of some education and influence,
but not an intellectual or aesthete; his foray into print was a consequence of
his Indian captivity. Nonetheless, he was familiar with the Natural Bridge
near his home in Botetourt County, Virginia, and the description of it by
Thomas Jefferson published in *Notes on the State of Virginia* (1782), and he
used that site as a benchmark for sublime scenery. He also was familiar with
the rhetoric of the sublime, and he used a cliché that dozens of more famous
writers would employ at Niagara Falls in years to come, the expression of
inexpressibility: "Such was the effect produced on me by surveying this
magnificent object, that when I attempted to express the astonishment of
my feelings to the officer who accompanied me, I could find no language to
give it utterance, and remained absolutely dumb" (307–8). Johnston's associations of Niagara with the sublime, and of the sublime with Thomas Jefferson's *Notes,* have become common since the 1780s, and the two together
offer an excellent point of departure for a study of sublime spectacles and

their importance in early American nationalism, landscape aesthetics, and attitudes toward wilderness.

By "sublime spectacles" I refer to wilderness not as an extensive quality of the natural landscape or habitat across a broad area, but to the intensive, striking scenes for which wilderness has long been valued and promoted in America. As Alison Byerly has written, the Sierra Club and other environmental organizations "rely on picturesque appreciation of the landscape to further their goals" (63). This wilderness picturesque is represented through aesthetically composed photographs taken at moments of ideal lighting and weather and is used to make appeals for donations and political support. The aesthetic pleasure of such scenic photographs is more broadly appealing than an ecologist's statement of the importance of a tract of wilderness habitat, much as the picturesque was, in the late eighteenth century, a popular or middlebrow aesthetic compared to the genteel cultivation of the sublime. And much as the sublime, as Kant defined it, is "an object (of nature) the representation of which determines the mind to regard the elevation of nature beyond our reach as equivalent to a presentation of ideas" (119), the ecosystemic extent of wilderness is an ideal concept beyond the reach of the ordinary observer, whereas the picturesque scene is designed to be an accessible, popular aesthetic. If we wish to find the closest approximation in early America to the modern popular relationship to wilderness landscape, the place to look is not in the representations of extensive wilderness per se, which covered most of North America at that time, but in the visions of these scenic spectacles that emblematized the wilderness around them. After all, as Byerly also writes, "the American wilderness . . . has been gradually reduced and circumscribed until it no longer seems to stretch into infinity" (53). For all that we may bemoan the fact, it is protected and celebrated on an intensive, not an extensive scale, and the long vistas that remain have become picturesque postcard scenes more than sublime experiences. But in the eighteenth century, before there was a sense that the space and natural resources of America had the practical limits we recognize today, there were already an aesthetic of the wilderness spectacle and controversies over how best to appreciate it. Chris Hitt has in a recent essay observed "the reluctance of ecocritics to engage literary representations of the sublime" (605) and has argued that "the traditional natural sublime, for all its problems, involves what look to us like ecocentric principles" (607). Indeed, an appreciation of this eighteenth-century aesthetic of sublime wilderness can provide historical context for modern aesthetic relationships between viewer and nature.

Niagara Falls, the Natural Bridge, and the confluence of the Potomac and Shenandoah Rivers (which Jefferson also described superlatively) are the three sublime spectacles I wish to examine. For Jefferson and others of his time, these were nationalist emblems of the American landscape. The scale and power of these sites became indices of the cultural and industrial potential of America. Landscape historians and preservationists have studied how conflicts between tourism, industry, and public space at Niagara Falls encapsulate the conflicts over the values of scenic preservation to Americans in the nineteenth and early twentieth centuries (McGreevey; Irwin; Sears). I aim to show that the roots of these conflicts go right back to the Revolutionary Era. This survey of eighteenth-century American wilderness spectacles will challenge common conceptions of the sublime as a Romantic concept opposed to utilitarian values. Although they often did repeat the aesthetic formulations of Burke and Kant, early Americans did not see the natural sublime as antithetical to the human goals or uses of natural resources. Moreover, a scientific or rational conception of these spectacles did not exclude the perpetuation of folklore about their marvels and mysteries.

THE PERIOD from 1775 to 1825 represents a gap in the academic account of American attitudes toward wild nature. Historians like Roderick Nash and Perry Miller have documented how seventeenth-century Puritan colonists regarded the surrounding wilderness with dread, as the domain of wolves and tempting demons. Many others have celebrated the affirmation of nature that Thoreau located in the same New England in a later period. But what of the intervening years? At the time of the Revolution and founding of the United States, the beauty and power of nature was already a source of pride and a locus of nationalism, yet the ways of looking at natural scenes were necessarily different than in the mid–nineteenth century. The scenic wonders of the western United States—Yosemite Valley, the Grand Canyon, the red rock spires and snowcapped peaks of postcard clichés—were yet unknown to Anglo-Americans. Many of the scenic spectacles which were celebrated, such as Passaic Falls in New Jersey or the Natural Bridge in Virginia, are now unknown or unexceptional to Americans living beyond the immediate area. Also yet unknown were the effects of the industrial revolution which later transformed Niagara and Passaic. In this deist, rationalist era there was not yet the Romantic sense that technology or science was opposed to the artistic or imaginative temperament. Moreover, the rituals of tourism, by which wilderness spectacles today are enshrined and defaced, deified, and commodified, had barely begun in America. Only a handful of men, such as Isaac Weld and the Marquis de Chastellux, traveled in the eighteenth century between major U.S. cities and these scenic sites, driven by the mere desire to see these places and write of their observations (Wills 260). A final important difference is that without photography, and before the popular explosion in American landscape painting beginning with Thomas Cole, scenic splendor was routinely conveyed in writing, and the influence of aesthetic theory on popular vision was far greater than it is today. Periodicals communicated scenic landscapes to readers not by simply reproducing a photograph, but by printing or reprinting the eyewitness accounts of travelers (sometimes alongside crude engravings), and the rhetorical formulas of the sublime served much as visual conventions do in landscape photography today. Something of this connection between visual and literary æsthetics is preserved in the word "cliché," which in French means photographic "snapshot." Thus the scenic wilderness spectacle was in this era already reified, already packaged into simulacra, but packaged not in visual representations, rather in literary ones.

Literary treatments of the American landscape in the revolutionary period also responded to the urgent project of forming a political and cultural union. Not only did the nation's small population and rudimentary infrastructure not measure up to those of England or France, but America lacked the very sources of aesthetic tradition: the classical civilizations of Greece and Rome. In European landscape painting and theorizing of the time, the ruins of Roman public edifices (such as in Piranesi's engravings) or of gothic churches (as in Wordsworth's "Tinturn Abbey" and J. M. Turner's painting of it) conveyed a sense of respect for the great achievements of the past and wonder at the forces which might have caused such decline and ruin. When Washington Irving traveled to England in 1815, he was the first American fiction writer to have achieved substantial fame in Europe, and he tried to balance the virtues of his native land with a need to absorb the culture of the Old World. Writing of his voyage in the pseudonymous *Sketch-Book of Geoffrey Crayon, Gent.* (1819–20), he claimed, "I visited various parts of my own country; and had I been merely influenced by a love of fine scenery, I should have felt little desire to seek elsewhere its gratification. . . . no, never need an American look beyond his own country for the sublime and beautiful of natural scenery" (54). Yet although "My native country was full of youthful promise; Europe was rich in the accumulated treasures of age. Her very ruins told the history of times gone by, and every mouldering stone was a chronicle. I longed to wander over the scenes of renowned achievement—to tread, as it were, in the footsteps of antiquity"

(54). In place of European ruins, scenes of cultural spectacle, America offered natural spectacles. These scenic landscapes might not convey a rich cultural past, but they did offer visual edification, as the title "sketch-book" suggests Irving's writing will do. Irving also claimed that "my idle humor has led me aside from the great objects studied by every regular traveler who would make a book" (55), and in place of sublime clichés, he wrote picturesque essays with titles like "Rural Life in England" and "The Country Church." Yet he also sought to synthesize the advantages of American and European scenery in the two famous tales that were first published in the *Sketch-Book*, "Rip Van Winkle" and "The Legend of Sleepy Hollow." He set both in the Hudson Valley, the first accessible scenic tourist destination in the United States. And both tales endowed the landscape with a sense of "mouldering" history which he claimed he had gone to Europe to find. The magical and uncertain legend of the Headless Horseman and the ghosts of Dutch colonists who entertain Rip are both folkloric "ruins" which imbue American landscapes with history and mystery. We will see that Niagara Falls inspired similar legends.

Irving's preface offers a sense of how literary conventions of landscape in European literature were adapted to America. Nature could take the place of culture as a goal for travelers and a locus of pride for natives. In the same period, the United States was developing its own scenic tourist sites. By the 1820s there were hotels and spas along the Hudson Valley, such as the Catskill Mountain House and Ballston Spa near Saratoga Springs (Robertson 191). The year 1825 marked the opening of the Erie Canal, connecting the Hudson Valley to Lake Erie. Not only was this event crucial as the opening of a trade route connecting the Great Lakes region or Old Northwest with the eastern seaboard, but it also made it possible for tourists to travel with relative ease to Niagara Falls. The canal caused Niagara Falls to change from a wilderness to a tourist spectacle. By restricting this study to the pre-canal period, I exclude a great body of literature about the Falls from the mid–nineteenth century, including many famous names like Margaret Fuller, Charles Dickens, Anthony Trollope, and William Dean Howells. But there were at least two dozen accounts of the Falls written by travelers prior to 1800, including Chateaubriand, Crèvecoeur, and Swedish naturalist Peter Kalm. Many of the longer and more provocative descriptions were by writers all but forgotten today, such as Isaac Weld, who traveled to all three of the sites on which I focus, and who quoted extensively from Jefferson's book in his *Travels through the States of North America and the Province of Upper and Lower Canada, During the Years 1795, 1796, and 1797*. By drawing upon amateur writers of nonfiction, I also hope to retain the diagnostic value of Niagara as a wilderness spectacle in the Early Republic. For, as Roderick Nash has written (without referring to Niagara specifically), by the 1830s the notion of wilderness as a sanctuary from society and commerce "appeared regularly in periodicals, 'scenery' albums, literary 'annuals,' and other elegant, parlor literature of the time. The adjectives 'sublime' and 'picturesque' were applied so indiscriminately as to lose meaning" (61). In the earlier period, these terms retained stricter definitions, meanings worth examining in detail.

FOR LANDSCAPE VIEWERS and artists of two hundred years ago, steep mountains and raging rapid rivers were sublime, verdant pastures, and quiet streams were beautiful or picturesque. English aristocrats in the eighteenth century who cultivated their landscape aesthetics on the "Grand Tour" through Italy and France celebrated Salvator Rosa and Claude Lorraine as the quintessential artists of the two moods. The former was known for rugged mountain scenes of gnarled trees and steep cliffs, frequently peopled with *banditti* prepared to pounce on wealthy travelers (such as those who later bought his paintings and engravings). The cult for these gothic landscapes was so pervasive that Horace Walpole, originator of the gothic literary genre with his *The Castle of Otranto* (1764), reduced it to a shorthand list: "Precipices, mountains, torrents, wolves, rumblings, Salvator Rosa" (qtd. in Monk 211). Salvator captured the sense of self-conscious fear that would become the trademark emotion of the sublime for Kant. By contrast, Claude (for some reason the artists' first names were always used) favored pastoral, picturesque scenes with softer contours. In this conception, Salvator stands for the sublime and for wilderness, with all the associations that the latter term had in pre-1800 America: danger, fear, spiritual depravation, and temptation. Claude represents the pastoral and picturesque modes of composed, pleasing scenes of nature, in which rugged mountains are relegated to the distant background. When Jefferson wrote that "The Ohio is the most beautiful river on earth. Its current gentle, waters clear, and bosom smooth and unbroken by rocks and rapids" (10), he expressed a Claudean picturesque scene. When he wrote of how the Potomac and Shenandoah Rivers "rush together" against the Blue Ridge and "have torn the mountain down from its summit to its base," leaving "piles of rock on each hand" (19), he consciously evoked the Salvatoran mood.

The two painters provide convenient tags for the opposition between the sublime and the picturesque. Byerly, in her provocative article on the influence of landscape aesthetics on wilderness policy in the United States, also employed the terms, writing that "The American idea of the wilderness might seem closer to the aesthetic category of the sublime than to the picturesque. In fact, the American wilderness has gradually been transformed from a sublime landscape into a series of picturesque scenes" (53) in a process similar to the tourist development and reification of Niagara Falls during the 1800s. As quoted above, wilderness "has been gradually reduced and circumscribed until it no longer seems to stretch into infinity but is contained and controlled within established boundaries" (53). The Salvatoran sense of fear and awe which a backpacker might feel has been for most people replaced by a Claudean picturesque simulacrum, in which the sport utility vehicle replaces the shepherd as pastoral mood accessory. The infinite, ungraspable scale of the sublime scene was a key tenet of Burke's theory: "Infinity has a tendency to fill the mind with that sort of delightful horror, which is the most genuine effect, and truest test, of the sublime" (73). Likewise, the extensive, ecosystemic breadth of wilderness is beyond the scale of the momentary human sensation, while the picturesque is designed around the scale of the viewer: "It is the spectator who engages the machinery of the picturesque æsthetic, mentally manufacturing a work of art where before there was a work of nature" (Byerly 55). Byerly lumps both Claude and Salvator together as picturesque, reserving the sublime for a purer form of wilderness experience, one which escapes aesthetic representation. Yet the sublime is a subjective effect dependent upon the presence of the spectator, just as the picturesque is. The passage from Burke quoted above continues: "There are scarce any things which can become the objects of our senses that are really, and in their own nature infinite. But the eye not being able to perceive the bounds of many things, they seem to be infinite, and they produce the same effects as if they were really so" (129–30). This is the aesthetic effect which Isaac Weld wished to attest to when he wrote of Niagara Falls that "It is impossible for the eye to embrace the whole of it at once" (Dow 1: 102). The paradox that, as Byerly states it, "The visitor to a wilderness area should find a place that has not been visited" (57) is, in fact, characteristic of the sublime, as a sensation which overwhelms sensation, a place so extensive that a rational conception of it must be intuited from an intensive sensation.

Burke, Kant, and earlier writers often defined the sublime in paradoxes, in contradictory terms like "delightful horror." In Jefferson's writing this contradiction or confrontation of opposites was often mapped onto the landscape, as mountain and river, or even into the aesthetic categories themselves, the picturesque in contrast to the sublime. Jefferson, though we might not regard him as an ecological thinker, was among the leading wilderness aestheticists of his day. His *Notes on the State of Virginia*, the only book he published in his lifetime, is an amalgam of science, geography, and ethnography but, as one scholar has written, "is now most remembered for its descriptions of the passage of the Potomac River through the Blue Ridge Mountains, and of the Natural Bridge" (Lawson-Peebles 177). These two famous landscape descriptions both capture the dialectical quality of the sublime and its dependence upon the spectator who feels its paradoxical effects. In the passage on the Natural Bridge, Jefferson used the grammatical second and first person to try to convey the emotional affect to the reader:

> You involuntarily fall on your hands and feet, creep to the parapet and peep over it. Looking down from this height about a minute, gave me a violent head ach. If the view from the top be painful and intolerable, that from below is delightful in an equal extreme. It is impossible for the emotions arising from the sublime, to be felt beyond what they are here . . . the rapture of the spectator is really indescribable! (24–25)

We know that Jefferson read Edmund Burke's *A Philosophical Enquiry into the Origin of our Ideas of the Sublime and the Beautiful* (1759), and this passage echoes Burke (Lawson-Peebles 173), not only in the contrast of perspective ("we are much more struck at looking down from a precipice, than at looking up at an object of equal height" [128]), but also for the empiricist theory of stimulus and response. The beautiful, according to both Burke and Kant, produced pleasure or delight, while the sublime inspired pain (Burke) or fear (Kant), in tension with the former sense of pleasure. Burke explained that although an excess of terror, like an excess of labor, causes pain, a moderate degree could produce pleasure. Whereas at the edge of the precipice the fear of falling was real, at the bottom the sense of height was pleasing. The two combined produced a paradoxical or dialectical sublime affect, such as had been described by Englishman John Dennis, who in 1693 was perhaps the first writer in English to find mountain scenery pleasing, writing that "the dreadful Depth of the Precipice . . . produc'd different emotions in me, viz. a delightful Horrour, a terrible Joy" (qtd. in Monk 207). Dennis did not use the term "sublime," but he began to define the oppositions of pain/pleasure, mountain/valley, sublime/beautiful, which Jefferson drew upon. And Jefferson reinforced this dichotomy by adding that from below the bridge, looking down the gorge, "The fissure continuing narrow, deep and streight for a considerable distance above and below the bridge, opens

a short but very pleasing view of the North mountain on one side, and Blue
Ridge on the other, at the distance each of them about five miles" (54). As
both Robert Lawson-Peebles and Garry Wills have noted, this view was
not in fact visible from below the bridge. Jefferson had composed a framed,
picturesque view, improving the site as a landscape gardener might wish to
do, and he was forced to admit his error and correct the passage in 1817 by
adding a handwritten note in the leaves of his own copy of his book. Jefferson's innovation upon the aesthetics of Burke was to show how the sublime
was not a rarefied, elite phenomenon above and beyond the picturesque or
beautiful, but that the two moods were dialectically dependent upon one
another.

THE OPPOSITION between the landscapes of Claude and Salvator, river
and mountain, pleasure and pain, therefore pervades Jefferson's aesthetics
even more than those of Kant and Burke. If Jefferson proposed a dialectical
synthesis of the two in his Natural Bridge passage, Niagara Falls and the
confluence of the Potomac and Shenandoah both work to deconstruct these
binary oppositions through a surprising reversal of the poles of landscape
aesthetics. Andrew Ellicot in 1789 described the topography that creates the
Falls:

> conceive that part of the country in which lake Erie is situated to be elevated
> above that which contains lake Ontario, about three hundred feet. The slope
> which separates the upper and the lower country . . . may be traced from the
> north side of lake Ontario, near the bay of Toronto, round the west end of
> the lake; thence its direction is generally east; between lake Ontario, and lake
> Erie it crosses the strait of Niagara. . . . It is to this slope that our country is
> indebted, both for the cataract of Niagara and the great falls of the Cheneseco
> [on the Genesee River]. (Dow 1: 91–92)

This "slope" is today known as the Niagara Escarpment. It is in some spots
a gentle hillside, in others a cliff or series of stepped cliffs. The Falls once
cascaded off the very lip of the escarpment but have gradually eroded the
soft shale and receded southward, creating the Niagara Gorge in a geologic
process we examine more below. The key point here is the sense that, contrary to the sublime associations around the figure of Salvator, these mountains are linear and well ordered. The sublime spectacle occurs when a river
breaks through the line of a mountain. Against the orderly, linear mountains flows the dynamic, passionate element of water. Much as the Niagara
"forces its way amidst the rocks" in Isaac Weld's 1796 account (Dow 1:

100), a linear mountain is "cloven asunder" by the "Patowmac" in Jefferson's other famous sublime scene. Both are examples of what Paul Shepard has called the "cross-valley syndrome," the phenomenon of a river cutting through a high ridge of mountains, rather than forming a valley alongside the range. In the case of the Columbia River Gorge and the Hudson River Valley, a large river passes through mountains as flatwater, even tidewater, but in the places under our examination here, the resulting waterfall or rapids is even more sublime:

> The passage of the Patowmac through the Blue ridge is perhaps one of the most stupendous scenes in nature. You stand on a very high point of land. On your right comes up the Shenandoah, having ranged along the foot of the mountain an hundred miles to seek a vent. On your left approaches the Patowmac, in quest of a passage also. In the moment of their junction, they rush together against the mountain, rend it asunder, and pass off to the sea. (19)

Even more than in the Natural Bridge scene quoted above, Jefferson uses the second person to invite the reader to become a spectator to the scene. But unlike the Natural Bridge passage, the dialectic of pain and pleasure, sublime and beautiful, is not achieved by a change in the viewer's perspective. The elements of the landscape itself play these two roles. In this "war between rivers and mountains" (20), the Potomac and Shenandoah Rivers are not, like the Ohio, a figure for Nature's maternal bounty, pastoral purity, or commercial utility, but a dynamic and destructive, even phallic force, which breaks through a mountain ridge. The continuation of the passage is a narrative orgasm, as well as a template for landscape aesthetics. The "junction" of the two rivers, whose libidinal urges had been building for a hundred miles of frustrated flow at the foot of an Appalachian ridge, leads to a sublime "rending," then concludes in a picturesque scene of bliss:

> the distant finishing which nature has given to the picture is of a very different character. It is a true contrast to the fore-ground. It is as placid and delightful, as that is wild and tremendous. For the mountain being cloven asunder, she presents to your eye, through the cleft, a small catch of smooth blue horizon . . . inviting you, as it were, from the riot and tumult roaring around, to pass through the breach and participate of the calm below. (19)

This calm in the background of the scene is the pastoral, yeoman farmer landscape with which Jefferson and Crèvecoeur are often associated, the thickly settled Mid-Atlantic region of "Frederic town and the fine country round that" (19). Among many previous critical discussions of this scene are comments on its painterly composition (Jones 359; Lawson-Peebles 178), on the contrast between the pastoral, cultivated East and the wild, untamed West (Seelye 68–70), and the sexual innuendo of looking through the "cleft," or "breach" (Kolodny 27–29). This eighteenth-century aesthetics of the "cross-valley syndrome," of the erotic war between water and rock in an era before erosion was well understood, seems to have extended beyond Jefferson. John Seelye finds it in the description of the union of the Allegheny and the Monongahela Rivers in Gilbert Imlay's novel *The Emigrants* (158–59). In his account of Niagara, Isaac Weld also employed an orgasmic sequence: "The river forces its way amidst the rocks with redoubled impetuosity, as it approaches toward the falls; at last coming to the brink of the tremendous precipice, it tumbles headlong to the bottom, without meeting any interruption from rocks in its descent" (Dow 1: 100). Weld, having also visited the Natural Bridge and read Jefferson's *Notes*, goes on to disagree, as Johnston did in the epigraph, about the honor of America's most sublime scene: "The passage of the rivers through the ridge at this place is certainly a curious scene, but I am far from thinking with Mr. Jefferson, that it is 'one of the most stupendous scenes in nature' and 'worth a voyage across the Atlantic'" (244).

Contrary to the typical aesthetic sublime of Alpine scenery in European Romantic literature, in *Notes on the State of Virginia* mountains appear to represent Enlightenment values of order and restraint, while rivers stand for the wild powers of nature. "[O]ur mountains are not solitary and scattered confusedly over the face of the country," wrote Jefferson of the Appalachian chain in the opening lines to his Query IV on "Mountains," rather "they commence at about 150 miles from the sea-coast, are disposed in ridges one behind another, running nearly parallel with the sea-coast" (18). As with the ongoing project of renovating his architectural masterpiece, Monticello, Jefferson's love of order and symmetry conflicted with practical goals he might otherwise wish to promote. The parallel ridges of Appalachia did and still do pose a much greater barrier to transportation and economic development than would a number of much higher mountains "scattered confusedly over the face of the country." From the perspective of settlement and commerce, the river is the civilized or picturesque, the mountain the wild or sublime principle. After all, at this time there was no inkling of railroads; rivers were the only means of large-scale transportation and commerce, and when the paths of rivers did not follow the needs of trade, canals such as the Erie Canal were the only answer. A waterfall or the rapids of a water gap created a barrier to the progress of trade and settlement.

At the conclusion of his survey of Virginia's rivers in Query II, Jefferson considered trade and foresaw that "There will therefore be a competition between the Hudson and Patowmac rivers for the residue of the commerce of all the country westward of Lake Erié" (15). As a Virginian, he wanted the Potomac route to become the most used, and it was in this light that he first mentioned Niagara Falls in *Notes on the State of Virginia:* "When the commodities are brought into, and have passed through Lake Erié, there is between that and Ontario an interruption by the falls of Niagara, where the portage is of eight miles" (44), more, he claimed, than the total land carriage distance on a route linking the Ohio, Youghegheny, and Potomac Rivers. Yet others did not agree with Jefferson's measurements. Weld reported of Niagara: "It is said, that it would be practicable to cut a canal from hence to Queenstown, by means of which the troublesome and expensive process of unlading the batteaux, and transporting the goods in carts along the portage, would be avoided. Such a canal will in all probability be undertaken one day or other" (Dow 2: 137). Unfortunately for Jefferson and the South, the Erie Canal was able to avert the problems of Niagara by digging straight across New York from the Mohawk valley to Lake Erie. Then the canal Weld envisioned, from Port Colborne to St. Catharines, Ontario, was completed in 1829. Both routes were more level than the Allegheny ridges of central Pennsylvania.

Thus by the early nineteenth century, the sublime challenge which Niagara Falls posed to commerce and transportation had been overcome. And there were strong suggestions, even before *Notes on the State of Virginia,* that eighteenth-century observers did not always regard the sublime spectacle of Niagara Falls as emblematic of man's humility before nature. Hitt's essay begins by acknowledging recent critiques of the sublime aesthetic, such as Paul deMan's comment that Kant's sublime inscribes "a reconquered superiority over a nature of which the direct threat is overcome" (604). Niagara appears to support this conclusion. If the beautiful, placid river connoted trade and transportation, the rapid river or waterfall suggested power. William Irwin in his study of Niagara uncovered a 1799 treatise entitled *The Political Economy of Inland Navigation, Irrigation, and Drainage, with Thoughts on the Multiplication of Commercial Resources and on Means of Bettering the Condition of Mankind, by the Construction of Canals,* in which one William Tatham proposed a scheme to use Niagara Falls' own power to solve the problem that it posed for navigation. A mill would drive a giant escalator, lifting ships up an inclined plane from the level of Lake Ontario to that of Lake Erie. In fact, mills had already created an industrial landscape

in some places in America, using the power of falling water to perform
what steam and internal combustion would later do. By 1791, Passaic Falls,
New Jersey, an earlier waterfall tourist attraction, was the site of manufacturing mills (Robertson 204). Tatham's plan was not so outrageous for its
time as one might think, and as Patrick McGreevey has shown, it was only
the first of many far-fetched utopian schemes for technological and social
innovation around Niagara Falls.

Another variation on the industrial development of Niagara was offered
in the 1771 proto-nationalist poem "The Rising Glory of America," written by Princeton graduates Hugh Henry Brackenridge and Philip Freneau
for their commencement ceremonies. The neoclassical historiography of the
poem imagined America as replicating the grandeurs of the Old World, and
they smoothed the barrier that Niagara posed to commerce through an engineering feat of vague but millennial proportions:

> And thou Patowmack, navigable stream,
> Rolling thy waters thro' Virginia's groves
> Shall vie with Thames, the Tiber or the Rhine,
> For on thy banks I see an hundred towns
> And the tall vessels wafted down thy tide.
> Hoarse Niagara's stream now roaring on
> Thro' woods and rocks and broken mountains torn
> In days remote far from their ancient beds
> By some great monarch taught a better course
> Or cleared of cataracts shall flow beneath
> Unincumber'd boats and merchandize and men. (77–78)

The present Potomac stands for the Thames as the Romans saw it and the
Tiber as it was before Rome was built, a place filled with potential for great
civilization. The "days remote" for Niagara are not in the geologic past but
the potential future, when its waters will be "cleared of cataracts" and lev-
eled for trade. These eighteenth-century dreams and schemes demonstrate
that the phenomenon Leo Marx called the "rhetoric of the technological
sublime" has its roots in the pre-industrial age. The difference is that instead of using images derived from machines such as the railroad to hail
the fulfillment of pastoral ideals of leisure and plenty, Freneau and Jefferson
saw industrial or commercial potential as inherent in the sublime landscape
itself. This pattern has been analyzed by Wayne Franklin in *Discoverers, Explorers, Settlers*. He asserts that "The idea of use, of exploitation, lurks everywhere in the discoverer's paean to American nature" (23), and he writes
of Jefferson's "confluence" passage that "an aesthetic order lies implicit in

the channels of commerce . . . the landscape seems to unfold itself according to the urgent human principle of navigation" (29). For example, at the
very end of the Natural Bridge passage, Jefferson notes that Cedar Creek,
running beneath the arch, is "sufficient in the driest seasons to turn a grist-
mill" (25). Of the bridge itself, Jefferson wrote that "it affords a public and
commodious passage over a valley, which cannot be crossed elsewhere for
a considerable distance" (25), and Isaac Weld wrote that "it seems to have
been left there purposely to afford a passage from one side of the chasm to
the other" (Dow 1: 221). The sublime wilderness spectacle was fully compatible with humans' practical needs and even, as with the Natural Bridge,
worked to satisfy these needs. While the picturesque might thrive on pastoral agricultural landscapes, the sublime made the leap from wilderness
to industrial landscape.

These eighteenth-century observers did not express a Romantic sense
of the sublime spectacle as a sacred place, of Niagara Falls or the Natural Bridge as manifestations of God's power in the form of natural beauty
which it would be sacrilege for man to alter. Although they shared some
of Kant's notions of the sublime, they did not see beauty in nature as defined by Kant's famous dictum of "purposiveness without purpose." They
were inclined instead to see the hand of the Creator as mimicking the works
of humans, or vice versa. A sense of natural theology undergirding a conservation ethic, so familiar in the later nineteenth century from quotations
taken from the writings of Muir and Thoreau, had not yet developed in the
period 1775–1825. Approaches to sublime spectacles varied from the self-
consciously aesthetic, as when Jefferson echoed Burke in his views of the
bridge from upon it and below it, to the utilitarian, seeing the bridge as
bridge, to occasional neoclassical personifications. It is surprising that the
deification of Niagara or other spectacles as figures for American nature
were not more common in the Early Republic. John Seelye has written that
John Neal's epic poem of the War of 1812, *The Battle of Niagara*, is a rare early
instance of this Romantic ethic in America, that it "runs against the full tide
of Enlightenment faith in internal improvements" such as the Erie Canal
(354). Yet oddly, Neal apostrophizes not to the Falls, but to "ONTARIO.
Dark blue water hail! / Unawed by conquering prow, or pirate sail, / Still
heaving in thy freedom—still unchained!" (27). Lake Ontario, of course,
is below the Falls and would not be much affected by a canal taming the
cataract.

KANT WROTE: "The beautiful in nature is a question of the form of the
object, and this consists in limitation, whereas the sublime is to be found

in an object even devoid of form, so far as it immediately involves, or else by its presence provokes, a representation of *limitlessness*" (90). Jefferson seems to ignore the criterion of limitlessness, for he wants to have his sublime and measure it, too. The Natural Bridge in Query V is already measured before Jefferson evokes the emotions and raptures it inspires. He provides five separate dimensions, in feet, and a geometer's description: "The arch approaches the semi-elliptical form; but the larger axis of the ellipsis, which would be the cord of the arch, is many times longer than the transverse" (54). The measurement of Niagara Falls was a lively controversy ever since Louis Hennepin, the first European to view them, in 1678, claimed they were "above 600 foot in depth" (Dow 1: 21). The subsequent realization that in fact the cascade drops only about 150 feet was a key factor in the evolving cliché of the traveler's disappointment upon viewing the Falls. Jefferson again scorns Niagara when he compares its deflated height to Virginia's own Falling Spring at the opening of Query V, "Cascades": "This cataract will bear no comparison with that of Niagara, as to the quantity of water composing it . . . but it is half as high again, the latter being only 156 feet, according to the mensuration made by order of M. Vaudreuil, Governor of Canada, and 130 according to a more recent account" (21).

There were ways, however, by which Niagara Falls defied explorers' attempts to measure and master them. As well as sublime, the Falls were gothic, hiding death and mystery behind foaming, roaring waters. The promise of a technological Niagara, and the rational inquiry which motivated the scientific analyses of all three sublime spectacles, were occasionally disrupted by gothic mysteries. Annie Dillard's dictum that "knowledge does not vanquish mystery" (241) held true, if just barely, in this pre-Romantic Age of Reason. When Jefferson observed that a cave near North Mountain in Virginia had nearly the same temperature as the cellars of Paris, or described the "blowing cave," which "emits constantly a current of air" (23), he prompted himself to consider mysteries concealed within the Earth. "There is a wonder somewhere" (33) he wrote apropos of theories about the formation of marine fossils in mountains far from the sea. Jefferson posited the Earth's interior as a common substrate for inquiry which he might share with learned men in Europe, yet it also offered an opportunity to speculate about mysteries which defied any rational explanation. Leslie Fiedler has written of how gothic novels employed "the device of the explained supernatural" (139–40), titillating readers with ghosts and scenes of horror only to offer at the end of the novel a rational or scientific explanation for these phenomena, much like episodes of the animated television series *Scooby Doo*. Thus in the late eighteenth century "At a moment when everywhere rationalism had triumphed in theory and madness reigned in fact" (138), popular fiction tried to have it both ways. Similarly, Niagara Falls inspired dreams of technological mastery of distance, water, and gravity, yet also became the focus of speculation about mysterious, unmeasurable depths behind and beneath its roiling waters. It led to important early analyses of the operation of erosion, and these in turn inspired a sense of awe and mystery at the scale of geological time.

Several of the common tropes of this "Gothic Niagara" find expression in another long poem about the Falls, Alexander Wilson's *The Foresters* (1805). This 2200-line work, in heroic couplets, was written by a Scottish-born ornithologist who is little known today, but, suitably enough, he was recognized in the fields of both literature and science in his own time. Wilson wrote dialect poetry on the heels of the popularity of Macpherson's *Ossian*, and he compiled a nine-volume illustrated *American Ornithology* (1808–14), which was the standard work until that of Audubon twenty years later. *The Foresters* is a travel poem recounting the journey of the author and two companions from Philadelphia to Niagara. When they finally arrive, after having been rescued from a "frail bark" in the midst of a storm on Lake Ontario, Wilson stresses the fear and religious awe with which he faces the sublime spectacle. He compares his pilgrimage to that of Muslims to "Mahomet's tomb . . . Such were our raptures, such the holy awe / That swell'd our hearts at all we heard and saw" (169). The Falls' power evokes that of a vengeful God, as Wilson seems to suggest in tales of the fate of animals who were swept over the edge:

> Fragments of boats, oars, carcasses unclean,
> Of what had bears, deer, fowls, and fishes been,
> Lay in such uproar, midst such clamour drown'd,
> That death and ruin seemed to reign around. (171)

Although Wilson claimed to have seen this debris, Swedish naturalist Peter Kalm in 1751 had written that no such clues survived the ride over the Falls: "The French told me they had often thrown whole great trees into the water above, to see them tumble down the Fall. They went down with surprising swiftness, but could never be seen afterwards; whence it was thought there was a bottomless deep or abyss just under the Fall" (Dow 1:62). Kalm says he doubts this story of the secret crypt but reports it anyway, suggesting that Niagara Falls might violate the conservation of matter. Kalm also wrote of a controversy over whether "the abundance of birds found dead below the Fall" was the result of some hypnotic force which the spectacle induced in them (McKinsey 29, Dow 1: 42).

Many early descriptions of the Falls described the challenge of climbing down into the gorge and walking behind the sheet of falling water, much like a descent into a dungeon or underworld. And like those mythic journeys, its factual basis is uncertain. The Baron de Lahontan visited the Falls in 1688 during one of the frequent battles between the Iroquois and the French colonists with their Huron allies. His brief account claimed that "Between the surface of the water that shelves off prodigiously, and the foot of the Precipice, three Men may cross in a breast without any other dammage, and a sprinkling of some few drops of water" (137). "JCB," a French soldier in the Seven Years War whose full name is not known, claimed he was the first writer to actually climb down the cliff and into a cavern behind the falls (Dow 1: 40–41), even though years earlier Kalm had reported that rockfall had closed up the cavern. Nonetheless, Alexander Wilson also reported the feat of climbing behind the cascading water:

> Our Bard and pilot, curious to survey
> Behind this sheet what unknown wonders lay,
> Resolved the dangers of th'attempt to share
> And all its terrors and its storms to dare; . . .
> There dark, tempestuous, howling regions lie,
> And whirling floods of dashing waters fly.
> At once of sight deprived, of sense and breath,
> Staggering amidst this caverned porch of death (172)

Others explained that the deep cave was inaccessible because it repelled explorers with an asphyxiating atmosphere. Weld in 1796 wrote that "my breath was nearly taken away by the violent whirlwind that always rages at the bottom of the cataract" and that none of his party would "attempt to explore the dreary confines of these caverns, where death seemed to await him that should be daring enough to enter their threatening jaws" (Dow 1: 106). The Falls were gothic; they concealed depths and mysteries which awed and terrified the spectator, yet, like the gothic, these mysteries were susceptible to being redescribed and dispelled by a scientific discourse. And this gothic aesthetic reflects the sublime one, insofar as the faculty of reason is briefly stifled or overwhelmed, only to return and succeed in comprehending its object (see Hitt 608).

This great o'erwhelming work of awful Time,

In all its dread magnificence sublime,

Rose on our view; amid a crashing roar,

That bade us kneel and Time's great God adore.

(ALEXANDER WILSON, "The Foresters," 169)

IT WAS the conception of time that revived the sublime power of Niagara Falls, that imbued it with a significance which transcended Thomas Jefferson's utilitarian landscape aesthetics. Sublime time can also offer the key to an ecological aesthetics of wilderness spectacle today, one which challenges any anthropocentric preference for framed picturesque landscapes of pleasure by challenging the very scale of the human senses. Kant wrote, in one of his lengthy sentences in *The Critique of Judgement:*

> The feeling of the sublime is, therefore, at once a feeling of displeasure, arising from the inadequacy of imagination in the aesthetic estimation of magnitude to attain to its estimation by reason, and a simultaneously awakened pleasure, arising from this very judgement of the inadequacy of the greatest faculty of sense being in accord with ideas of reason. (106)

In this section, subtitled "The Mathematically Sublime," it is the scale of numbers, extending both infinitesimally and astronomically beyond either end of the scale of human senses, which invites reason to exceed and comprehend imagination. Yet Kant did not conceive of the best metaphor of all for the mathematical sublime, geological "deep time." Nor did Jefferson, who in his account of the confluence of the Potomac and Shenandoah Rivers evoked a geological past, yet proposed a biblical, catastrophist image of the formation of the spectacle. The central section of the passage, sandwiched between the violent rending and the pastoral scene "through the cleft", reads:

> The first glance of this scene hurries our senses into the opinion, that this earth has been created in time, that the mountains were formed first, that the rivers began to flow afterwards, that in this place particularly they have been dammed up by the Blue ridge of mountains, and have formed an ocean which filed the whole valley; that continuing to rise they have at length broken over at this spot, and have torn the mountain down from its summit to its base. The piles of rock on each hand, but particularly on the Shenandoah, the evident marks of their disrupture and avulsion from their beds by the most powerful agents of nature, corroborate this impression. (19)

This natural dam break is not an "unscientific" explanation, for modern geologists describe the same phenomenon on a much larger scale in the draining of a primordial Lake Missoula in a tremendous deluge down the Columbia River. Jefferson might be supposed to have used this theory to explain the presence of marine fossils on Allegheny ridges. Yet in Query VI he considered and rejected this theory. Nor did he use this hypothesis to support a belief in the Noachian deluge, for Query VI also attempts to rationalize that biblical story as an instance of a similar dam break in the ancient Mediterranean. Instead, this violent cataclysm seems to be offered simply as a natural historian's explanation for the subjective affect of the sublime. It is ironic, therefore, that Niagara Falls invoked the opposite, a gradualist theory of geological creation by erosion.

As early as 1768, an anonymous writer on Niagara observed the scene from the edge of the escarpment above Queenston and commented, "At this place it is probable that the falls originally were, and broke up by slow degrees, to their present situation, which is seven miles higher" (Dow 1: 67). Andrew Ellicott in 1789 clarified this theory: "The cataract of Niagara was formerly down at the northern side of the slope . . . but from the great length of time, added to the great quantity of water, and distance which it falls, the solid stone is worn away, for about seven miles, up towards lake Erie" (1: 92). Isaac Weld repeated the theory, adding as evidence that "the falls have receded very considerably since they were first visited by Europeans, and that they are still receding every year" (2: 112). The rejection of the biblical chronology which this implied does not seem to have caused any consternation so long as no explicit estimate was made of the time involved. Charles Lyell, widely credited as the founder of modern geology, used the Niagara Gorge as an example of the powers of erosion in the first edition of *Principles of Geology* (1830). In this account, he blithely sidestepped the issue of biblical time:

> There seems good foundation for the general opinion, that the falls were once at Queenstown, and that they have gradually retrograded from that place to their present position, about seven miles distant. If the ratio of recession had never exceeded fifty yards in forty years, it must have required nearly ten thousand years for the excavation of the whole ravine; but no probable conjecture can be offered as to the quantity of time consumed in such an operation, because the retrograde movement may have been much more rapid when the whole current was confined. (1: 181)

Lyell had not seen Niagara when he wrote this, but he did in 1841 and wrote of the Falls in some of the twelve later editions of his great work and in *Travels in North America; with Geological Observations* (1845). His suggestion in the passage that rates of erosion varied avoided the outright attack on the six-thousand-year biblical chronology which he would later take up more aggressively, but the matter of the exact date is less significant than the sense of "deep time" which any such estimation inspires. We might say that geological time is the greatest post-eighteenth-century instance of the sublime and the one which best preserves the aesthetic subtleties of an era which did not share our sense of eternity. Geologic time surrounds humanity yet is on a scale which defies the human imagination; it is a creation of scientific measurement, yet it mocks the arrogance of this measurement. Like the early accounts of Niagara Falls, sublime time is both scientifically and spiritually edifying, and it can communicate to us, two hundred years later, the sense of wonder with which early Americans regarded sublime wilderness spectacles. Yet a sublime sense of deep time did nothing to prevent the construction of hydroelectric projects which now divert one-third of the water from Niagara Falls through subterranean tunnels.

If as Chris Hitt suggests, "the concept of the sublime offers a unique opportunity for the realization of a new, more responsible perspective on our relationship with the natural environment" (605), while, as Alison Byerly insists, today's commodified picturesque stands in the way of any sublime experience of wilderness, can these eighteenth-century American spectacles return us to a sublime aesthetic of nature? They can only if we acknowledge the paradoxes that were contained by the sublime from its foundation. Like the Gothic, the sublime tempts reason to abandon itself, only to return and reclaim sovereignty. The wilderness spectacle invites an image of nature untouched by humans but also suggests the means for industry, commerce, and commodification of that nature. The American sublime inspired Romantic idylls of mystery and awe but also puffed up nationalist pride and invited schemes for mills, canals, and bridges. If Thomas Jefferson had visited Niagara Falls, he might have agreed with Johnston that it was the greatest sublime spectacle of American Nature, but if he had then proclaimed that no canal or mill would ever tame its raging waters, it might well have been only because he wanted to build one between the Ohio and Youghigheny instead.

REFERENCES

Burke, Edmund. *A Philosophical Enquiry into the Origin of our Ideas of the Sublime and the Beautiful*. 2nd ed. London: Dodsley, 1759.

Byerly, Alison. "The Uses of Landscape: The Picturesque Aesthetic and the National Park System." *The Ecocriticism Reader*. Ed. Cheryll Glotfelty and Harold Fromm. Athens: U of Georgia P, 1996. 52–68.

Chastellux, François Jean, Marquis de. *Travels in North America*. Chapel Hill: U of North Carolina P, 1963.

Dillard, Annie. *Pilgrim at Tinker Creek*. New York: Bantam, 1974.

Dow, Charles Mason. *Anthology and Bibliography of Niagara Falls*. 2 vols. Albany: J. B. Lyon, 1921.

Fiedler, Leslie. *Love and Death in the American Novel*. 1960. New York: Anchor, 1992.

Franklin, Wayne. *Discoverers, Explorers, Settlers: The Diligent Writers of Early America*. Chicago: U of Chicago P, 1979.

Freneau, Philip. "The Rising Glory of America." *The Poems of Philip Freneau, Poet of the American Revolution*. 2 vols. Ed. Fred Lewis Pattee. Princeton: Princeton U Library, 1902. 1: 49–84.

Hennepin, Louis. *Déscription de la Louisiane*. Paris: Sebastien Huré, 1683.

Hitt, Chris. "Toward an Ecological Sublime." *New Literary History* 30.3 (1999): 603–23.

Imlay, Gilbert. *The Emigrants*. 1793. New York: Penguin, 1998.

Irving, Washington. *The Sketch-Book of Geoffrey Crayon, Gent. The Works of Washington Irving*. Vol. 1. New York: Cooperative Publication Society, n.d. 49–402.

Irwin, William. *The New Niagara: Tourism, Technology, and the Landscape of Niagara Falls*. University Park: Pennsylvania State UP, 1996.

Jefferson, Thomas. *Notes on the State of Virginia*. Ed. William Peden. Chapel Hill: U of North Carolina P, 1955.

Johnston, Charles. "A Narrative of the Incidents Attending the Capture, Detention, and Ransom of Charles Johnston . . ." *Held Captive by Indians: Selected Narratives, 1642–1836*. 1973. Ed. Richard VanDerBeets. Knoxville: U of Tennessee P, 1994. 243–318.

Jones, Howard Mumford. *O Strange New World; American Culture: The Formative Years*. New York: Viking, 1964.

Kant, Immanuel. *The Critique of Judgement*. Trans. James Creed Meredith. Oxford: Clarendon, 1952.

Kolodny, Annette. *The Lay of the Land: Metaphor as Experience and History in American Life and Letters*. Chapel Hill: U of North Carolina P, 1975.

Lahontan, Louis-Armand de Lom d'Arce, Baron de. *Nouveaux Voyages de M. Le Baron de Lahontan, dans l'Amerique Septentrionale*. The Hague, 1703. Trans. London, 1703.

Lawson-Peebles, Robert. *Landscape and Written Expression in Revolutionary America: The World Turned Upside Down*. Cambridge: Cambridge UP, 1988.

Lyell, Charles. *Principles of Geology*. 3 vols. 1830–33. Ed. Martin J. S. Rudwick. Chicago: U of Chicago P, 1990.

Marx, Leo. *The Machine in the Garden: Technology and the Pastoral Ideal in America.* New York: Oxford UP, 1964.

McGreevey, Patrick. *Imagining Niagara: The Meaning and Making of Niagara Falls.* Amherst: U of Massachusetts P, 1994.

McKinsey, Elizabeth. *Niagara Falls: Icon of the American Sublime.* Cambridge: Cambridge UP, 1985.

Miller, Perry. *The Errand into the Wilderness.* Cambridge: Harvard UP, 1956.

Monk, Samuel H. *The Sublime: A Study of Critical Theories in XVIII-Century England.* New York: Modern Language Association, 1935.

Nash, Roderick. *Wilderness and the American Mind.* New Haven: Yale UP, 1967.

Robertson, Bruce. "The Picturesque Traveler in America." *Views and Visions: American Landscape before 1830.* Washington, D.C.: Corcoran Gallery of Art, 1986. 187–210.

Sears, John. *Sacred Places: American Tourist Attractions in the Nineteenth Century.* New York: Oxford UP, 1989.

Seelye, John. *Beautiful Machine: Rivers and the Republican Plan, 1755–1825.* New York: Oxford UP, 1991.

Shepard, Paul. "The Cross-Valley Syndrome." *Landscape* 10 (1961): 4–8.

Weld, Isaac. *Travels through the States of North America and the Provinces of Upper and Lower Canada, During the Years 1795, 1796, and 1797.* 1807. New York: Johnson Reprint Corp., 1968.

Wills, Garry. *Inventing America: Jefferson's Declaration of Independence.* Garden City, N.Y.: Doubleday, 1978.

Wilson, Alexander. "The Foresters: Description of a Pedestrian Journey to the Falls of Niagara." *Poems and Literary Prose of Alexander Wilson.* Vol. 2: *Poems.* Ed. Rev. Alexander B. Grosart. Paisley, Scot.: Alex. Gardner, 1876. 2: 111–73.

Landscapes of Hope and Destruction

Ecological Poetry in Spanish America

URUGUAYAN ESSAYIST Eduardo Galeano offers a grim vision of the links between ecological problems in Latin America and multinational capitalism. U.S. companies move south across the Mexican border, "attracted by dwarfish salaries and the freedom of pollution"; European and U.S. companies produce and sell in Latin America fertilizers, pesticides, and cars banned in the First World; one-crop farming in Colombia produces tulips for Holland, roses for Germany, but "Holland gets the tulips, Germany the roses, and Colombia's left with rock-bottom wages, a damaged land and poisoned, overexploited water"; nowhere is the level of lead in the blood as high as in the inhabitants of Mexico City; indigenous women working in the coastal plantations of Guatemala feed their children with the most contaminated breast milk on the planet ("La ecología" 55–58).[1]

Clearly, the struggle for "sustainable development" is doubly difficult when the most basic needs are yet to be covered, and there is widespread resentment toward First World ecological advice and pressure: *you* got fat destroying your environment, so what right do you have to tell *us* to curb our development, clean up our act, and preserve what you seem to consider this supposedly last remaining paradise in the world? The paradoxes, of course, are blatant: the money that comes from ecological abuses in Latin America fills not only pockets abroad but also the pockets of the local elite without "filtering" down to the bulk of society: for the poor, all too often, it just means greater injustice, greater pollution, and a more and more infertile land. And as many ecologists point out, blaming others is an easy alibi for local exploiters and polluters.

The first major blow to American ecosystems was the Conquest, and in many ways it has been downhill ever since. Alfred Crosby, in 1989, wrote *Ecological Imperialism: The Biological Expansion of Europe,* and Elinor Melville, in 1994, wrote of "a plague of sheep" that arrived with the Spaniards in Mexico. But it was more than just sheep. "Chickens, pigs, donkeys, goats, sheep, cattle, horses, and mules" were all part of the ecological revolution

brought about by the European invasion, radically altering traditional indigenous cultures (Melville xi). In "La lámpara en la tierra," the opening
section of *Canto general* (general song), Chilean Nobel Prize winner Pablo
Neruda (1904–73) begins his American version of *Genesis* with famous first
words that designate a clear environmental cutoff point: "*Antes de la peluca
y la casaca / fueron los ríos, ríos arteriales*" (Before the frock coat and the wig /
were the rivers, arterial rivers), running through a fertile, nurturing world
that was "beloved of the rivers," "mother of metals": a "new womb of
the world" in which man, "tender and bloody"—like nature itself—"was
earth, vessel, eyelid of tremulous mud, form made of clay" (*Obras completas* 1: 417). Neruda's feminized nature even joins in the fight against the
conquistadors:

> The grave river Bío Bío
> said to Spain: "Stop."
> The forest of maitines whose green threads
> hang like a tremor of rain
> said to Spain: "Do not go on." The larch,
> titan of the silent frontiers,
> pronounced its word in a peal of thunder.
> But to the depths of my country,
> fist and dagger, the invader arrived. (485)

In these same years, maternity was an omnipresent theme in the poetry
of Chile's other Nobel Prize winner, Gabriela Mistral (1889–1957), in the
forms of frustrated mother, rural teacher (mother of other children), poetic
creator, and an earth which has the "attitude of a woman with a child in
her arms" (*Desolación* 202). From the 1940s onward, Mistral was writing of
"Gea"—more recently the Gaia of Lovelock—blending classical mythology
with Quechua ideas of the Pachamama and mentions of Saint Francis, as
a concrete personification of an exuberant, untouched American paradise
which she contrasted with alienated, urbanized, war-stricken Europe: while
the "Old Mother" burned,

> only the American Gea
> lives her night with the scent of clover,
> thyme and marjoram and listening
> to the rumour of martens and beavers
> and the blue flight of the chinchilla.
>   (*Desolación, Ternura* 206)

The deep-rooted link between woman and nature is enhanced by the auto-biographical speaker's childhood experiences of Chilean women working in the orchards and enjoying a direct physical and spiritual contact with the earth that men could not experience: in her poetry men exploit, destroy, and are unable to communicate with the voices of her animistic world. While "Men feel more / manly when they hunt," Mistral's speaker describes herself as a woman: that is, "an absurd thing that loves and loves, / that praises and will not kill," incapable of "those great things / they call 'exploits' " ("they," of course, meaning "men") (*Poema* 135). Patrick Murphy has pointed to the patriarchal connotations implicit in the use of Gaia imagery in recent decades,[2] and Mistral does indeed (like certain traditionalist ecofeminists) see women's difference as biological and not the product of their patriarchal culture. Woman is governed by the maternal instinct: "be she a professional, a worker, a peasant or just a simple lady, a woman's only raison d'être in the world is maternity, both material and spiritual maternity, or only the spiritual for those of us who have no children" (*Lecturas* 15).[3]

TOWARD THE END of the 1960s in Spanish America, as in the rest of the world, a growing ecological awareness started touching the poets. Neruda himself published *Fin de mundo* (The end of the world), which offers a disenchanted rereading of his earlier political poetry. In 1969 he was not far from being the world's "official" communist poet and was the Chilean Communist Party's candidate for the forthcoming presidential elections (the alliance with Salvador Allende's Socialist Party would lead him to stand down), but in *Fin de mundo*, which offers—as though it were written thirty years later—a panoramic view of the "century of death" in its death throes, Neruda has seen that *both* sides in the Cold War have viciously plundered and abused their environments. Nowhere, not even Latin America, is immune:

> You could no longer walk
> in 1970
> through the streets and the fields:
> the worn-out locomotives,
> the pitiful scooters,
> the failed automobiles,
> and aeroplane bellies
> invaded the end of the world:
> they wouldn't let us pass by,

they wouldn't let us blossom,
they filled beaches and valleys,
they suffocated belfries:
you couldn't see the moon any more.

Venice disappeared
beneath the petrol,
Moscow grew so big
that the birches died
from the Kremlin to the Urals
and Chicago grew so high
that it suddenly collapsed
like a box of dice.

I saw the last bird flying
near Mendoza, in the Andes.
And remembering it I shed
tears of penicillin
                    (*Obras completas* 3: 453–54)

THE HORRORS of Hiroshima and Nagasaki are present in this book by Neruda, along with a growing consciousness of the renewed threat of mass destruction (there are two poems entitled "Bomba"). The nuclear theme appears, too, in several other Spanish American poets. Wooed and exploited by the United States, the continent was unavoidably implicated in the Cold War: the Cuban Revolution had offered not only a hope for radical political change—hopes of justice, equality, freedom—but also a potential foothold for the expansion of Soviet interests. So nuclear matters were no alien subject: the 1962 Cuban missile crisis is proof enough. Another Chilean poet, Oacutescar Hahn (1938), is one of the more interesting "nuclear" poets. His initial and his last name, which he shares with Otto Hahn—inventor of nuclear fission and Nobel Prize winner for chemistry in 1944—seem to have condemned him to return obsessively, again and again, to the subject of nuclear war. A surrealist twisting of apocalyptic imagery from biblical and Sanskrit sources leads to poems such as his "Visión de Hiroshima":

Old men fled, decapitated by the fire,
angels ran aground on sulphurous horns
decapitated by the fire,
virgins with radioactive haloes

were stranded, decapitated by the fire.
All the children emigrated, decapitated by the sky.
Over the molten street we saw
not the limbless eye, not the maimed skin, not blood:
but lovers transfixed in public
and the wife of Lot
turned into a column of uranium.
The heated hospital runs out through the drains,
your frozen heart runs out through the pipes,
they are crawling under the beds,
they are crawling like green and cindered cats
mewing ash. (60–61)

THE CUBAN REVOLUTION coincided with and fomented a literary explosion in Spanish America, which includes not only the famous novelists of the "boom" (Gabriel García Márquez, Mario Vargas Llosa, Julio Cortázar, Carlos Fuentes, and others) but also socially minded "conversational" or "colloquial" poets whose revolutionary impulse has later, in some cases, tended toward ecological themes. In the following pages I allude to four poets who have undergone a similar evolution: Chilean antipoet Nicanor Parra (1914–), Mexican poets José Emilio Pacheco (1939–) and Homero Aridjis (1940–), and Nicaraguan poet Ernesto Cardenal (1925–).

NICANOR PARRA, fellow traveler of the Beats whose ironic and desacrilizing *Poemas y antipoemas* (1954) was vital in levering aside the dominant lofty grandiloquence, became a major influence—perhaps the major influence—for poets in the 1960s. Three decades later, the antipoet became an *ecopoet*. In 1972, in an iconoclastic box of postcards, the *Artefactos*, Parra's efforts to erase the distance between life and art, with his violently ironic criticism of ideological polarization, caused uproar in a bitterly divided Chile: a prime example is his parodic butchering of the left's slogan for political unity (*La izquierda unida / jamás será vencida* [The left united will never be defeated]) into "La izquierda y la derecha unidas / jamás serán vencidas" (*Artefactos*). In 1983 Parra published a second set of postcards which, alongside anti-Pinochet protest, attack right- and left-wing governments—this time for their environmental blindness—once more relying for their effect on graffiti-type texts, punchy slogans, fiery sarcasm, and wit:

We're no longer asking
for bread, clothes or a roof
We'll make do
with just a little
AIR
YOUR EXCELLENCY

Good News:
the world recovers in a million
years
It's us who disappear

Childhood memories:
the trees didn't yet have the form of tables
and raw chickens maneuvered through the landscape.

(Chistes)

THE EARLY POETRY of Homero Aridjis, president of the Pen Club, founder and director of the environmental organization *el Grupo de los Cien* (The group of the hundred), celebrated nature in arcadian terms, yet little by little the paradisiacal setting took on concrete forms—those of the land where he was raised—and his personal experience as a child. As in so much modern writing, the adult poet living in the city looks back and idealizes the lost paradise of his childhood environment. For Aridjis's speaker, however, this paradise is doubly lost: the forests in which once he wandered and which he considered his home are now being destroyed, and the native species whose language he learned in his childhood are disappearing. The oyamel forests around Contepec are one of the few winter habitats of the monarch butterfly, and much of the poet's work with the Group of the Hundred has been involved in the protection of this area. One of the poems from *Tiempo de ángeles* (Time of angels) contrasts the harmony of the butterflies in their (and the poet's) environment—the perfect, peaceful, nocturnal coexistence of animal, forest, and village—with the brutal destruction brought about, in glaring daylight, by modern man:

At night, the frost-coated forests
of my village await the lights of dawn.
Like closed leaves, the Monarch butterflies

cover the tree's branches and trunk.
Lying one on the other, they form a single organism.

It's midday. In the perfect silence the noise can be heard
of an electric saw advancing toward us
knocking down trees and slashing wings. Man, with his thousand
naked and hungry children, comes screaming his needs
and stuffing his mouth with fistfuls of butterflies.

(*Tiempo* 32)

The Romantic roots to Aridjis's poetry are traumatized by the annihilation
of the natural world he knew as a child: the nostalgia colors his writing still
more, as he laments and at the same time re-creates on the printed page
what is lost, but the life-giving material is gone:

Now the oyamels of your childhood trees have been felled, where will you listen
to the voice of the poem that flew, like a wounded serpent, through the branches?

(*Antología* 435)

While his former poetry suffered like a wounded serpent, Aridjis has tended progressively toward a simpler, more didactic, and at times cheerlessly
ironic style and content, inverting biblical texts in ironic rewritings such as
"Descreación" (Decreation):

Once the world had been made
man arrived
with an axe
with a bow
with a gun,
a harpoon
and a bomb
Once his hands and feet had been armed
with evil intentions and teeth
he killed the rabbit
he killed the eagle
he killed the tiger
he killed the whale
he killed man (342–43)

Likewise, Aridjis rewrites mythological and literary representations of
rivers and speaks of those that once glimmered as they flowed down to
Tenochtitlán but "today diminished, heavy with waste / and bloated with

excrement, go lowing through tubes" (398), utterly different from the gran-
deur and lyrical power of Pessoa's Tagus, the Seine of Apollinaire, Push-
kin's Neva, and Lorca's Guadalquivir (449).[4]

At the same time, as the language of nature disappears, the poet has to
learn a new language inscribed in the signs and symbols of city life:

> I read above the sea of cars
> the letters of lead
> that form in tomorrow's space
> the prophecy of an imminent ending
> to old Tenochtitlán, (318)

Apocalyptic warnings and nightmare images of Mexico in the future
abound in Aridjis's most recent books: both countryside and city are ecologically devastated. Language is contaminated. Human beings are spiritually
crippled, unable to love: in a hellish Mexico City with its yellow sky, its
cathedral sunken like a grey ship, its hills treeless, and its dogs, children,
and daisies suffering "the bitter death of the rain and the air," man's funeral
is anticipated by a lover's kiss from a "viscous, metallic mouth" (464).

MEXICO CITY, one of the most polluted cities in the world, is "today the
paradigm of urban disaster, the archetype of the growing environmental
and social problems of third world cities" (Ezcurra 1) and has driven another poet of Aridjis's generation, José Emilio Pacheco, toward ecological
themes. From his earliest work, Pacheco seemed to gravitate around fixed
obsessions of passing time, suffering, and poetry itself; the green perspective of later years has developed and added new shades of meaning to these
supposedly timeless subjects. The passing of time and the traditional dialectic of life and death, of permanence and brevity, stumble now against
indestructible, nature-defying products such as the plastic container "that
lasts seconds in the hand that tears into it; centuries upon centuries in burial
grounds of waste" (*Tarde* 232); and against the extinction of whales and or-
chids and of all forms of life in Mexico City—an "island of asphyxiation"
(*Los trabajos* 89). These are the dire consequences of "the drunkenness of
believing ourselves, by God's will, eternal owners; / wizards capable of
chaining down the world and sacking it at our pleasure" (*Tarde* 62).

Pacheco, too, offers an apocalpytic image of both present and future.
The poem "Séptimo sello" (Seventh seal) alludes explicitly to the biblical
Revelation, but this is a human-made, godless—and indeed a hopeless—
apocalypse:

> And little by little we devoured the earth
> Poisoned to its roots
> not a tree was left, not the trace of a river
> The air was all putrefaction
> and the countryside oceans of litter
> I am the last man
> I survived the ruin of my species
> I can reign over the world
> but what's the point
>
> (*Tarde* 132)

Poetically self-reflexive and constantly questioning his techniques and motives as a writer, Pacheco, like Aridjis, realizes that the ecological crisis demands structural changes in his writing: his former, and intermittent, faith both in the timelessness of good poetry and in the eternal cycles of nature and history tends to disappear, and his use of analogies or allegory to make sense of present-day problems starts to falter. The plastic ruins of our throwaway culture cannot be compared to the ruins of ancient cultures: the analogy does not work; the old dialectic of life and death no longer holds, or not, at least, in equivalent terms.

Modern poetry has always swung, according to Octavio Paz, between the extremes of analogy and irony, which "tear at the conscience of the modern poet": this analogy corresponds to a mythical, cyclical concept of time; irony, however, is the child of linear, unrepeatable time, and is "the wound through which analogy bleeds itself dry" (*Los hijos* 109–10). Pacheco's poetry veers radically toward irony. Idyllic and apparently timeless pastoral scenes are cut down in the final lines of his poems with grotesque images of present-day squalor (*Tarde* 112, 174).

A short poem in prose called "El infierno del mar" (The sea's hell) analyzes metapoetically what lies at the root of this poetic change: the old symbols no longer work when the reality they sprung from no longer exists: "You, too, like everyone else, called it mirror of eternity, foil to the earth, path that unites, abyss that separates," the speaker says, taunting himself for his blind repetition of clichés made obsolete not through overuse but by a change in the basic referent:

> If you, like Euripides, believed that the sea washes away the filth of the world,
> take a look at what we throw into it from this shore: lead, copper, mercury,
> cyanide. Sail out and you'll see oil slicks littering its paths. Viscous death cov-

ers life with obscurity, dishonors the flight of the birds, and gloomily corrodes the fishes.

The reasons for poetic change—just take a look at what is happening—open up into an ecological plea for change in the real world:

> For centuries we could abuse the sea and plunder, unpunished, everything its waves contained. Today as we kill it we are dying. When the sea dies we will have no more oxygen. The apocalypse will not descend from the sky, the world will not end with a sigh. The sea's hell will take hold of us—and the final irony of a return to our origins—we will die gaping like fishes out of water. (*Tarde* 230)

BUT DESPITE this insistent and inescapable imagery of destruction, there are other voices in Spanish America that present images of hope. The "emergence" of indigenous poets in recent years is particularly important, as can be seen in Mapuche writers such as Leonel Lienlaf and Elicura Chihuailaf, whose worldviews explicitly question the materialism and destructiveness of modern (Chilean) life and celebrate the possibility of an existence in greater harmony with the universe. Just as important, from an ecological or ecocritical perspective, is the way these poets have been so suddenly "discovered," published, and grafted onto the canon.

Paradigmatically, Lienlaf's *Se ha despertado el ave de mi corazón* (The bird of my heart has awoken) appeared in 1989 from one of Chile's foremost publishers, Editorial Universitaria, with a prologue by Raúl Zurita, one of the country's leading poets.

But perhaps the most optimistic and influential of Spanish American ecological writers is Ernesto Cardenal, poet, ex-priest, important figure in liberation theology, and minister of culture in the postrevolutionary Sandinista government. His poem "Apocalipsis" (1965)—an apocalypse that does (unlike Pacheco's) descend from the sky—is a carefully worked rewriting of the biblical Revelation. He, too, like Saint John, is ordered to relate what he sees:

> And it came to pass
> that I saw an angel
> (and all his cells were electronic)
> and I heard a supersonic voice
> that told me: Open your typewriter and write
> and I saw a silver-plated projectile that was flying

> and from Europe to America it arrived in 20 minutes
> and the name of the projectile was the H-Bomb

The scenes of destruction outdo all memories of the Second World War:

> and I saw over New York a mushroom
>   and over Moscow a mushroom
>   and over London a mushroom
>   and over Peking a mushroom
> (and Hiroshima's fortune was envied)
> And all the shops and all the museums and libraries
> and all the earth's beauties
>   evaporated
> and became part of the cloud of radioactive particles
> that floated over the planet, poisoning it

But as in the Bible, the apocalyptic destruction is part of the divine punishment and brings with it the hope of a new world: in Cardenal, the last lines speak of a new Evolution, a New Planet, a new species of *homo sapiens* consisting not of individuals but of free human beings that form together a single organism, and a New Canticle which is "a song of love" (*La hora cero* 32–36).

In 1969, *Homenaje a los indios americanos* (Homage to the American Indians) offered a celebration of American indigenous peoples and their harmonic relation with the Mother Earth, as opposed to predatory colonial and modern Western societies, while *Oráculo sobre Managua* (Oracle of Managua) gives a dramatic image of the way environmental problems hit hardest in the poorest sectors of society:

> That's where Acahualinca begins, the houses of cardboard and tin
>   where the sewers emerge . . .
>   Streets smelling of prison
> with that characteristic stench of prisons, of
> shit and rancid urine
> houses of bags of cement petrol cans refuse old rags.
>   That's where the sewers end
> On the shore of the lake the children play making holes
> with a stick to see who can pull the most flies from their hole
> In the water cotton wool, toilet paper, condoms.
> Nearby the market. On the rubbish vultures.
> A stream of milky sewage flows into the lake

on the right, the poisoned lagoon of Acahualinca, tender-green . . .
hovels in the plain where the trucks unload
(or unloaded) Managua's rubbish
plain full of cans paper plastic glass the skeletons of cars
vultures on the posts waiting for more trucks

(*Oráculo* 9–10)

Cántico cósmico (Cosmic chant), a vast work which combines physics, politics, biology, and religion, returns to the idea of a new world announced at the end of "Apocalipsis." One of the canticles is dedicated to Gaia (*Cántico cósmico* 78): Lovelock's anti-Darwinism and sense of harmonic unity correspond closely to Cardenal's worldview; indeed, many liberation theologians feel identified with central tenets of *deep ecology*. The disastrous sequels of capitalist exploitation of nature are frequently signaled in the book, and, interestingly, Cardenal sees—or perhaps saw—in the Sandinista revolution an opportunity to set back the clocks: social changes must necessarily be ecological, too. Thus, a polluted river in Leon can function as a paradigmatic image of the injustices under the dictator Somoza:

Poor River Chiquito! Your misfortune
is that of the whole country. Somoza's regime is reflected in your waters.
Leon's River Chiquito, fed by springs
of sewage, residues from tanneries and soap factories,
white water from the soap factories, red from the tanneries;
plastic on the river's bed, basins, rusty iron. That
is what Somoza's regime left us.

After the revolution, the speaker insists that everything will change. The revolutionaries are part of the ecological avant-garde:

We'll recover the forests, the rivers, the lakes.
We are going to decontaminate Managua's lake.
Not only humans were anxious for freedom.
All ecology was growing. The revolution belongs also
to lakes, rivers, trees, animals (141–42)

The wishful thinking and naive idealism of Cardenal can best be seen, perhaps, in the rather artificial analogy he establishes between revolutionary triumph and the return to the wild of some parrots that were caught while being smuggled to the United States:

My friend Michel is military chief in Somoto,
   there near the Honduran border,
and he told me he'd discovered some parrots
that were going to be smuggled into the United States
so they could learn to speak English.
There were 186 parrots, and 47 had already died in their cages.
And he took them back to where they'd been caught
and when the lorry drew near to the place called Los Llanos
near the mountains those parrots came from
   (huge mountains loomed behind Los Llanos)
the parrots got nervous, started flapping their wings
   and pushed against the bars of the cages.
And when the cages were opened
they all flew off in the same direction like arrows toward the mountains.
That's just what the Revolution did with us, I think:
it took us out of the cages in which they were going to take us to speak English.
It gave us back the Homeland they'd torn from us.
The compañeros, green like the parrots, gave the green mountains back to the
   parrots.
   But 47 of them died. (146)

Cardenal's utopian worldview offers an uplifting moment of optimism amid the growing number of ecological poets who are writing today in Spanish America. His nostalgia for the lost Golden Age of pre-Columbian America and his tenacious faith in its return in a postrevolutionary future (which the Sandinistas did not, in the end, deliver) may seem naive but is perhaps—as Jonathan Bate argues for others in his magnificent *The Song of the Earth*—responding to a deep-rooted human need:

> Idealization of the supposed organic communities of the past, like idolization of the aboriginal peoples who have supposedly escaped the ills of modernity, may often serve as a mask for the oppressions of the present. But the myth of a better life that has gone is no less important for being myth rather than history. Myths are necessary imaginings, exemplary stories which help our species to make sense of its place in the world. (25)

IN *La otra voz* (The other voice), one of the last essays published during his lifetime, Mexican Nobel Prize winner Octavio Paz pointed the way toward a new poetry in Latin America, able to address the "central theme" of the

turn of the century—"the human race's survival on a ravaged and poisoned earth"—without falling into the traps of so much political poetry, but
rather "suggesting, inspiring, insinuating. Not demonstrating, but showing." Inevitably, the urgency that draws poets to the ecological crisis tends
to hamper their possibilities of a subtle, oblique approach to the subject, and
besides, from a political point of view, being indirect all too often means
being ineffectual. But then again, how politically effectual has any direct,
tub-thumping declaimer ever been? The ways of poetry are slower, more
insidious. And whereas Jonathan Bate sees in myth a way of curbing ecological mayhem, Paz places his hopes in a poetry bound together analogically
with itself and the universe:

> Mirroring cosmic fraternity, the poem is a model of what human society could
> be. Faced with the destruction of nature, it shows the brotherhood between
> planets and particles, between chemical substances and our consciousness.
> Poetry moves our imagination and thus teaches us to recognize differences
> and discover similarities. The universe is a live web of affinities and oppo-
> sitions. Living proof of universal fraternity, each poem is a practical lesson
> of harmony and concord, although its theme be a hero's anger, the loneli-
> ness of an abandoned girl or the mind's immersion in the still waters of a
> mirror. Poetry is the antidote to technology and the market. The function of
> poetry, today and tomorrow, is reduced to that. No more? No less. (*La otra*
> 187–89)[5]

NOTES

1. Here, and elsewhere in the text, the translations are mine.

2. "It seems highly unlikely that Gaia imagery can be used without invoking any
of the Greek patriarchal baggage attached to the symbol" (Murphy, *Literature* 59).

3. It would be interesting to study how this binding of maternal and natural imagery has been rewritten in a radically different manner by contemporary women
poets such as Nicaraguan Gioconda Belli, whose best-selling novels offer a curious
amalgam of revolutionary Sandinismo, feminism, and ecologism, which can also be
found in her poetry.

4. For translations of this ("The Poets' Rivers") and other texts by Aridjis, see *ISLE*
5.2 (1998): 105–10.

5. This essay is part of the project *En defensa del planeta: ecología en la poesía hispánica*
(In defence of the planet: Ecology in Hispanic poetry), which has been financed by
a research grant awarded by the Fundación Caja de Madrid. Ecocritical readings
of Spanish and Spanish American literature are rare. Noteworthy exceptions are an
article in English by Forns-Broggi ("Ecology and Latin American Poetry") and the

special issues of *Hispanic Journal* (ed. Patrick Murphy and Roberto Forns-Broggi) and *Ixquic* (ed. Jorge Paredes and Benjamin McLean), which are all listed in the references below.

REFERENCES

Aridjis, Homero. *Antología poética (1960–1994)*. [Mexico]: Fondo de Cultura Económica, 1994.

———. *Tiempo de ángeles*. [Mexico]: Fondo de Cultura Económica, 1997.

Bate, Jonathan. *The Song of the Earth*. London: Picador, 2000.

Belli, Gioconda. *El ojo de la mujer*. Madrid: Visor, 1992.

Cardenal, Ernesto. *Cántico cósmico*. Madrid: Trotta, 1992.

———. *La hora cero y otros poemas*. Barcelona: El Bardo, 1971.

———. *Oráculo sobre Managua*. Buenos Aires: Carlos Lohlé, 1973.

Crosby, Alfred W. *Ecological Imperialism: The Biological Expansion of Europe, 900–1900*. Cambridge: Cambridge UP, 1989.

Ezcurra, Exequiel, et al. *The Basin of Mexico: Critical Environmental Issues and Sustainability*. New York: United Nations UP, 1999.

Forns-Broggi, Roberto. "Ecology and Latin American Poetry." *The Literature of Nature: An International Sourcebook*. Ed. Patrick D. Murphy. Chicago: Fitzroy Dearborn, 1998. 374–84.

Galeano, Eduardo. "La ecología en la marca de la impunidad." *Ecología solidaria*. Ed. Fernando Mires et al. Barcelona: Trotta, 1996. 55–62.

Hahn, Oscar. *Tratado de sortilegios*. Madrid: Hiperión, 1992.

Lienlaf, Leonel. *Se ha despertado el ave de mi corazón*. Santiago: Universitaria, 1989.

Melville, Elinor G. K. *A Plague of Sheep: Environmental Consequences of the Conquest of Mexico*. Cambridge: Cambridge UP, 1994.

Mistral, Gabriela. *Desolación*. Santiago: Andrés Bello, 1988.

———. *Desolación, Ternura, Tala, Lagar*. [Mexico]: Porrúa, 1986.

———. *Lecturas para mujeres*. [Mexico]: Porrúa, 1976.

———. *Poema de Chile*. Barcelona: Pomaire, 1967.

Murphy, Patrick D. *Literature, Nature, and Other: Ecofeminist Critiques*. New York: State U of New York P, 1995.

Murphy, Patrick D., and Roberto Forns-Broggi, eds. Spec. issue of *Hispanic Journal* 19.2 (1998).

Neruda, Pablo. *Obras completas*. Vol. 1: *De "Crepusculario" a "Las uvas y el viento,"* *1923–1954*. Barcelona: Galaxia Gutenberg/Círculo de Lectores, 1999.

———. *Obras completas*. Vol. 3: *De "Arte de pájaros" a "El mar y las campanas,"* *1966–1973*. Barcelona: Galaxia Gutenberg/Círculo de Lectores, 2000.

Pacheco, José Emilio. *Tarde o temprano*. [Mexico]: Fondo de Cultura Económica, 1986.

———. *Los trabajos del mar*. Madrid: Cátedra, 1983.

Paredes, Jorge, and Benjamin McLean, eds. Spec. issue of *Ixquic* 2 (2000).

Parra, Nicanor. *Artefactos*. Santiago de Chile: Ediciones Nueva Universidad, 1972. N.p.

————. *Chistes par(r)a desorientar a la (policía) poesía*. Santiago de Chile: Ediciones Galería, 1983.

Paz, Octavio. *Los hijos del limo*. Barcelona: Seix Barral, 1990.

————. *La otra voz: Poesía y fin de siglo*. Barcelona: Seix Barral, 1990.

PART 2

Reaching Out
to Other Disciplines

LISA LEBDUSKA

How Green Was My Advertising

American Ecoconsumerism

Gifts that remind us why this planet is a
special place, and why it should stay that way.
catalog ad copy for Bloomingdale's "Serengeti ceramic serveware"

People have been wearing the Greenpeace logo for twenty years now.
Choosing items from the Greenpeace catalog is one way to show
your commitment to the organization and the environment.
Greenpeace catalog letter to "Dear Friend"

AMERICAN ECOCONSUMERISM, a form of postmodern commodification shaded green, poses problems of theory and praxis for cultural studies theorists and environmentalists alike. Both the wasting and acquiring (conserving) of nonhuman-made resources, ecoconsumerism encompasses environmental commodification as well as commodified environmentalism. In other words, ecoconsumerism consists of "greenwashing" (commodifying nature to produce capital) and "greening" (commodifying nature to produce capital to be used in the conservation of nature). Ecoconsumerism engages rhetoric, ideology, and ecology in a perpetual consideration of borders; for if, as Marshall Blonsky puts it, "we can use the sign to lie" (viii), and greenwashing and greening use similar signs, can we distinguish between the "lies" that each tells? Furthermore, to what extent do environmental goals depend on the need to distinguish between the two? And, finally, can environmentalism participate in the commodity system without being co-opted by it?

For radical ecologists, the first border drawn is the ideological boundary between "green" (lowercase) and "Green" (uppercase). As Andrew Dobson explains, "green," which is also known as shallow or light green ecology, signifies environmentalism and its attendant acts such as recycling, attaching catalytic converters to cars, and appending scrubbers to industrial smokestacks. By contrast, "Green," also known as deep or dark green

143

ecology, signifies ecologism, "a political ideology in its own right" which argues for substantial political structural changes in the way resources are used (Dobson 5). The environmentalist, for example, seeks to recycle the aluminum can whereas the ecologist argues against producing the can in the first place. The environmentalist consumes differently; the ecologist consumes less. For purposes of clarity, I follow Dobson's lead and distinguish between the two movements using "environmentalism" and "ecologism."

Because ecologism contests consumption itself, it remains ideologically opposed to capitalism, unlike environmentalism which often exists comfortably, even collusively, within a capitalist frame. Advertising, which perpetuates consumption, and often unthinking consumption at that, is inherently anti-ecologic because it starts with the premise that consumption is desirable. In a similar fashion, dolphin jewelry, whale notecards, and polar bear wrapping paper (all of which are featured in the Greenpeace catalog) are at best environmental rather than ecologic statements because they, too, promote an unquestioning consumption of the Earth's resources. As a study of advertising, therefore, this essay is already situated within the environmentalist project; nevertheless, it endeavors to explore the possibilities for moving toward the ecologic given such constraints.

At this particular moment, popular culture makes no distinction, erects no borders, between environmental projects. Although a Bloomingdale's catalog offering elephant teapots and giraffe pitchers would appear to have little in common with Greenpeace's exhortation to "ask yourself if you really need" a product before buying it (itself a contradiction when one considers Greenpeace catalog items), popular culture unites capitalist and seemingly ecologic ideologies. For example, after naming Earth the Man of the Year in 1988, *Time* magazine went on to announce happily in 1991, "Doing well by doing good, merchandisers join forces with environmentalists" (Cramer 48). The article featured such ecoconsumerisms as the licensing of the National Wildlife Federation logo and credit card companies' donating of an unspecified "small percentage" of their earnings to "nature advocate" groups. Informing the article, and the various acts of ecoconsumerism it featured, was a quiet depoliticizing of the environment (natural resources, land, and its inhabitants); or, in other terms, a substitution of the environmental for the ecologic.

Although some environmental groups like the National Wildlife Federation have leaped into the commodity pool while simultaneously rejecting the politicization of the environment, other groups such as Greenpeace have attempted to maintain a more marginalized position from which to critique the commodification of nature. This denaturalizing of nature (i.e., an unmasking of systemic exploitive environmental practices) does not, of course, sit comfortably with the American consumer, whose ecopolitical dis-ease was best expressed by Chester Sackett, a disgruntled Greenpeace contributor:

> Your editorial, "Towards a New Environmentalism," has a highly political flavor. Issues of racism, social justice, economic fairness and democracy are certainly vital, but I don't contribute to *Greenpeace* to deal with them.

Underlying Sackett's letter is a longstanding tradition—the myth of the apolitical landscape—and it is upon this myth that ecoconsumerism has built its success.

The myth of the apolitical landscape is constructed by and through most dominant conceptualizations of "American," but it is perhaps most relevant to the frontier hypothesis and American transcendentalism, which both construct the individual through his/her relationship to nature. As Henry Nash Smith's classic *Virgin Land* points out, Frederick Turner's influential frontier hypothesis was based on the insistence that "democracy [is] born of free land" (253) and that the opening of the West acted as a political equalizer because it provided equal opportunity for land acquisition. Under Turner's hypothesis American land becomes a means by which to avoid the notion of political struggle; land is used to signify the apolitical. Thus, the signs of nature (such as Native peoples, plants, and animals) are used to mask the exploitations of their material referents. Although a number of critics in addition to Smith (most notably Annette Kolodny and Richard Slotkin) have pointed out the exploitations masked by Turner's frontier hypothesis and its attendant myths, a brief examination of Turner's land "democracy" is nevertheless useful for understanding the power of contemporary ecoconsumerism's "apolititicism."

The success of Turner's frontier "hypothesis" (read "myth") derives its strength largely from its ability to effectively erase the actual political struggles of Native Americans, women, and white laborers. While almost any passage from Turner would serve to illustrate my point, one of the excerpts chosen by Smith is particularly revealing:

> European men, institutions, and ideas were lodged in the American wilderness, and this great American West took them to her bosom, taught them a new way of looking upon the destiny of the common man, trained them

in adaptation to the conditions of the new world . . . opened new provinces,
and dowered new democracies in her most distant domains with her material
treasures and with the enobling influence that the fierce love of freedom . . .
furnished to the pioneer. (qtd. in Smith 254)

Native Americans in this passage and in other similar myths are, of
course, neatly bound up in the conceptualization of wilderness. Because
they represent the savage they are justifiably conquered in the quest for
civilization. They constitute a necessary element in cultural representations,
forming, to use Slotkin's phrase, a "fatal environment" that the heroic,
Christ-like white man must overcome in order to justify his presence.

Women, too, are effaced by frontier myth, even when they are not relegated to the savage realm. In the above passage, for example, the feminine
is mapped onto American land, thus conflating female subjugation with
land exploitation. As Annette Kolodny shows in *The Lay of the Land*, the
dual quality of this feminine mapping, which renders the land both maternal and sexual, ultimately constructs the frontier as an account of male
conquest and alienation.

Additionally, even the white men who were supposed to benefit from
land democracy saw little of it. Once the Great Plains were "opened" for
white settlement, for example, "[t]he railroads grabbed the largest share—
181 million acres of land . . . for building half a dozen rail links with the
West; and in consequence they became the largest landholders in the country" (Bowen 80). Other speculators used various means of deception to ac-
crue large portions of land under the Homestead Act. Ultimately, despite
any official rhetoric to the contrary, "half a billion acres of U.S. land went to
major landholders and only 80 million to homesteaders" (Bowen 80). The
discourse of democracy (e.g., Turner's "destiny of the common man") constructs land in such a way as to mask the exclusionary practices of corporate
interests.

Literary representations of land contribute further to the depoliticization
of land. As David Wyatt points out, "In America the charting of consciousness has often begun as an act of mapping landscape" (17). Wyatt offers
Thoreau's "Solitude" ("landscape provides opportunity for self-reflection")
and the Emersonian transparent eye to support his thesis that "in classic
[literary] American accounts of landscape, landscape tends to disappear"
(33). As landscape is textualized it recedes, becoming a mere backdrop to
and for the search for self and in-dividualism (undividedness). This quest

for self ultimately legitimates all self-serving practices, including those that are used to exploit other groups or even other individuals.

Within the symbolic order, the quest for self is played out, in Lacanian terms, as a desire for the fictional unity of the imaginary, a wholeness with which various objects, represented as "other," seem to be invested but which cannot return the subject to the pre-symbolic unity of the mirror stage. Through its participation in the symbolic order of language, the Lacanian subject is constituted as a desiring subject, and it is this act of desiring which makes it the ideal site for capitalism. The consumer frontier becomes the unpurchased (and therefore unconquered) array of goods and services promising a civilized wholeness.

Functioning within a capitalist ideology, ecoconsumerism supplies an ever-changing frontier of natural images, textualizing nature into a quest for individualism, a psychic chase through an endless woods in pursuit of the gurgling brook, the majestic vista, the carefree otter "other" whose capture will allow us, like the traveler in Frost's "Directive," "to be whole again beyond confusion." Often, in both greenwashing and greening, the referents themselves—whether they are a nuclear power company or the struggle to prevent one of its plants from opening—are completely effaced, unimagined, and the real exploitive practices producing those referents fade further still, out of focus, out of mind, out of reach.

Ecoconsumerism assumes a variety of guises, using texts to create natural images for products, to signify environmental harmlessness, and to proclaim environmental activism. Quite often, greening and greenwashing become indistinguishable, as both create codes and consuming subjects which are at best money green. Nevertheless, certain borders of difference may still be constructed between the two ecoconsumerisms, and it is within these margins that environmentalism can begin to use the commodity system to politicize nature without falling prey to the co-optation of its capitalist project. An exploration of representative advertisements from corporate interests such as AT&T, the U.S. Council for Energy Awareness, and the American Forest Council as well as an interrogation of Greenpeace promotions (the largest of the political environmental movements within the United States) helps to illustrate my point.

An AT&T print ad offers an on-line Thoreau, "Dave," isolated in a mountain hide-away, alone except for his coffee cup, his keyboard, and his CRT. A disembodied "voice" in the form of quoted text speaks in phrases and ellipses as it tells Dave's story:

> It's his first national story . . . so Dave goes up there to get away from it all. Got himself a first-class communications setup . . . all AT&T . . . interviews over the phone . . . he goes for a run . . . answering machine takes messages . . . his editor calls and he faxes rewrites . . . makes every deadline . . . series starts tomorrow.

The copy at the bottom informs "you, the professional home worker" that, "With AT&T, on your own means never going it alone," accompanied by the ubiquitous tagline, "AT&T: The right choice."

Dave, the ecoconsumer, white, professional, and male, would seem to exploit nature at leisure, but both he and nature sit and wait to be exploited by a larger system of forces. The ecoconsumer retreats to the natural environment to get away from "it" all, but it is "it" that follows him, "it" that dictates his time, "it" that grows him, sprouting him from the keyboard, his gaze the gaze of the terminal, myopic and unable to gain the perspective of the land that surrounds him. Technology does not offer to free him from the chains that bind; it merely extends his tether, and like a hooded falcon he may try to fly (or run), but ultimately he remains fixed, answerable to the machine, the fax, the deadlines that keep him productive.

Nature's image offers the promise of reauthoring (Thoreau's, "The surface of the earth is soft and impressionable by the feet of men"), but the ecoconsumer does not rewrite himself through nature; his is a rewriting conducted through the image of nature. He does not write himself; technology writes him. The answering machine is now his voice, his mark of lack, his "I." It speaks him. The fax machine, too, authors him, sending him (his product) out to the world of "it" that he has gotten away from and then returning himself to himself, like the Lacanian signifier, which "represents a subject not for another subject but for another signifier" ("Of Structure" 194). He is dictated by his editor and sent as a "fax," a facsimile, a reproduction of a reproduction, a true simulacrum.

Nature does not intrude on the production of the ecoconsumer; with the mountain vista decidedly in the background (a history of success built on exploitive land practices now forgotten), the ecoconsumer remains both above and protected from it, perched on his deck, surrounded by a railing, safely fenced in from community, land, and his past. Despite the absence of telephone lines which would violate the view (his image of the land), the ecoconsumer remains remarkably connected, attached by the tendrils of fiber optics to a vast network of cultural, political, and economic power. Though he tries to achieve undividedness or "other" unity by being on his own, his quest is an impossible one, filled with the contradictions of postmodern consumption: "With AT&T, on your own never means going it alone."

The locus of the power, the disembodied voice, remains unlocatable, dispersed. Retreating to nature, the ecoconsumer goes to get away from "it," but "it" has no referent. Nothing has preceded it; nothing follows it. It is pure present, total immediacy, both everywhere and nowhere; hidden in the mountains, lurking in the terminal, waiting in the home which is now a place of work. And all this, "The right choice"—the correct choice, the choice of the political right—constitutes a conservative choice. But this "choice" is a nonchoice dedicated to maintaining the interests of those whose power rests on the ability to exploit land to their own advantage.

The U.S. Council for Energy Awareness takes the naturalization of power through land exploitation a step further by omitting people from its print ads. Its tagline, "Nuclear energy means cleaner air," depends on a mountain lake panorama and educational copy which in part reads as follows:

> In the words of the President's National Energy Strategy, "Nuclear power is a proven electricity-generating technology that emits no sulfur dioxides, or greenhouse gases."
>
> In fact, nuclear energy helps reduce air-borne pollutants in the U.S. by over 19,000 tons every day. That's because the 111 nuclear plants now operating in this country don't burn anything to generate electricity.

This text promises the imaginary in the clear, unmoving reflection of the mountain lake. Here, unrepresented by any human agents, the ecoconsumer disappears, becoming the Emersonian transparent eyeball ("I am nothing; I see all"). Nuclear energy clears the vista by providing invisible fallout—radioactivity can neither be seen nor smelled. The nuclear ecoconsumer is the one who seeks only to look. Narcissus-like, the ecoconsumer need only gaze and, seeing nothing but her/his own reflection (no yellow haze, no puffs of smoke) does nothing, and in doing nothing becomes nothing.

This ecoconsumer takes in and is taken in by the virgin landscape of Mother Nature in order to fulfill the desire for pre-oedipal unity that the womb provides. Nature, like the womb, is pre-symbolic, untainted, unbiased by language and the system(s) which produce it. It constitutes the "outside opinion" obtained "[t]o confirm the benefits of nuclear energy" and announced in truthful black-and-white headline typeface. The lack of the desiring subject is further filled with numbers (themselves as "truthful" and as pure as nature) which create a fiction of knowledge. The ecocon-sumer, constructed as knowing subject-scientist (able to quote quantities of airborne pollutants and numbers of nuclear power plants) remains safely removed from the taint of politics, an objective decision maker, blissfully informed and molded by numbers that say nothing of radioactive waste tonnage, cancer rates, or even half-lives. The lake's surface, like those of nuclear waste sites across the country, remains peacefully undisturbed, per-fectly concealing of the leaks and faults that lurk beneath.

The ecoconsumer, given the full advantage of vision through the cam-era's wide angle, takes in the scene's serenity, beauty, and majesty, a true aesthete, a genuine lover of nature who need not know history. Chernobyl, Three-Mile Island, and Sellafield need not exist; the ecoconsumer of nuclear energy is an individual who recognizes that "the more plants we have, the more energy we'll have for the future of our planet." Produced through his ability to consume ceaselessly and increasingly, the ecoconsumer becomes a commodity for the sustained growth of the nuclear industry.

The ecoconsumer of the American Forest Council is also produced by and against an image of nature, but he (the ad features a man) is an activist, not in the subversive sense of challenging and problematizing the status quo, but in his ability to support and identify with corporate interests. A print ad that appeared in the *Smithsonian*'s special environment issue mark-ing the twentieth anniversary of Earth Day spread a mountain vista across two pages. The ecoconsumer, a bearded white male, squats atop a hill, in-tently planting a pine sapling. The ad speaks directly to "you," constructing a second-person hero ecoconsumer who is celebrated more for his identi-fication with corporate interests than for his love of nature. The ad begins with a parade-like congratulation: "This Earth Day, we salute those of you who do something that forest products companies and private landowners do 6 million times a day. Plant a tree."

The jubilee continues with a ticker-tape–like list of sponsors ranging from ITT Rayonier to Scott Paper that runs across the bottom of the page. The list separates itself from the rest of the ad with a thin black rule which acts as both dividing line and law. The American legal system has, for the most part, protected corporate interest over the environment (witness, for example, the on-going rollback of the Clean Air Act, the ability of industry to move from state to state or even overseas in the search for lax environ-mental laws, or the EPA's offer of a partial cleanup of Superfund toxic waste sites). The list of sponsors runs quietly underneath the ad, seemingly small but noticeable, safely protected by a border of its own devising.

The parade's honoree, the vigilant ecoconsumer, remains in the picture, but he is like the visitor to the World Trade Center in Michel Certeau's "Practices of Space" whose "altitude transforms him into a voyeur. It places him at a distance. It changes an enchanting world into a text" (123). The ecoconsumer stands at the summit, his face turned down and hidden by hardhat and beard. His beard (signifying maleness, "naturalness," and rebellion) lies overshadowed by his hardhat, the protection he brings to both construction and destruction. Seedlings hang from a bag at his side, a strap-on womb partially lost from the picture, unfortunately necessary to an image that is so fully male (the ubiquitous plaid shirt, heavy construction boots, and beard). His hands are gloved; protected from both tree and land, he works the symbols of nature but remains unsullied by them. He is a land manager, a construction worker of natural resources whose desire is not to exist as part of the land, but to control it and bring it under his will.

"For Us, Every Day Is Earth Day," the text announces, and indeed in an era where "Marketers see green in the greening of America" (Begley 61), Earth Day has become a true marketing event, a sign of corporate America, sponsored and produced by interests such as Union Carbide, Domino's Pizza, and the maker of Glad plastic bags. And who can forget prime time's "The Earth Day Special," with Bette Midler as a dying Mother Earth, waiting for rescue by the ecoconsumer who need simply consume the proper product ("Only you can save the planet!" declares the Waldenbooks' Greenshelf) in order to fulfill his desire for unity with the Earth.

The ecoconsumer here engages in renewal, but it is a renewal of resources for capitalist interests in which he engages. The ecoconsumer uses his labor to build (plant) the very products he will consume. Trees and tree planting are part of an assembly-line process dependent upon the surplus value of the ecoconsumer's labor. The ecoconsumer has no face because he needs no identity; he is an undifferentiated consumer/laborer. In a similar fashion, the text which erases his difference also fails to distinguish between old-growth and new-growth forests and the wildlife each supports. A Derridean "supplement," the excess and remainder of this difference spill beyond the borders of the text because as the language of mass production and mass consumption offer "renewal" as a code for the exploitation of natural resources, environmental cost in the form of air pollution, water pollution, and soil erosion erupt, producing the ultimate nontextual silence:

Extinction.

As environmental movements increase their participation in the commodity system through such actions as the Nature Conservancy's partnership with Nature Company and the publication of a Greenpeace catalog (filled with the "signs" of ecology—dolphin shirts, penguin mugs, and
shark puppets), ecologists have begun to question the extent to which such
participation constitutes co-option. Can an ecologic code which would create a politicized ecoconsumer function within a capitalist system? The promotion of any consumption, but particularly the consumption of luxuries
such as jewelry, note cards, and wrapping paper, is inherently anti-Green
because it involves an unnecessary use of natural resources. Nevertheless,
while the practice itself is at best environmental rather than ecologic, the
codes informing these practices may begin to work toward producing an
ecoconsumer who is more green than greenwashed.

The ecoconsumer produced by the Greenpeace code is perhaps the most
interesting because s/he is constantly shifting, as if afraid of occupying one
position for too long. The ecoconsumer of Greenpeace checks, for example,
is both faceless and voiceless (no people appear in the ads); a former writer
of "silent checks" who, through purchasing and using Greenpeace checks,
becomes an activist; "Now you can speak out for Greenpeace with every
check you write." Check writing is substituted for political activism, as the
ecoconsumer is no longer a grass-roots activist, but a check-writing member
of a large institution that will carry out environmental goals without using
the deadly sign "politics."

This ecoconsumer need never speak; the checks speak for her/him,
showing that s/he "want[s] clean rivers and lakes and seas" and "saying
'No' to the production of toxic waste and 'Yes' to the protection of threatened marine mammals and other endangered species, human beings included."

This ecoconsumer need never know how her/his desire is to be fulfilled,
either. The message s/he sends through the check is bewildering, as the
check becomes a stop to communication, cryptically pronouncing "Let the
Oceans Live" (written over a dolphin silhouette against a sunset sky), or
"You Can't Sink a Rainbow" (masterful etching of the Greenpeace ship *Rainbow Warrior*), and, for the purist, "Greenpeace" (the world on a Greenpeace
buoy).

Each of these checks carries with it a different signifier which in turn produces a different type of ecoconsumer. The dolphin as signifier has come to
represent a sort of benign environmentalism. Seeming to smile perpetually,
the dolphin signifies the animal world's joyful acceptance of human pres-

ence. The dolphin is the happy mammal of the *Flipper* TV show or Florida's SeaWorld, where visitors pay a fee to frolic with them in their pens. Palatable and pleasant, this dolphin does not speak of exploitation.

The dolphin of the Greenpeace check is a dolphin cartoon, a pastel sign that rejects all traces of drift net lacerations and the political ideologies that produce and perpetuate industrial tuna fishing practices. This dolphin is a signifier airbrushed of all its political consequence, filled only with its ability to produce a how-cute, anthropomorphized smile.

By contrast, an advertisement for Greenpeace action which appeared on the back cover of *Greenpeace* magazine (in 1992 Greenpeace abandoned its magazine in favor of a more environmentally benign newsletter) featured a very different kind of dolphin and a very different kind of ecoconsumer. The ad is a black-and-white photograph in the photojournalistic style. A dying dolphin lies cradled in a woman's arms. This dolphin, like the tortured prisoner of Foucault's *Discipline and Punish,* bears the visible marks of coercive power, its body covered with drift net gashes.

The ecoconsumer here is the woman-nurturer who seems to take the mammal's pain upon herself. The ad's headline announces, "So far, we've found 7 dolphins in 60 miles of driftnet. That only leaves 999,940 miles to go." But even this ad, with its attendant journalistic political "truths" about exploitive fishing practices, does little to address the political and economic systems which produce, encourage, and demand those practices. The ecoconsumer remains a consumer of goods first; no political border or boundary has been challenged or even questioned. The ecoconsumer as resisting subject is again constructed solely in terms of his/her buying power, which in this case is the ability to make a financial contribution to Greenpeace Action. The knowledge base producing our conceptualization of the ecoconsumer remains safely in place.

This Greenpeace advertising dilemma again asks us to consider the compatability of environmental and capitalist agendas. The problem of the Greenpeace campaign, as I see it, is not that it chooses to participate in the market system, but rather that it fails to address the knowledge bases informing that system. If it were to deploy advertising in such a way as to foreground systemic exploitations, Greenpeace and other environmental groups would ultimately construct ecoconsumerism in terms of its ecology rather than its consumerism—ECOconsumerism as opposed to ec(h)o-CONSUMERISM. However, such a reconstruction demands acknowledging and publicizing the very political nature of nature, and until American environmentalists undertake this task, popular culture will remain a right (or politically "wrong") vehicle that has been enabled to drive uninterrupted along a highway of good intentions, leaving us all in the wake of its exhaust.

REFERENCES

Begley, Sharon. "The Selling of Earth Day: Marketers See Green in the Greening of America." *Newsweek* 26 March 1990: 60.

Blonsky, Marshall, ed. *On Signs*. Baltimore: Johns Hopkins UP, 1985.

Bowen, Ezra, series ed. *This Fabulous Century*. New York: Time-Life, 1970.

Certeau, Michel. "Practices of Space." *On Signs*. Ed. Marshall Blonsky. Baltimore: Johns Hopkins UP, 1985. 122–46.

Cramer, Jerome. "The Selling of the Green." *Time* 16 Sept. 1991: 86.

Dobson, Andrew. *Green Political Thought*. London: Unwin Hyman, 1990.

Kolodny, Annette. *The Lay of the Land: Metaphor as Experience and History in American Life and Letters*. Chapel Hill: U of North Carolina P, 1975.

Lacan, Jacques. "Of Structure as an Inmixing of an Othemesa Prerequisite to Any Subject Whatever." *The Structuralist Controversy*. Ed. Richard Macksey and Eugenio Donate. Baltimore: Johns Hopkins UP, 1972. 186–271.

Plant, Christopher, with David H. Albert. "Green Business in a Gray World: Can It Be Done? An Introduction." *Green Business: Hope or Hoax?* Ed. Christopher Plant and Judith Plant. Philadelphia: New Society, 1991. 1–8.

Sackett, Chester. Letter. *Greenpeace* Nov./Dec. 1990.

Seligman, Jean, and Linda Buckley. "The Selling of Earth Day." *Newsweek* 26 March 1990: 60–61.

Slotkin, Richard. *The Fatal Environment: The Myth of the Frontier in the Age of Industrialization, 1800–1890*. New York: Atheneum, 1985.

Smith, Henry Nash. *Virgin Land: The American West as Symbol and Myth*. Cambridge: Harvard UP, 1950.

Wyatt, David. *The Fall into Eden: Landscape and Imagination in California*. New York: Cambridge UP, 1986.

Dominion, Empathy, and Symbiosis
Gender and Anthropocentrism in Romanticism

ANIMALS have arguably been the oldest metaphor used to define human-ity, to construct human identities by symbolizing what humans are and are not. Appropriated for whichever rhetoric they serve, animals occupy a Pro-crustean bed of order and disorder, innocence and depravity, violence and peacefulness, masculinity and femininity, monarchy and democracy, wis-dom and ignorance, as well as sacrifice, sexuality (both innocent and de-praved), gluttony, drunkenness, and other seemingly disparate qualities. Mary Midgley, for instance, has drawn attention to the contradiction con-tained in the disparate uses of the very terms *animal* and *beast*, the former of which can encompass a wide range of connotations from "spiritual" to "bes-tial" (Midgley 36–37). These contradictions have been attributed by Tim In-gold to "our propensity to switch back and forth between two quite differ-ent approaches to the definition of animality: as a domain of the 'animal kingdom' including humans, and as a state of condition, opposed to hu-manity" (Ingold 4). Contradiction therefore pervades the entire discourse of zoology, from purportedly objective scientific texts to more openly subjec-tive representations of animals in imaginative literature and art. The animal in art has been considered so entirely rhetorical that its role is sometimes explained away as an incidental shell (Bettelheim 75, 177) whose kernel is the "cultural values, relationships, and problems of human society" (Tap-per 57).

Insofar as Romanticism is a coherent movement, animals are central to its holistic symbolism and a prominent feature of its art. This centrality notwithstanding, the Romantic animal is delineated as the Other and, like all human representations of animals, is toggled between alterity and iden-tity in the process of human self-definition (both masculine and feminine). This ambivalence and alternation may be traced to the conceptual discrep-ancy toward the superiority of Man (not Woman) over other beings that has been inherited by mainstream Western thought through its two major tributaries, Greece and Judeo-Christianity.[1] These discrepancies can be seen pervading not only art and literature but also religion, scientific taxonomy, and even the law.[2]

The most influential modern reinforcement of the dualist position came, of course, from Descartes, whose 1637 *Discours de la mèthods* contained the notorious *bêtemachine* theory that animals were mere bodies, no more than automata. Both human and animal bodies could be considered automata, but speech and the soul separated the human from the animal. The animal body operated purely on mechanical principles, and any sounds made by the animal—including its cries of pain—were the products of its machinery.

At the time of Descartes's death in 1630, no country in Europe had a law granting animals any rights, an absence that would remain unchanged for more than a century (Maehle 93). Violent sports, such as hunting for the upper classes and cock- and dogfighting, bullbaiting, and bull running for the lower, were widely practiced (Malcolmson 49–50). Country fairs often featured performers who entertained spectators by eating live animals (such as cats and foxes), as well as activities like "goose-pulling" and "sparrow-mumbling," entailing competitions to pull off the head of the live creature concerned (E. S. Turner 61–62). But the thought of late-eighteenth- and early-nineteenth-century England, the intellectual period that has been constructed as "Romantic," can be considered to be a turning point for the way in which animals—and the human-animal relationship—were viewed in Europe. This revolution was part of a shared discourse that was manifested at the scientific, the philosophical, the literary, and the practical levels, as well as at the parliamentary level in England.

Before the so-called Enlightenment, taxonomic systems had been purely emblematic or anthropocentric, with little distinction made between real and mythical animals. Pliny's first-century *Natural History* freely mixed folk tradition with observation, elephants with dragons, and moral evaluation with empiric observation. Even a millennium and a half later, purportedly scientific taxonomies were based on subjective categories, such as edible/inedible, wild/tame, useful/useless, and even "sweet/foul smelling." Richard Brookes's *Natural History of Quadrupeds* (1763) concluded that the obvious division of animals was into "the Domestic and the Savage." The Linnaen system (*Systema Naturae* [1735]), accepted in England from the 1760s, reflected the Enlightenment and was the first taxonomy that seemed to base itself on objective criteria rather than mere anthropocentrism. Linnaeus's system was based upon establishing distinct categories to classify each animal as well as to ascertain its relative place within the natural order, and to the horror of many he firmly grouped *Homo sapiens* with other mammalian species and specifically with other primates under the order *Anthro morpha*. Devising a binomial system of nomenclature, Carl Linnaeus used one Latin (or Latinized) word to represent the genus and a second to distinguish the species. Although he was not wholly convinced about the fixity of the genera, he was about the species, and his influence is based on his atemporal stance. Within a few decades, however, the fixity of the Linnaen mode of classification would be superseded by modes in which the immutability of species was no longer a given. Well before the end of the eighteenth century, Erasmus Darwin's *Zoonomia* (1794–1796) had appeared, and by 1800 Jean Baptiste de Monet (the Chevalier de Lamarck) had proclaimed his earliest public statement of his own theories of evolution (or "transformism") in his lecture "Système des animaux sans vertèbres" (Lecture on the systems of invertebrate animals). Both men had arrived at their conclusions independently and had anticipated a theory of evolution but were unable to establish how exactly evolution took place. Erasmus Darwin, basing his conclusions on vestigial organs and the metamorphoses of animals during development, deduced that transmutation of the species took place through the satisfaction of desires and needs, while Lamarck based his theories of transformism on his belief in the inheritance of acquired characters. Lamarck's theories were further developed in *Philosophie zoologique* (1809) and *Histoire naturelle des animaux sans vertèbres* (1813–1822), which emphasized the harmonious organicism of the environment through the active role it played in transformism—a far cry from the struggle for survival that was to be the hallmark of Charles Darwin's natural selection.

Despite the dominant trends of Enlightenment objectivity and Cartesianism, there lingered a strong current that ran counter to both modes of thought. Although Linnaeus's method of classification was widely accepted by the mid–eighteenth century, objectivity clearly vied with unconcealed anthropocentrism until well into the nineteenth century. Even Linnaeus had included orders such as "beasts of burden" (*iumenta*) in his taxonomy. Georges Leclerc Buffon, on the other hand, was more undisguisedly subjective, and he dismissed objectivity as a goal, following relationships rather than essences: the most "natural" way to classify an animal therefore became its relationship to man.

Likewise, Cartesian dualism appeared on the surface to reign supreme, but several philosophers throughout Europe had been unconvinced by Descartes. In France both Voltaire and Diderot had been skeptical of the *bête-machine* theory (with Voltaire providing proof of animal intelligence in his article on animals in *Dictionaire philosophique*), while in England John Locke ridiculed Descartes's theory, stating that scientists believed it "only because their work required it." Bernard Mandeville, himself a vegetarian, called Descartes a "vain reasoner" in his "Fable of the Bees." By the 1760s some philosophers had begun to concede the possibility of human-animal continuity by accepting the concept of animal "sagacity" (intelligence). The Scottish philosopher David Hume acknowledged that animals had the power of "experimental reasoning," while England's David Hartley attributed the human disbelief in animal rationality to human ignorance of animal communication (Thomas 125).

Long-lasting and far-reaching though the philosophers' impact might have been, a more immediate influence on the thought of eighteenth-century England was produced by some men of religion who attempted to dissociate Christianity from exploitative dominion over animals. Among these were Humphry Primatt, whose 1776 *Dissertation on the Duty of Mercy and Sin of Cruelty to Brute Animals* labeled cruelty toward animals a heresy and a sin, drawing attention to the elevated status given to animals in other religions. Likewise, James Granger's 1772 sermon *Apology for the Brute Creation or Abuse of Animals Censured* had attempted to link kindness to animals with Christianity and to warn that cruelty to animals would lead to cruelty to humans—a claim that is still the subject of debate today (Felthouse and Kellert 710–17). Both tried to focus attention on biblical passages in Exodus (20:10, 23:12) and Deuteronomy (5:14, 22:6–7, 25:4) and especially Proverbs 12:10 ("A righteous man regardeth the life of his beast") and away from Genesis 1:26–28 and 9:2–3, the two passages that had been used to deny accountability toward animals.[3]

Meanwhile, vegetarianism was acquiring many ardent advocates who decreed that meat eating should be avoided on several grounds: its cruelty, its unnaturalness, its repulsiveness, and its potential to produce bad breath. John Oswald, a Scottish officer stationed in India, was sufficiently influenced by the teachings of Hinduism to give up meat and persuade others to do likewise in *The Cry of Nature, or an Appeal to mercy and Justice on behalf of persecuted animals* (1791). Joseph Ritson's *Essay on Abstinence from Animal Food As A Moral Duty* (1802) had a profound influence on Shelley, who in turn urged against animal slaughter in *Vindication of Natural Diet* and *Essay on the Vegetable System of Diet*. Meat was almost England's national symbol, but by the middle of the eighteenth century vegetarianism in one form or another, though certainly not widespread, was no longer an unknown habit for the English. Its converts had included Aphra Behn, Lord Chesterfield, and James Boswell, as well as its more vocal advocates. Likewise, the traditional habit of serving, at the dining table, smaller animals with their heads attached gradually ceased to be seen as aesthetically enhancing and slowly all but disappeared (Thomas 287–300).

Before 1800 the law had occasionally punished "wanton, intentioned, or malicious" cruelty to animals (for acts like tearing out the tongues of live animals that were someone else's property), but only on account of the animals' role as human property; animals had no legal protection in their own right. When Sir William Pultney presented to the House of Commons the first bill seeking this protection in 1800, the concept was considered ludicrous by Parliament and the press. Intended to prohibit the baiting of bulls, the bill was opposed by William Windham (who was then the secretary of war and an ardent defender of bullbaiting) and lost by a vote of 43 to 41. (The issue, opined the *Times* editorial of 25 April 1800, was tyranny and beneath the dignity of Parliament: "whatever meddles with the private personal disposition of a man's time or property is tyranny direct.") This did not deter Lord Erskine of Restormel, a former lord chancellor, from attempting (albeit unsuccessfully) in 1809 to persuade Parliament to accept a bill, entitled "Preventing Wanton and Malicious Cruelty to Animals," which would establish the principle of animals' legal rights (Erskine, cols. 553–71). He was joined in these endeavors by Richard Martin (later the MP for Galway and popularly known as "Humanity Dick" for the nickname given him by George IV). Despite a number of initial failures, Martin succeeded in establishing Europe's first law against cruelty to animals in the 1822 act to "prevent cruel and improper treatment of Cattle," which was followed by the 1835 Cruelty to Animals Act outlawing animal-baiting sports, and then the 1849 act "for the more effectual Prevention of Cruelty to Animals."

Some of this feeling culminated in the foundation in 1824 of the Society for the Prevention of Cruelty to Animals (SPCA). With Princess (soon to be queen) Victoria as one of its patrons, it could add *Royal* to its name, becoming, in 1840, the RSPCA, and it became a major force in the policing of the laws that had gone into effect and in spreading the movement of animal welfare to France, Germany, and other European countries (Brown 24).

All attempts at benevolence toward animals were not fostered by an acknowledgment of the human-beast continuity and often stemmed instead from two countervailing forms of anthropocentrism. The first was that cruelty toward animals would eventually lead to cruelty toward humans, as Hogarth illustrated through the lesson of Tom Nero in the engravings entitled *The Four Stages of Cruelty*. Tom Nero, who begins as a juvenile animal torturer and develops into a murderer, is eventually hanged and dissected. The second was that animals were indeed inferior creatures and were *therefore* worthy of protection and kindness. As Thomas notes, "The paradox, therefore, was that it was out of the very contradictions of the old anthropocentric tradition that a new attitude would emerge" (Thomas 156). For David Hartley the human was to the animal what God was to the human: a guardian with inherent duties and responsibilities; for Jeremy Bentham the question to be asked was neither "Can they *reason*? nor Can they *talk*? but Can they *suffer*?" (Bentham 412).

Literary Romanticism not only reflected but actively produced the changes of time, and the poets who later became known as the Romantic poets frequently made public and poetic statements about animals that reflected the influence of pantheistic doctrines on their thought. These statements produced enduring effects—both active and contemplative—on public opinion and frequently were cited by the pamphleteers and even were quoted in speeches in Parliament. Blake's lines "A robin redbreast in a cage / Puts all heaven in a rage" became a slogan linking human and animal freedom, while in "The Lamb" and "The Tyger" he deconstructed the anthropomorphic view of these two animals. "A Fly" highlighted the human-animal continuum:

> Am not I
> A fly like thee?
> Or art thou not
> A man like me?
>
> For I dance
> And drink and sing
> Till some blind hand
> Shall brush my wing.

Robert Burns went even further than Blake in apostrophizing not only the humble "fellow-mortal" mouse but the decidedly unromantic louse as well. Cowper's *The Task* declared that its speaker would banish from his "list of friends . . . the man / Who needlessly sets his foot upon a worm." Wordsworth's poems abound in the lessons taught to him by the animal world. "Hart-Leap Well" empathetically re-creates the terror of a hart during a chase, exhorting the reader of 1800 "never to blend our pleasure or our pride / With sorrow of the meanest thing that feels." Coleridge's "Rime of the Ancient Mariner" (1798) explores the guilt produced by the wanton killing of an albatross, while the eponymous hero of his poem "To a Young Ass" receives the salutation "I hail thee *Brother.*" Percy Shelley's *A Vindication of Natural Diet* (1813) and *Essay on the Vegetable System of Diet* linked animal slaughter with disease and crime, which flow from unnatural diet: since meat can only be gained violently, its consumption would inevitably produce violence. Angling, according to Byron, was not only the crudest but also the stupidest sport. Keats characterized his own poetic ability as the "camelion" (chameleon) power of empathy that enabled the poet to enter the being of other creatures: "if a Sparrow come before my Window I take part in its existince and pick about the Gravel" (Keats, 186).

Blake, William Wordsworth, Coleridge, Byron, Percy Shelley, and Keats compose the Big Six who have exclusively dominated the canon of Romanticism for more than a century and a half, supposedly because there "were no women" writing at the time and because their work was far from trivial or insignificant: it was certainly widely read and widely sold. These explorations have shown that far from being the monolithic movement it was once considered, the literature of this period encompasses several Romanticisms, including what Anne Mellor has termed a "masculine" Romanticism and a "feminine" one (Mellor, *Romanticism and Gender* 3–4), and that the exclusion of women from the Romantic canon has been based on the privileging of the masculine.[4]

This exclusion appears to be in danger of infiltrating the nascent canon of green literature. Anthologies of literature promoting green issues or humaneness to animals seldom exclude detailed excerpts from the Big Six. Mary Shelley has gradually entered both canons, but unfortunately little if any mention is made of the less canonical women writers of this period, such as Anna Barbauld, Sarah Trimmer, Dorothy Wordsworth, and Mary Wollstonecraft, who anticipated many of the axioms of ecofeminism.[5] These women used the pen (perhaps in less prestigious genres than the men) to inculcate moral awareness rather than abstract speculation, frequently championing creatures like caterpillars and spiders for humane treatment, unlike the male poets whose causes tended to be "cuter," more anthropomorphous animals.[6] Emphasizing rationality rather than mysticism as the foundation of benevolent compassion, they had a lasting effect on middle-class morals. Some incited the wrath of established writers like Charles Lamb and Coleridge for their desire to ban nursery rhymes and fairy tales that promoted cruel irrationality or cruel behaviour, such as the Mother Goose nursery rhymes that taught children "heartless fancies in which the cow with the crumpled horn tossed the dog that worried the cat that killed the rat that ate the malt . . . of cats down the well, of mice docked by carving knives, blackbirds baked in pies" (E. S. Turner 76).

The best known of these women was probably Anna Letitia Barbauld (1743–1825), who was in fact one of the most popular living poets at the end of the eighteenth century. In addition to her poetry and her well-known political pamphlets against slavery, she wrote fables and verses for children. Her *Hymns in Prose for Children* instructs children to think of the world of animals as the manifestation of God but also to see in the animal kingdom exemplars of order and hierarchy. The poem "The Mouse's Petition" was prompted by a visit to Joseph Priestley's house and the sight of a caged mouse destined for a respiratory experiment with brewery gases. It is an ironic reminder to Priestley that Unitarianism (which Priestley founded) is "a resurgence of Stoic and early Platonic views of God as pervading mind" (Wordsworth and Hebron 15). Positing the possibility of a pantheistic link between humanity and the animal world, the poem through the use of its animal speaker simultaneously emphasizes pantheism and the need for anthropocentric compassion:

> The well-taught philosophic mind
> To all compassion gives;
> Casts round the world an equal eye
> And feels for all that lives.
>
> If mind, as ancient sages taught,
> A never dying flame,
> Still shifts thro' matter's varying forms,
> In every form the same,
>
> Beware, lest in the worm you crush
> A brother's soul you find;
> And tremble lest thy luckless hand
> Dislodge a kindred mind
>
> Or, if this transient gleams of day
> Be *all* of life we share,
> Let pity plead within thy breast
> That little *all* to spare.

The "petition" (spoken by the mouse) was attached to its cage. It had its desired effect, and the mouse was soon released (E. S. Turner 78).

Her other animal poems include some stock apostrophes to the dog and skylark, as well as the romanticized "India" and "Animals, and their Countries," which are catalogs of the animals of the colonies. Despite the exoticism they obviously exploit, they create a sense of wonder without the suggestion of human, masculine, or European dominion that such descriptions usually entailed.

Barbauld's subtle use of shifting perspective is highlighted in "The Caterpillar." "No helpless thing, I cannot harm thee now," is the opening line of its female speaker, who then proceeds to detail with photographic accuracy the beauty of the creature, "the silver line that streaks [its] back / The azure and the orange that divide / [Its] velvet sides." But it is not because of the creature's beauty or its helplessness alone that the speaker refrains from killing it, for she acknowledges having taken part in the "slaughter" of other creatures, having "crushed whole families beneath [her] foot." The anthropomorphism of her reason might seem trite were it not infused with her refusal to attach moral superiority to her own act of seeming mercy, her ability to recognize the occasional egocentrism of altruism without denying the validity that that altruism possesses. She compares her act of saving the one caterpillar to the act of a triumphant victor who savors the "roar of canon and the clang of arms" and who has no "soft relentings" for "the work of death and carnage." Yet when he sees

> A single sufferer from the field escaped,
> Lift his imploring eyes,—the hero weeps;
> He is grown human, and capricious Pity,
> Which would not stir for thousands, melts for one
> With sympathy spontaneous:

The unflinching recognition of the sentimentalism and anthropomorphism of this capricious act, which is "not Virtue" but the "weakness of a virtuous mind," is characteristic of the combination of compassion and rationality that appears in Barbauld's work.

Sarah Trimmer (1741–1810), on the other hand, adopted a more firmly anthropocentric and moralistic position in advising children to learn compassion for animals but not the "contrary fault of *immoderate tenderness*." When her *Fabulous Histories Designed for the Instruction of Children Respecting Their Treatment of Animals* was written (1786), the keeping of pets had only recently become fashionable, and the *Histories* were originally conceived as a series of animal fables and often reprinted under the title *The History of the Robins.* Each incident is designed to teach children Harriet and Frederick Benson (and their contemporaries) enlightened attitudes toward animals, as well as to give them the robins' perspective of humankind. Their mother's determination to teach them kindness does not alter her conviction that "we should prefer the happiness of mankind to that of any animal whatever." She regrets "that so many lives should be sacrificed to preserve ours; but we must eat animals or they would at length eat us, at least all that would otherwise support us." Nor does she question the dictum that animals must give "us" their bodies because they have nothing else to give; they have "been expressly destined by the *Supreme Governor* as food for mankind," and by giving their wool and milk some animals are permitted to "return their obligation to us." Interspersed with the children's adventures is the story of a family of robins—named Robin, Dicky, Flapsy, and Pecksy— whose parents try to teach them the humanized virtues of self-sacrifice and obedience. Trimmer's stories also include the themes of hunting and other blood sports. Through the mother character—who is invariably Trimmer's own mouthpiece—Charlotte and Henry of *An Easy Introduction to the Knowledge of Nature* are guided to think of "the poor little frightened creature" and its suffering.

Mary Wollstonecraft (1759–1797) modeled her *Original Stories from Real Life with Conversations Calculated to Regulate the Affections and Form the Mind to Truth and Goodness* (1788) on Sarah Trimmer's work. Mrs. Mason, who narrates the stories, clearly receives Wollstonecraft's endorsement as a model of exemplary thinking and is governess and spiritual guide to Mary and Caroline, two rich girls. Her love of animals extends to snails, caterpillars, and spiders, which she allows to crawl onto her hand, emphasizing the fact that annoyance and disgust cannot be grounds for killing: "You are often troublesome—I am stronger than you—yet I do not kill you." She raises several issues that are still unsolved in animal rights discourse today, such as animal euthanasia and the slaughter of vermin and animal "pests." Although her compassion and anthropocentrism are not in conflict with each other ("Be tender-hearted . . . it is only to animals that children *can* do good. Men are their superiors"), she even raises the issue of animal communication and language: "dumb they appear to those who do not observe their looks and gestures; but God, who takes care of every thing, understands their language; and so did Caroline this morning." While she does not endorse the slaughter of "pests," her position toward euthanasia leans in favor of being cruel to be kind: upon seeing two birds injured from a gun fired by an obnoxious boy, she instructs Mary and Caroline to take up one of them so that she may bind the wing together in the hope of healing it, but she believes that to permit the other bird to "die by inches" would be simply "selfishness or weakness," and saying this "she put her foot on the bird's head, turning her own another way."

This period was hardly the first time that animal stories and fables had been used to instruct either adults or children, but we see the dictum that the animal is incidental to the animal tale dismantled by these women writers, who actually use the animal fable to teach *about* animals, even though their ultimate goal might be greater humanity.

Although a well-known writer in her own right, Wollstonecraft's reputation was both highlighted and obscured by that of her famous (or infamous) family, as was also the case with Mary Lamb (1764–1847) and Dorothy Wordsworth (1771–1855). Mary Lamb's "The Rook and the Sparrows" illustrates the frequent human denial of the malevolence of the natural world and the resulting anthropomorphic tendency to valorize "cute" animals above others. She describes a little boy who feeds a hungry sparrow with crumbs of bread but withdraws this "kind bounty" when he observes a great blackbird taking away the smaller bird's "share." The speaker wishes she could have told the child that "rooks live by food / In the same way that sparrows do," and that "Birds act by instinct, and ne'er can / Attain the rectitude of man." Dorothy Wordsworth, like Mary Lamb, was a prolific writer whose reputation was overshadowed by her brother; her journals often reveal observations that were appropriated by William for his own poetic purposes. Her work is permeated with observations of the animals that occupied her quotidian routine, and in many ways she may be seen as the most representative Romantic woman writer, a writer whose contribution to Romanticism is most fully illustrated by comparison with her brother's.

Neither William nor Dorothy constructs a nature red in tooth and claw. William presents almost exclusively a rosy picture of animals, and unlike the women or the other members of the Big Six, he shows animals only in conflict with humans. Dorothy does not dwell on the malevolence of nature either but shows its potential destructiveness curbed and softened by nurture and care. William's animals are usually diminutive and seldom described in minute detail. "White as milk" or "white as snow" are the most visual descriptors of animals that he employs, unlike Dorothy's photographic re-creation of the "sheep bleating & in lines & chains & patterns scattered over the mountains," or the crows that "become white as silver as they flew in the sunshine," then becoming like "shapes of water passing over

the green fields" as they gain distance. For William, animals are distinctly
"inferior kinds" and *therefore* worthy of compassion. Animal nature is something to be incorporated but transcended, as is female nature. Keith Tester's
observation that animal rights are usually extended only to "nice, cuddly
mammals," ones that are easy to anthropomorphize (Tester 16) might well
be applied to William. The few nonmammals that are idealized in his poems are visually appealing birds or butterflies.[9] For Dorothy, the hierarchy
between humans and animals might be implicitly intimated through the
theme of nurture that runs through her work, but the symbiosis that accompanies this nurture undermines the hierarchy.

A comparison of Dorothy's "Mary Jones and her Pet-lamb" and
William's "The Pet-Lamb" will focus on some of these differences.[8] One
of Dorothy's only narratives, "Mary Jones" tells the story of a little girl
who cares for a young lamb brought home by her father (anticipating by
thirty-odd years the nursery rhyme "Mary Had a Little Lamb"). The lamb's
mother has died; it tries to run away, but Mary is able to rescue her pet and is
in turn rescued by her parents. William's poem "The Pet-Lamb" focuses on
a similar incident: little Barbara Lewthwaite also cares for a lamb brought
home by her father.

Both Dorothy and William use the lamb to construct a human identity.
For Dorothy, the identity is created through Mary's bonding with the lamb.
The lamb tries to run back into the hills where it was born, but Mary asserts
her human control of the lamb not through the power of human language
but through nurture, protectiveness, and mothering. Nature thus becomes
domesticated through feminine symbiosis rather than masculine dominion,
its potential violence withheld and subsumed in the harmony between humans and animals: just as the humans vow never to take a knife to the
lamb, the bees never sting Mary or the lamb and become a feature of the
landscape. As Levin points out, they "hover over, perhaps guarding, her
lamb's final resting place" (Levin 58). Dorothy's barely noticeable narrator
explores the parallelisms between the family community of the humans,
the symbiotic relationship between Mary and her pet animal, and the gentle
domestication of nature without confirming or denying the hierarchy that
these parallelisms constitute.

For William, however, the lamb serves as a launching pad to explore the
distinctness between the world of nature and the world of human (male)
consciousness. Like Blake before him (who rhetorically asked, "Little lamb
who made thee? . . . Gave thee life and bid thee feed?"), William cannot see
the lamb without imposing a teleological structure on its role in the uni-

verse, using it to speculate on the relationships between creation, literary creation, and the limits of language. William's focus on the narrator contrasts sharply with Dorothy's evasion of self. The "I," the hallmark of masculine Romanticism, is seldom present in the work of the female Romantics and is virtually absent in Dorothy's work. "She could not, would not analyze," claimed Elizabeth Hardwick, demonstrating the absence of contemplation that has been considered her strength as well as her weakness (Hardwick 163).

The triangle in Dorothy's story is the girl, lamb, and parents, who all work symbiotically: girl rescues lamb, lamb tries to provide warmth for girl, parents rescue both. In contrast, William's triangle is composed of lamb, girl, and narrator. William's intrusive narrator keeps trying to imagine what Barbara is saying, unable to see the lamb except in anthropocentric terms (and Barbara except in androcentric terms). William's pantheistic musings, in fact, highlight the difference between man and animal. Animal and human identities are interwoven, but with distinct divisions among the three (narrator, girl, and lamb), with the clearly male narrator distanced from both girl and lamb. This distancing recalls the distancing of animal and female nature in the identity constructed by William in "Tintern Abbey," in which the narrator wistfully recalls, but believes he has transcended, the "coarser pleasures" and "animal movements" of his youth, when he "bounded o'er the mountains" as spontaneously as a roe, animal joys that he links with the female as he reads these "former pleasures" in Dorothy's eyes, where he can see a hint of his "former"—and inferior—self.

In spite of its purported organicism, William's masculine Romanticism, however benevolent and compassionate, actually emphasizes the dualism between man and animal. While Dorothy's animal establishes a link between nature and human, the animal for William becomes a means to privilege the human and male, to explore the distinctness between the natural and the conscious worlds, and to appropriate both the animal and the female for his own voice and "ballad."

To some extent the epistemological heritage of the male and female writers was a shared one, but the epistemological *concerns* of the women differed from those of the men. Masculine Romanticism sought to construct an identity grounded in the duality between the poetic voice and the outside world, based on "the quest for permanence," "the correspondent breeze," or the dialectic of "nature and consciousness," or "natural supernaturalism."[9] But the male writers' preoccupation with the so-called hallmarks of Romanticism—with poetic voice, the epistemology of the creative imagination, and with the limits of Adamic language—was not shared by the women writers, who focused instead on what has been called an "ethic of care" (Gilligan 174). As Anne Mellor has observed, "They grounded their notion of community on a cooperative rather than possessive interaction with a Nature troped as a female friend or sister," resisting the "model of oppositional polarity (as the foundation of both the natural and the human worlds) for one based on sympathy and likeness" (Mellor, *Romanticism and Gender* 3).

Speaking with a rather tired (and tiresome) Eurocentrism, Freud observed in the early years of the twentieth century that "there is a great deal of resemblance between the relations of children and of primitive men toward animals. Children show no trace of the arrogance which urges modern adult civilized men to draw a hard-and-fast line between their own nature and that of all other animals" (Freud 126). Undermining this "hard-and-fast line" between the animal and the human is one of the central impulses of Romanticism, and regardless of gender, compassion and sympathy are omnipresent in its impulse. Yet few Romantic texts can be said to culminate in a convinced affirmation of unity or to display a confident movement out of dualism—either to monism or to pluralism. Rather, the paradigm of most masculine Romantic texts is an open-ended exploration of the dialectic between the adult, male consciousness and its constructed Other. Texts that appear to dismantle instead reinscribe the appropriative dualism between man and animal that is at the heart of masculine Romanticism, a duality that feminine Romanticism's symbiotic bonds frequently question.[10] By subverting the polarities of dualism, and therefore of ambiguity, the texts of feminine Romanticism dismantle the hegemony of man.

NOTES

The research for this essay was supported by grants from the Office of the Dean of Research (College of Arts and Sciences) at the University of Puerto Rico (Mayagüez) and from Fondos Institucionales of the University of Puerto Rico, which I gratefully acknowledge. I am also grateful to Jeff Cowton, registrar of the Wordsworth Museum in Grasmere, for permitting me to consult manuscript material, and to Carmen Amorós and Luis Marin of the University of Puerto Rico (Mayagüez) general library for their assistance with interlibrary loan material.

1. Greek thought characterized by Aristotle, Socrates, Plato, and Pythagoras can be seen permitting an anthropocentric view of the universe as well as the notion of continuity between all living things. Aristotle, for instance, ascribed *anima nutritiva*, the feeding principle, to all living beings—human, animal, and vegetable—but *anima sensitiva*, the principle of sensation, only to humans and animals. Although *anima*

rationalis was a human faculty, this was essentially a distilled form of *anima sensitiva*, and all living beings shared the common bond of *anima*, the life principle (Noske, 44).

Judeo-Christianity posed problematic demarcative boundaries, especially in the attribution of a soul to man alone, whose twice-given dominion over other creations could be interpreted as divine sanction for exploitation of animals. In addition, scholastic Aristotelianism in its Christianized interpretation by the thirteenth-century Schoolmen augmented this division. The contradictions in Christianity are encapsulated by the opposed views of Lynn White Jr. and Donald Worster. White has referred to Christianity in its Western form as "the most anthropocentric religion the world has ever seen" ("Historical" 1205), while Worster, among others, has drawn attention to the leanings of "left-wing" Protestantism as well as the assumption of accountability inherent in the Christian concept of stewardship that undermine the anthropocentric exploitation attributed to Christianity by White (Worster 187–88).

2. For instance, the official church denial of animal souls notwithstanding, pre-Christian Celtic and Germanic animistic influences had endured in European jurisprudence to the extent that animals were known to have served as witnesses to crimes or to have been executed for crimes (Ritvo, *Animal Estate* 1–2).

3. See, for instance, the following passages. Exodus 23:12: "on the seventh day you shall abstain from work, so that your ox and your ass may rest"; Deuteronomy 22:6–7: "When you come across a bird's nest by the road, in a tree or on the ground, with fledgling or eggs in it and the mother-bird on the nest, do not take both mother and young. Let the mother-bird go free, and take only the young; then you will prosper and live long"; Deuteronomy 25:4: "You shall not muzzle an ox while it is treading out the corn"; Genesis 1:26–28: "Then God said, 'Let us make man in our image and likeness to rule the fish in the sea, the birds of heaven, the cattle, all wild animals on earth, and all reptiles that crawl upon the earth' "; Genesis 9:2–3: "The fear and dread of you shall fall upon all wild animals on earth, on all birds of heaven, on everything that moves upon the ground and all fish in the sea; they are given into your hands. Every creature that lives and moves shall be food for you; I give you them all, as once I gave you all green plants."

4. Mellor states, however, and aptly demonstrates through her reading of John Keats and Emily Brontë, that "gender-biased romantic ideologies are grounded not on biological sex but rather on socially constructed and therefore fluid systems of discourse" (Mellor, *Romanticism and Gender* 4).

5. Dorothy Wordsworth is included in the *Norton Book of Nature Writing* (Finch and Elder 1990) and Mary Shelley in Derek Wall's *Green History: A Reader in Environmental Literature, Philosophy, and Politics* (1994), but none are included in either Ivo Mosley's *The Green Book of Poetry* (1993) or Jon Wynne-Tyson's *The Extended Circle: A Dictionary of Humane Thought* (1990).

6. Even Cowper declared that man could exterminate "creeping vermin, loathsome to the sight," without blame.

7. Yet Dorothy's journal records William's telling her "how they used to kill all

the white ones [butterflies] when he went to school because they were frenchmen" (D. Wordsworth 78).

8. "Mary Jones and her Pet-lamb" was first published in Susan Levin's *Dorothy Wordsworth and Romanticism* (238–41), and all quotations are taken from this text.

9. Titles of books on Romanticism by David Perkins, M. H. Abrams, Harold Bloom, and M. H. Abrams, respectively.

10. Karl Kroeber, on the other hand, maintains that "at their best [the Romantics] were skeptical of claims that a divine origin and future personal redemption distinguished mankind from all other natural beings." His reading of the biases of the (male) Romantics as "proto-ecological" rather than appropriative emphasizes the ecological nature of their acknowledgment of duality: "the highest attainment that the romantics can imagine for a human being is a capacity to endure violently contradictory emotions. Ambivalence must characterize the most intense experiences of creatures at once natural and cultural, whose finest achievements necessarily express awareness of the irresolvably dubious implications in that duality" (52).

REFERENCES

Barbauld, Anna. *Hymns in Prose for Children.* New York: Garland, 1977.

———. *Poems.* London: Joseph Johnson, 1773.

Bentham, Jeremy. *An Introduction to the Principles of Morals and Legislation.* Ed. Wilfrid Harrison. Oxford: Oxford UP, 1948.

Bettelheim, Bruno. *The Uses of Enchantment.* New York: Vintage, 1977.

Brown, Anthony. *Who Cares for Animals? 150 Years of the RSPCA.* London: Heinemann, 1974.

Buffon, Georges Leclerc (Count de). *Natural History: General and Particular.* Trans. W. Smellie. 20 vols. London: W. Wood, 1812.

Erskine, Thomas. Speech to the House of Lords. *Parliamentary Debates* (15 May 1809), cols. 553–71.

Felthouse, A. R., and S. R. Kellert. "Childhood Cruelty to Animals and Later Aggression against People: A Review." *American Journal of Psychiatry* 144 (1987): 710–17.

Finch, Robert, and John Elder, eds. *The Norton Book of Nature Writing.* New York: Norton, 1990.

Freud, Sigmund. *Totem and Taboo: Some Points of Agreement between the Mental Lives of Savages and Neurotics.* 1913. Trans. J. Strachey. New York: Norton, 1950.

Gilligan, Carol. *In a Different Voice: Psychological Theory and Women's Development.* Cambridge: Harvard UP, 1982.

Hardwick, Elizabeth. *Seduction and Betrayal: Women and Literature.* New York: Vintage, 1975.

Ingold, Tim, ed. *Companion Encyclopedia of Anthropology.* New York: Routledge, 1994.

Keats, John. *The Letters of John Keats, 1814–1821.* Ed. Hyder Rollins. Cambridge: Harvard UP, 1958.

Kroeber, Karl. *Ecological Literary Criticism: Romantic Imagining and the Biology of the Mind*. New York: Columbia UP, 1994.

Levin, Susan. *Dorothy Wordsworth and Romanticism*. New Brunswick, N.J.: Rutgers UP, 1987.

Lévi-Strauss, Claude. *The Savage Mind*. Chicago: U of Chicago P, 1966.

Maehle, Andreas-Holger. "Cruelty and Kindness to the 'Brute Creation': Stability and Change in the Ethics of the Man-Animal Relationship, 1600–1850." *Animals and Human Society: Changing Perspectives*. Ed. Aubrey Manning and James Serpell. London: Routledge and Kegan Paul, 1994. 216–17.

Malcolmson, Robert. *Popular Recreations in English Society, 1700–1850*. Cambridge: Cambridge UP, 1973.

Mellor, Anne. *Romanticism and Gender*. New York: Routledge and Kegan Paul, 1993.

————, ed. *Romanticism and Feminism*. Bloomington: Indiana UP, 1988.

Midgley, Mary. "Beasts, Brutes, and Monsters." *What Is an Animal?* Ed. Tim Ingold. New York: Routledge and Kegan Paul, 1994. 35–46.

Mosley, Ivo. *The Green Book of Poetry*. Kirstead, Eng.: Frontier, 1993.

Noske, Barbara. *Humans and Other Animals: Beyond the Boundaries of Anthropology*. London: Pluto, 1989.

Plumwood, Val. *Feminism and the Mastery of Nature*. London: Routledge and Kegan Paul, 1993.

Regan, Tom, and Peter Singer, eds. *Animal Rights and Human Obligations*. Englewood Cliffs, N.J.: Prentice-Hall, 1976.

Ritvo, Harriet. *The Animal Estate: The English and Other Creatures in the Victorian Age*. 1987. Harmondsworth, Eng.: Penguin, 1990.

————. "Animal Pleasures: Popular Zoology in 18th- and 19th-Century England." *Harvard Library Bulletin* 33.3 (summer 1985): 239–79.

————. "Learning from Animals: Natural History for Children in the Eighteenth and Nineteenth Centuries." *Children's Literature* (Annual of the Modern Language Association's Division on Children's Literature) 13 (1985): 72–93.

————. "New Presbyter or Old Priest? Reconsidering Zoological Taxonomy in Britain, 1750–1840." *History of the Human Sciences* (Great Britain) 3.2 (1990): 259–76.

Rowland, Beryl. *Animals with Human Faces: A Guide to Animal Symbolism*. London: Allen and Unwin, 1974.

Singer, Peter. *Animal Liberation: Towards an End to Man's Inhumanity to Animals*. 2nd ed. London: Jonathan Cape, 1990.

Sorabji, Richard. *Animal Minds and Human Morals: The Origins of the Western Debate*, Ithaca: Cornell UP, 1993.

Tapper, Richard. "Animality, Humanity, Morality, Society." *What Is an Animal?* Ed. Tim Ingold. New York: Routledge and Kegan Paul, 1994. 47–62.

Tester, Keith. *Animals and Society: The Humanity of Animal Rights*. New York: Routledge and Kegan Paul, 1991.

Thomas, Keith. *Man and the Natural World: Changing Attitudes in England, 1500–1800*. London: Allen Lane, 1983.

Trimmer, Sarah. *Fabulous Histories*. New York: Garland, 1977.

Turner, Ernest Sackville. *Heaven in a Rage*. Fontwell, Eng.: Centaur, 1992.

Turner, James. *Reckoning with the Beast: Animals, Pain, and Humanity in the Victorian Mind*. Baltimore: Johns Hopkins UP, 1980.

Wall, Derek. *Green History: A Reader in Environmental Literature, Philosophy, and Politics*. New York: Routledge and Kegan Paul, 1994.

White, Lynn, Jr. "Continuing the Conversation." *Western Man and Environmental Ethics*. Ed. Ian Barbour. Reading, Mass.: Addison-Wesley, 1973. 55–64.

———. "The Historical Roots of Our Ecologic Crisis." *Science* 155 (10 March 1967): 1203–7.

Wollstonecraft, Mary. *Original Stories from Real Life*. Oxford: Woodstock, 1990.

Wordsworth, Dorothy. *Grasmere Journals*. Ed. Pamela Woof. Oxford: Oxford UP, 1993.

Wordsworth, Jonathan, and Stephen Hebron, eds. *Romantic Women Writers*. Kendal, Eng.: Wordsworth Trust, 1994.

Worster, Donald. *Environmental History and the Ecological Imagination*. New York: Oxford UP, 1993.

Wynne-Tyson, Jon. *The Extended Circle: A Dictionary of Humane Thought*. London: Cardinal, 1990.

KB in Green

Ecology, Critical Theory, and Kenneth Burke

The cure for digging in the dirt is an idea; the cure for any idea
is more ideas; the cure for all ideas is digging in the dirt.

KENNETH BURKE

IT IS A FACT widely reported that the term "ecocriticism" was first coined
by William H. Rueckert in his 1978 essay "Literature and Ecology: An Experiment in Ecocriticism" (second of a pair of essays published jointly as
"Into and Out of the Void"). It would appear that Rueckert has produced
no larger body of work elaborating the critical practice he sketches in this
essay, no overt further instance of his pursuing the "experiment" he conducts in that one piece.[1] In a diffuse yet important sense, though, Rueckert
has been pursuing an "ecocriticism" of sorts all along. He has done so by
contemplating the formulations of a thinker whom in that originary essay
he dubs "one of our first critical ecologists" (76). This is Kenneth Burke,
the great American critic about whom Rueckert wrote repeatedly and with
whom he corresponded for more than forty years until Burke's death in
1993, at the age of ninety-five.[2] While Rueckert is generally only mentioned
and rarely stressed in discussions of ecocriticism, his mentor Burke is virtually invisible. This, I think, is a larger, more important omission.

My purpose in this essay is to raise Burke's profile as a "critical ecologist," a creator of adaptive terminologies who warrants the attention of
those who would further such a critical project. I do so not for the historical
record but in response to present needs. An ongoing challenge for ecocritical practice is to get critical theory and ecology to address each other in ways
they do not now sufficiently do. To pointedly oversimplify the situation, I
would say that critical theory, in its fixation on the constructed character of
representation, neglects ecology; and ecology, in turn, must suffer its embarrassment in employing theory that threatens always to tar it as "foun-
dationalist." I hope through Burke to suggest some ways that this neglect
and embarrassment might be mitigated.

Let me amplify this suggestion with regard to "ecocriticism" and critical theory in general. The originary emphasis of an ecological criticism, as proposed in Rueckert's essay and in the work of such other critics as Joseph Meeker, Glen Love, and Karl Kroeber, is at once normative and pragmatic, heedless of disciplinary proprieties, broadly concerned with the "environmental impact" of textual productions upon biological dispensations. Its spirit and intent are amenable to Burke, who in seventy years of transdisciplinary peregrinations insistently acted upon what he took as criticism's imperative, to "use all that there is to use" (*Counter-Statement* 108).[3] But while Burke's pragmatic impulses and, later in life, his particular critical agenda bear comparison with "ecocriticism" as such, his invariable point of departure is not ecology but language. His critical projects are more strictly comparable with those of such grand formulators of postmodernist thought as Foucault, Derrida, Rorty, and others, whose theoretical precepts Burke has not just complemented but often by decades anticipated.[4] However usefully these other thinkers may be "applied" to environmentally inflected critical endeavors,[5] in their own work they evince next to no acquaintance or concern with the natural environment. Ecology may address them, but they do not address ecology. Here again, Burke is different. He offers at once a nonfoundationalist theory of language and a critique of environmental dilemma; he cures (or seasons) his ideas with digging in the dirt.

Since Burke as much as any of these critics defies summary, I will sketch the differences and consonances I find by means of illustration. Let me start by reciting some ways that we, as a public, talk about spotted owls. The owl is an endangered species, threatened as its habitat vanishes, accorded value in proportion to that threat. It is a predator, which we understand in hierarchical terms as the uppermost of life forms in a given habitat. We may figure the predator metaphorically as the pinnacle or capstone of a pyramid, in that it takes a whole lot of lower life to prop up just a little of this higher sort. The figure of a pyramid accords with our understanding of the owl as an animal of status, one of the ruthless, beautiful few who lord it over the many—monarch of the ancient forest. Yet we could liken it also to the head of a single organism: if that's lopped off, the rest dies; or if the body goes, the head follows.

Of course, the spotted owl is a head or pinnacle of another sort, dialectical or rhetorical. It's a synecdoche for a larger biological context our metaphors can't encompass. It's an "entitling" of the political struggle played out over the whole feathered, wooded, peopled mess we designate the "ancient forest." It's a "representative anecdote" which, unfolded, parsed out, and pushed for implications, can stand in for a whole order of such struggles and the terms in which they're waged.

Synecdoche, entitlement, and representative anecdote are all critical notions that readers of Burke may recognize.[6] Burke's parlance can be further applied to what the spotted owl anecdote represents. As tropes or formulas, the pyramid with capstone and the organism with head correspond, respectively, to what Burke sees as the alternative "ultimate vocabularies" available to us: what he calls metaphysics and his punning variant, metabiology. This distinction Burke summarizes in a formula: "Things move, people act." Whereas metaphysics, stressing things in motion, is a reductionist, mechanistic orientation, metabiology is a poetic or, as Burke would have it, "dramatistic" orientation, stressing the motivated action of persons and "the operations of biologic growth" (*Permanence* 230). If we consider that it's "biology" that Burke makes "meta" here—that it's things and not creatures that he puts in contradistinction to people—we have grounds for seeing configured in these paired terms the far ends of the conflict our owl entitles. The metaphysical stance, as held for example by the spectacularly ill-named "wise use coalition" of loggers, miners, developers, and four-wheelers, sees the forest as thing: commodity, resource, or trove of raw materials. The metabiological stance, as expressed for instance in the "deep ecology" movement, understands the forest as drama or poetry, the interplay of actors or factors whose relations are embodied, not literally but faithfully, in story and myth. Thus the "ancient forest," in turn, is a synecdoche for orientations these two "ultimate vocabularies" construe and, again as Burke would have it, are impelled to "perfect," their adherents striving in effect to complete (or finish off!) the world in those terms.

It is broadly typical of Burke that myth, science, psychology, and economics should so interpenetrate with imperatives of social order as they do in this brief discourse. I wish to stress, however, that my choice of a specifically ecological anecdote is not arbitrary. Burke's talk of motion and action is not just descriptive; Burke coins such a notion as "metabiology" to propose it *in preference to* metaphysics, the reductionist turn of mind he finds underlying modern predicaments of every stripe, including, quite explicitly, environmental ones. While the term "metabiology" drops away from his critical lexicon in later works, the action-motion distinction it articulates is Burke's career-long fixation, articulated further in ways more central to his work, particularly in the notion of "Dramatism" as such, Burke's title for his critical orientation. These other articulations, in turn, are never divorced, I would insist, from the concern with natural processes evident in the terminological novelty I have described. It is evident as well, I might note, in the tangible circumstances of this man who, in his home in rural New Jersey, enacted his critique of modernity, choosing to live without electric power (until 1951) or running water and indoor plumbing (until the mid-1960s, when his wife's illness forced his hand).[7] Burke knew firsthand what it meant to cure ideas by digging in the dirt. His notions of natural process, of "the thinking of the body," are literally grounded.

Though these affinities suffuse his thinking throughout his life, Burke's most explicit concern with ecological matters comes quite late in his career, in works of the 1970s and 1980s. His most sustained original project of this late period is a satire on technology and pollution, combined with a rationale for and analysis of that satire, the entire project entitled Helhaven.[8] The satire itself is a fantasia involving a "culture-bubble" habitat of that name being built on the moon as a refuge from a terminally befouled planet Earth. This lunar habitat, this perverse "womb-heaven," as Burke calls it, which its promoters tout as the culmination of human progress, represents the perfection of the worldview or mindset that Burke at this stage in his writings is calling "Technologism." In opposition to this, Burke espouses a "Humanism" (capital H) of a reformed type. In his Heinz Warner Lectures of the period (1971), published as *Dramatism and Development,* he remarks:

> Today, it seems to me, our quandaries sum up the need for a kind of Humanism that would be defined as antithetical to "Technologism." [. . .] As distinct from mere technology, "Technologism" would be built upon the assumption that the remedy for the problems arising from technology is to be sought in the development of ever more and more technology. (53)

I want to remark on the consonance of this formulation to that proposed by ecologist and environmental historian David Ehrenfeld some years later in his book *The Arrogance of Humanism,* a powerful critique of the mindset Burke is indicting. A glance at Ehrenfeld's title makes clear that the term "humanism" (small h) in his usage has entitlements quite other than those Burke wants to ascribe to it. But Ehrenfeld's "humanism" and Burke's "Technologism" are clearly the same beast. As Ehrenfeld depicts it, the creed of humanism takes as its core assumption the belief that "All problems are soluble," inserts the implied agent to read "soluble by people," and proceeds through a number of correlate assumptions to the effect that problems not soluble by technology—and it's assumed most are—are susceptible to social solutions, and that in a pinch we (or our technologists) will find out what we need, work things out, and survive (16–17). Ehrenfeld illustrates with a litany of instances in which the founding assumption Burke cites for Technologism—that problems of technology require yet more technology—has been honored, with catastrophic results.

How is it that Burke can posit something called "Humanism" in opposition to precisely that which Ehrenfeld calls "humanism"? A short answer is that to Ehrenfeld the term covers a diagnosis, to Burke a prescription and prospect. Ehrenfeld means to be comprehensive, to offer a perspective from which what are normally taken as conflicting entities—science and religion, for instance—can be seen as founded on shared, and mutually suspect, assumptions. His version of humanism is a merger of grand proportions, a total ideational dispensation in relation to which institutionalized science and religion play out merely schismatic rivalries against a backdrop of essential consensus. Burke's Humanism, on the other hand, results from an act of division. Burke means to differentiate the Humanism he recommends from other, earlier modes of humanism, and he sees its opposite number, Technologism, as itself arising out of a version of humanism. His way of deriving this pair of terms rests on a distinctly nonanthropocentric (Ehrenfeld would say nonhumanist) view of the import of being human:

> [A]n anti-Technologistic Humanism would be "animalistic" in the sense that,
> far from boasting of some privileged human status, it would never disregard
> our humble, and maybe even humiliating, place in the totality of the natural
> order. (*Dramatism* 54)

This view of an "animalistic" Humanism is fundamentally opposed to the deep-seated arrogance of the humanism Ehrenfeld indicts. Faced with this confusion of humanisms, we might almost prefer Max Oelschlaeger's practice, in *The Idea of Wilderness*, of calling this whole Earth-forsaken posture "Modernism" and hope we're headed to its posterior side.

Not that Burke believes we are headed any such way: early and late in his career he views this mindset and our modern plight as more than likely intractable. The longer he lived, the more fatalistic, even deterministic, he was to grow. By 1983, with his afterwords to new editions of his volumes from the mid-1930s, his earlier notions of "technological psychosis" and "Technologism" have given way to an attitudinal monolith he calls "Counter-Nature." Considering how people seem compelled to complete and perfect an attitude or terminology even to the point of disaster (to be "rotten with perfection," as he mordantly quips), Burke suggests that this "exponentially developing Counter-Nature" presents us with a situation in which the earthly *end* of human history is manifest *already,* in our predicaments *now*—and particularly by reason of the fact that Technology can be neither criticized nor corrected without recourse to still more Technology. The *opportunities* to produce further "generations" of contrivances are indistinguishable from the *compulsions* to do so. (*Attitudes* 396)

Again, this is Ehrenfeld's version of humanism—an attitude perfected, yielding a perfect fix.

But why can't we depend on Ehrenfeld and Paul Ehrlich and their ilk—ecologists and activists as such—to spread this chilling message? Why drag the word-crazed Burke in to echo it? Since with Burke it's a student of word craziness in itself who is framing such warnings, in ways integral, not incidental, to his study of language and culture, I look to him as an exemplar of critical theory of a certain sort: the sort I have described as addressing ecology, not awaiting its address. Loosely described, this is theory which may fall into, or be claimed for, various of the overlapping camps called postmodernism, anti-foundationism, social construction, or whatever other term may fit a critical stance which doesn't totalize, doesn't sweat epistemology, and dwells on social dimensions of language. Yet it is theory consonant with a biocentric perspective and concerned with its articulation in ways most other language- or culture-based critical stances are hardly at all.

The difference is heralded in expressions I've used or cited above. I've noted, first, that Burke wants a Humanism that is "animalistic." This late proviso is only one manifestation of a continuing preoccupation with peoples' biological status, a fixation integral to his critical system. "Man is the symbol-using animal" begins his "Definition of Man" in *Language as Symbolic Action*—a definition he reworked over the years, finally arriving at this: humans are "Bodies That Learn Language." This central equation, like all Burkean pairs, can be shifted back and forth for heuristic emphasis. Whereas for most postmodern purposes (and for most of Burke's as well) the phrase would be read, "Bodies That Learn *Language*," the possibility and need for a reverse emphasis exist as well: "*Bodies* That Learn Language." Both are indispensable, for Burke's whole account of social order through symbolic action hinges on the fact that it is *biological* needs that humans linguistically construe, no different in principle from those of other animals. "Do you really believe you are an animal?" asks Gary Snyder in "The Etiquette of Freedom." Burke believes it, insists on it; like Snyder he "come[s] back to it over and over again, as something to investigate and test" (15). Most critics working adjacent turf seem not to.

I cite but one example of this, a key one, I think, because it is influential. This is Richard Rorty's assertion that the ocular metaphors for knowledge he investigates in Western culture are purely arbitrary and accidental, the outgrowth of some peculiar and ungrounded whim of Plato's that has stuck to us like a bad tattoo ever since.[9] Now, it's clear that such metaphors did not have to come into play in just the way they have, and in that sense they were and remain "contingent." Other cultures don't slice things thus. But it strikes me as blinkered to think that a metaphor linking eyes with knowledge is arbitrary. The talk of dogs might be expected to betray an epistemology of scent. What we see is mediated and thus may be thought "constructed"; but our eyes *grow*, and no one's talk can tell them how.

Yet mediation as well, symbolic action in all its forms, is to Burke not distinct from our biological estate. "All living things are critics," he announces in *Permanence and Change*, proceeding to derive humankind's special critical prowess from how language enables us to criticize our criticisms, to manipulate and transmit them. Burke is concerned to show that the prospects and perils, the dialectical ups and downs of symbolic action, are essential to our natures. Learning language is what *these* bodies happen to do, with certain consequences, which are structured but not determinate and not determined. Orientation is always partial, situated, and purposeful, for humans as for any life form.

And orientation can go wrong, as it has for us with results that, upon our own partial terms, must seem paradoxical. The "third clause" of Burke's "Definition of Man" (sic) reads, "Separated from his natural condition by instruments of his own making" (*Language* 13) such that in the exercise of capacities natural to them, humans have somehow ceased to act naturally. This is the core conundrum in any biocentric formulation of the current human condition; it is a problem central to Burke, yet a nonentity to much critical theory, which dismisses outright the notion of a "natural condition" for humans. Burke, late in life, says of the transformations of technological "Counter-Nature" that

> they introduce conditions of livelihood (including grave manmade threats to survival) quite alien to the state of nature to which our prehistoric ancestors successfully adapted. Paradoxically, our ancestors bequeathed to us the potentialities for constructing dangers (of both *kind* and *concentration*) from which they themselves were protected. (*Permanence* 296)

What Burke says here suggests what advocates of deep ecology have been especially concerned to explore: that like any animal, we humans have an evolutionary heritage, which is in certain indeterminate, loosely configured ways literally *embodied*. If this sounds too categorical, we can discount the recognition in some roughly pragmatist fashion and say this: If we understand ourselves to be animals—as we are enjoined to not only because we have no warrant to doubt it but because, in our circumstances, it seems a better, more promising thing to believe—then what we understand to be true of every other animal we must take to be true of ourselves. We must explore the consequences accordingly, without, however, believing we can determine them. A critical perspective which took seriously this premise would insist that historicist accounts of human action range widely enough (rhetorically as well as temporally) to encompass evidence of some broad consonance in human life patterns over far the greater part of our interpretable past as a species. It would think this consonance to have import— it would think *about* this consonance *in order* to have import—as speaking to but not dictating to us about our present state. A story told from this stance would most likely not be Rorty's "Whiggish" one about how our cave-dwelling ancestors struggled upward toward our present eminence, kicking their ladders aside after each stage of the ascent. [10] If anything, it would more nearly resemble Paul Shepard's story of a population gone pretty well insane in some strict sense of the word, roughly eight or ten thousand years ago, to the ultimate regret of those others who kept their moorings.

Yet a story told from this stance is not to be nostalgic; it will not exhort us to "go back" toward some primeval condition reputed to lurk in our genes. We do not move, we *act*, this metabiology would insist; we never "prophesy" any human condition *except* "after the event." Instead it would enjoin us to make what understanding we can of it, renaming what has passed to reclaim what persists, to create and sustain conditions of human well-being which, *as such*, are not peculiar to humans—conditions, for instance, that a spotted owl might preside over as well. The effort to do so, this story might suggest, is without foundations, but it could not be ungrounded if it tried.

This story of grounds without foundations, of unconstructed biological "substance" (as Burke paradoxically reads the term), [11] may appear to depict Burke as a totalizer after all, bent on stopping history by sequestering it within the confines of his formulas. This is hardly his intent; his atemporal terministic schemes are joined to a project of cultural "redescription" in Rorty's sense, one which remains deeply situated in every historical context Burke occupies over his long career. But if stopping history is not his intent, it may still be his desire. For if history seems bent on stopping itself for good—if the story of "Counter-Nature" or an arrogant humanism is valid— one is impelled to hope (though not to believe) that it might somehow be stopped short of its ending. Thus the question of whether or how history gets stopped or "moves forward" gets vexed, even paradoxical, precisely in light of *present* historical contingencies. Burke's approach to the conun- drum, broadly speaking, is to think about how contingency might be nor- malized, how history might be not stopped but stabilized through a sort of rhetorical or interpretive homeostasis. His every pronouncement on ed- ucation hovers about this prospect. [12] At a certain level, this is not so dif- ferent from what Rorty hopes for; the utopian stories, the solidarity Rorty sees underpinning public morality and procedural justice, are to serve a similarly steadying effect. Something like redescription is central to both. Burke's "Pentad" and allied formulas constitute both an account of proce- dures and materials available for such a purpose and also an argument for a particular redescription (a "definition of man") itself. [13] Rorty's ongoing "conversation" provides the dynamic element of a social existence which, though founded on nothing, nevertheless sustains itself, by virtue of the private ("abnormal") redescriptions which surface to reinvigorate and cor- rect it.

Yet the character of the redescriptions these two offer is very different, and the difference can be understood to hinge, I would argue, upon Gary Snyder's question. Burke, I've said, continually reenacts his engagement with our biological estate. Rorty, by contrast, does not really believe he is an animal. His every mention of other animals, of biological states, of evolutionary theory, betrays his skepticism on this count. His remarks on John Dewey's metaphysics are a most telling instance of this: the one aspect of Rorty's own pragmatist predecessor and hero's thought that he takes pains to repudiate is exactly Dewey's organicism, as embodied in his no- tion of experience—a notion which, on its face, looks very much more like a metabiology than the metaphysics it's billed as. [14]

The reluctance to acknowledge that humans have anything other than a social nature is far from peculiar to Rorty but is instead common to him and most of his putative adversaries, whose debates take place well within the set of assumptions Ehrenfeld calls humanism. Rorty's principle of human- ity's endless powers of self-revision is a corollary expression of humanism's core assumption, that all problems are soluble by people; his rhetoric of ever-new conversations and continually expanding discursive "space" re- capitulates in its attitude, I believe, the frontier mentality of endless expan- sion into untouched terrains, of problem solving by abandonment. Burke's

Pentad is a far cry from this psychic expansionism; in the recursiveness of its terms, it impresses upon the questing mind the necessity of coming to rest back within its essential perimeters, of knowing well the place where it comes to rest.

In this it seems an extrapolation of an ecological metaphor, from a critic who first used ecology as a metaphor for discursive practices as early as 1937. The presence in Burke, and the absence in critics like Rorty, of an incipiently ecological or biocentric sensibility or, for that matter, any concrete acknowledgment of environmental concerns at all, connects finally with the problems of history and contingency outlined above. The story Burke tells about history has a beginning, middle, and end, three acts which he would like to entitle (as he says of his original three-part scheme for *Permanence and Change*) Orientation, Disorientation, and Reoriention. But in his story of history as in his book, Burke is not able to end with return or recovery or transformation. He can offer only a question mark and a set of interlocked conditions that may be "contingent" (in the sense that they did not *have* to take this form) but nonetheless are *permanent*. This quality of permanence is not a metaphysical category but instead can be taken in Nelson Goodman's discounted sense of being durable indeed, in something of the way, for instance, we might think the ancient forests have been and ought to be permanent.[15]

This is the effectual sort of permanence sought for the effectiveness, say, of a nuclear waste repository, commensurate with the longevity of what we place there. It's a permanence sought no less for any sign system we might design for such an installation, in faint hope of warning or scaring away any still-inquisitive descendents of ours who happen across it, whom no barriers can be counted upon "permanently" to restrain. Those who are now contemplating the design of such a system—which is to say, who contemplate the character of such descendents—are in principle coming to grips with the recognition that environmental concerns, as Glen Love points out, are *not a crisis;* to call them such is pernicious in that it implies they will go away (202–3).[16] The designers deal with conditions, not crises; they are weighing in practical ways the question that Burke believes education should take as "a major concern": "What does it mean to be a talking animal?" (*Attitudes* 355). They have no choice but to presume some effectual permanence, some continuity in the nature of that talking animal, every aspect of whose talk must certainly be transformed over the ten- or twenty-thousand-year lifespan of radioactive wastes. The designs they conjure are difficult, probably chimerical, not least because contemplating human survival over such

a "permanent" expanse—survival without institutional memory (i.e., repetition in language) of the character of such a thing as a crypt of nuclear
poison—assumes quite a bit. It assumes, first, a rupture or drift from our
current technological dispensation, which acknowledges in principle no
limits to its prowess and continuity and thus to its communicability over
time. And it anticipates a subsequent level of success on the part of these
future humans in surviving and perhaps even healing what Burke calls the
"divorce from our home in nature"—a further aspect of what he takes as
education's enduring concern.

However chimerical, such a prospect is a chimera to live with, even to
savor, especially in light of its largest assumption of all—the assumption
of our essential kinship, identity, *consubstantiality* with these imagined suc-
cessors, which leads us to imagine we would like to speak to them, even
if only to warn them away. If we can just keep talking, the idea goes, we
will end up becoming those other talking creatures, still endangered but
again at home, whose words are transformed but whose substance is our
own. The prospect sustains itself in the choices we make of the stories we
repeat to ourselves now. These in turn must depend, I imagine, on a certain
piety toward what Burke calls "Something or Other not of man's making"—
something not constructed, something comprehending organic creation,
which category encompasses the talking animal itself.

NOTES

The epigraph repeats one of Burke's aphorisms, called "Flowerishes," quoted in
Rueckert, *Encounters with Kenneth Burke* (1994).

1. The dearth of further overtly critical work by Rueckert may help explain why
repercussions of his essay among professed ecocritics seem seldom to extend beyond
mention of the term's titular origins. A notable exception is John P. O'Grady's "Unhandling Our Perspective," which discusses the essay at some length mainly in order to fault Rueckert's uses of the terms "ecology" and "ecologist," neither of which
O'Grady finds used with sufficient acknowledgment of the "vagaries" of the sciences
and scientists to which they refer. Since the essay appeared in *ISLE*, I will register my
objections to O'Grady's complaints. I do not see how Rueckert's appropriation of
"ecology" can be both insufficiently "precise" and yet "remarkably limited" on account of its reliance upon such popular ecologists as Aldo Leopold and Ian McHarg
rather than upon the "scientific literature"; I would think precision of the latter sort
would impose yet more severe limitations for the sort of practice Rueckert envisions.
Further, I find that O'Grady conflates "ecology" with "the science of ecology," as if
the term had not already escaped that disciplinary orbit and become pertinent and
useful, or at least subject to legitimate contention, in a larger discursive sphere—

in the work of Kenneth Burke, for instance, whose references to and metaphorical applications of the term are among our earliest, dating to 1937. And I question what I read as O'Grady's positing the "overarching metaphor," "trope," and "poetics" of ecocriticism in opposition to the "methods" of ecology as a science, as if metaphor did not pervade, for instance, not just Rueckert's poetic extensions but also the uses in thermodynamics of such a term as "energy." Rueckert's mentor Burke can give us all an education in such interanimation of scientific and poetic rhetorics.

2. Some particular ways in which Rueckert has pressed the point of Burke's ecological predilections have become widely available only recently, with the 1994 publication, in *Encounters with Kenneth Burke*, of a pair of MLA session papers delivered in 1980 and 1981, respectively: "Logology and the Rhetoric of Ecology" and "Poetry, Logology, Technology, Admonology: Kenneth Burke in 1981—from Counterstatement to Counter-nature."

3. Frank Lentricchia (54) remarks on how discomfiting to "disciplinary chauvinists" is the critical practice represented in this often-repeated credo of Burke's.

4. Lentricchia, for example, finds in Burke's *A Grammar of Motives* (1945) a "full-blown structuralism in advance of the French structuralist movement," but also asserts that "Burke, in several keenly self-conscious moments in his book, forecasts the critique of structuralism mounted in the work of Foucault and Derrida" (67). This is a characteristic, not peculiar, assessment of Burke's accomplishment with regard to certain staples of postmodern theory.

5. They are applied, for instance, in the "constructive postmodernisms" of Max Oelschlaeger and Neil Evernden, both of whom draw often upon Rorty in particular.

6. "Synecdoche" is treated as one of "The Four Master Tropes" in Burke's *A Grammar of Motives*, 503–17. "Entitlement" is the key term (and a prime instance of what the term refers to) in "What Are the Signs of What? (A Theory of 'Entitlement')" in Burke's *Language as Symbolic Action*, 359–79. "Representative anecdote" is first discussed in *A Grammar of Motives*, 59–61.

7. Rueckert, *Encounters*, 56 and 90. Many passages in Burke's correspondence with his lifelong friend Malcolm Cowley describe the labor of planting and pond digging at his place in Andover, New Jersey, where he moved in the early 1920s and, except for numerous lecture and visiting scholar gigs, stayed for the rest of his life.

8. The Helhaven project is comprised primarily of two pieces, "Towards Helhaven: Three Stages of a Vision" and "Why Satire, with a Plan for Writing One"; Burke makes mention of the project as well in *Dramatism and Development*.

9. See chapter 3 of Rorty's *Philosophy and the Mirror of Nature*, especially 157–59, for an important version of the critique of ocular metaphors central to his project. Rorty's discussion is, of course, more subtle and substantive than my crack gives it credit for. Nevertheless, it issues some fairly astonishing outcomes. An exhibit: "We must get the visual, and in particular the mirroring, metaphors out of our speech altogether" (371). If thine eye offends thee . . .

10. For the "Whiggish" story of progress, see Rorty's *Philosophy and the Mirror of Nature*, 344. For an example of ladder kicking, see his *Contingency, Irony, and Solidarity*, 96.

11. Burke's discussion of "the paradox of substance," whereby what is most essential to an entity (its "substance") is defined by what is peripheral to or outside it (its "sub-stance," what it stands upon), is found in *A Grammar of Motives*, 21–58.

12. An important pronouncement is found in the rhetorical question with which Burke ends *Permanence and Change:* "But might it not be possible that, were an educational system designed to that end, this very fluctuancy could be intelligently stabilized, through the interposing of method?" (294).

13. Burke's best-known critical instrument, the Pentad, is a set of five terms or factors which Burke insists must be accounted for in any complete statement about human motives: Act, Scene, Agent, Agency, and Purpose. Not the terms themselves, especially, but rather the relations or what Burke calls the "ratios" between them are what's crucial. The Pentad is introduced and elaborated in extraordinary fashion in *A Grammar of Motives*.

14. For Rorty's critique of Dewey, see "Dewey's Metaphysics," *Consequences of Pragmatism*, 72–89. Passages crop up fairly frequently in Rorty's work that in some way or other evince the orientation I am critiquing. To further detail my claim, I might cite such exhibits as these: Rorty's contention that "what ties us to the non-language-using beasts" is, more than anything, *pain* (*Consequences* 94), an assumption informing his discussion of the attribution of feelings to babies, animals (with faces more or less "humanoid" in character), robots, or Martians (*Philosophy* 187–91); also, his reading of Darwinian theory as essentially completing the project of mechanistic Newtonian physics, eventuating, with Freud, in the fortuitous ability to "see oneself as a Rube Goldberg machine that requires much tinkering" (*Essays* 152). This attitude toward the mechanical worldview that informs what Burke calls Technologism is further manifest in Rorty's willingness to concede in principle that "Every speech, thought, theory, poem, composition, and philosophy will turn out to be completely predictable in purely naturalistic terms" (*Philosophy* 387)—a concession which, besides being increasingly recognized as wrong even *in* "naturalistic terms," is proffered with unseemly confidence and sanguinity. Finally, more subtly, I might remark on the strangeness that can ensue when Rorty ventures a demonstration using something terrestrial and organic (rather than with robots or Martians or Galactics or Antipodeans). This can be seen with his use of cherry blossoms as a running figure in an essay about Heidegger: for instance, in his description of the items on Heidegger's list of "elementary words of Being" as being "contingent as the contours of an individual cherry blossom"—as if what were most notable about a tree in bloom was the peculiar character of each individual blossom (*Essays* 37). It seems fitting, somehow, that in the photo of Rorty decorating the covers of his recent books, the flowers in the backdrop are well out of focus.

15. Goodman likens permanence as expressed in terms of durability to truth as expressed in terms of credibility, saying in effect that continuous credibility renders the question of permanent and thus unattainable truth moot: such truth can be discarded "in favor of total and permanent credibility, which though equally unattainable is explicable in terms of what is attainable, just as permanence is explicable in terms of durability" (124).

16. This design is a concrete problem (so to speak) to contemporaries of ours. See, for instance, Alan Burdick's article "The Last Cold-War Monument" for an account of the activities of Department of Energy panels charged with this task. Love is reporting the view of Lord Ashby, as quoted in an article by Victor B. Sheffer.

REFERENCES

Burdick, Alan. "The Last Cold-War Monument: Designing the 'Keep Out' Sign for a Nuclear-Waste Site." *Harper's Magazine*, Aug. 1992, 62–67.

Burke, Kenneth. *Attitudes toward History*. 3rd ed. Berkeley: U of California P, 1984.

———. *Counter-Statement*. Berkeley: U of California P, 1968.

———. *Dramatism and Development*. Barre, Mass.: Clark UP, 1972.

———. *A Grammar of Motives*. 2nd ed. Berkeley: U of California P, 1969.

———. *Language as Symbolic Action: Essays on Life, Literature, and Method*. Berkeley: U of California P, 1966.

———. *Permanence and Change*. 3rd ed. Berkeley: U of California P, 1984.

———. "Towards Helhaven: Three Stages of a Vision." *Sewanee Review* 79 (1971): 11–25.

———. "Why Satire, with a Plan for Writing One." *Michigan Quarterly Review* 13 (Winter 1974): 307–37.

Ehrenfeld, David. *The Arrogance of Humanism*. Oxford: Oxford UP, 1981.

Evernden, Neil. *The Social Creation of Nature*. Baltimore: Johns Hopkins UP, 1992.

Goodman, Nelson. *Ways of Worldmaking*. Indianapolis: Hackett, 1978.

Kroeber, Karl. *Ecological Literary Criticism: Romantic Imagining and the Biology of Mind*. New York: Columbia UP, 1994.

Lentricchia, Frank. *Criticism and Social Change*. Chicago: U of Chicago P, 1983.

Love, Glen A. "Revaluing Nature: Toward an Ecological Criticism." *Western American Literature* 25 (1990): 201–15.

Meeker, Joseph. *The Comedy of Survival: Studies in Literary Ecology*. New York: Scribner's, 1972.

Oelschlaeger, Max. *The Idea of Wilderness*. New Haven: Yale UP, 1991.

O'Grady, John P. "Unhandling Our Perspective." *ISLE: Interdisciplinary Studies in Literature and the Environment* 2.1 (1994): 117–21.

Rorty, Richard. *Consequences of Pragmatism*. Minneapolis: U of Minnesota P, 1982.

———. *Contingency, Irony, and Solidarity*. Cambridge: Cambridge UP, 1989.

———. *Essays on Heidegger and Others*. Cambridge: Cambridge UP, 1991.

———. *Philosophy and the Mirror of Nature*. Princeton: Princeton UP, 1979.

Rueckert, William H. *Encounters with Kenneth Burke*. Urbana: U of Illinois P, 1994.

———. "Into and Out of the Void: Two Essays." *Iowa Review* 9 (1978): 62–86.

Shepard, Paul. *Nature and Madness*. San Francisco: Sierra Club, 1984.

Snyder, Gary. *The Practice of the Wild*. San Francisco: North Point, 1990.

Tales of the Wonderful Hunt

In 1924 an anatomy professor named Raymond Dart, analyzing a collection of fossilized bones found in a South African limestone quarry, concluded that he had found an ancestor of humanity, a bipedal man-ape he dubbed *Australopithecus Africanus*. Because it was found with the remains of small animals, Dart concluded that Australopithecus was a hunter and scavenger. Over the next few decades more Australopithecine fossils were found amid the remains of larger mammals, which led Dart to believe that Australopithecus was a more capable, daring, and brutal hunter than he had at first imagined. In a 1953 article called "The Predatory Transition from Ape to Man," he argued that our ancestors' hunger for meat and thirst for violence, and our subsequent ability to use weapons, not only distinguished humans from apes but accounted for the evolution from simian to human. With a vividness shockingly uncharacteristic of a scientific paper, Dart described Australopithecines as "confirmed killers: carnivorous creatures, that seized their living quarries by violence, battered them to death, tore apart their broken bodies, dismembered them limb from limb, slaking their ravenous thirst with the hot blood of victims and greedily devouring writhing flesh." From fractured jaws that could have been smashed by bones wielded as clubs, and from skull holes that looked like the work of horns used as daggers, Dart concluded that at times Australopithecus turned its bloodlust on its own kind. It was a cannibal as well as a killer. In Dart's misanthropic view, that genetic background accounted for the "blood-bespattered, slaughter-gutted archives of human history" (qtd. in Cartmill 10–11).

By the 1970s Dart's analysis, especially as popularized by Robert Ardrey, became known as the "hunting hypothesis," and it made its way as received knowledge into anthropology texts. But in a 1981 book entitled *The Hunters or the Hunted?*, zoologist C. K. Brain, looking at the same evidence, reached conclusions very different from Dart's. Rather than being hunters with an appetite for the kill and its meaty rewards, says Brain, Australopithecines were the hunted, threatened by leopards and two now-extinct carnivores: a hunting hyena and a relative of the saber-toothed tiger called *dinofelis* which was beautifully equipped for attacking and eating primates and hominids. The Australopithecine skulls were smashed not by bone clubs but by rock settling atop them; the holes in the skulls matched the teeth of leopards; and the caves containing Australopithecine bones were littered with bones of other large animals not because Australopithecines scattered them there but because they were all, Australopithecines included, dragged there by efficient predatory carnivores.

Paleoanthropologists now believe *Australopithecus Africanus* is not our direct ancestor but a distant relative. Still, it was descended, and none too distantly, from our common ancestor, so the scientific debate has profound implications for our conception of what human nature is—and what role hunting has in that nature.

HIKING on the Appalachian Trail in Maine, accompanied by my friends Pesch and Joe Dunes, I lay plans to test the Brain and Dart hypotheses. Perhaps I am inspired by the familiar notion, reduced to the status of cliché, that backpacking is a way for us to get "back to nature." What is usually meant by that is a combination of getting reacquainted with the world around us and rediscovering something of our essential self, our own nature, once all the foofaraw of contemporary civilization is left behind. Though I am no scientist, I outline an experiment to see if a certain representative human subject can find it in his nature to hunt. I volunteer myself, knowing that my experience with hunting is uncontaminated by training, for I have never hunted. And yet, I have nothing against hunting. I am thankful for all the green space labeled "State Game Lands" on the map of my home state of Pennsylvania. I eat meat, and I think there's something to the argument that it is an environmentalist act to have some firsthand knowledge of where that meat comes from.

And so, entering the still expansive forests of Maine, in the name of gathering empirical evidence, I inwardly proclaim my intent to kill something by my own hands and eat it. Not a moose or a bear or anything like that—that would be both difficult and illegal. Something like a squirrel or a raccoon or a frog. Something that ought to taste like chicken.

MY SECOND MEANS of testing the conflicting analyses of hominid nature will be to examine the evidence found in stories. Hunting has long been a prominent motif in American literature. In general, our writers' early answers to the question raised by Brain suggest that we were the hunted.

Cotton Mather, for instance, warned of the toothy terrors of the forest primeval, among them "Dragons," "Droves of Devils," and "Fiery Flying Ser-
pents," but worst of all "the rabid and howling *Wolves* of the *Wilderness*
[which] would make . . . Havock among you, *and not leave the Bones till the
morning*" (*Wonders* 13, 85; *Frontiers* 10). Until the late eighteenth century
Americans may have felt overwhelmed by the New World's vast and mostly unknown wilderness. Early descriptions of the American wild are full
of terrifying accounts of forest predators. But almost concurrent with the
birth of the United States as a political entity, American writers began to
produce a rich body of folklore and fiction that, in general, presents man—
if not woman—as an enthusiastic hunter, finding his essential self fulfilled
through the hunt and seeming to glory in the violent contest with nature.

The dominant motif in our hunting literature is that of the wonderful
hunt, which has been called "America's favorite tall tale" (Dorson, *American Folklore* 45). In its pure form, as identified by folklorist Stith Thompson,
the wonderful hunt involves incredible success on a hunting adventure; related motifs feature a remarkable hunter, remarkable animals, and a natural world of astonishing fecundity (522–34). Wonderful hunt stories seem
unequivocal about the joy of hunting, but not far under the surface they reveal some uneasiness or uncomfortable ambiguity about human aggression
and its effects on the natural world. To illustrate, let me tell a story, a folk
tale that I heard told by the late storyteller Marshall Dodge, set somewhere
in the woods of Maine. To be true to the oral tradition, I will not attempt
an exact transcription of either his recorded version or the version he once
presented on *A Prairie Home Companion*. Instead I'll tell it as I remember it
(you'll have to imagine the phony Down East accent and the dance of flames
in our shared campfire)[1]:

> It was settin' in to be a hard winter. When that first snow come, I took stock
> of my pantry and decided I was in need of some meat, so I took down my
> gun with the side-by-side barrels, from where it was hangin' there above the
> stove, and set off into the woods. Well, I hadn't gone but about twenty yards
> when I seen some rabbit tracks, and I went on down the trail a-followin' 'em.
> Hadn't gone but about another twenty yards when I was distracted by a terri-
> ble snarlin', and I looked up and there was a mountain lion up in a tree. Well,
> I looked at the mountain lion, and the mountain lion looked at me, and I lifted
> my gun with the side-by-side barrels, and he was all set to pounce down upon
> me when we was both distracted by a terrible howlin', and there was a pack of
> wolves settin' upon us. I looked at the mountain lion, mountain lion looked at

me, and we decided whatever our differences was, we'd best team up to take care of the immediate problem of the wolves.

Well, I hadn't but just barely got the stockade built . . . when those wolves was upon us. I fired my gun with the side-by-side barrels and dispatched several of those wolves, and those that made it up over the stockade fence was dispatched by the mountain lion, and afore too long that en-tire pack of wolves was dispatched. Then I looked at the mountain lion, mountain lion looked at me, and we decided whatever our differences was we'd done right by each other, and so we'd best part as friends. So he went on up the trail and I went on down the trail, a-followin' them rabbit tracks.

I hadn't gone but about another twenty yards when I was distracted by a terrible growlin', and there was a big ole bear chargin' t'wards me. I lifted my gun with the side-by-side barrels and let go with the first barrel. Well, that startled him some . . . but the bear kept a-comin'. Then I fired the second barrel. *That* startled him some . . . but the bear kept a-comin'! I set about reloadin' so as to let that bear have both barrels at once, but afore I could lift my gun that bear was upon me, so I reached inside his mouth, grabbed ahold of his tail, and pulled that bear inside out. Well, *that* startled him some! But the bear kept a-comin'!! 'Course, by now he had run right on past me, headin' up the trail, and I headed on down the trail, a-followin' them rabbit tracks.

Afore too long I come to a stream, and I was hoppin' across on some rocks when I looked across and there was a pair of foxes, about twenty feet apart. I looked from one to the other, tryin' to decide where to aim, when I was distracted by a loud honkin' overhead. There was a dozen geese flyin' by. I looked at the geese, and at the foxes, and was considerin' the situation, when I was distracted by a loud quackin', and there was a dozen ducks flyin' by overhead. Well, I was at a bit of a nonplus, so I just aimed somewhere sort of at random, and fired both barrels. The shot hit a rock, split it apart, and killed both foxes. The kick from the shot was so powerful that it blew the gun apart. One barrel flew up and knocked down a goose, t'other flew up and knocked down a duck, and the recoil knocked me backward into the stream. When I come to, I had one hand on an otter's head, one hand on a beaver's tail, and my trouser pockets was so full of trout that a button popped off my fly and killed . . . the rabbit."

Elements of the wonderful hunt have been frequently adapted for serious purposes in our literature in such classics as Cooper's Leatherstocking series, Melville's *Moby-Dick*, Faulkner's "The Bear," and Hemingway's *The Old Man and the Sea*. But Dodge's "Rabbit Hunting" story is clearly

more akin to comedic, vernacular tall tale uses of the motif—Thomas Bangs
Thorpe's "The Big Bear of Arkansas," for instance, or the Davy Crockett almanac stories, or William Gilmore Simms's delightful "How Sharp Snaffles
Got His Capital—and Wife." Stories like these served several purposes during their heyday in nineteenth-century America: they expressed fears of the
wilderness that still seemed to dwarf American civilization while also providing a means for coping with and overcoming those fears and celebrating
the richness of nature in America. Perhaps these stories remain popular in
the twenty-first century because they capture the thorough optimism of our
culture, the sense that our endeavors can lead to unprecedented success.
Or, as Henry Wonham argues, perhaps tall tales serve Americans "as an
ironic comment about their own inflated dreams" (284). But in searching for
their national identity American storytellers have rehearsed an age-old inquiry into human identity. In a way these stories present another version of
the paleontological puzzle of Australopithecus, exploring questions about
our place in nature's pecking order. Perhaps the questions have seemed of
special significance in America, given the historical prevalence of wild nature in our land and the continuing prevalence of violence in our culture—
for as Richard Slotkin has noted, violence as a means to fortune, freedom,
and power has been "the structuring metaphor of the American experience" (5).

Like our Australopithecine predecessors, the narrator in "Rabbit Hunting" contends with fearsome natural antagonists. Dinofelis, the hominid
hunting relative of the saber-tooth tiger, was the stuff nightmares are made
of, and Americans through the nineteenth century seem to have felt themselves tormented by creatures equally fierce and—the key word here—primordial. Mountain lion, wolf, and bear—repeatedly in our literature these
are the foci of our hunters' fear. And legitimately so. New World versions
of these animals were often more sizable and fierce than their Old World
relatives—consider the grizzly—and certainly they were more prevalent.
The creatures of the wild here were seen as larger than life, often supernat-
urally so—like the bloodthirsty panthers in Charles Brockden Brown's 1799
novel *Edgar Huntly,* the "creation b'ar" of Thorpe's "Big Bear of Arkansas,"
or "Old Ben" in "The Bear," even Moby-Dick, or, more recently, the enormous shark in *Jaws*. These are the sorts of creatures that long kept Americans wondering if they are dominant over the wild or threatened by it. Of
course, we do not feel that way much any more, not at least in the eastern
United States, where there simply is not enough wilderness to make us feel
dwarfed by nature. Except, maybe, in Maine.

IN MAINE civilization seems remote, and the hiking is magical. In Mahoosuc Notch the Appalachian Trail winds over, through, and under piles of boulders that have poured down both mountains above the cleft. Occasionally, we hear water trickling underneath. A couple of times we see ice—in midsummer. Heading northeast to the center of the state, the Trail ascends through evergreen forests to rocky tops with great names like Old Speck, Baldpate, Moxie Bald, Whitecap, and Nesuntabunt. In one place it winds through electric green moss in dark first-growth forest. This is the forest primeval. I keep looking around for knights on horseback and maidens in distress, or at least a gnome or hobbit or two. We camp by lakes where loons cackle and hoot into the night, where water drips like star flecks from the antlers of moose at sunrise.

One day Pesch finds something marvelous. In a pool by a spring, a garter snake has caught a frog from behind. I had thought that snakes swallowed their prey head-on, but this is evidently not always the case. The snake has downed about half the frog. The hind legs are gone. Only the head and the front legs protrude from the snake's mouth. And here's the really strange thing: the snake's sides are heaving as it breathes—and so are the frog's! It's still alive! Occasionally the frog paws pathetically at the ground with its two paltry front legs, but it can't get any purchase to hop anywhere. Every so often, the snake gulps a bit, and a little more panting frog is captured by the snake's widening grin. It all happens very slowly. We watch for almost an hour and leave before the meal is done.

I remember a line from Margaret Atwood's *Snake Poems*, in which she describes a snake as:

> an endless gullet
> pulling itself on over the still alive prey
> like a sock gone ravenous, like an evil glove. (88–89)

I'm reminded too of my vow to go a-hunting. I could have killed the snake and frog together and had a two-course appetizer. But they were both pretty small. Besides, that scene was too remarkable to interrupt. And I have to admit to my own discomfort. Not only do I get queasy at the thought of killing something, but I also worry about my reputation among hikers. I don't need the food. To kill something out here for my own spiritual profit—that's an act of selfish, if not senseless, destruction. I may as well start voting Republican.

On the other hand, as a symbolic gesture it would prove something important. As a backpacker, I am only a visitor to the wild. I carry in what

I need, carry out what I use. That's good low-impact camping. But after almost two thousand miles on the Trail I want to know if I could survive out here, or more, if I could feel like I belong, if I could truly make a home or at least a living in the wild. To kill and eat even a small portion of my dinner would prove that I *could* do it, even if I'm not *actually* doing it. And now I know what to hunt—a snake. There have been plenty on the Trail throughout Maine, garters mostly. It should be an easy matter to whip one by the tail and smash its head against a rock, or just bash it with my hiking stick. Skinning it should be simple—just cut a slit down the middle of the yellowish belly, hang it up and let the blood drip out, then peel off the skin and fry up the meat. I'm sure it'll taste like chicken.

PREDATOR AND PREY: the fossil evidence of Australopithecus is ambiguous about which role we play. So, too, the folkloric evidence of wonderful hunt stories. Is the narrator of "Rabbit Hunting" the hunter or the hunted? Much of the evidence suggests that he is the hunter. His survival depends on a successful hunt, and he embarks on the hunt with a certain zeal, and he is indeed successful. But his success owes more to luck than skill; in fact, it comes despite—or maybe even as a result of—incredible incompetence. And though he sets off as hunter, for much of the story he finds himself fending off attacks from creatures more predatory than himself. In the confrontations with mountain lion, wolf, and bear, he is more the hunted than the hunter.

What are the implications of all this? Possibly, if we believe with Jung that folktales offer clues to the collective human psyche, we can conclude from "Rabbit Hunting" that hominids are not particularly well equipped to hunt, but that they take it up for self-defense and for survival. The fact that the narrator just sort of falls into his success—or rather, it falls *onto* him— might support theories that we were always more opportunistic scavengers than hunters. But there's another possibility, too. The "Rabbit Hunting" story suggests our uneasiness at acknowledging our hunting nature even as we depend on it. The narrator conducts a successful hunt without ever really hunting—or at least without doing much intentional killing. The foxes, the goose, the duck, the otter, the beaver, the trout, the rabbit—they are all bagged by mistake; the narrator does not so much as aim at them. The only thing he kills on purpose are the wolves, but in describing that encounter he euphemistically replaces the word *kill* with *dispatch*. Besides, the responsibility for the wolf killing lies just as much with the mountain lion which is hunting him and the wolves, so the narrator seems to be merely taking part in some natural process. For the most part, his hunting is harmless, or is made to seem so. In the confrontation with the mountain lion, both parties relinquish the contest. In the confrontation with the bear, *Ursus* is impervious to his gunshots and does not even seem much the worse for wear when he's pulled inside out.

But if the narrator is ineffectual as hunter, he does not quite play the role of predatory victim either. The charging bear passes right through him, and the mountain lion teams up with him. All this suggests a bit of wish fulfillment: that we succeed in the hunt without trying—without, that is, ever having to unleash the violent side of our natures—and that carnivores neither mean us harm nor are capable of doing us any harm. For all the attacking and shooting and killing in the story, the narrator's relationship with the natural world seems quite harmonious—an effect furthered by the humorous tone. Joseph Meeker contends in *The Comedy of Survival* that comedy is inherently ecological: it recognizes that we are "a part of nature and subject to all natural limitations and flaws"—the flaws (like incompetence) which are the subject of comedy—and that we must adapt to our environment (37). Looked at another way, though, perhaps the humor of wonderful hunt stories produces the antithesis of ecological awareness. The comedy in "Rabbit Hunting" allows us to avoid recognizing the consequences of our actions in the natural world. From a biocentric perspective, the narrator's wonderful hunt is ecological catastrophe, but the story de-emphasizes the abundant, perhaps excessive, killing inherent in the hunt.

Up on Bemis Mountain the blueberries are ripe. The bushes emerge from moss growing in depressions in the stone. We intend to fill our liter-sized water bottles for pancakes in the morning. There are so many berries that the collection process shouldn't take too long, except we keep eating as many as we bottle. I wander around the flat summit. After picking the choice offerings off a bush I look around for the next. That's when I see the snake, just a few feet away. It's the biggest one I've seen so far, only about three feet long but wrist-fat. It's motionless, lying in a series of lazy S's. I take a step. He doesn't move. I bend down and reach out my hand. Pause. No movement. Is he dead? Asleep? The eyes are open, but of course snakes have no eyelids. Their eyes are always open, awake or asleep. I lower my hand and bend my knees further.

This is not how I caught snakes when I was a kid. Back then I used the quick snatch and grab. Now I'm being slow and methodical. If he's asleep, can he still see through those open eyes?

Just inches above the back of the snake's head now, and then there's sudden silent motion and I'm bitten. From the fleshy V on the back of my hand between the base of thumb and forefinger, drops of red bubble up. I make urgent references to the snake's Oedipal proclivities. It has scooted a few feet away and stopped. I'm seething. I take my hiking stick and jab it, pressing the snake's neck hard into the rock. (Of course, the whole snake is neck, but I mean the spot right behind the head.) The rest of the snake writhes in angry semaphore. I stoop and clutch, lift and support the snake with both hands, hurry off to show my prize to my friends.

THE CONFUSION over who hunts whom, the remarkable success of the hunt despite the less-than-remarkable skill of the hunter—these observations about "Rabbit Hunting" apply, with some variations, to other American versions of the wonderful hunt. In "The Big Bear of Arkansas," for instance, the title refers to both man and bear, and the two shift in their roles as hunter and hunted throughout. The human "Big Bear," Jim Doggett (which, yes, sounds like Crockett) talks a good hunt, but his prowess is undercut when at the climactic moment of the chase he is caught in midpoop with his pants around his ankles. The bear dies, says Jim, seemingly of his own volition, as if he decided it was his time. In Simms's "Sharp Snaffles" the hunter, out to earn a fortune so that he can in turn earn his prospective father-in-law's permission to marry his sweetheart, falls into a hollowed-out tree and discovers a mother lode of honey, then falls out of the tree and kills a bear.

In serious, more consciously "literary" versions of the wonderful hunt, many of the same patterns hold. Ahab, for example, sets off to hunt the whale but ends up the hunted. The hunters in serious wonderful hunts are not necessarily incompetent, but they are typically incomplete or infirm or maimed in some way; all fall short of the ideal of a natural hunter. Ahab seems mad in his fixation with the white whale. Hemingway's Old Man has seen his best years pass him by. In "The Bear" the most expert hunters, Ike McCaslin and Sam Fathers, abstain from the hunt, and the slayer of Old Ben is the buffoon-like Boon Hogganbeck. Even the greatest "remarkable" hunter in our literature, Cooper's Natty Bumppo, is flawed by his lack of social grace. He's also inconsistent: he scorns the slaughter of pigeons and argues for conservation, but he is capable of shooting down an eagle simply to show off.

Comedic and serious versions of the wonderful hunt differ mainly in terms of consequences. While the often-incompetent hunters of comic wonderful hunt stories meet with unaccustomed success, the hunters in serious treatments of the theme, more likely to be skillful, end up tragic figures despite their prowess. Meeker points out that tragedy assumes conflict between human and natural forces, and it concerns itself with humanity's attempt to render itself superior to those forces, suffering in the attempt, and usually ending up dead (22–24).[2] Cooper's Natty Bumppo, for instance, ultimately faces the inevitable Catch-22 of the frontiersman's life: the better he does his job of taming the wild by hunting down its creatures, the sooner he enables civilization to move in, and so the sooner he finds himself out of a lifestyle. He is pushed ever further westward by the forces of civilization and dies a lonely man on the Great Plains. Though Hemingway's Old Man kills the big marlin, all he is able to tow home is its skeleton. Ahab, Queequeg, Tashtego and the rest of the Pequod's crew (excepting Ishmael) are sucked up by the sea, perhaps in punishment for their pride in contesting against nature. While the ecological consequences of bountiful hunting "harvests" are ignored in comedic wonderful hunts, a conservationist impulse often seems to underlie these tragic versions.

The tragic emphasis dominates recent hunting fiction, often exacerbated by a sense that human dominance over nature has denied us roles as either hunter or hunted. Rarely are the hunts of contemporary stories in any sense "wonderful." Hunters in contemporary stories are often inexperienced and incompetent, but not comically so, and often their unintended prey is human. In David Quammen's "Walking Out," a boy mistakenly shoots his father; in Tobias Wolff's "Hunters in the Snow," the pathetically insecure protagonist shoots an overly sarcastic friend. When hunters in contemporary stories are successful, they are often remorseful about their success, like the girl who kills her first deer in David Michael Kaplan's "Doe Season." In just two centuries we have gone from fearing the wild to finding ourselves irrevocably and miserably distanced from it. Human dominance over nature has left us nothing to hunt but each other, with no predator seeming threatening enough to make us feel like the hunted.

It's an eastern garter I've caught, mostly brown, yellow-striped, of course, with red-flecked scales showing through when he bends and stretches. It's my imagination, I know, but I start to wonder how sure I am that it's a garter and not a copperhead gone astray from its usual habitat. As I wonder, the snake's head seems to swell and triangulate. The blood on my hand seems to come from twin puncture holes. This worries me, since I thought garters have a semicircular row of teeth. I jam his mouth open with a stick. No fangs.

Pesch and Joe Dunes are not nearly as impressed as I had hoped they would be. They are more impressed with the bounty of blueberries they've picked, which does put my efforts to shame. The day is grey, about to rain, and it's hot and muggy, and the snake's musk, the smell of his fear mixing with mine, is dizzying. Atwood calls snake odor "part skunk, part inside / of a torn stomach" (87). There's something else, too—something that smells like chicken. The black flies are going nuts around me. They're fierce, relentless. I get bit in the eyelid. I need my hands to swat so I throw the snake into a bush. End of hunt. I try to pick more berries, but the bugs won't leave me alone; they're picking on me. I give up and hike on down the mountain, finding relief only when a gentle rain falls.

That night, we have blueberry pancakes for dinner. On one of my pancakes, a black fly gets caught in the honey we're using for syrup. I'm too hungry to be fastidious, so I swallow it down.

WHILE HUNTING is an important theme in Anglo-American literature, it is even more prominent in Native American stories. Maine is, or was, Abenaki territory, and the Abenaki story of "Gluscabi and the Game Animals" offers a neat contrast with Anglo-American wonderful hunt tales like "Rabbit Hunting." The Abenaki story concerns the fantastic hunting adventures of Gluscabi, a trickster figure who formed himself out of the dust left over from the creation of people. Equipped with a magic bag made by Grandmother Woodchuck, a bag that always has room for more game, Gluscabi tells all the animals in the world that the sun is about to go out and the world will be destroyed, but they will be safe in his game bag. After they fall for his trick, he boasts to Grandmother Woodchuck that he will never again need to hunt for food. But she reprimands him, saying that the animals will "sicken and die" in the bag, leaving nothing for his children. She also points out the virtues of hunting, telling Gluscabi that "It is . . . right that it should be difficult to hunt" the animals, because "you will grow stronger trying to find them. And the animals will also grow stronger and wiser trying to avoid being caught. Then things will be in the right balance" (Bruchac 113). Gluscabi opens the bag and lets the animals go.

It is likely that American Indian hunting myths were an important source for Anglo-American wonderful hunt stories. After all, wonderful hunts are inevitably set on the frontier where Anglo-American culture came into contact with Native American cultures. So it is not surprising that the story of Gluscabi resembles stories like "Rabbit Hunting," most prominently in the fanciful exaggeration. Gluscabi's capture of all the animals in the world puts the rabbit hunter's haul to shame. The stories are similar, too, in that the protagonist reaps the rewards of the hunt without doing any hunting. The differences between the stories, though, are far more telling than the similarities. While there is humor in the exaggeration of "Gluscabi and the Game Animals," the moral dimension of Gluscabi's story takes precedence over the joke. But the serious purpose does not imply tragedy. Hunting is not seen as something that ruins us or debases us or makes us something less than human. To the contrary, it makes us better and it makes the world better. Rather than being avoided or its implications skirted, hunting is welcomed as part of our nature and part of the natural harmony, not a threat to either. That sense of harmony means that Gluscabi never feels threatened by predators, nor does he keep the excessive harvest of game gathered on his hunt. The harmony also includes women, who in Anglo-American hunting stories are almost always depicted as the hunted (like Louisa Grant in Cooper's *The Pioneers*, who faints away when attacked by a panther but is rescued by the unerring shooting of Hawkeye/Natty Bumppo). In the story of Gluscabi, it is a female spirit who recognizes the rightful place of hunting in human culture and in the balance of nature.

So considering these American versions of the wonderful hunt, do we have an answer to Brain's question? Does the evidence of our literature tell us if we're at heart hunter or hunted? Not really. Clearly some differences in human conceptions of our hunting role are culturally determined: Native American stories show that hunting can be reconciled with a vision of natural harmony that includes people, while Anglo-American stories suggest skepticism about that premise. Those Anglo-American writers who see violence as inherent in the proposition that humans are hunters by nature portray it as inevitably leading to tragedy, for we are ultimately punished for our hunting success. On the other hand, comedic writers (and storytellers) in the Anglo-American literary tradition seem unwilling to admit to the violence; we succeed in the hunt despite ourselves, and we seem to do no real harm to the natural world. Perhaps the ability to euphemize violence is especially important in a nation that prides itself on lofty ideals about the virtues of the common citizen, but that at the same time won its identity as a nation through the violent act of a revolution, maintained a system of slavery through selective violence, retained its national identity through a Civil War, and today tolerates an incredible rate of violent crime.

The unwillingness to admit to our power over the natural world is also important in a country where pride of place coexists with faith in progress, even when that faith means depleting natural resources.

Cultural considerations may also account for Raymond Dart and C. K. Brain's different interpretations of the hard skeletal evidence of Australopithecus. In his study of "Hunting and Nature through History," Matt Cartmill points out that both Dart's hypothesis and the reactions against it were products of their times. World War II, the Holocaust, the Cold War—to Dart and his supporters these were proof of human depravity and our violent nature, proof that they found substantiated by fossil evidence. Cartmill points out, though, that the "reaction against the hunting hypothesis" itself had "a political basis," grounded in the post-1960s pacifism and feminism of the academically entrenched political left. Some scientists implicated Dart and his supporters in the horrors of war, seeing in his argument an attempt to legitimize violence and warfare (especially in Viet Nam) as simply part of human nature. Feminists decried the hunting hypothesis for promoting and justifying male aggression and dominance (18–19).

But the twentieth-century debate about the hunting hypothesis is just another exchange in a much longer conversation about the morality of hunting. Cartmill traces Western civilization's ambivalence about hunting back to ancient Greece, and he shows that social considerations have always influenced our conceptions of hunting. When hunting was an exclusive privilege reserved for the upper classes, for instance, criticism of the cruelty of hunting also served to condemn the cruelty of the ruling classes. In truth, says Cartmill, hunting has never been the sole source or even primary source of human sustenance—we have been scavengers, gatherers, and farmers more than hunters. Cartmill claims, too, that hunting has always been the pursuit of a minority—as it remains today, when only 12 percent of Americans hunt (230).

My own hunting adventure was more farcical than comic or tragic. Perhaps my failure to discover my inner hunter reflects my immersion in the culture of backpacking, where, as the saying goes, we take from the woods nothing but pictures, leave nothing but footprints. Or maybe it suggests something about my own personality and upbringing. Maybe I'm one of the natural majority who does not find it in his essential nature to hunt. But ultimately I hesitate to read anything grandiose about human nature into my encounter with the garter.

Who knows—maybe the findings of Dart and Brain can likewise be traced back to some personal origin. Might not a scientist named *Dart* be predisposed to emphasize the role of weaponry in human development? On the other hand, might not a scientist named *Brain* be predisposed to think that without a highly developed intellect, Australopithecines would have been fairly helpless creatures? Whatever the source of their different conclusions, cultural or personal, the findings of science turn out to be as ambiguous and indeterminate and open to interpretation as any story. Neither science nor fiction provides firm answers to Brain's question about whether we were or are the hunter or the hunted. But in the various considerations of humanity's proclivity for hunting we do have a provocative dialogue, conducted by storytellers as well as scientists, Grandmother Woodchuck as well as Davy Crockett. Emerging from the dialogue are questions that get at the heart of our existence: What is human nature? And what is the nature of our relationship with nonhuman nature?

NOTES

1. For a fine collection of faithfully transcribed Down East tall tales, see Richard M. Dorson, *Jonathan Draws the Long Bow*, especially the wonderful hunt stories on pages 111–18. I have chosen here to be more storyteller than scholar and to rely on a wonderful hunt version told by a humorist (and modified by my own telling) rather than one transcribed by a scholar from an "authentic" source to make the point that the oral tradition is still alive on the Appalachian Trail. It is the told version of the story, fluid and changing, not the one captured on the page, that is part of the literary canon of the Trail. At least it has been on two occasions when I've told the rabbit hunting story to Boy Scouts with whom I shared a campsite.

2. My point that tall tales gloss over ecological consequences of the hunt and that a conservationist impulse often underlies tragic versions of the wonderful hunt obviously differs from Meeker's finding. But his analysis focuses on drama, mine on narrative.

REFERENCES

Ardrey, Robert. *The Hunting Hypothesis: A Personal Conclusion concerning the Evolutionary Nature of Man*. New York: Atheneum, 1976.

Atwood, Margaret. *Selected Poems II: Poems Selected and New, 1976–1986*. Boston: Houghton Mifflin, 1987.

Brain, C. K. *The Hunters or the Hunted? An Introduction to African Cave Taxonomy*. Chicago: U of Chicago P, 1981.

Bruchac, Joseph. "Gluscabi and the Game Animals." *Native American Stories*. Golden, Colo.: Fulcrum, 1991. 108–13.

Cartmill, Matt. *A View to a Death in the Morning: Hunting and Nature through History*. Cambridge: Harvard UP, 1993.

Dorson, Richard M. *American Folklore*. Chicago: U of Chicago P, 1959.

———. *Jonathan Draws the Long Bow*. Cambridge: Harvard UP, 1946.

Kaplan, David Michael. "Doe Season." *Comfort*. New York: Viking Penguin, 1987.
    1–22.

Mather, Cotton. *Frontiers Well-Defended*. Boston, 1707.

———. *The Wonders of the Invisible World*. London, 1862.

Meeker, Joseph. *The Comedy of Survival: Studies in Literary Ecology*. New York: Scrib-
    ner's, 1972.

Quammen, David. "Walking Out." *Blood Line: Stories of Fathers and Sons*. St. Paul,
    Minn.: Graywolf, 1988. 1–41.

Slotkin, Richard. *Regeneration through Violence: The Mythology of the American Frontier,
    1600–1860*. Middletown, Conn.: Wesleyan UP, 1973.

Thompson, Stith. *Motif-Index of Folk Literature*. Vol. 5. Bloomington: Indiana UP, 1955.

Wolff, Tobias. "Hunters in the Snow." *In the Garden of the North American Martyrs*.
    New York: Ecco, 1981. 9–26.

Wonham, Henry B. "In the Name of Wonder: The Emergence of Tall Narrative in
    American Writing." *American Quarterly* 41 (1989): 284–307.

Going to Bashō's Pine

Wilderness Education for the Twenty-first Century

THE GREAT seventeenth-century Japanese haiku poet Matsuo Bashō, when asked by a student to describe the source of inspiration, is said to have replied, "If you want to know the pine, go to the pine." There are many ways to follow master Bashō with a group of university students in the wilderness classroom.

Say the particular pine is ponderosa pine, the classroom is the high plateau of backcountry Zion National Park in late May, the course is natural history of the Colorado Plateau, and there are twelve learners who are nearing the end of an eight-week field program.

First, there is the taxonomy describing the tree. Over the spring we have come to know other members of the *Pinaceae,* but we have not encountered ponderosa before: *Pinus ponderosa,* long-needle leaves in threes, ruddy puzzlebark, cones with prickles on the scales, grows mostly above 1,600 meters in Utah in open stands, the most widespread pine in western North America. These forests provide habitat for birds and mammals new to us—songs from the olive-sided flycatcher and Swainson's thrush float down from the canopy. There are human uses of ponderosa pine to discover. The tree is cut and milled for construction lumber, and the needles make a resinous tea high in vitamin C. "Like drinking the forest," remarks a student.

Then (science aside) there are various cultural constructions of ponderosa pine. The entire pine family is shot through with mythos, and "pine" conjures up many images in our group. We talk about what they mean, sharing a bit of our personal history with trees as we connect with a larger cultural story.

This forest near Sawmill Spring was cut heavily some seventy years ago, and today the millsite is a green meadow and a pond with a springbox. We find giant stumps in the nearby woods which butt against our concepts of national parks as pristine nature. This partially logged forest in a nature reserve is a place where human and natural histories intertwine.

Still, we return to the pine. The afternoon assignment is to go off into the forest, find a spot to sit, observe avian activity and make a field journal entry, and then sit with the trees for a time and reflect on the day's activities. In this wild classroom, before science, history, and culture, the ponderosa pine is always present as a being-in-place, like us, alive and growing.

Characteristics of Wilderness Education

Wilderness education, as a new kind of environmental education, blossomed in the 1970s as the burgeoning public awareness of ecology combined with college student demands for alternative education. Almost immediately, this movement differentiated into two parallel streams. Adventure education programs (Outward Bound, the National Outdoor Leadership School, and a host of nonprofits serving special-needs groups) focused on the noncredit teaching of outdoor skills, leadership, and personal growth through wilderness experience. Though college-age students made up the majority of adventure education participants in to the 1980s, today's programs are increasingly geared toward corporate professionals.

The second stream, academic wilderness education, offering credit toward undergraduate degrees, may be more radical in philosophy, goals, and methods. Wilderness education seeks to educate the whole person through, as Jonathan Fairbanks suggests, "a blend of reading, study, and experience that creates a sense that learning is part of a greater whole, that academic experiences contribute to life rather than merely serving as a formal prelude to it" (22). There are many ways, of course, to accomplish such learning, but academic wilderness education is unique because the field classroom is alive, a fundamental ally in learning. Living places from vacant lots to wild mountains and deserts are essential for wilderness education whether the length of study is an afternoon, a week, or a semester.

Along with dependence on living classrooms, academic wilderness education blends experiential learning (learning by doing) with the traditional transmission model of higher education (learning by information assimilation). The transmission model represents students as passive, empty vessels waiting to be filled with expert knowledge through lectures by professors. Though much empirical educational research shows the ineffectiveness of this transmission approach, the model and practice persist. It is difficult to describe precisely why universities do not often support academic wilderness education. Reasons include liability concerns, perceived loss of oversight due to off-campus locations, and a lack of institutional support for education theories and practices that deviate from the status quo.

Beyond these two shared traits there are many variations between academic wilderness education programs. The Audubon Expedition Institute, for example, places a premium on environmental studies with attention to group process. Audubon students spend significant amounts of class time building community through shared decision making. Since the program is bus-based, much field time is spent car-camping and visiting regional and local experts throughout the country. Wildlands Studies is research-project oriented. These programs focus on a specific bioregion's environmental issues or work to collect data on species or ecosystems at risk. The wilderness and civilization program at the University of Montana explores the nature/culture boundary with a humanities emphasis. In this program, students begin the semester with a two-week backpack and then return to campus to pursue group studies in literature, history, and philosophy with wilderness themes. (For a list of programs see the appendix.)

I taught my first wilderness education program in the southern Appalachians in 1975 for Antioch College and have worked in the wild classroom for several universities. Since 1982 I have directed the Sierra Institute wilderness studies program at the University of California Extension in Santa Cruz. Founded in 1974, the Sierra Institute (SI) offers three-, five-, and eight-week undergraduate environmental studies programs taught in backcountry areas throughout western North America, Belize, and Chile. It has been over a decade since I last surveyed the field ("The University of the Wilderness"), and it is time for a re-evaluation. For the balance of this essay, I will use SI to portray specific wilderness education methods (especially those with an emphasis on using literature) before spotlighting future issues that will challenge all outdoor classroom programs in the twenty-first century.

Practice in the Wild

Through the stories we hear who we are.

—LESLIE MARMON SILKO, "Landscape, History, and the Pueblo Imagination"

WE WERE CAMPING in Grand Gulch, a sixty-mile gash eroded out of the southern edge of Cedar Mesa in southern Utah. The group was at that stage in a long hike where, if you are lucky, you feel the weight of industrial civilization lift off your shoulders and your perception sharpens. The zen-bell song of the canyon wren. Tinkle of water over sandstone slabs. Angle of afternoon light. Day's work ahead: present an outline of Anasazi cultural stages and how we define them, hike a few miles in search of the ruin, and give an in-class writing assignment that ties the day's learning together.

My lecture is straightforward, though I emphasize the material culture field marks of dwelling sites and rock art panels that allow one to estimate when and how the place was inhabited. We pack for the day hike and set off.

The ancestral Pueblo (Anasazi) people lived densely in Grand Gulch, and their sign is everywhere. Students are fascinated by the Anasazi for two main reasons. First, contact with any prehistoric Native people feeds the inclination to romanticize Indians. Second, most people just cannot conceive of how any humans could flourish in this dry desert place.

After a bit of searching against the eastern cliff we discover the ruin, remarkably intact. The Anasazi left seven hundred years ago, but we find a yucca fiber sandal, a very large potsherd among hundreds, numerous corn cobs, red-painted figures on rock walls, a small intact kiva, and more. The place is magical, mythical, prehistoric, and also in the present, here and now.

Later, we draw together below the ruin. The Anasazi left no written accounts, but two nights ago we read and discussed Leslie Marmon Silko's essay "Landscape, History, and the Pueblo Imagination." Referring to the Old Ones, Silko begins, "You see that after a thing is dead, it dries up. . . . The spirits remain close by. They do not leave us" (83–84). We have just spent an hour inhaling the dust of this ruin. I give out the assignment: Pick an age (child, teen, adult, elder) you want to be. Pretend you are an Anasazi who lives here and describe what you did around home today, using what you know about ancestral Pueblo culture, what you have discovered here, and your imagination.

We are to meet back at camp in a few hours.

What might happen when a student mixes academic learning and knowledge of "the facts" with the living place where facts are born? How might a learner mix into this educational crucible his or her own creative impulse along with the experiences of peers who are engaged with the same place and the same problems? Just as the body can be connected to the mind by a backpack full of books, wilderness education works best when relationships are developed beyond the simple act of holding class in the great outdoors.

To educate the whole person, wild teaching is concerned primarily with connecting across boundaries in four key relationships:

place/learning
doing/knowing
individual/group
reflection/action

Place and Learning. David Orr has written that "place has no standing in contemporary education" (*Ecological Literacy* 126), but in academic wilderness education place is paramount. The wild classroom provides a wholeness that allows for profound learning. SI instructor Leslie Ryan calls this wholeness "physical integrity . . . often, for the first time in their lives, students' days are not split into bits. On the trail, in general, people experience an unprecedented freedom from distraction" (letter to author, 5 January 1999).

In Grand Gulch, the search for and discovery of the Anasazi site, the feel of knobby corncobs, the tangy odor of ruin pack-rat urine, the sheer presence of the place, all drew us into deep learning. Stories were being created long before I gave the assignment.

Epiphanies are common in the wilderness classroom. Three springs ago in the Eel River country of the California Coast Range, Gina, a student in a field ecology program, was engaged in a difficult assignment: observe a single species for an entire day and record its behavior in your field journal. This work can be exciting, but often, like much of field biology, it is incredibly boring. Gina watched a clump of budding wild onion, and nothing happened for six and a half hours. Packing to leave and feeling that the day was wasted, Gina glanced down at the plant—and one flower popped open soundlessly. Then, one after another, in rapid succession, all five buds blossomed in the evening air. And then tiny flies appeared to feast on ripe pollen . . .

I have taught ecology and natural history in the field and in campus classrooms, and there is no substitute for observing species in the context of habitat. Like Gina, I have not observed flowers opening or pollinators at work in the lab—such behaviors have been selected against by the act of collecting a mere slice of life for display indoors.

Literature, however, is not dysfunctional indoors, and it may be that reading Edward Abbey in the canyon country does not confer any special benefit to students. But there is more to literature than style and substance. In addition, there is the need to grasp what claim the canyons had on Abbey in the creation of *Desert Solitaire*. After teaching Abbey both indoors and out, I believe that this text cannot be understood without some familiarity with the canyons where the book was born. And further, when the study of literature includes exploration of one's own creativity, wild classrooms offer the opportunity to express one's own response to the land, as well as endless inspiration. Thoreau could not have written *The Maine Woods* if he had not journeyed beyond Walden Pond. The Great Salt Lake could offer refuge to Terry Tempest Williams only if she first had intimate contact with its birds and waters.

Doing and Knowing. "Aren't they just backpacking for credit out there?" Well, no—these are college classes taught outdoors, where learning by doing is married to assimilating information. Though universities certainly prefer abstract knowledge to learning by doing, wilderness teachers do not privilege experience. Outdoors, both kinds of learning are attended to, giving students the opportunity to test assumptions about Native peoples and plant phenology with their own direct encounters.

The anthropological construction of Anasazi culture helped students make sense of the ruin we visited, but it could never capture fully those people or their place. And maybe the framework was invalid—what direct evidence of its legitimacy could we find at the site?

In the field classroom, teachers are learners, too. Educator Alison King believes that instructors must play active roles in the joining of theory with practice. She suggests that teachers act as "guides on the side" instead of "sages on stage" (17). I have learned that the more I model active learning, the easier it is for students to become engaged with their own educational process.

Each autumn on the Colorado Plateau, Leslie Ryan and Alec Cargile teach an SI program with coursework in literature and ethics that beautifully integrates doing and knowing. Though reading and writing play a significant role in their program, Leslie and Alec begin by teaching tracking and orienteering: "We consider tracking as a form of reading and orienteering to the landscape as a form of ethics" (letter to author, 5 January 1999). While students develop these skills, they also read and discuss David Abram's *The Spell of the Sensuous*, plumbing the diverse character of language and varieties of reciprocity. Both human and other beings are available to "test" Abram's work. Students write on a daily basis; journal entries, sketches, and simple, descriptive poems are assigned, with lots of reading aloud around the campfire.

By the third week of the eight-week program, students begin to work on a draft of what will become their major project. They start to engage in an intensive revision process which Leslie describes as analogous to learning about a place, or falling in love. . . . A conversation is about to take place between the story and the student. The student re-reads: the story speaks while the student listens. The student revises: the student speaks while the story listens. A raven cries in the distance, a rock falls, a shadow crosses a knee: the landscape enters the conversation; the student and the story listen.

On the final hike of the program, Leslie and Alec spend an average of four hours with each student, attending to the final stages of this revision process. As Leslie states, "as the process goes on, the human teacher is able to stand farther and farther back, as the student gains trust and confidence in his or her direct communications with these other beings, the great friends, inspirations, and teachers who have, at least for the moment, all the time in the world."

Group and Individual. My students have been out alone gathering stories and now it's time to welcome them home.

After supper, we are cradled in darkness and firelight. Everyone takes turns reading aloud from their Anasazi story. One by one, the students are transformed: a child in a cradleboard watches ravens play in a blue desert sky; an old man with a feeble leg dreams back to the time he hunted desert bighorn above the canyon rim; a sister and brother out gathering rice grass get lost and together solve the puzzle of where home lies; a hunter paints a wall and prays for vision. Some of the details of the students' tales don't fit ancestral Pueblo reality, but these can be discussed later through my written feedback. The point is that the stories resonate, spring from a ruin in a real canyon inhabited by oaks, lizards, spirits, and a group of young explorers willing to share.

Every SI instructor has favorite ways to knit individuals into community. Many use journal sharing and various read-aloud techniques to encourage group voice. These methods work well whether the class is on natural history or nature writing. Greg Gordon, who teaches literature and environmental issues in the northern Rockies, assigns an eco-autobiography in which students write and share a nutshell version of how their relationship with nature evolved. Later, these stories are passed around the group and can also be developed further into an individual's final project.

Backcountry community life is far richer than what occurs on campus. Teachers and students share a journey—you backpack and camp together. Students may find that though the instructor knows all the plants or is a scholar of contemporary American nature writing, this same teacher is a weak hiker who tends to miss trail junctions. The footing is more equal in the backcountry around the mundane tasks of daily living. Beyond common ground, participants have common educational interests and goals. Students also take the same classes, so study groups form naturally. Individuals with particular strengths share expertise. Community support encourages individual safety in backcountry living and creativity in learning. For most participants, the result is a great expansion of sense of self, a deep sense of membership in an intimate human group, and a definition of community that includes the wild.

Reflection and Action. A young man spins a story about his first backpack with his dad. A woman takes the revision of her paper down to a hidden pool, washes her face, and sits against a juniper to watch the sun dip below a rock rim. Another woman crouches by an unopened flower all day and nothing happens until . . .

Many theorists agree with educators Pat Hutchings and Allen Wutzdorff that "reflection transforms experience into learning" ("Experiential Learning" 15). Students, however, are less and less capable of doing reflective learning because modern life and large lecture halls do not often allow for it. The outdoor classroom is built around active learning, but reflection must also be accommodated and at many scales. In class, I sometimes like to work with what educator M. B. Rowe calls "wait time," where ample space is allowed for thinking between questions and responses. Mountains at evening are excellent facilitators of "wait time" and reflection. In the high country an hour before dark, each group member goes off (with journal and headlamp) to find a place, sit quietly, watch the world, and not return to camp till darkness is complete. Being still with the world is an experience that only a handful of students have ever had, I have found over my twenty-five years of teaching. But what better way is there to begin to learn, in the words of ethnobotanist Gary Nabhan, "to live well with the 'others' around you" (63)?

Future Issues

ACADEMIC WILDERNESS EDUCATION, despite its strengths, is not in a strong position at the dawn of the new millennium. Since I surveyed the field in 1988 ("University"), most of the problems I described then have become worse. Here is a short list of what is of most concern to me.

Loss of Habitat. The biodiversity crisis that biologists warn about continues unabated. Yes, there were more acres of protected land in the United States in 1999 than there were in 1970, but wildernesses are increasingly fragmented biologically from unprotected roadless lands. Though wilderness education does not depend on legal wilderness, it does require a certain amount of relatively "wild" habitat. And habitat degradation, combined with an increasingly urban population, makes it more difficult to access places that retain a semblance of ecological integrity. What writer Robert Michael Pyle describes as "the extinction of experience" goes hand in hand with the extinction of species.

Dominance of Technocratic Society. Life in the United States continues to become more technological, specialized, and rapid-paced. And so do the schools that serve American society. This does not bode well for kinds of learning that require commitments of time and reflection. The use of computers, for example, almost defines membership in today's university communities, but users forget that such technologies amplify some forms of knowledge (explicit, context-free, digitalizable) while reducing other forms (tacit, contextual, memory-based). Support for technical education (business, engineering, computer science), as measured by budget dollars and numbers of student majors, is increasing dramatically. At UC Santa Cruz, students have less flexibility to take elective credits outside major requirements. They are encouraged to "stay on track" and not stray beyond campus boundaries. In 1987, author Wendell Berry wondered how universities could train "responsible heirs and members of human culture" in the face of such forces (77). Recently, Berry has been joined by a host of voices trumpeting alarm at the growing influence of technocracy on learning. Yet Berry's standard is left unmet as teachers and students increasingly "become makers of parts of things" (77).

Decreasing University Support. At UC Santa Cruz, the environmental studies department has recently been forced to reduce by 50 percent its support for its only intensive field program. Field biologists nationwide bemoan the loss of such courses. With fewer field courses in which to participate, students have less access to the wild classroom. Enrollments at SI and other programs appear to be holding steady, but most program administrators report that they are spending more money and staff time to maintain the status quo.

Finally, even after thirty years there is still a paucity of empirical research on wilderness education methods and results. Does it really work better than the campus classroom? If so, how? No studies have elucidated what optimal trip length or intensity might be, or even what instructor qualities or specific activities might contribute to greater learning. The few recent studies (which are very narrow in design) report only that results are inconclusive and more research is needed.

What Is "Wilderness"? In a recent essay, "The Trouble with Wilderness," historian William Cronon suggested that "The time has come to rethink wilderness" (67). Cronon's view reveals changing attitudes toward wild nature in the United States—in fact, distinctions between people and nature are under re-evaluation by many intellectuals, if not by the general public. What this debate holds for academic wilderness education is unclear. But I sense that those who cling to strict dichotomies between nature/culture, wild/tame, raw/cooked, will find these views less useful as the new century unfolds. After all, it matters little whether a sacred mountain, population of native onions, Anasazi ruin, or city lot are labeled as natural or cultural artifacts. What is important, according to education philosopher Thomas Colwell, is "the particular ways in which and degrees to which they are interconnected" (8) and how much these relationships elicit compassionate behavior from us.

Going to Bashō's Pine

TWO THOUSAND FEET above the Pacific in California just south of the canyon where Big Creek spills fresh water into the salty deep, there is a place of singular beauty and ecological significance. The beauty is easy to grasp—you face due west in open grassland on a dome at the end of one ridge among many ridges north and south, all diving steeply into endless blue waters. Close behind, giant trees speckle the grassland, waving their thick arms toward the ocean. These are ponderosa pines, far isolated from their nearest kin to the east, the westernmost population of the species in North America. How did they come to live here?

I brought my students to camp in this place in 1984, to sleep under a silver moon, to listen to night tides, and to puzzle over the pines. We watched the moon rise late, slept away from land's edge, and over several days examined and discussed the trees while counting seedlings. There were very few. The population appeared to be winking out.

In 1987, the Rat Creek fire torched 60,000 acres of Big Sur, burning the mature ponderosas into dull black snags. The seedlings never had a chance.

Twelve seasons from the first visit and eight years after the fire, I returned to the pines with students. I shared the 1984 data, told the fire's story. We hiked to the old snags, and though many had toppled, several still threw out their branches to the wind. And in dense patches here and there under the snags, young green trees stood two to three feet high. We surveyed hundreds.

Pinus ponderosa prefers a hot burn. Fire incinerates thick grass, exposes mineral soil. Cones open to the heat, and seeds disperse in the sea breeze.

"If you want to know the pine, go to the pine."

You can't count seedlings in a classroom. More important, you can't sense directly that culture, like fire-prone pines, is dependent on larger processes, deeper relationships that are ongoing and wild.

If our task is to grow a new culture in the New World, "a civilization that can live fully and creatively together with wildness," as Gary Snyder suggests (6), then a first step is to go to Bashō's pine to discover that the tree is whole and in relation, whether young or old, green or black, censused or left alone.

The learning is in the tree.

The tree endures.

APPENDIX: PARTIAL LIST OF ACADEMIC
WILDERNESS EDUCATION PROGRAMS

Audubon Expedition Institute
PO Box 365
Belfast, ME 04915
207–338–5859

Environmental Field Program
Antioch College
Yellow Springs, OH 45387
513–767–9001

Environmental Studies Department
Prescott College
220 Grove Ave.
Prescott, AZ 86301
520–778–2090

School for Field Studies
16 Broadway
Beverly, MA 01915–4499
www.fieldstudies.org (last checked 26 August 2002)

Sierra Institute
740 Front Street
Santa Cruz, CA 95060
831–427–6618
sierrai@cats.ucsc.edu
www.ucsc-extension.edu/sierra/ (last checked 26 August 2002)

Wildlands Studies
3 Mosswood Circle
Cazadero, CA 95421
707–632–5665
WildInds@sonic.net

Wild Rockies Field Institute
PO Box 7071
Missoula, MT 59807
406–549–4336
www.wildrockies.org/wrfi/ (last checked 26 August 2002)

REFERENCES

Abram, David. *The Spell of the Sensuous*. New York: Pantheon, 1996.
Berry, Wendell. "The Loss of the University." *Home Economics*. San Francisco: North Point, 1987.
Bowers, C. A. *The Culture of Denial: Why the Environmental Movement Needs a Strategy for Reforming Universities and Public Schools*. Albany: State U of New York P, 1997.
Colwell, Thomas. "The Nature-Culture Distinction and the Future of Environmental Education." *Journal of Environmental Education* 28.4 (Fall 1997): 4–8.
Cronon, William. "The Trouble with Wilderness; or, Getting Back to the Wrong Nature." *Uncommon Ground: Toward Reinventing Nature*. Ed. William Cronon. New York: Norton, 1995. 69–90.

Drengson, Alan. "Wilderness Travel as an Art and as a Paradigm for Outdoor Education." *Quest* 32.1 (Winter 1980): 110–20.

Fairbanks, Jonathan. "The Elastic Classroom." *Journal of Environmental Education* 11.3 (Summer 1980): 22–24.

Gillet, D. P., G. P. Thomas, R. L. Skok, and T. F. McLaughlin. "The Effects of Wilderness Camping and Hiking on the Self-Concepts and Environmental Attitudes and Knowledge of 12th Graders." *Journal of Environmental Education* 22.3 (Summer 1991): 33–44.

Grumbine, R. Edward. *Ghost Bears: Exploring the Biodiversity Crisis*. Washington, D.C.: Island, 1992.

——. "The University of the Wilderness." *Journal of Environmental Education* 19.4 (Fall 1988): 3–7.

Hanna, Glenda. "Wilderness-Related Environmental Outcomes of Adventure and Ecological Education Programming." *Journal of Environmental Education* 27.1 (Winter 1995): 21–32.

Herreid, Clyde F. "Why Isn't Cooperative Learning Used to Teach Science?" *BioScience* 48.8 (July 1998): 553–59.

Hutchings, Pat, and Allen Wutzdorff, eds. *Knowing and Doing: Learning through Experience*. San Francisco: Jossey-Bass, 1988.

King, Alison. "Inquiry as a Tool in Critical Thinking." *Changing College Classrooms*. Ed. Diane F. Halpern and Associates. San Francisco: Jossey-Bass, 1994. 13–38.

Mattingly, Hayden F. "Seeking Balance in Higher Education." *Conservation Biology* 11.5 (October 1997): 1049–52.

Meffe, Gary, and Ronald Carroll, eds. *Principles of Conservation Biology*. Sunderland, Mass.: Sinauer, 1997.

Miles, John. "Wilderness as a Learning Place." *Journal of Environmental Education* 18.2 (Winter 1986–87): 33–40.

——. "Teaching in Wilderness." *Journal of Environmental Education* 22.4 (Fall 1991): 5–9.

Nabhan, Gary P. *Cultures of Habitat*. Washington, D.C.: Counterpoint, 1997.

Nash, Roderick. "Wilderness Education Principles and Practices." *Journal of Environmental Education* 11.3 (Summer 1980): 2–3.

Noss, Reed. "The Naturalists Are Dying Off." *Conservation Biology* 10.1 (February 1996): 1–3.

Noss, Reed, and Allen Cooperrider. *Saving Nature's Legacy*. Washington, D.C.: Island, 1994.

Orr, David. *Ecological Literacy*. Albany: State U of New York P, 1992.

——. "Speed." *Conservation Biology* 12.1 (February 1998): 4–7.

Pyle, Robert Michael. *The Thundertree*. Boston: Houghton Mifflin, 1993.

Rowe, M. B. "Wait Time and Rewards as Instructional Variables, Their Influence on Language, Logic, and Fate Control, Part I: Wait Time." *Journal of Research in Science Teaching* 11 (1974): 81–94.

Rumrill, Gene. "Academic Horizons in Wilderness." *Journal of Environmental Education* 11.3 (Summer 1980): 4–6.

Silko, Leslie Marmon. "Landscape, History, and the Pueblo Imagination." *Antaeus* 57 (Autumn 1986): 83–94.

Snyder, Gary. *The Practice of the Wild*. San Francisco: North Point, 1990.

Yung, Laurie, Bob Yetter, Wayne A. Friemund, and Perry J. Brown. "Wilderness and Civilization: Two Decades of Wilderness Higher Education at the University of Montana." *International Journal of Wilderness* 4.2 (July 1998): 17–20.

Ten+ (Alternative) Films
about American Cities

CINEMA has always been an urban art form, requiring concentrations of people in order to maintain an adequate audience for regular exhibition. And since moviegoers have always relished the experience of seeing familiar, as well as exotic, places in the movie theater, urban centers have been a popular filmic subject since the invention of the Cinématographe. Many, if not most of the early Lumière films depict aspects of Lyons, Paris, and other European cities; and a substantial number of the earliest American films focus on two of the cities that have remained familiar locations for motion pictures of all kinds: the Library of Congress currently distributes, online, two series of early films under the rubric "American Memory," <http://lcweb2 .loc.gov/ammem/papr/mpixhome.html> (last checked 26 August 2002), one focusing on New York City at the beginning of the twentieth century and the other on San Francisco before and after the earthquake and fire of 1906.

This interest in the city has remained relatively constant throughout the history of commercial film, both silent—for example, Chaplin's *The Kid* (1921), Harold Lloyd's *Safely Last* (1924), Fritz Lang's *Metropolis* (1927), King Vidor's *The Crowd* (1928)—and sound: virtually the entire history of *film noir* takes place in urban centers and is often about the compromises and brutalities necessary to the development of the modern metropolis. In recent decades especially the expansion of Los Angeles has inspired a memorable series of *film noirs: Chinatown* (1974), *One False Move* (1991), *Devil in a Blue Dress* (1995), *LA Confidential* (1997), to name a few. Gangster films too are nearly always set in urban locales, as are many suspense thrillers and a wide variety of films from other genres, even sci-fi, which frequently offers premonitions of urban-centers-to-come.

Given the considerable history of the use of the modern city as setting for popular film, those interested in using films as part of an exploration of the history and representation of American place need not look far for

Fantasia (Cynda Williams) and Ray (Billy Bob Thornton) on the road, in *One False Move* (1991), Carl Franklin's film noir about American urban and rural life.

useful instances. And yet, to rely solely on the commercial cinema for ex-emplary texts is to waste a remarkable opportunity, for the modern city has been the subject of a good many accomplished documentaries and avant-garde films, ever since Charles Sheeler and Paul Strand collaborated on what is widely considered the first American avant-garde film, *Manhatta* (1921). As Jan-Christopher Horak has explained, *Manhatta* provides a re-markable instance of the intersection of American Romanticism (in its use of intertitles—and a title—derived from Whitman) and the arrival of Mod-ernist art in post–World War I America (Horak). During the following de-cade, the modern city became the topic of one of the first distinctive gen-res of documentary and avant-garde film (both histories claim the genre): the City Symphony. A triad of European films—Alberto Cavalcanti's *Rien que les heures* (*Nothing but the Hours,* 1926), Walther Ruttmann's *Berlin, die Sinfonie einer Grosstadt* (*Berlin: Symphony of a Big City,* 1927), and Dziga Ver-tov's *The Man with a Movie Camera* (1927)—defined the form and have re-mained three of its masterworks. Each depicts a composite day in the life of that urban metropolis most central to a particular national identity (Paris, Berlin, Moscow, respectively), and each does so using a style that reflects an ideology that can be read as characteristic of, or at least appropriate to, its location.

Elements of the European City Symphony quickly found their way into American films, first in a series of American City Symphonies in the early 1930s[1] and in the landmark collaboration between Ralph Steiner and Willard Van Dyke, *The City*, produced by the American Institute of Planners for the 1939 World's Fair. And I have argued elsewhere ("City") that the City Symphony form has found its American epitome in more recent years in Spike Lee's *Do the Right Thing* (1989). But this is to grossly oversimplify the remarkable range of alternative films about American cities produced by filmmakers working alone, with very limited budgets. Since many of these films are not only not widely known (and can be difficult to find for someone not intimately familiar with independent cinema), a brief discussion of a few of them seems appropriate and timely. While I have numbered the following sections, my numbering is not evaluative: all the films are of considerable interest and pedagogical value. And as will be clear, my listing means to provide only a hint of what's available in the remarkably underutilized wide world of alternative cinema.

Note: When using the films discussed in the following list, good 16mm (or in the case of No. 5, video/35mm) projection, in a screening room designed for showing films well, is essential. Disrespectful presentation destroys much of the power and subtlety of these films.

1. *Under the Brooklyn Bridge* (1953) by Rudy Burckhardt (15 minutes; black and white)

IT IS UNLIKELY that any filmmaker spent more time filming New York City than the late Rudy Burckhardt (he died in 1999), who emigrated to the United States from Switzerland in 1934. In the 1940s, he produced a trilogy of city films—*Up and Down the Waterfront* (1946), *The Climate of New York* (1948), and *Under the Brooklyn Bridge*—that established the approach he was to use in the dozens of films he produced during the decades that followed. Unlike the European City Symphonies of the 1920s and the earliest American imitations, Burckhardt did not see his New York films as a polemic for national identity. His fascination with New York was, and remained, that of a visitor taken with how the city looks and feels. In general, Burckhardt filmed from street level, editing the imagery he collected into clusters that argue nothing more than his interest in particular visual phenomena. On the other hand, his refusal to see himself as outside the city spaces he records suggests a fundamentally democratic urge that is also reflected in Burck-hardt's frequent return to such locations as 14th Street and Central Park.

Under the Brooklyn Bridge is filmed near the Brooklyn Bridge, in both Manhattan and Brooklyn. It begins with a catalogue of architectural details of doors and windows and several panoramic shots of the bridge. A second sequence documents the demolition of a building near the bridge; it is fol-lowed by a sequence of workers on lunch break. A fourth section focuses on several young boys skinny-dipping under the bridge on the Brooklyn side; a fifth, on workers leaving places of work at the end of the day. The film concludes with shots of empty streets at dusk and classic imagery of the Brooklyn Bridge with the Lower Manhattan skyline behind it in the twi-light. There is a somewhat somber musical soundtrack.

What makes *Under the Brooklyn Bridge* memorable is a function of Burck-hardt's strictly observational approach. The film reveals dimensions of American society that may have seemed rather mundane in 1953, but which, half a century later, are surprising. Most obviously, perhaps, the nude boys swimming in the East River around collapsed docks and build-ings not only recall our parents' warnings to avoid such places but reveal that there was a time when young people could be unselfconscious around the camera. These boys seem quite comfortable in their nudity, despite their awareness of Burckhardt filming, and they remind us of the degree to which our bodies have been "colonized" by film and television during recent dec-ades. Also notable now is the considerable, seemingly comfortable inter-play between working-class whites and blacks, as they labor, eat, and leave work together. What Peter Hutton (see section 8 of this discussion) has said about the photographer Atget is equally true of Rudy Burckhardt: "At first, those images didn't seem to have any great value—they were too familiar— but as time has gone on, they've increased in value. They've become minia-ture museums" (see Hutton interview).

Filmmakers' Cooperative, c/o The Clocktower Gallery, 108 Leonard St., 13 Floor, New York, NY 10013 (212–267–5665; film6000@aol.com; www .film-makerscoop.com [last checked 26 August 2002]): $35.

2. *N.Y., N.Y.* (1957) by Francis Thompson (15 minutes; color); and *Panorama* (1982) by Michael Rudnick (12 1/2 minutes; color)

FRANCIS THOMPSON'S *N.Y., N.Y.* was, well into the 1960s, as widely pop-ular as any American city film has been; and so long as one has a good 16mm print of the film (when renting *N.Y., N.Y.* from the Museum of Modern Art, be sure to ask for a print that has not faded toward red, as older 16mm color prints tend to do), it remains a considerable pleasure. *N.Y., N.Y.,* subtitled *A Day in New York,* presents New York ("New York," here, meaning Manhattan) as a visual phantasmagoria. Using a variety of lenses that shatter, multiply, and bend the city scenes he records, and an upbeat soundtrack composed by Gene Farrell, Thompson captures the wonder and romance of New York and transforms the City Symphony form into jazzy comedy.

With its evocations of such landmarks as the Brooklyn Bridge and Grand Central Station, and apparent allusions to American artists such as Charles Sheeler and Lionel Feininger, *N.Y., N.Y.* seems infused with New York's then-rising importance in the world art scene. Nowhere is this clearer than in Thompson's obvious enjoyment in being able to produce effects at least as wildly experimental as those in the commercial cinema of his era. Even when he seems to provide a visual comment on the downside of modern city life—in, for example, one shattered image of a man reading a newspaper with the headline "Doom!"—the film's visual inventiveness and gorgeous color suggest that, whatever doubts we may have about modern urban life, we might just as well admit that despite its problems, New York is also, for many of us, a wonderful place to visit and live.

MoMA: Circulating Film Program, 11 W. 53rd St., New York, NY 10019 (212–708–9530): $30.

In 1982, Michael Rudnick finished *Panorama,* a depiction of San Francisco that is remarkably close in spirit to *N.Y., N.Y.*—though at the same time it reflects a rough distinction between New York and San Francisco city films: while depictions of New York tend to rely on the composite-day structure that developed in the 1920s, depictions of San Francisco tend to reflect that city's preeminence with the photographic panorama during the late nineteenth century.[2] Over the period of a year, Rudnick filmed the city from in and around his fourth-floor apartment in the Russian Hill area, in time-lapse. The finished film alternates between leftward pans and shots made with a nonmoving camera. Rudnick's apartment offers a variety of vantage points that include both distant events and mini-events going on within the apartment.

The original inspiration for *Panorama* was a comment by Helen Almazán (Rudnick's wife), on returning home at the end of a vacation, that San Francisco was dreary. Rudnick's film was an attempt to rescue his city from this charge; and certainly his panoramic time-lapsing transforms San Francisco and environs into a phantasmagoria of human and meteorological

Distorted automobile in Francis Thompson's *N.Y., N.Y.* (1957).

activity, punctuated with good humor. During the year of filming, Rudnick discovered tiny visual miracles and created jokes within his composi-
tions. The mood of the film is epitomized by a blimp that, as a result of the
time-lapsing, scoots around the sky like a waterbug, accompanied by Rock
Ross's wry, minimal soundtrack. The wacky blimp seems to encapsulate
what Rudnick sees as the Bay Area's energy and high spirits.

Rudnick, 312 Texas St., San Francisco, CA 94107 (415–863–7105): $30.

3. *Castro Street* (1966) by Bruce Baillie (10 minutes)

DURING THE 1960s, Bruce Baillie came to see the Bay Area filmmaking
scene's spirit of place. He was a crucial figure in the development of Canyon
Cinema, at first an exhibition cooperative and subsequently (and still) a distribution cooperative, and his films were widely seen and admired. In his
films and in his comments about them, Baillie often portrayed himself as
a cinematic knight errant, a "holy fool," and his 16mm camera, his sword,
and the resulting films, quests for the Holy Grail of film art. For Baillie the
challenge was to create beauty without ignoring the unattractive realities of
modern life. This is most obvious, perhaps, in *Castro Street*, the film that, he

would claim later, "blew my fuses for life" (Baillie). *Castro Street* is certainly not a conventional city film, and it has nothing to do with Castro Street in San Francisco's Castro District. The Castro Street Baillie filmed is located across the Bay in Richmond, in an industrial area dominated in the 1960s by railroad switchyards and a Standard Oil refinery.

Baillie's quest in *Castro Street* was to come to grips with a set of paradoxes that underlie the relationship of nature and technology in any modern, industrial society. Baillie knew, of course, that San Francisco's reputation as a beautiful city has always depended on the willingness of boosters and tourists to eliminate unattractive sectors of the city from both film and consciousness. Rather than participate in this pattern, Baillie was determined to confront his area's industrial zone, recognizing that without such landscapes, modern cities are inconceivable. By the 1960s, the romance of the industrial had faded, and industrial zones had become "blemishes" on the landscape, visual emblems of this nation's addiction to overconsumption and wastefulness. For Baillie, the quest was to retrieve something of the earlier Romantic pleasure in the industrial, while simultaneously retrieving nature, as an ideal and a reality, from the ravages of modern industrialization.

The resulting film is a hand-crafted, multilayered montage during which we move along both sides of Castro Street (on one side from right to left; on the other, from left to right) simultaneously. The railroad switchyards are imaged in black and white; the refinery, in color. Baillie creates a kaleidoscope of gorgeous texture and color that simultaneously honors tiny spaces of flowers and grasses that grow among the industrial machinery *and* sees various dimensions of industrial structures as evocative of natural forms. As a-natural as the Richmond industrial zone might seem, Baillie suggests that it is a product of nature, not only in the obvious sense—industry is built within nature, exploits natural resources—but in a spiritual sense as well: the same force that grows the flowers has inspired humans to "grow" the material flowers of their imagination. If nature is the physical manifestation of the divine spirit, modern culture—and the industry that sustains it—is the manifestation of the human spirit in the process of emulating divinity. Recognizing this parallel, Baillie implies, provides hope that within the relentless accumulation polemicized by so many, we can recognize the original sources of our power and find new, healthier ways to honor them.

Canyon Cinema, 2325 Third Street, Suite 338, San Francisco, CA 94107 (415–626–2255; films@canyoncinema.com; www.canyoncinema.com [last checked 26 August 2002]): $35.

4. *Walden, Reel 1* (1968) by Jonas Mekas (43 minutes)

WHEN Jonas Mekas and his brother, Adolfas, arrived in New York in 1949—they fled their native Lithuania as the Nazis arrived, were later captured, and spent the late 1940s in a German labor camp—their first important purchase was a 16mm movie camera, with which Jonas Mekas immediately began to document the Lithuanian exile community in Brooklyn. Gradually, he transferred his focus to the developing community of independent film artists (and supporters) that soon became his aesthetic home. Transferring the free-form, Whitman-esque poetic line he had developed in Lithuania (Mekas remains a well-known Lithuanian poet) to an increasingly gestural tactic of moving the camera and exposing frames, Mekas began a filmic quest to recapture the rural life he had loved in his native land within his adopted home, the quintessential modern metropolis.

In 1968, Mekas finished the first of several long films that critics would call "diary films": originally entitled *Diaries Notes & Sketches* (a.k.a. *Walden*), the film has become known simply as *Walden*. *Walden* divides into four sections, the first of which is as good an introduction to Mekas's sensibility as any. Part 1 of *Walden* uses Manhattan as its home base, though it does record trips to upstate New York (to Timothy Leary's home in Millbrook), to New Jersey, and to France (Marseilles, Cassis); it intercuts between visual imagery and diaristic intertitles (both are accompanied by a soundtrack of city sounds, especially the subway; music, often made by Mekas himself; and bits of narration: "I make home movies; therefore I live; I live, therefore I make home movies"). Mekas's frequent juxtaposition of the intertitle, "Walden," with imagery of Central Park, and especially the lake, becomes a motif in *Walden, Part 1* and helps to define his sense of modern life and the relationship of Thoreau to it.

Despite the widespread popular sense that Thoreau lived in the wilderness for two years before writing *Walden,* we know that, in fact, Walden Pond was just outside the important village of Concord, itself quite near a major urban center served by the train that regularly passed by Walden Pond. *Walden* and Thoreau's *Journal* are demonstrations of the complexity and richness of nature close to home and its potential for transforming our day-to-day lives. Mekas's *Walden* goes one step further, by depicting "Walden" *within* urban experience, not only in the sense that Central Park is within the commercial/industrial grid of Manhattan streets, but by visually noting the wide range of ways in which the natural and the urban coexist.

Central Park in Jonas Mekas's *Walden* (1968).

Mekas's *Walden* is full of flowers and bird sounds, sunsets and rainy days—and, most of all, creative people of all ages who, in person and in their art, seem attuned to the particulars of their natural-urban surround. The long, final section of *Walden, Part 1*, "Notes on the Circus," provides a metaphor for the kaleidoscopic visual richness of Mekas's world, and his erratically pixilated, multilayered evocation of the circus reveals a childlike fascination with the overwhelming visual richness of the world that seems closely related to Thoreau's.

Warning: For those first experiencing a Mekas diary, the idiosyncrasies of his style—and especially the "unstable" physicality of his erratic exposure of frames and his camera movement—are nearly always disconcerting, even frustrating. Of course, this style is a radical critique of the conventions of commercial media and its comparatively seamless hard sell.

Film-makers' Cooperative, c/o The Clocktower Gallery, 108 Leonard St., 13 Floor, New York, NY 10013 (212–267–5665; film6000@aol.com; www .film-makerscoop.com [last checked 26 August 2002]): $75.

5. *Symbiopsychotaxiplasm: Take One*
(1972) by William Greaves (75 minutes)

DURING the same year that Mekas was editing *Walden,* William Greaves
was involved in planning and shooting a very different, though equally
remarkable, film that, like *Walden,* used Central Park as a location and as a
crucial metaphor. Unlike Mekas, Greaves did not consider himself an avant-
garde filmmaker. Having established himself in the 1940s and 1950s as an
actor on Broadway, as a songwriter, and as an actor in several Black Underground films, as well as in one of the major "Problem Pictures" of that era
(the "Problem Pictures" were low-budget Hollywood films that focused on
serious social issues), *Lost Boundaries* (1949), Greaves left the States, where
there were no opportunities for fledgling black filmmakers, and moved to
Canada, where he trained to be a documentarian at the National Film Board
of Canada. Returning to New York in the 1960s, Greaves became a productive, relatively conventional documentary filmmaker (and part-time acting
teacher at the Actors' Studio), and by 1969, he had attracted "angel financ-
ing" from a friend and former acting student for any film he desired to
make. The result was one of the more bizarre and interesting experiments
of the era, *Symbiopsychotaxiplasm: Take One.*

The title is Greaves's variation on social theorist Arthur Bentley's "sym-
biotaxiplasm," a term designed to refer to any functioning social organism.
Greaves's addition of "psycho" indicated his interest in focusing on the production process of a film as a social organism with its own particular psychology. Greaves organized a shoot in Central Park and directed his crew
to film not only pairs of actors performing a scene he had written (a man
and a woman argue: she is furious at the abortions he's pressured her into
and his apparent homosexual escapades; he temporizes, pretending that
he's just not ready for a child), but also the crew shooting this scene *and* the
events in the Park surrounding the shoot. Originally, Greaves had planned
to make a series of films, "Takes," but in the end was able to complete only
Take One and that not until 1972.

Symbiopsychotaxiplasm: Take One uses Frederick Olmsted's first great park
as its most basic metaphor. Just as Central Park provides an interruption
in the grid of Manhattan and the urban world of business and commerce,
Symbiopsychotaxiplasm was an interruption in Greaves's career as a commercial documentarian. And just as Central Park was conceived as a space
where New Yorkers of all classes and ethnic groups could escape the rig-

William Greaves during the shooting of
Symbiopsychotaxiplasm: Take One (1968/1972).

ors of the workaday world and experience the salutary effects of nature, Greaves's production process provided an "open" space within which his multi-ethnic, mixed-gender crew and cast (and a variety of bystanders) could collaborate. Of course, Greaves understood his crew would hardly be inclined to feel at ease during the production. He did what he could to loosen his directorial control so that his collaborators could be free in new ways, and in the end he instigated several mini-rebellions, as crew and cast vented their frustrations with Greaves's openness. Further, the film is full of interventions by people visiting the park, including a homeless man whose opening question, "Oh, it's a *movie* . . . so who's moving whom?" cuts to the heart of Greaves's quintessential 1960s film.

Available in 35mm or as VHS only, from Greaves, 230 W. 55th St., New York, NY 10019 (800–874–8314): call for rate.

6. *Zorns Lemma* (1970) by Hollis Frampton (60 minutes)

Even among those familiar with American independent cinema, *Zorns Lemma* is not generally thought of as a film about place, but as a landmark "structural film" (a film in which a radically unconventional structure is the most obvious element), or as a film about epistemology: each of the film's three sections creates a different relationship with the viewer, and these successive relationships reflect the ways we learn. But each section of the film *is* a depiction of place, and the three sections together offer a vision of urban and rural life.

The brief first section (about 2 minutes) presents a reading of alphabetic verses from North America's first English grammar book, *The New England Primer* ("In Adam's fall we sinned all / Thy life to mend God's book attend) and no imagery: the viewer—or really the listener—sits in a darkened room. In the long second section (47 minutes), Frampton presents set after set of alphabetized, environmental words: each word is on-screen for one second, and each set of twenty-four letters (Frampton uses a twenty-four-letter version of the Roman alphabet: i/j and u/v are treated as single letters) is separated from the next by one second of darkness. No sooner does the viewer (this section of the film is silent) become accustomed to the one-image-per-second, alphabetic rhythm than Frampton begins to replace each letter with one-second moments of ongoing processes/actions that we return to, again and again. This section ends once each of the twenty-four letters has been replaced by an ongoing image. During the final section (12 minutes), we watch a man, a woman, and a dog cross a snowy field from the foreground and enter a wood on the far side of the field, in four continuous approximately 3-minute shots, while we hear six female voices read—one word at a time, and one second per word—a passage from Robert Grosseteste's "On Light . . . ," an eleventh-century treatise on the structure of the universe.

The three sections roughly chart Frampton's assumptions about how he (and we) tend to develop as thinking beings.[3] The short first section represents childhood, which for Frampton was a time of intellectual darkness: whatever bits of learning were offered were wrapped in moral or religious instruction. The second section represents, first, the excitement of learning to read and to conceptually access the world (the flood of fifty-eight-words-per-minute creates a verbal phantasmagoria for the viewer) and then the process of coming to understand larger patterns and learning to function practically in the world. The concluding section suggests that a deeper wis-

Word photograph by Hollis Frampton.

dom comes with age and with the attempt to make sense of the nature of existence.

What makes *Zorns Lemma* relevant to this discussion is Frampton's use of location. If the first section locates us in no particular place (Frampton felt that childhood was "nowhere"), the long second section is definitely located in New York City, and specifically in Lower Manhattan and Brooklyn where Frampton lived during the seven years when he was collecting environmental words. Read as a city film, the second part of *Zorns Lemma* suggests that cities are, above all, places where verbal signification is everywhere, where reading controls perception (as Frampton was to say later, "Once we can read, and a word is put before us, we cannot not read it" (Frampton interview 49). For 47 minutes, the hundreds of alphabetized words (and most of the replacement images) imply, and often reveal, city scenes and city activities; and since the series of alphabetized words roughly suggests a daily cycle, this section of *Zorns Lemma* is simultaneously an elaborate exploration of New York and an evocation of the City Symphony form. Indeed, even when, in the final section, Frampton's film arrives in the country, the one-word-per-second reading of the Grosseteste text suggests that the urban experience is so powerful that, even when we leave the city, we cannot leave its relentless rhythms behind.

Replacement image for S in middle section of *Zorns Lemma* (1970).

Few films challenge conventional media viewing, and especially the assumption that experiences of media cannot be intellectually invigorating,
more obviously than *Zorns Lemma*. For this reason it is an exciting film
to work with in the college classroom, especially since it reflects Frampton's impatience with the modern tendency to separate the arts and the
sciences. *Zorns Lemma* is nearly obsessively verbal, but its structure is rigorously mathematical and evokes mathematician Max Zorn's "lemma," the
eleventh axiom of set theory: stated (crudely) in words, the "existential axiom" argues that in any set of sets, there is a further set made up of a comparable instance from each of the previous sets. For those in environmental
studies and other fields dedicated to closing the gap between art and science, Frampton's film is of particular value.

MoMA: Circulating Film Program, 11 W. 53rd St., New York, NY 10019
(212–708–9530): $150.

7. *New York Portrait, Parts 1, 2,* and *3* by Peter Hutton (15 minutes)

FOR MORE THAN a quarter century, Peter Hutton has been making films that resist the seemingly endless acceleration of modern life and modern cinema. Instead of presenting viewers with more and more images to consume, Hutton has dedicated his filmmaking to slowing things down and developing patience, even serenity, in film viewing. The resulting films not only retrain the overstimulated contemporary eye but model a more balanced consciousness outside the movie theater.

Hutton has divided his energies between films that focus more fully on his natural surroundings, the Hudson Valley in New York State (Hutton teaches at Bard College and has made a series of films in homage to the Hudson River School of American painting), and films that focus more fully on urban reality. Hutton's urban films themselves divide between depictions of foreign cities—for example, Budapest, in *Budapest Portrait (Memories of a City)* (1986), and Lodz, Poland, in *Lodz Symphony* (1993)—and New York City, which he depicted first in *New York Near Sleep for Saskia* (1972) and subsequently in a series of *New York Portraits* (*Part 1*, 1979; *Part 2*, 1981; *Part 3*, 1990). For purposes of this brief discussion I'll focus on the first *New York Portrait:* it is both remarkable and typical of the series.

As is true in all his films to date, in *New York Portrait, Part I* Hutton forgoes the use of color, as well as conventional strategies of editing developed during the history of narrative film. *Part I* includes only thirty-two shots (the film is 15 minutes long) and with a few exceptions, each individual shot is divided from the next by a moment of darkness. Indeed, these interruptions are emphasized by Hutton's use of fade-ins and fade-outs. The imagery itself is quite different from most imagery of urban spaces. Hutton is drawn to quiet moments and to details often ignored. While his considerable skill with composition and chiaroscuro renders his imagery quite beautifully (and is often evocative of classic photography and painting), Hutton neither explicitly nor implicitly polemicizes for or against city life. For him, New York is merely another place where one can live and be aware of the experience of light in time, of texture and movement, of the inevitable intersection of technology and nature. In the film's sixth shot, for example, we observe a downtown Manhattan skyline in silhouette, stretching across the bottom of the image; above the buildings is a cloud-filled sky. As happens so often in Hutton's films, the image is so still that, at first, we aren't positive that it's not a photograph. But the extended length of the shot allows us to adjust, so that just as we are about to decide that it *is* a photograph, we realize that the clouds are gradually shifting through the image. Instead of taking the conventional route of locating a moment of "action" within the "world" of the frame, Hutton implicitly locates the space of the frame within the shifting natural forces that determine both the look of the city and the quality of his image.

In recent years I've found no filmmaker simultaneously as unconventional as Hutton and as accessible to general audiences. His films feel like a reprieve from the usual near-hysteria of our lives; and while on one level they feel nostalgic (the length of Hutton's shots and his use of black and white are reminiscent of the earliest motion pictures and particularly of the Lumière Brothers), they are very much a product of the late twentieth century, an interruption of our rhythms of perception and a plea for a more meditative sensibility. The very subtlety of Hutton's films, however, requires excellent screening conditions: a room that can be made quite dark and a projector with good light.

Canyon Cinema, 2325 Third Street, Suite 338, San Francisco, CA 94107 (415–626–2255; films@canyoncinema.com; www.canyoncinema.com [last accessed 26 August 2002]): $30.

8. *Water and Power* (1989) by Pat O'Neill (54 minutes)

It is hardly surprising that the technique of time-lapsing has played an important role in the modern city film. By condensing the time during which urban activities occur, the complex patterns of city life are dramatically revealed. The use of time-lapse for a city film is certainly not new—Dziga Vertov used the technique with remarkable invention in *The Man with a Movie Camera* (1929)—but since the 1960s, it has become so common as to verge on cliché. In her high-spirited depiction of New York, *Go! Go! Go!* (1964), Marie Menken uses time-lapse to miniaturize the city and reduce the City Symphony form to a more human scale. In *Organism* (1975), Hilary Harris uses it to develop a parallel between the human body and the "organism" of the city: time-lapse renders the flow of traffic analogous to the flow of blood in the body. For Harris the city is a macrocosmic version of the body. Both Godfrey Reggio, in *Koyaanisqatsi* (1984), and Peter Von Ziegesar, in *Concern for the City* (1985), are simultaneously fascinated with the intricate urban choreography revealed by time-lapse and frightened by the implications of our ultra-technological urban society. But in his portrait of Los Angeles,

Blimp between skyscrapers in Peter Hutton's *New York Portrait, Part II* (1981).

Water and Power, Pat O'Neill has taken the use of time-lapse one step further than any of these filmmakers, in a film that deconstructs the fundamental dichotomy on which the City Symphony rests: the distinction between city and country.

O'Neill has long been recognized as a master of the optical printer, a device that allows a filmmaker to rephotograph previously filmed imagery and manipulate it in a variety of ways. In *Water and Power* O'Neill combines time-lapsed imagery and optical printing to conflate very disparate spaces: most obviously, modern LA and the Owens Valley, where the Owens Valley aqueduct to LA begins. Indeed, LA's relentless expansion has come at the cost of the Owens Valley (described so beautifully in Mary Austin's *The Land of Little Rain* (1903)): where the water table has been drained so completely as to render the area a new Death Valley. In *Water and Power* we see both places simultaneously—with time-lapse revealing their urban and rural rhythms—as part of the same cinematic image and moment, O'Neill's way of suggesting that in modern city building, the urban and the rural are parts of the same constructive/destructive reality.

Water and Power is a remarkably complex film that works with a variety of conflations of reality—of Los Angeles's past and present, of commercial filmmaking and independent filmmaking, of black-and-white and color—to produce an experience that is simultaneously an engaging visual phantasmagoria *and* a meditation on the possible disaster our ever-more-frenetic urbanization may be leading to. The film's opening image of a man jumping off a bridge colors everything that follows.

Water and Power is available in both 35mm and 16mm. While there is a video version, my experience is that in much conventional video projection, crucial details are lost. When I tried to use a video version in class, the opening suicide, which occurs in extreme long shot, was entirely invisible.

Canyon Cinema, 2325 Third Street, Suite 338, San Francisco, CA 94107 (415–626–2255; films@canyoncinema.com; www.canyoncinema.com [last accessed 26 August 2002]): $150.

9. *Side/Walk/Shuttle* (1991) by Ernie Gehr (41 minutes)

ERNIE GEHR has established himself as one of avant-garde cinema's most inventive magicians, often using his filmmaking as a means of discovering the unused cinematic potential in the aspects of film we take most for granted. The most remarkable instance in recent years is his *Side/Walk/ Shuttle*, a film that ignores perhaps film's most consistent visual convention: that the film frame must replicate our usual way of thinking about and depicting up, down, left, and right. In nearly all film (as in nearly all painting and photography), the top edge of the frame is assumed to be synonymous with up, the bottom of the frame with down, the left and right edges with left and right. Using San Francisco as his topic, Gehr decided to see what he could reveal about us as spectators and about his experience of living in San Francisco by not adhering to this convention: that is, by seeing the film frame as a means for reframing our sense of sight both inside and outside the theater.

Gehr took his inspiration from another San Francisco artist whose exploration of how we see changed the world and helped to instigate film history: the photographer Eadweard Muybridge. Before he became famous for his motion study photographs, which analyzed motion into photographic components, and his Zoopraxiscope, which resynthesized the components of motion into the illusion of motion (the Zoopraxiscope was a crucial step in the development of the movie projector), Muybridge had distinguished

Los Angeles as surreal city in Pat O'Neill's *Water and Power* (1989).

himself as a photographer of nature and Native peoples and as the preeminent maker of panoramic photographs: his large panoramic photographs of San Francisco remain the most notable instances of the form. For *Side/Walk/Shuttle* Gehr filmed on Nob Hill, the site of the Muybridge panoramas—specifically from an elevator on the outside of the Fairmont Hotel, as it moved up and down the building. But instead of restricting his view to the usual panorama of the city visible from the elevator, Gehr composed his successive extended shots of his trips in the elevator (each shot is as long as an uninterrupted elevator trip up or down the Hotel) so as to reveal the remarkable variety in the ways in which his camera could represent this one scene.

While a few early shots reveal San Francisco in a more or less conventional way, as the elevator climbs high enough to reveal Coit's Tower, the Embarcadero, and the harbor, Gehr's inventive framing continually alters the way we see the view from the elevator, so that later shots create first mystery, then disorientation. By the final third of *Side/Walk/Shuttle*, buildings seem to fall slowly from the sky, and viewers seem to have entered a filmic universe where there is no clear up and down, left and right, and

Time-lapsed person against backdrop of Owens
Valley in O'Neill's *Water and Power* (1989).

where even an apartment building we have seen over and over seems to be
an entirely new structure. While Gehr has spent most of his life in cities, especially New York and San Francisco, he continues to experience the kinds
of disorientation the modern city can create for newcomers; and for a San
Francisco resident, the precariousness of urban life seems particularly evident, since earthquakes or, in the fantasies of some, Divine Retribution *could*
cause buildings to fall from the sky.

Gehr's new form of panoramic photography is accompanied by a form
of auditory panorama. While some of his trips up and down the elevator are
silent, others are accompanied by a variety of sounds, recorded at various
times in various cities: in Grand Central Station in New York, in Geneva,
Switzerland; in Venice, London, and Berlin. These sounds reflect a lifetime
of travel and the frequent disorientation that comes with living in one place
amid powerful memories of others.

All in all, the experience of *Side/Walk/Shuttle* is more remarkable than
any brief description can suggest, and this experience reminds us that the
velocity of urban development during the past century has forced all of us

to continually rethink our relation to history and to the larger society of which we are part. Since the nature of the life around us is always evolving, we are never still either; we are always in motion, though the direction of this motion remains fundamentally ambiguous. Our lives are continually turned upside down.

Canyon Cinema, 2325 Third Street, Suite 338, San Francisco, CA 94107 (415–626–2255; films@canyoncinema.com; www.canyoncinema.com [last accessed 26 August 2002]): $35.

10. *Weegee's New York* (195?) by Weegee (Arthur Fellig) (21 minutes)

WHILE the other films included in my listing are presented in the order of their completion, I am ending with *Weegee's New York*, which was shot before any of the other films listed, in order to draw attention to a crisis facing the entire field of avant-garde cinema. Because these films are rented so infrequently, compared to major and minor works in the other arenas of film history, even by those who might profit the most (in their teaching, in their research, in their pleasure) from screening them, new prints are not struck, and the remaining prints of some films sometimes show considerable wear and tear. And because the academic film establishment seems to have concluded that presenting "films" using newer technologies—video, DVD, laser disk—is more cost effective than renting, or buying and maintaining, 16mm prints, those academic libraries that were developed during recent decades are closing down, and the few remaining prints of some landmark films sometimes fall out of distribution altogether. This is what has happened to *Weegee's New York*, as remarkable a film as any I've discussed here and probably more influential than any of them. For a time, an excellent print of the film was available from the University of Minnesota; but recently Minnesota closed down their 16mm distribution collection, and I have not been able to find a print anywhere else. Remember, when you rent the films discussed in this listing, you help to keep this remarkable cinematic world alive and help assure that the next generation will have access to it as well.

The completion date of *Weegee's New York* remains ambiguous since the details of its production are uncertain. What seems clear is that during the late 1940s or early 1950s Weegee filmed a number of kinds of New York City imagery; and when Amos Vogel, director of Cinema 16 (the New York Film Society; Weegee was a member), decided he wanted to present Weegee's

New York imagery, he edited the film into its current shape. *Weegee's New York* begins with a 7 1/2-minute section called "New York Fantasy" in which we see imagery of the Manhattan skyline, Times Square, and New York harbor in a variety of expressionistic styles, such as time-lapse and shooting through a lens that creates a blurred multiple image. The beautiful, even Romantic, imagery of "New York Fantasy" is followed by "Coney Island," which is Weegee at his witty, photographically invasive best. This 13 1/2-minute section provides color imagery of sunbathers, lovers, walkers, swimmers of a wide range of ethnicities negotiating a remarkably crowded beach, all accompanied by popular records of the era. Even more fully than the skinny-dipping sequence of *Under the Brooklyn Bridge*, Weegee's "Coney Island" reveals people seemingly at ease with their bodies, even at times under the persistent gaze of the camera. It is as if these New Yorkers understood what most of us have forgotten: that a holiday should be not only freedom from work, but also freedom from the necessity of maintaining media-constructed models of correct physical appearance. As politically and morally uptight as we imagine the 1950s to have been, Weegee reveals and celebrates a society that comes to life precisely when it is not being "productive"—a people who seem to have little interest in what others think of them.

NOTES

1. William Urrichio discusses several early American City Symphonies in "The City Viewed: The Film of Leyda, Browning and Weinberg."

2. For a history of the photographic panorama in San Francisco, see Peter B. Halls, *Silver Cities*.

3. Frampton discusses the structure of *Zorns Lemma* in my interview with him.

REFERENCES

Baillie, Bruce. Interview by author. *A Critical Cinema 2: Interviews with Independent Filmmakers*. Berkeley: U of California P, 1992. 109–38.

Frampton, Hollis. Interview by author. *A Critical Cinema: Interviews with Independent Filmmakers*. Berkeley: U of California P, 1989. 48–60.

Halls, Peter B. *Silver Cities: The Photography of American Urbanization, 1839–1915*. Philadelphia: Temple UP, 1984. 41–82.

Horak, Jan-Christopher. "Paul Strand: Romantic Modernist." *Making Images Move: Photographers and Avant-Garde Cinema*. Washington, D.C.: Smithsonian Institution Press, 1997. 79–97.

Hutton, Peter. Interview by author. *A Critical Cinema 3: Interviews with Independent Filmmakers*. Berkeley: U of California P, 1998. 249.

MacDonald, Scott. "The City as the Country: The New York City Symphony, from Rudy Burckhardt to Spike Lee." *Film Quarterly* 51.2 (1997–98): 2–20.

Urrichio, William. "The City Viewed: The Film of Leyda, Browning and Weinberg." *Lovers of Cinema: The First American Film Avant-Garde, 1919–1945.* Ed. Jan-Christopher Horak. Madison: U of Wisconsin P, 1995. 287–314.

PART 3

New Theoretical and Practical Paradigms

Literary Activism and the Bioregional Agenda

Activists will continue to press for Congressional term limits.
Unfortunately, academe has contributed little to the debate.
Chronicle of Higher Education, 28 April 1995

PRACTITIONERS of the Foxfire approach to education say that students whose work gains purpose learn the most. Apprehending the products of scholastic endeavors makes a difference in the way the learning process itself proceeds. The proverbial paper chase and the appeal of good grades rarely prove satisfying goals in themselves. But factor in a practical consequence to those same academic exercises, add an element of instrumentality, and the learning game gains elevated stakes. Foxfire founder Eliot Wigginton, when teaching high school in the Appalachian Mountains of northern Georgia in 1966, set out to invigorate his classrooms by dispatching his students into the community to gather information on folkways and folklore, crafts and arts, material culture and religious experience, all of which students collected into *Foxfire,* a quarterly magazine that was eventually printed in a series of illustrated commercial anthologies. As bioregionalist Kirkpatrick Sale has remarked of those early scholarly efforts, "Though not every place has kept its history properly alive, a fountain of information still exists if we will but tap it—as shown, for example, in the wonderful Foxfire books, the recent collections of Indian lore, and many other projects of oral history and folk knowledge" (45).

For those Foxfire students in Georgia, printing research and preserving knowledge gave their education meaning. Doubleday published the results of their labors in 1972 and sold millions of copies. For adult writers, however, the process and product of research and publication may be less fulfilling. As much as we may believe in the value of conducting scholarly dialogs, of advancing knowledge and offering new perspectives, a misgiving may begin to gnaw—that most professors win grants, deliver papers, and write articles and books chiefly to gain tenure and promotion. As much as we may underscore for student writers the value and necessity of the writing process, we still privilege the product in our writing careers more than we admit, still value destinations more than the journeys by which we get there. And even if we can agree that research and publication are inherently worthwhile, we may continue to wonder whether we are lured by the bait of fame, say, or by that elusive "disinterest" Matthew Arnold named the sine qua non of the highest scholarly criticism. Neither goal is sufficient in itself. Nor do the rewards of the tenure and promotion system always prove sufficient compensation. What is disparaged today as political correctness is in fact a sign that scholars are finding the relative inconsequentiality of much conventional research to be stifling and daunting. One key to getting beyond PC is to forge past narrow academic confines.

Bioregionalism may be broadly defined as the process of rediscovering human connections to the land. Although learning the lore implies the study of humanity's interpenetrations and interpretations of nature, Alexander Pope's injunction that "the proper study of mankind is man" must be rejected. The study of humankind cannot be conducted separately from the biological processes that nourish us and that have allowed us to become the dominant species. All of us can walk the fields and forests of the particular regions we inhabit, learn to name flowers and identify bird songs, gain a sense of how the snowbanks melt into the streams that become the river. The range of temperatures, the yearly precipitation, the creatures and species of the wild, the impacts of our own kind on the region—these details form the foundation of the sustainable culture that is the ultimate goal of bioregionalism. As it applies to the study of American literature, too, bioregionalism becomes a useful critical orientation insofar as it informs the mass of writing tied so intimately to nature, writing by people as varied as Anne Bradstreet and Gretel Ehrlich, Thomas Jefferson and Robinson Jeffers, Mark Twain and Willa Cather, as well as naturalists like Josselyn, Bartram, Audubon, and Muir. Admittedly, such an approach would have scarce bearing on the likes of Henry James, Edith Wharton, and many of the postmodernists, alienated by the natural world or, at the very least, separated from its embrace.

Sociologists say altruism ranks among the highest designs of humankind, near the pinnacle of the supposed hierarchy of needs. If this is so, then reason tells us that scholars in the arts and letters need to conduct research that actually can effect change. Injustice is a menace even in the ivory tower. Yet we seem to suffer a rhetorical deficit, a vagueness of purpose. The most accomplished writing in other professions not only informs the unaware and prepares the uninitiated, not only renders an affective function and influences opinion, but also seeks to accomplish something hard and fast. It matters. Part of the anguish of John Berryman's poetic persona, Henry, arises from his belief that his works and days bear few consequences. The great literature he reads bores him, his friends bore him, "the tranquil hills, & gin look like a drag" (16). Once he publishes a book, he waits expectantly but can say nothing more about it than "no harm resulted from this" (82). Nor should it come as a surprise that unhappy Henry's author, feeling out of touch and ineffectual in his society, took his own life in 1972.

One of Berryman's younger peers, Robert Bly, prompts clever chuckles in some circles for his book *Iron John* and his work in the men's movement, chuckles that demonstrate how writing meant to render some social change is decried, twisted, misunderstood. (Foxfire founder Wigginton's name likewise has been blighted by the news of his seducing students.) Bly was a prominent poet and critic in the 1960s and 1970s, a champion of the Deep Image school of poetry, one of the few canonized writers to infuse his work with political opinions. Learning from the poetic practices of European and South American artists, he practiced a free verse that decried U.S. involvement in the Vietnam War. And in a series of essays, notably "Leaping Up into Political Poetry," he promoted a heightened awareness and a poetics of commitment that countered most canonized efforts in American letters. Bly argued that a "husk" had grown around the best impulses in the American psyche, and that those impulses require social outlets; but "the friction of the civil rights movement and the Vietnam War have worn the husk thin in a couple of places now" (246). A new swiftness and intensity is needed, Bly insisted, that would draw upon Whitman's critiques of the Civil War, Thoreau's objections to the Mexican War, and the scope of history that informs Ezra Pound's *Cantos.*

The politics of the 1960s charged American scholarship—as interest in matters of race, class, and gender still attest. Scholars have appropriated the tools of the social sciences and skillfully applied them in the letters and the arts. We still pay too much attention to scholarly audiences, though, attention that limits our rhetorical resources and stunts the written word's potential to engender much-needed change. In "Trading on the Margin: Notes on the Culture of Criticism," Henry Louis Gates Jr. comments on the enervation possessing contemporary critics: "that it's mostly make-believe, that the brilliant Althusserian unmasking of the ideological apparatus of film editing you published in *October* won't even change the way Jon Peters

or Mike Ovitz treats his secretary, let alone bring down the house of patriarchy" (181).

And he is right. So much well-intended scholarly writing lacks a realistic
purpose, lacks luster. It is not reaching the readers who need most to hear
and heed its message. Standard academic journals too often become the
chief targets of learned discourse. Writers accordingly continue to preach to
the converted and to overlook the most salient and essential questions. In
these pages I propose a middle course between the demands of the academy
and the needs of the American psyche as Bly defined them. In doing so I
address not only scholarly writers but also poets, not only essayists but also
novelists and playwrights, all of whom may influence those administrators
charged with evaluating faculty performance.

THE OPENING EXAMPLE of the Foxfire teaching method is not a gratuitous analogy. The deep engagement of Foxfire pupils, the student-centered
learning, the student role in shaping curricula, and above all the practical
consequences of the work itself serve as paradigm for what may be called a
literary activism, by which I intend all advocacy scholarship. In the case of
the early Foxfire students, the purpose was not only to inform and motivate
readers but also to preserve ancient and traditional forms of knowledge and
thereby to weaken the powerful grasp of technology in contemporary life.
It was a revolutionary agenda, a quiet one that practiced bioregionalism
before the term came into currency.

Some of the great stigmas Whitman and Thoreau, Pound and Bly, suffered in their time are sure to distort the ideas of scholars like Kirkpatrick
Sale who sanction bioregionalism. Sale and others promote a scholarship of
advocacy, a literary activism. Not content merely to delineate his topic, Sale
passionately advances the bioregional vision in books that range through
sociology and economics, history and mythology, literature and science.
Key to this philosophical agenda is "learning the lore" of the bioregions
we inhabit, Sale insists, which forms a first step toward altering society as a
whole. Yet interdisciplinary scholarly approaches, however highly touted,
are more conspicuous in lip service than in practice, more observed in the
breach than in actuality. If such allegiance were sincere, bioregionalism
would offer a tool to offset the trajectory of postmodernism on the one hand
and the wide-eyed reverence of much American nature writing on the other.
From the bioregional vision, a muscular literary activism can result, one as
useful for belles lettres as for scholarship, as pertinent to scholarly reader-
ships as to the needs of government managers and the public at large.

The tools of the colonial historian and cultural critic are especially valuable in understanding bioregionalism. Imperialism—ecological as well as social—has become an ongoing pattern in America. Just as the Native Americans were crushed and overrun, wild species are reeling from the impacts of overharvesting, habitat eradication, and pollution. Native languages, indigenous as well as immigrant, originally spoken in distinct regions have been obliterated and the speakers forced to adapt to centralized and homogeneous standards; diverse forms of religion, a great cultural wealth, are stymied. As David McCloskey has noted, the latest phase is the decline of vitality of our city centers and hometowns, the depopulation of most rural areas, and a slow but steady urban sprawl that detaches people further from the Earth (3–4). Just as subjugation of nature involves the domination of people, subjugation of peoples involves domination of nature. Flora, fauna, and people all suffer when a place is plundered. The resulting loss of diversity and vitality produces a double displacement, both natural and human, under an industrial global monoculture (7–8). Gary Snyder, a prominent spokesman for the movement, has defined bioregionalism as "the entry of place into the dialectic of history" (41)—the poet's vote of confidence for the historian's long view.

Ecologies and communities are two banks of the same stream. Having been lost together, they can also be restored together. Such a hope is central to the bioregional project of helping to seed new "ecocultures" of peoples who know, love, and care for their lands. If the basic problem is displacement, one answer is reinhabitation of our bioregions. Again, with a poet's beguiling simplicity, Gary Snyder would remind us, "To know the spirit of a place is to realize that you are a part of a part and that the whole is made of parts, each of which is whole. You start with the part you are whole in" (38). Bioregionalism, then, aspires to replace arbitrary political jurisdictions with integrated native regions; to allow watersheds, ecoregions, and larger bioregions to become the basis of analysis, planning, and resource management. Scientifically, bioregionalism would join ecology to anthropology through geography by linking ecosystem, region, and culture. And from a sociological perspective, bioregionalism would generate a fresh social bond, one that would annul the ties of both ethnicity and bureaucracy. Politicians and political scientists like Frank Bryan and John McClaughry in Vermont are realizing how efficiently decentralized state governments can function. Such a new regionalism does not advocate a return to tribalism, nor does it reinforce provincialism. Rather, it calls for a new kind of ecocultural bond that is deeply rooted in the place itself.

My bioregion is known as the Palouse, a high area of rolling hills and fertile soil that encompasses two watersheds, one flowing west across the Columbia Plateau, the other south to the confluence of the Snake and Clearwater Rivers, both ultimately draining into the Columbia River and west to the Pacific. The rainfall is slight, snowpacks heavy, winters long, winds high, summers often sudden, dusty, short. The bunchgrasses indigenous to the region, along with lupine and paintbrush, penstemon and ponderosa pines, created rich diversity for species now extirpated—gray wolf and grizzly bear, caribou and wolverine, sharptail grouse and prairie chicken. The native grasses have been all but supplanted by exotic invaders, human-introduced, including cheatgrass in the early 1900s and yellow star thistle in the 1980s. Wheat and peas and lentils, crops on which the economy relies, blanket the hills. As timber prices rise, logging proceeds at a rapid pace; as more dams impede the wild streams, salmon species fail; as farmers rely increasingly on chemical inputs to maintain crop yields, the soil of the region grows less stable and the waters less clear. But this litany of losses does not enervate the hopefulness of local activists; it does not overtop the optimistic and tenacious spirit of community. A tangible connectedness binds human inhabitants to one another and to the land, a bond that prompts a tacit satisfaction when bull moose wander into town, when wild onions and morel mushrooms become ripe.

THERE ARE tight connections between bioregionalism and literary local color, known also as sectionalism or regionalism. American writers who identify closely with a geographical locale have historically endured the critical onus of provincialism, an onus grounded in insecurities that stem from comparisons to European culture. No one should forget how William Faulkner, irredeemably identified with rural Mississippi, had to struggle in relative obscurity for the first decades of his career. It took a Malcolm Cowley to persuade readers to look beyond Faulkner's regional setting to the universal themes that energize his work. Inherited wisdom still confers the belief that the chief features of regional literature include attention to the speech, manners, dress, dialect, and folkways of given geographical sections of the country. Yet readers who exercise due sensitivity to the finer dimensions of literary regionalism find that its focus on the more antique and outmoded forms of knowledge recommends it. Herbalism, today considered separately as botany and medicine, sprang from the study of the species of a given region. Herbalism is one example of ways of knowing—often ignored by the study of belles lettres—that flourish in local color fiction. Regionalism offers abundant reminders that attending to "philosophy" in previous centuries meant reading all the physical sciences.

Approaching American literature bioregionally allows us to sift our indigenous from our derivative cultures, our grassroots themes and motifs from the European inheritance, a task scarcely begun. Richard Dorson wrote surveys of early American lore—*Jonathan Draws the Longbow* and *America Begins*—but few literary critics have seen fit to reference these valuable resources. Bioregionalism legitimizes such studies and investigates the ecological values and biological currents that run through so much American literature written before widespread urbanization. (Urban dwellers, likewise, need to know that they rely on the countryside for many resources and can also act according to a bioregional vision.) To read American letters through varied strains of popular religion—prodigies, portents, supernatural wonders, myths, and lore—is to help level the social classes, to intermix the highbrow and the lowbrow, and to generate more comprehensive portraits of the periods. Just as essential for the bioregional approach, however, as novelist Thomas Hardy knew so well, is how mythic constructs reveal an intimate knowledge of place that owes no allegiance to the more conventional forms of wisdom inherited from other cultures and countries.

Colonialist David D. Hall identifies a "lay tribalism" (156) that underlies the more salient and famous Puritanism, one that springs from intimate affiliations with locale. The sickness of souls, the war Satan wages against Christ, the providence God offers righteous men and women, these are placeless themes. But the unique dynamics of Congregationalism in New England also lent themselves to the growth of "cunning folk," as they became widely known—indigenous herbalists and wizards ostracized from dominant Christian circles. Young Goodman Brown of Nathaniel Hawthorne's famous tale undergoes his ordeal because the belief system of his community suggested it, because community culture had sown the seeds of his malaise. And everyone remembers the way that most memorable of literary cunning folk, Roger Chillingworth of *The Scarlet Letter*, uses his potent herbs and elixirs to poison the Reverend Arthur Dimmesdale. But scholars can look further than fiction for examples. The life of American diarist and midwife Martha Ballard, read and presented in a Pulitzer Prize–winning book by Laurel Thatcher Ulrich, shows how a cunning woman integrated with the early national folk culture of New England.

Just as Antaeus relied upon keeping feet firmly planted on the Earth to gain his power, so folk cultures remain most vital when their bioregional origins continue intact. The religious schisms that beset the seventeenth century may be understood in part as dictates imposed from outside the bioregions, exotic dogmas of continental origin. Jonathan Edwards, preaching and writing in the more rational eighteenth century, understood the threat of lay tribalism and tried to arrest it by personifying a deity whose potential for wrath—overshadowing the powers of nature and place—would briefly succeed in recapturing the sway that popular religion had come so near usurping. Never mind how sensational these early spiritual quests may sound to modern sensibilities; they are the stuff of which our most vivid early literature is made. Sarah Orne Jewett's solitary souls in rural Maine owe much to their indigenous literary ancestry. Brockden Brown, Poe, and Melville created psychic dramas whose ties to bioregional roots have been unrecognized or neglected.

In a deceptively simple book of essays that includes "The Regional Motive," Wendell Berry explored bioregionalism before the term came into being. The Kentucky farmer and poet, writing in the wake of a supposedly reactionary agrarianism, may be said to have first given bioregionalism shape as it is today. Berry found "regionalism" in 1972 "a term [that] very quickly becomes an embarrassment or an obstruction." More than just diminutive in usage, the word for Berry can carry the negative freight of both nationalism—insular and patriotic—and of condescension, "which specializes in the quaint and the picturesque, and which behaves in general like an exploitive industry" (63). This is an especially pertinent comparison, given bioregionalism's intimate relationship with the environmental movement today. Berry's environmental bent is evident throughout but is compounded with an insistence that "local life is intricately dependent, for its quality but also for its continuance, upon local knowledge" (67). "The Regional Motive" accordingly celebrates the correspondence of human beings with biological processes, and it would remedy the sad fact that "the history of the white man's life on this continent has been to an alarming extent the history of the waste and exhaustion and degradation of the land" (63).

To moderate this historical trajectory, bioregionalism explores numerous routes to sustainability—that is, routes to sustain both agriculture and human culture. Less a theoretical construct imposed from afar than a delineation of human cultures as they clash or mesh with biological cultures, it seeks to perpetuate the natural processes on which our economies rely and to reach a steady-state cultural balance that can likewise be sustained. This breed of ecological criticism would use bioregionalism as the vehicle to drive toward the key goals of establishing a useful cultural criticism, reinvigorating the merit of scholarship, and practicing an ethics of responsible activism.

WRITERS of belles lettres increasingly are putting their talents to work toward activist ends. Gary Snyder's reading tours in the 1980s sometimes perplexed audiences who expected poetry but instead got lectures promoting bioregional principles. Terry Tempest Williams, a scientist by training, has turned to highly emotional writings and readings that explore alternatives to human dominations of the land. Before their recent deaths, Wallace Stegner and Edward Abbey crafted novels and essays that are as political as they are artistic in advocating the preservation of the wild. These writers all write from the West, a measure not only of the heated battles over environmental issues but also of the importance of wild spaces to the western imagination. Insofar as writing constitutes an activism when it is wielded to effect political change, evidence of literary activism in the West is rife. Not content merely to inform or influence, the bioregional writer derives creative energy from what is widely known as *"praxis*, the union of philosophy and activism" (Scarce, 32), a union not limited to radical actions. Such a union is essential. If philosophy that lacks a complementary impulse toward activism characterizes most impotent scholarly writing in the arts and letters, then the impulse toward activism without a basis in concrete philosophy can degenerate into polemic or anarchy.

Initiating a large departure in American nature writing, Rick Bass, author of *Oil Notes* and *The Ninemile Wolves*, set aside a career as a petroleum engineer and moved to Montana to devote himself to full-time writing on nature and the environment. In "20515 House, 20510 Senate," he articulates both the literary tensions and the activist passions that are combining in so many American writers. The title of Bass's essay offers a mnemonic for folks who want to know the zip codes for the addresses of Congress. Bass first characterizes the conflicting demands of politics and art, then hits upon a metaphor that crystallizes the key issues: "Suppose you are given a bucket of water. You're standing there holding it. Your home's on fire. Will you pour the cool water over the flames or will you sit there and write a poem about it?" Affective and instrumental ends conflict; art pulls the writer one way, practical duty another. The bucket of water may be construed as the writer's talent; the house afire is environmental degradation; the courses of action divide between politics and art. Bass follows with a passionate plea to lovers of nature writing to take the steps necessary to save Montana's Yaak Valley bioregion—"a sanctuary, a harbor, for wild things, and for diversity" (4)—and in so doing to assure that nature writers continue to enjoy the bioregions on which the art relies.

Just as a bucket of water is a feeble way to thwart a house afire, a single letter to Congress may seem futile beside the efforts of Washington lobbyists paid by special interests. The momentum of national politics often appears too imposing; the writer or would-be activist feels ineffectual and defeated from the start. But talented writers and speakers and organizers need not stop at a letter to Congress or even a letters campaign. In 1906, Upton Sinclair spurred the federal government to enact the Pure Food and Drug Act when he investigated the American meat-packing industry with his novel *The Jungle*. The values of literary activism, using bioregional approaches, include an ability to have an impact on wide audiences with well-placed books or articles; the opportunity to practice truly interdisciplinary forms of writing and research, not only within disciplines but across the genres; and the inherent rewards of altruistic efforts that can bring about social change. The bioregional agenda does not insist that environmental activism is more worthy in itself than activism for human rights, say, but it does insist that the subjugation of nature always involves domination of people, and the subjugation of peoples involves the domination of nature.

Scholar-critics are well adapted to oppose spoken and written mandates of government officers who undercut some bioregional efforts. Documents generated by out-of-touch civil servants who are ineffectually safeguarding the public trust can be obtained and read using the same critical skills we use to read literature. Environmental impact statements, offers of timber sales on public lands, state water appropriations bills, bids on livestock-grazing allotments, and proposed legislation of all sorts are publicly available and often subject to public appeal. Erik Ryberg of the Ecology Center at the University of Montana, now stationed in McCall, Idaho, received graduate training in English and has successfully appealed a number of grazing-allotment renewals; he insists such documents are "easily deconstructed." Combining critical discernment and bioregional knowledge learned first-hand from knowing the land, literary activists can offer perspectives on key issues that involve the well-being of all living creatures.

Participation in the democracy is at stake. With political apathy high and voter turnouts low, civil servants welcome public participation. The most vocal players involved in the democratic process today—members of the so-called wise-use movement—often have the greatest economic interests at stake and thus constitute an alarmingly partial point of view. Moreover, the most active participants sometimes also represent absentee interests—investors from outside the state or region who are apt to care less for the land than do those who live on it. Many land managers welcome public input and are sensitive to the concerns of environmentalists and bioregionalists—as the advent of the three-thousand-member Association of Forest Service Employees for Environmental Ethics attests—yet their hands often are tied by organizational superiors and by a hidebound tradition of business as usual. The would-be appellant or activist need not be versed in matters scientific or political to succeed; language is the vehicle by which most governmental officials conduct business, and language is subject to scrutiny and interpretation, as everybody knows. Hidden motives of the writer(s), undue solicitude to special interests, lapses and lacunae in the arguments: the critical eye can discern such irregularities as these and refute them. Praxis, the union of philosophy and activism, can afford the authority and urgency required to effect change.

In the following case study, I try to demonstrate these principles by deconstructing a document generated by the U.S. Forest Service (USFS). To constitute a fully bioregional study, of course, the discussion also would have to address the varied needs of Native Americans to maintain their cultural continuity and spirituality that rely upon intact ecosystems and bioregions, a task I am now undertaking through conversations with the Colville Tribe. Again, subjugation of nature always involves the subjugation of peoples.

HORSESHOE BASIN is a high meadow on the extreme east side of the Pasayten Wilderness, part of the Okanogan National Forest (ONF), a popular recreation area in the North Cascades of Washington State. Legends tell of stirrup-high bunchgrasses that once flourished here and throughout the Pasayten, grasses now supplanted by ankle-high sod grasses and other weedy species. Water filtration has been severely curtailed, the dirt pounded for years by thousands of hooves. Each summer some 1,200 sheep feed through the area as part of a grazing allotment. Associated ecological impacts of livestock grazing in the North Cascades—impacts surely not unique to the region—include high elevations and correspondingly short growing seasons, the close proximity of mining claims and grazing allotments, and the problem of hungry livestock grazing on "erosion control seedings," that is, on trees and grasses that are planted at taxpayer expense to diminish other ecological damages incurred by extractive industries.

In the checkerboard of state lands, federal lands, parks, and private inholdings that constitute the North Cascades, the ONF attempts to support about seventy-five separate grazing allotments, some founded before the turn of the century, many around the time of the Great Depression, others as late as 1973. These allotments are forced to carry the weight of more than 14,000 animals, of which 11,756 are cattle. Range elevations vary from 2,500 to as high as 7,000 feet, and ONF maps demonstrate how very much of the forest is covered by livestock during the grazing season, usually 1 June to 15 October, and how many allotments directly abut one another, even in fragile alpine sections. Short growing seasons, combined with relatively long grazing seasons, pose a grave danger to the overall health of the bioregion.

Area management plans reveal the high priority given to livestock interests. Passages in the unpublished and unpaginated ONF grazing report show how land managers often defer to a vocal constituency of cattlemen and miners. The agency "can not legally authorize grazing" on patented mining claims, it claims, for these are "classed private land." The report also notes, without any evidence of irony, that inactive mining claims above the Methow Valley "are situated on the steep south slope" and thus "do not have any significant impact on livestock grazing," as if mining claims might infringe on grazing privileges, whether or not such claims were on slopes too steep for stock to travel. The language reminds us that the acronym DNS, standing for "demonstration of non-significance," may be used to appease a variety of commodity-based interest groups competing for public lands resources.

But commodity-based uses of the bioregion are not always competitive and antagonistic, as the following passage shows: "Logging roads and skid trails have made additional feed areas accessible for grazing." That is, access roads and trails constructed to facilitate logging, inevitably damaging to wildlife populations and migrations, furnish forage sites for grazing cattle. What emerges from such observations is evidence of a sort of symbiotic relationship between logging and ranching. Both loggers and grazing permittees benefit from USFS roads that open up and scar the wilderness. Moreover, of course, logged tracts increase light available for growing plants and thus increase the forage available to cattle and sheep. In the North Cascades, as in much of the West, the Bureau of Land Management (BLM) and the USFS often are forced to mediate between competing claims of livestock and logging interests, the most vocal champions of our much-abused public "land of multiple uses."

In a faint concession to critics of public grazing, ONF officials try to encourage grazing permittees to vary "turn-on locations," that is, the sites at which livestock are released or "turned on" to allotments each spring.

Not only are herds most evident at these sites, but damage to stream banks and vegetation is most conspicuous. Resource management again becomes a game of appearances, played by means of ruses, like the screen of trees left standing between a highway and a clear-cut forest, a trick that logging companies in the Pacific Northwest are learning with the hired help of landscape architects. If campers, hunters, and such "multiple-use beneficiaries" do not witness the damage sheep and cattle cause in wilderness, then for all practical purposes no damage has occurred, and Old West ways can continue unabated. Grazing seasons terminate just prior to the opening day of the state general hunting season, mid-October, a date that means cows must be out before hunters encounter them and grow suspicious that livestock compete for forage against game animals. Most fauna in the West—deer, elk, black bear, and grouse, for instance—cannot live well in livestock-larded habitat (Jacobs, 292–305).

But the most telling abuse of grazing privileges in the Okanogan bioregion is that scientists have been forced to serve cowboy functions. Grazing pressures on sensitive riparian zones in the ONF formerly were thwarted by state or federal employees "riding" herds of private livestock to disperse them—an absurd image and a scandalous use of public funds. Riding herds keeps them from bunching up and inflicting too much damage to the land. However, managers recently have advised permittees to begin "doing their own riding. The cattle need to be kept well dispersed especially out of plantations and out of riparian zones, off the main roads particularly in the fall when they bunch up against cattleguards." Again, appearances are foremost. The authors of the report do not detail what environmental damages might occur; merely, they advise owners to ride herds because other users of the public land might object to cattle defecating in streams and congesting busy roads.

The land seems to be developing mechanisms to defend itself. Grazing permittees, range science specialists, and USFS employees alike have been chagrined to witness the proliferation and migration of poisonous and spiny varieties of weedy species like Russian and star thistles, halogeton, white top, tansy ragwort, and knapweed. Some of these exotic species, which often compete with or prey on native species, ironically also prove toxic to the domestic animals that help to spread them. How do officials choose to deal with incursions of such plants? In heavily infested areas, the weeds are mowed and burned so seeds will not generate new plants; in other districts, herbicides are sprayed, much to the jeopardy of the bioregion at large; and in some districts, including parts of the North Cascades, noxious weeds are pulled by hand. The image is absurd—a government-hired laborer or scientist on public lands, bending over or falling to hands and knees to uproot weeds, his salary paid by tax dollars, his energy expended for the welfare of cattle ranchers and their herds first responsible for the spread of the weeds (Devine 44).

Sheep and cattle barons in the Old West fought range wars over pasture lands and waterways, real estate and market shares. But stakes in the New West have changed, and range wars now rage over issues like the preservation of native wildlife habitats and biological diversity. The combatants include not only ranchers who graze their herds on public lands but critics armed with the latest data from conservation biology and economics. One of the largest unbroken wildernesses in the lower forty-eight states, the North Cascades warrants an immediate reprieve from cattle and sheep.

ACADEMIC WRITING demands a sense of consequentiality to give purpose to the work. Yet many educational practices in American schools isolate individual students and overemphasize learning by rote. Consequently students gain few or no experiences in interdisciplinary approaches, enjoy little say in the direction of their studies, and find it difficult to relate the studies to life outside a classroom. Many of these same problems beset writers and researchers in colleges and universities. A lack of applicability characterizes a great deal of the work produced by professionals in the letters and arts. Writers yearn to prompt some practical consequences with their studies, yet such effects are rarely evident. Research projects often seem irrelevant to life beyond the professional conference or the library walls. The common saying "It's an academic question" demonstrates how many issues prove immaterial or unanswerable. The Foxfire method addresses this defect by assuring that the work is characterized by student action rather than by the passive reception of processed information. Literary activism, by any other name, possesses the same potential for adult writers and researchers.

The most rudimentary knowledge of bioregionalism can provoke fresh perspectives in the disciplines. As a complement to the emerging ecocriticism, it offers scholars in the humanities a vital approach, one that would tie the humanities back to the land before they float off into an academic void. The greening of America, sometimes considered a feeble vestige of the 1960s counterculture, shows no sign of diminishing in significance for either urban or rural dwellers, requisite as it is to the survival of species and culture alike. And although space may be the final frontier, social and biological ecology now are dominating much of our historians and artists, history and art. Interdisciplinary approaches in scholarship, which encourage a merging of the sciences and arts, can prompt collaboration among researchers in disparate fields. But bioregionalism is more than mere philosophy or pedantry, more than some theory nice to contemplate. It truly gets us where we live. It teaches us the means by which we can reinvestigate our living regions and reinvest our selves.

REFERENCES

Bass, Rick. *Oil Notes*. Boston: Houghton Mifflin, 1989.

———. *The Ninemile Wolves*. Livingston, Mont.: Clark City, 1992.

———. "20515 House, 20510 Senate." *American Nature Writing Newsletter* 5.1 (Spring 1993): 3–5.

Berry, Wendell. *A Continuous Harmony: Essays Cultural and Agricultural*. New York: Harvest/Harcourt, 1972.

Berryman, John. *The Dream Songs*. New York: Farrar, Straus and Giroux, 1969.

Bly, Robert. *American Poetry: Wilderness and Domesticity*. New York: Harper and Row, 1990.

———. *Iron John: A Book about Men*. Reading, Mass.: Addison-Wesley, 1990.

Bryan, Frank, and John McClaughry. *The Vermont Papers: Recreating Democracy on a Human Scale*. Chelsea, Vt.: Chelsea Green, 1989.

Devine, Robert. "Environment: The Cheatgrass Problem." *Atlantic* 271 (May 1993): 40, 44, 46–48.

Dorson, Richard M. *America Begins*. New York: Pantheon, 1950.

———. *Jonathan Draws the Longbow*. 1946. New York: Russell and Russell, 1970.

Gates, Henry Louis, Jr. *Loose Canons: Notes on the Culture Wars*. New York: Oxford UP, 1992.

Hall, David D. *Worlds of Wonder, Days of Judgment: Popular Religious Belief in Early New England*. New York: Knopf, 1989.

Jacobs, Lynn. *Waste of the West: Public Lands Ranching*. Tucson, Ariz.: Lynn Jacobs (P.O. Box 5784), 1991.

McCloskey, David. "Ecology and Community: The Bioregional Vision." Unpublished essay, 1991.

Okanogan National Forest. "Livestock Use by Allotment." 1989.

Ryberg, Erik. Interview by author. Dixie, Idaho, 30 May 1993.

Sale, Kirkpatrick. *Dwellers in the Land: The Bioregional Vision*. San Francisco: Sierra Club, 1985.

Scarce, Rik. *Eco-Warriors: Understanding the Radical Environmental Movement*. Chicago: Noble, 1990.

Snyder, Gary. *The Practice of the Wild*. San Francisco: North Point, 1990.

Ulrich, Laurel Thatcher. *A Midwife's Tale: The Life of Martha Ballard, Based on Her Diary, 1785–1812*. New York: Random House, 1990.

Ecocriticism

What Is It Good For?

To the memory of Charles Bernheimer

REPRESENTATIONS of nature in literature, as Lawrence Buell has recently pointed out, have typically been dealt with and understood in the twentieth century not as images of literal or factual reality (regarded as interesting or valuable in itself) but in terms of the formal or symbolic or ideological properties of those representations—which is to say that nature (leaving aside the question of whether it can be portrayed accurately or even adequately in literary texts) is important not for what it physically is but for what it conceptually means or can be made to mean. Thus professors of literature, "whatever their behavior in ordinary life," Buell provocatively remarks, "easily become anti-environmentalists in their professional practice" (85). Not only, that is, do they frequently set aside the literal reality of place or environment that they encounter in their reading—writing off that reality as a textual construction or effect and focusing instead on what they take it to encode—but they teach their students to do the same and to regard the result as the essence, the sine qua non, of literary understanding. The consequence of such understanding, however, can often be not simply the disconnection of literature from the world that animates it but the estrangement of readers from the world in which they read.

With the advent and (for better or worse) increasing institutionalization of "ecocriticism" over the last several years, along with the effort to open the literary canon to a fuller sampling of nature writing and the literature of place, both historical and contemporary, growing numbers of writers and critics are attempting to reverse this situation and to bring environmentalist values into greater relation to what and how they read. This project is based on the understanding that we live in what David Abram calls a "more-than-human world" (as opposed to one in which nature is always something to be tamed or overcome, so that the natural and the human are necessarily at odds), and it is based as well on the conviction that literature can reflect the reality of such a world with reasonable success, despite real obstacles to representational precision. To be sure, in a time of poststructuralist orthodoxy, with its insistence that there is nothing outside the text, the effort to read ecologically involves a renewed attention to the referential capacity of literature and to the reality of even "fictional realities," as Buell refers to literary representations in his own attempt to show how environmental texts render and recover the object-world of nature, a rendering, as he demonstrates, that sometimes seems to demand recourse to "outright fiction or distortion" (88, 103). This effort also involves a new and broader understanding of language and perception as themselves natural processes, conditioned by the environmental matrix in which they emerge.[1] Indeed, in *The Spell of the Sensuous*, David Abram provides such an understanding and manages to revitalize Ralph Waldo Emerson's mythic "language of nature," when he demonstrates not only that words (or the letters of the alphabet which constitute them) are originally linked to the natural world, but that the sensible, natural environment, for oral cultures which lack a written analogue to their speech, is, in fact, a text, a literal book of nature.[2] Thus, for such cultures, it is the land that is the "primary visual counterpart of spoken utterance, the visible accompaniment of all spoken meaning"; and it is the land that is "the sensible site or matrix wherein meaning occurs and proliferates" (139–40)—as opposed, of course, to the abstract discursive systems (beginning with the alphabet) which, in literate cultures, as Abram argues, have tended to displace nature and to disrupt their relation to it. Hence, in these cultures, nature has often suffered the fate of the mountain described by Wallace Stevens in a late poem that begins: "There it was, word for word, / The poem that took the place of a mountain" (*Palm* 374).

My concern here, however, will be less with such theoretical issues than with what I see as the environmental character of literary texts and with ecological reading considered in terms of critical practice. Specifically, I am proposing both to assert and to test the assumption that all texts are at least potentially environmental (and therefore susceptible to ecocriticism or ecologically informed reading) in the sense that all texts are literally or imaginatively situated in a place, and in the sense that their authors, consciously or not, inscribe within them a certain relation to their place. To do so, I shall be looking at several passages and poems by writers ranging from Jane Austen to Wallace Stevens to Gary Snyder, a range eclectic enough to cover a variety of discourses and to allow for consideration of what happens to a text when it is read not in its intended mode (of romance, say, in the case of Austen) but in terms of its implied or unconscious orientation toward the environment.

Although it is clear that some texts are more environmentally responsive and therefore more environmental than others—or, as Buell puts it,
that environmental representation "is at least faintly present in most texts
but salient in few" (7)—ecocriticism becomes most interesting and useful,
it seems to me, when it aims to recover the environmental character or orientation of works whose conscious or foregrounded interests lie elsewhere.
One object of ecocriticism, as I see it, is to read in such a way as to amplify
the reality of the environment in or of a text, even if in doing so we resist
the tendency of the text itself (or of our own conditioning as readers) to
relegate the environment to the status of setting, so that it becomes a place
chiefly interesting because of the human events that unfold in it, or to see its
significance as primarily symbolic, so that it becomes something essentially
other than itself.

My interests also extend to the nature of ecocriticism or ecological reading per se, and my sense of what such reading involves should already
be emerging here. Often defined simply and vaguely as the study of the
relation between literature and the environment, ecocriticism, for perhaps
obvious reasons, can sometimes be a tendentious, adversarial enterprise.
Indeed, given the enormity of the ever-growing number of threats to the
Earth, its air and water, its habitats and species, such aggressiveness is understandable and even, one might think, long overdue. Nevertheless, in my
sense of it, ecocriticism is and should be more than merely the latest form of
literary or textual policing, one whose agents, on their beats in the already
suspect canon, keep their eyes peeled for violations of conceptions of environmental integrity and biospheric health that were simply unavailable to
earlier literary historical periods. Such violations are not hard to find, even
in texts commonly regarded as founding sources of contemporary nature
writing, including Emerson's *Nature* and Thoreau's *Walden*.[3]

Hence in my approach to it, ecocriticism, ultimately a form of environmental advocacy, is primarily a critical and literary tool, a kind of reading designed to expose and facilitate analysis of a text's orientation both
to the world it imagines and to the world in which it takes shape, along
with the conditions and contexts that affect that orientation, whatever it
might be. Texts, in this outlook, are environmental but not necessarily environmental*ist*. But ecocriticism, I would argue, becomes reductive when
it simply targets the environmentally incorrect, or when it aims to evalu-
ate texts solely on the basis of their adherence to ecologically sanctioned
standards of behavior, as if one were to adopt, as a critical principle, Aldo
Leopold's "land ethic," for example, and apply it to literature. "A thing,"

Leopold wrote (and, we may hypothesize, a text), "is right when it tends
to preserve the integrity, stability, and beauty of the biotic community. It is
wrong when it tends otherwise" (262). Since the literary value of a text, however, depends on more than the ethical or ecological attitudes it expresses,
to read literature in the light of such a principle, we may feel, is precisely *not*
to read it as literature, but as policy or doctrine, to be accepted or rejected
out of hand. Moreover, if literacy and language themselves, as Abram has
suggested, have adversely affected humanity's relationship to nature, then
perhaps no text can be "right," in any ultimate sense, with respect to the
health or preservation of the more-than-human world.[4] To read and to write
we must inevitably turn away from the environment, however briefly.

AMONG THOSE TEXTS that we might regard, from a modern environmentalist perspective, as least right (in Leopold's sense) are probably the descriptions of nature, few and far between as they are, that we find in the
fiction of Jane Austen, a writer for whom the idea of the world as more-than-
human must be close to unthinkable. Indeed, what we most likely remember from her novels, and even from recent cinematic versions of them—
such as Emma Thompson's *Sense and Sensibility*, with its striking wide-angle
shots of what we have been trained to see as "Romantic landscape"—are
polite, witty conversations set in domestic interiors. Still, although Austen
is manifestly *not* a nature writer, and although her landscapes may seem to
be designed to encourage our anti-environmentalist tendencies as readers
eager to see something other than nature in representations of it, there is a
good deal of ecocritical interest in some of Austen's natural settings, particularly if one reads them against their grain, considering them apart from
the novelistic needs they may serve, and looks carefully at what they describe. Occasionally one even discovers something like a pro-environmental
stance on the part of Austen's narrator, although its expression may fulfill
her primary purpose to critically expose the attitudes of her characters and
maintain an ironic or satiric perspective upon their behavior.

In an early episode of *Pride and Prejudice*, for example, Elizabeth Bennet's sister Jane, having been caught in a downpour on her way to visit Mr.
Bingley's sisters at Netherfield, is forced to spend the night there and wakes
up ill the next morning. In her concern for Jane, Elizabeth decides to go to
Netherfield herself and, in the absence of a carriage, has no alternative but
to walk the three-mile distance through wet and muddy fields—a decision
to which her mother reacts with disbelief: "How can you be so silly . . . as
to think of such a thing, in all this dirt! You will not be fit to be seen when

you get there" (78). Mrs. Bennet's attitude here is echoed later by Bingley's sisters, one of whom remarks that Elizabeth "really looked almost wild" after her walk (81), while the other, Elizabeth's chief rival for the affections of Mr. Darcy, comments at length on what she sees as Elizabeth's lack of propriety: "To walk three miles, or four miles, or five miles, or whatever it is, above her ancles in dirt, and alone, quite alone! what could she mean by it? It seems to me to shew an abominable sort of conceited independence, a most country town indifference to decorum" (82). Exposing oneself to nature, in these terms, at least if one is a woman, is tantamount to a serious violation of acceptable civilized behavior. Indeed, to the extent that Elizabeth herself "really looked almost wild," exposure to nature becomes, in effect, identification with it.

Austen's narrator, on the other hand, sees Elizabeth quite differently, describing her on her walk as "crossing field after field at a quick pace, jumping over stiles and springing over puddles with impatient activity, and finding herself at last within view of the house, with weary ancles, dirty stockings, and a face glowing with the warmth of exercise" (79). The vigor of the description here, with its stream of present participles and detailed attention to the conditions of the walk and to the exertions required of Elizabeth, gives us direct access to a physical environment that few women, in the genteel world of the novel, ever want or have to deal with. If Mrs. Bennet and Bingley's sisters alike are more concerned with decorous appearances than with Jane's health or Elizabeth's selfless and affectionate concern for her, the narrator, acknowledging the hardship and the dirt of her journey, is also aware of its benefits in the final, redeeming detail of Elizabeth's glowing face—a glow, ironically, that catches the admiring attention of Mr. Darcy, who remarks, in a way that briefly links him with the narrator, that Elizabeth's eyes "were brightened by the exercise" (82). One notices, too, a certain balance of attitude in the narrator's presentation of the episode. Jane's exposure to the natural world results in a bad cold, but Elizabeth's makes her radiant, and this difference suggests a regard for nature, on the part of the narrator, as itself a balance—an awareness that sets the narrator apart from just about every character in the novel.

Later, when Elizabeth goes with her aunt and uncle, the Gardiners, on an excursion that takes them to Pemberley, Mr. Darcy's beautiful house and grounds in Derbyshire, we arrive at what is certainly the most important episode featuring a natural setting in *Pride and Prejudice:*

Elizabeth, as they drove along, watched for the first appearance of Pemberley Woods with some perturbation; and when at length they turned in at the
lodge, her spirits were in a high flutter.

The park was very large, and contained great variety of ground. They entered it in one of its lowest points, and drove for some time through a beautiful
wood, stretching over a wide extent.

Elizabeth's mind was too full for conversation, but she saw and admired
every remarkable spot and point of view. They gradually ascended for half a
mile, and then found themselves at the top of a considerable eminence, where
the wood ceased, and the eye was instantly caught by Pemberley House, situated on the opposite side of a valley, into which the road with some abruptness wound. It was a large, handsome, stone building, standing well on rising
ground, and backed by a ridge of high woody hills;—and in front, a stream of
some natural importance was swelled into greater, but without any artificial
appearance. Its banks were neither formal, nor falsely adorned. Elizabeth was
delighted. She had never seen a place for which nature had done more, or
where natural beauty had been so little counteracted by an awkward taste.
They were all of them warm in their admiration; and at that moment she felt,
that to be mistress of Pemberley might be something! (267)

After being admitted to the house, Elizabeth and the Gardiners are taken on
a tour of it by the housekeeper, and Elizabeth turns to a window "to enjoy
its prospect" and looks back at the landscape through which she has just
passed:

The hill, crowned with wood, from which they had descended, receiving increased abruptness from the distance, was a beautiful object. Every disposition of the ground was good; and she looked on the whole scene, the river,
the trees scattered on its banks, and the winding of the valley, as far as she
could trace it, with delight. As they passed into other rooms, these objects
were taking different positions; but from every window there were beauties
to be seen. The rooms were lofty and handsome, and their furniture suitable
to the fortune of their proprietor; but Elizabeth saw, with admiration of his
taste, that it was neither gaudy nor uselessly fine. (268)

What is taking place in this episode, which the narrator unfolds for us
from Elizabeth's point of view, is what Tony Tanner calls, in his excellent
introduction to the novel, the "education of [Elizabeth's] vision," an ongoing process of clarification and understanding in which her entry into

Pemberley becomes "both an analogue and an aid" for her "perceptual pen-
etration of the interior quality" of Mr. Darcy, so that the landscape and the
house come to signify the man himself (19). Everything that Elizabeth sees
at Pemberley, as Tanner goes on to say, represents "a visible extension of
[Darcy's] inner qualities" (24), a reflection of his values and taste and personality (and wealth!), and in this sense the landscape begins to take on
some of the aspects of Emerson's transcendentalist conception of nature as a
language, one whose signs, natural phenomena themselves, are ultimately,
for Emerson, symbols of spirit. In Austen's text, of course, it is Darcy's spirit,
so to speak, informed as it is by the assumptions and values of his culture
and class, that manifests itself in the natural and material forms ci his house
and its environment. Thus to admire Pemberley, and to take delight, as Elizabeth does, in every disposition of its grounds, is to be in touch with the true
character and worth of its owner.

Tanner's account of this episode, one in which the interests of nature are
quite subordinated to those of the scene's human actors, may be regarded
as a perfect example of what Buell would see as anti-environmentalist reading, although in this case Tanner certainly takes his cue from the text itself,
from the attitudes of the narrator and the characters, and most of all, perhaps, from Mr. Darcy, who has clearly organized or orchestrated the "whole
scene" at Pemberley in accord with the dictates of what Elizabeth and the
narrator are pleased to recognize as good taste and sound judgment. The
environment, through a sort of acculturation, has been thoroughly appropriated for human purposes, with the result that there is, in effect, little difference between the natural phenomena outside the house and the rooms
and furniture within it, since everything on view in both spaces has been
selected or arranged precisely to invite the sort of admiration that Elizabeth
feels. When she and her aunt and uncle, for instance, find themselves "at the
top of a considerable eminence, where the wood ceased," their eyes, we are
told, are "instantly caught by Pemberley House, situated [clearly by design
and for dramatic effect] on the opposite side of a valley." This catching of
eyes, evidently, has not been unforeseen or unplanned. Even more telling is
the "stream of some natural importance [which] was swelled into greater,
but without any artificial appearance," an effect, as the language hints, of
what one imagines to have been some strenuous efforts of earthmoving and
landscaping, and Elizabeth seems all but conscious of the extent to which
what she sees here is a calculated illusion. Indeed, much of the charm of
Darcy's landscaping lies in the way it has been hidden or disguised, so that
it appears "natural." Hence the stream's banks "were neither formal nor

falsely adorned," and Elizabeth "had never seen a place for which nature had done more, or where natural beauty had been so little counteracted by an awkward taste"—observations which, like the landscaping itself, seem reluctant to admit the reality of the situation. On the one hand, the place is *naturally* beautiful; but on the other, it has been altered, its beauty "counteracted," although "so little" as to exhibit hardly any signs of untoward or graceless human tampering.[5]

The reality, however, is that what is on display at Pemberley is not "nature" so much as an aestheticized reconstruction of it, one informed by the late-eighteenth-century notion of the "picturesque," which promoted the transformation of environment into artful landscape, a set of staged scenic effects meant to appeal to aesthetic tastes and standards derived more from visual art than from any actual natural environment.[6] Thus when Elizabeth looks back at the "hill" from which she had descended, what she sees is "a beautiful object," and as she passes from room to room in the house, she takes note of the "beauties to be seen" "from every window," as though the surrounding environment has been consciously divided up and framed in order to be apprehended as a series of pictures.

Curiously, the best criticism of Tanner's reading, and of the episode in *Pride and Prejudice* which elicits it, may come from none other than Ralph Waldo Emerson, when, in *Nature*, he breaks in upon his own discussion of the ways in which we are assisted by natural objects in the expression of our own meanings and wonders "whether the characters [or natural phenomena regarded as signs] are not significant of themselves. Have mountains, and waves, and skies," Emerson asks, "no significance but what we consciously give them, when we employ them as emblems of our thoughts?" (204). Before we assume, however, that Emerson's question is an environmentalist one, a protest on behalf of nature seen as valuable and meaningful in itself, we should recall that Emerson's approach to nature, in Buell's phrasing, is ultimately (but not exclusively) a "religiophilosophical" one (118), and that his aim here is to call attention to what he regards as the larger meanings of natural objects, meanings which are not finally natural or human but spiritual. As Emerson himself puts it, in "fortunate hours . . . the universe becomes transparent" for us, "and the light of higher laws than its own shines through it" (205). If anything, Emerson's transcendentalism here exposes the narrow humanism and materialism of the culture that Austen herself portrays, both sympathetically and critically, in her novel. Yet for both writers "nature" is clearly a "commodity" (and not only in a figurative sense) that has been refashioned to serve needs and represent values which have little to do with the physical environment as a reality in itself.

The point to emphasize, however, is that such a judgment is not merely a negative or critical one, and that it does not necessarily represent the goal or endpoint of ecocriticism, whose legitimate interests also include the history or evolution of the relations of culture to nature, whatever they might be, and of the perception of nature by culture. Austen's text, considered from such a perspective, might lead us to wonder about the filters or ideological and conceptual lenses through which we ourselves view "nature," or whether we ourselves can ever hope to perceive the physical environment "as a reality in itself." There are, in other words, links as well as differences between our attitudes toward nature and those inscribed in Austen's novel, and there is even a sense in which Mr. Darcy may be regarded as a sort of neoclassical or pre-Romantic environmentalist. What is also on display in the Pemberley episode, after all, if it is read ecocritically, is an image of Darcy's or his culture's conception of the proper relation between humanity and nature. Insofar as Darcy is committed to what was likely regarded in the late eighteenth century as the wise use and management of his natural resources, that relation may be characterized as "conservationist," although what he seems to aspire to, or pretends to espouse (now that his land, ironically, has already been altered), is more of a "preservationist" approach, one which seeks to maintain the environment in its own, unaltered state. But the basic issues—how to manage nature, how much management is too much, and what balance to strike between giving nature free rein and imposing our will upon it—clearly persist into our own time (in which they have become even more urgent), and this awareness ought to preclude easy criticism of Darcy, or of the book he inhabits, or of the culture that both represent, as environmentally pernicious. As Tony Tanner points out in a note to the Pemberley episode, the eighteenth-century vogue for landscaping and formal gardening often gave rise to reflection on issues basic to neoclassicism, such as the question (as he puts it), "to what extent does man with his art *correct* nature's faults and improve her, and to what extent does his art *follow* nature, helping her to realize her own most felicitous intentions and display her qualities to best effect?" (398). In other words, what should the precise relation between art and nature or, more broadly, between humanity and nature, be? Is nature itself artful, or is it in need of human control?

The assumption behind these questions, of course—an assumption still very much with us—is that it is a human understanding or assessment of nature's intentions and qualities that counts most, and that nature's self-realization achieves its greatest fulfillment only when it is in accord with human determinations of what is "most felicitous" and of what constitutes "best effect." These are philosophical and aesthetic issues, but also ethical and environmental ones—and because of Tanner's phrasing (dating from 1972), they become an object of ecofeminist concern as well, given his tendency here, prompted by the eighteenth-century attitudes he is articulating, to feminize nature and to place "her" in a position dependent upon and inferior to that of "man," who with his art corrects her faults and improves her and, even when his art *follows* nature, still helps her to realize her own best effects, which, it is assumed, she is unable to do on her own. For Mr. Darcy, and for the eighteenth-century tradition of neoclassicism embodied at Pemberley, the possibility that nature might validly pursue its own goals and intentions, without need of human (and specifically masculine) "improvement" or guidance, had not yet, apparently, come into view.[7]

As a form of what I have been referring to as "reading against the grain," ecocriticism, it should be clear, depends upon our willingness as readers to marginalize, if not completely overlook, precisely those aspects and meanings of texts that are traditionally privileged or valorized, by which I mean a whole range of anthropocentric attitudes and assumptions whose authority and even hegemony in reading and criticism are often still taken for granted. What ecocriticism calls for, then, is a fundamental shift from one context of reading to another—more specifically, a movement from the human to the environmental, or at least from the exclusively human to the biocentric or ecocentric, which is to say a humanism (since we cannot evade our human status or identity) informed by an awareness of the "more-than-human."[8] Some texts, clearly, will respond to such reading and context shifting more fully or convincingly than others, and the one I want to consider now, Wallace Stevens's "Anecdote of the Jar," may seem initially to be tailor-made for ecocritical treatment. Remarkably, though, it has rarely if ever received such treatment, perhaps because its speaker's act of placing a jar in Tennessee seems so patently fanciful and metaphorical that readers have felt licensed if not obliged to locate its meanings elsewhere. Some, for instance, have seen the poem as an ironic response to Keats's "Ode on a Grecian Urn"—and thus as a defiant dissent from (or as a sheepish concession to) the priority of British Romantic tradition by an American upstart or latecomer.[9] It is a poem, according to this reading, about literary history and the anxiety of influence. More typically, it has been read in terms of the endless Stevensian dialectic of reality and imagination and thus as a modernist text about the nature and status of the creative act and its relation to the world apart from art. In yet another reading (and act of context shifting), Frank Lentricchia sees the poem as political and anti-imperialist by virtue of its appearance in Michael Herr's book on the Vietnam War, *Dispatches* (1970), in which Stevens, as Lentricchia puts it, "is made by Herr to speak directly against the ideology of imposition and obliteration coactive in Vietnam with a strategy of defoliation." What Stevens or his speaker expresses, then, is an "imaginative imperialism" that is both "activated and subtly evaluated" in his poem (23).

With its concern about defoliation and thus *environmental* imperialism, Lentricchia's political reading begins to edge toward a more fully ecocritical account of "Anecdote of the Jar," one which, in our own era of escalating environmental degradation and what has been called the "malling of America," might seem hard to avoid. [10] In a poem dating from 1919, however, Stevens may be less concerned with the environment per se than with the more abstract issue, approached somewhat comically in his text, of the relation between culture and nature. Thus the poem dramatizes a face-off between the jar, a cultural artifact, and the apparently arbitrarily chosen natural environment of "Tennessee" (although the phonetic and metrical properties of "Tennessee" also clearly appeal to Stevens). Moreover, despite its presentation as a "slovenly wilderness," Tennessee at the same time is a state of the Union, which is to say a geographical space that has already been demarcated and named and thus humanized, itself a virtual artifact.

> I placed a jar in Tennessee,
> And round it was, upon a hill.
> It made the slovenly wilderness
> Surround that hill.
>
> The wilderness rose up to it,
> And sprawled around, no longer wild.
> The jar was round upon the ground
> And tall and of a port in air.
>
> It took dominion everywhere.
> The jar was gray and bare.
> It did not give of bird or bush,
> Like nothing else in Tennessee.
>
> (*Palm* 46)

The placing of the jar, from the perspective of the speaker, clearly produces some miraculous results. Tennessee appears tamed and transformed, no longer itself. As opposed to an inaccessible wilderness, it has become a humanly meaningful place, available now to human apprehension and use. One is led to think (especially by Stevens's phrasing in the poem's second line) of John Winthrop's ambition to create a "city upon a hill," an ideal Christian community, in the wilds of seventeenth-century New England; or, more broadly, of Thomas Jefferson, variously committed, in the words of the historians Peter Carroll and David Noble, to "the imposition of rational order upon the natural wildness of the earth" (55, 136). At the same time, though, one might also argue that Tennessee, with which the poem's first and last lines end, has remained quite itself, an intact and unchanged natural reality against which the jar appears merely "gray and bare," so that the "dominion" it has taken "everywhere" seems suddenly empty and irrelevant. The change in the landscape, we might feel, has been merely imagined. In terms of these alternatives, the poem seems constituted by an unresolvable tension in the mind of its speaker, who is torn between, on the one hand, a need to organize and thus gain access to Tennessee and, on the other, a sense that such organization or "dominion" amounts to a distortion of the vital and thriving organic reality that Tennessee already is (or was). Unlike Mr. Darcy, who has already reordered the environment at Pemberley and now seeks to maintain it in its new state, one whose "natural importance" has been "swelled into greater, but [we are assured] without any artificial appearance"—although maintaining Pemberley in its new state means sealing it off from any further change or natural process— Stevens's speaker seems much more concerned that his act of placing the jar is simply not in keeping with what is already there in the environment, and that his act has, in fact, introduced an element of artifice that has not only altered the environment's appearance but violated its essential nature. Read ecocritically, "Anecdote of the Jar" might be renamed something like "The Resource Manager's Lament," and what it records is its speaker's arrival at an incipient ecocentric awareness, which here includes his recognition that our encounters with the natural world inevitably change it, often in ways that we come to regret. He needs the ordering that he brings about, but he cannot overlook his sense of loss, or his sense of a difference between the jar's "dominion" and the wilderness itself, now "no longer wild."

IN THEIR INTERACTIONS with their respective landscapes, both Stevens's speaker and Mr. Darcy seem to be involved in a similar drama. Whereas Stevens's speaker, however, begins to question the validity of the order brought about by his placing of the jar, Darcy, we may assume, never doubts that he has improved Pemberley by, in effect, raising it out of the realm of the natural and into that of the aesthetic. Both have corrected and thereby partially rejected nature—although as a further result Stevens's speaker has also learned to see more fully into the life of nature, or what Gary Snyder calls the nature of nature, with its giving of "bird or bush." Seen against the background of that larger life, which continues to pursue its own processes, the imposed order of the jar suddenly loses its glamour for Stevens's speaker. Gray and bare, the jar exists apart from what it supposedly dominates, "Like nothing else in Tennessee," or like the inhuman "Jove in the clouds" in Stevens's "Sunday Morning," an inadequate deity, alien both to us and to the "sweet land" from which he holds himself aloof (*Palm* 6). The ecologically positive outcome of the speaker's effort to make the environment serve human interests is precisely his new and humble awareness at the end of the poem that such efforts have their limits, and this is so not only in the sense that our attempts to impose our interests upon nature are costly both to nature and to us, but also in the sense that nature will ultimately evade them.

"Each place," as Gary Snyder tells us in *The Practice of the Wild*, "is its own place, forever (eventually) wild" (27). And this wildness is the nature of nature—or, as he actually and more intensively puts it, "the nature of the nature of nature" (103), a phrase that deliberately evokes a sense of almost inaccessible depths, a reality beyond human range and certainly beyond our ability to order or alter it in any lasting way. In Snyder's conception, in fact, human orderings and alterations of the environment are simply absorbed or appropriated by it and become part of the totality and evolving history of its processes,[11] since a place, as he explains, is not solid or fixed but "has a kind of fluidity: it passes through space and time":

> A place will have been grasslands, then conifers, then beech and elm. It will have been half riverbed, it will have been scratched and plowed by ice. And then it will be cultivated, paved, sprayed, dammed, graded, built up. But each is only for a while, and that will be just another set of lines on the palimpsest. The whole earth is a great tablet holding the multiple overlaid new and ancient traces of the swirl of forces. (27)

Although Snyder seems to be reviving the old trope of the "Book of Nature"—elsewhere in *The Practice of the Wild* he explicitly and emphatically disowns this idea (69)—his interest here runs much more in the direction of the historicity and dynamism of nature, its ceaseless flow and changeability, and what Wendell Berry calls its "unforeseen" quality (245). If nature is a text at all, it is one that is constantly being revised and rewrit-

ten. Moreover, it is just this natural dynamism that stands in permanent opposition to the notion of the world as fixed and stable, and that undermines
any claim, such as the one Stevens's speaker makes, that the wilderness has
been tamed. It seems, even, to lead Snyder to disown the very conceptions
and articulations that constitute his discourse as a nature writer, as when
he declares, in the preface to *No Nature* (1992), that "Whatever [nature] actually is, it will not fulfill our conceptions or assumptions. It will dodge
our expectations and theoretical models. There is no single or set 'nature'
either as 'the natural world' or 'the nature of things.' " Given this radical
otherness, nature, apparently, will resist our efforts not only to control it
but even to name it. Snyder's propositions here, in any case, reduce the
very discourse that contains them to a merely provisional status. In addition, they seem to call for a poetics at odds with any notion of formal finish
or rhetorical finality or perfection. A poem for Snyder is thus not, say, a
momentary stay against confusion, a crafted order sealed off from a messy
world, but an opening to and an acknowledgement, often awed, of both
momentariness and confusion, although the latter is construed, positively
and without alarm, as the present moment or manifestation of an evolving
fluidity, "the swirl of forces." The early poem "Once Only" (*Back* 22) is a
simple and concrete example:

> almost at the equator
> almost at the equinox
> exactly at midnight
>> from a ship
>> the full
>
>> moon
>
> in the center of the sky.
>
>>>> Sappa Creek near Singapore
>>>> March 1958

The poem's shape derives from the experience that generates it, as the
speaker locates or *places* himself in the world, in time and space, in terms
of the remarkable coincidences (abstractions—equator and equinox—side
by side with visible realities—ship and moon) that make up the poem. Yet
it is not the speaker or his language that is foregrounded here, but the experience that takes place "once only," outside and around him, to which he
quite fully subordinates himself. As Annie Dillard remarks about the oc-
currence of beauty and grace in the world, which "are performed whether

or not we will or sense them," "The least we can do is try to be there" (8). In this poem Snyder is certainly *there*, although his being there is ecocentric, in the sense that as a self he is displaced, taken precedence over, virtually and grammatically, by what lies outside him.

FROM THE PERSPECTIVE of ecocriticism regarded as a form of reading against the grain, Snyder's work often turns out to provide a new grain, one in which place and the environmental appear not as symbol or setting but as themselves, in propria persona. In a poem like "Among," from the 1983 collection *Axe Handles* (10), the displacement of the human by the environmental, for which ecocritical reading calls, has already taken place. Or it may be more accurate to say that in such a poem the human assumes its proper place within the environment, since "place is part of what we are" (*Practice* 27):

> Few Douglas fir grow in these pine woods
> One fir is there among south-facing Ponderosa Pine,
>
> Every fall a lot of little seedlings sprout
> around it—
>
> Every summer during long dry drouth they die.
> Once every forty years or so
> A rain comes in July.
>
> Two summers back it did that,
> The Doug fir seedlings lived that year
>
> The next year it was dry,
> A few fir made it through.
> This year, with roots down deep, two live.
> A Douglas fir will be among these pines.
>
> > at the 3000-foot level
> > north of the south fork
> > of the Yuba river.

As opposed to Mr. Darcy, or Stevens's speaker in "Anecdote of the Jar," whose relation to and decisions about the land are, if not thoughtlessly abusive, then certainly anthropocentric, Snyder's speaker is consciously, actively, and sympathetically engaged with his surroundings here in a way that defines environmental awareness or ecocentrism not so much in terms of what Buell describes as a radical abandonment of the self or as a "thoroughgoing perceptual breakthrough" (144–45), but as an attainable, even practical state of being. In its understated, undramatic way, the poem considers the chances of survival for Douglas fir trees in a region barely hospitable to their growth. Like Thoreau taking the temperature of Walden Pond and keeping careful records of its changing depth, the speaker is motivated by curiosity but more importantly by a sort of neighborly solicitude for these more-than-human inhabitants of his local environment. The poem thus exists at a far remove from the Romantic nature lyric, with its interest in the experience and sensibility of the poet, and focuses instead, in an unusually direct and discursive way, on the trees and the local environmental conditions which they must overcome or adapt to in order to survive. Adapting to those conditions, it is clear, is something of a heroic achievement, one that the speaker regards with deep appreciation. The iambic pentameter of the poem's last line, moreover, underscores the extent to which it is an affirmation and gives it a formal and poetic authority that Snyder rarely invokes in his work.

The poem becomes most interesting, however, when it is seen as a counterexample, or an alternative to the sort of transcendental ecocentrism that constitutes a major motive or motif in American nature writing, and that Buell, in his account of it, calls "radical relinquishment," a gesture in which one gives up "individual autonomy itself" and forgoes "the illusion of mental and even bodily apartness from one's environment"—although we may wonder if these are real options for a human consciousness that would remain both human and conscious. Setting the stage for his own discussion of the possibilities and pitfalls of ecocentric expression, a discussion fully aware of "the heroic difficulty of achieving a thoroughgoing redefinition of the self in environmental terms" (167), Buell quotes Holmes Rolston III to the effect that "ecology does not know an encapsulated ego over against his or her environment," and then wonders, "what sort of literature remains possible if we relinquish the myth of human apartness? It must be a literature," he suggests, "that abandons, or at least questions, what would seem to be literature's most basic foci: character, persona, narrative consciousness." But then he wonders again, "What literature can survive under these conditions?" (145).

One answer to this question, it seems to me, is a poem like "Among," although it is necessary to see it not as an enactment of relinquishment but as a text whose speaker has already internalized, and thus takes for granted, what Buell sees as an essential questioning of the primacy of the self—

which is to say, "the validity of the self as the primary focalizing device
for both writer and reader" (179). Typically, Snyder's speaker here adopts
a style that is highly impersonal and self-effacing, not unlike the outer-
directed ecocentric mode of "Once Only" and other poems. Yet "Among"
also projects the sense that the self, like the Douglas fir which has sunk its
"roots down deep," and to which the poem pays tribute, is most truly itself, or can only become itself, "among" its surroundings, rather than as
an isolated, individual ego. "Our place is part of what we are," as Snyder
insists, because what we are has come about in response to place, or to the
worldly conditions, the environmental matrix, responsible for the kind of
being that we have (*Practice* 29). But it is also important to emphasize that
the self in a poem like this is not so thoroughly effaced or displaced by its
own ecocentric interests that it loses its autonomy and ceases to function as
what Buell calls a "superintending consciousness" (144). The consistently
iambic rhythm of the poem's final stanza is a clear sign that this is the case.
What is at stake in "Among" is not an abandonment of the ego, regarded
as a necessary condition for arriving at a fuller ecocentrism, but a correction of the usual imbalance between the human and the nonhuman, and a
recognition of the Douglas firs as environmental neighbors and partners.
Snyder, in any event, does not erase himself from the scene "in these pine
woods" and drift off, like Emerson in *Nature,* into universal currents of being, or imagine, like James Wright in "A Blessing," that "if I stepped out of
my body I would break / Into blossom" (57). Nor does his poem undergo
a corresponding dissolution or textual unraveling (since Buell is perfectly
right to point out that literature can hardly be expected to survive once we
give up the idea of our separateness from the environment). Instead Snyder's speaker acknowledges his presence within a larger, more-than-human
community, "among" trees whose presence enhances his own and on whose
behalf he speaks. Indeed, to the extent that he is committed to the ongoing
life of that larger community and to his own role as its spokesperson, it
is very much in his own interests *not* to forgo individual autonomy and
consciousness.[12]

    As a final point, it is worth noting how, both in "Among" and in "Once
Only" (and in other poems as well), Snyder registers his awareness of place,
or of the environment of his text, in a literal italicized footnote, a brief ad-
dendum, placed at the bottom of the poem. By this novel means he provides
information about the poem's setting, or about the spatial and temporal circumstances of its composition, which other poets indicate (if at all) in their
titles, one famous example being Wordsworth's "Lines Composed a few

Miles Above Tintern Abbey on Revisiting the Banks of the Wye During a Tour, July 13, 1798." Snyder's captions or subtitles, however, not only allow us to locate his speaker in a particular setting but also attest to the degree to which place plays a generative role in the production of the poem. In addition, they tend to insist upon the reality of the poem's external circumstances, as if to say, although this is a poem, it has a basis in real experience, in the actual, sensible world.[13] By means of this device, Snyder has, in effect, opened a channel for the expression not simply of environmental awareness but of awareness of the impingement of the environment upon the text— an impingement, I have been suggesting, by which all texts are affected, although often at levels too remote to recover.

Postscript: Because it is likely to be relatively widely read and regarded as an important, sophisticated, even defining example of the ecological reading of poetic texts, I want here to respond briefly to Bonnie Costello's recent article " 'What to Make of a Diminished Thing': Modern Nature and Poetic Response." Primarily, I want to take issue with the article's dismissive treatment of the work of Gary Snyder and with its virtual rejection of ecocentrism, or Buell's aesthetic of relinquishment, which it construes (reductively) as a hyper-Romantic mode of being and writing based on an outmoded impulse to escape from a cultural world that is too much with us into a static pastoral retreat outside it. Readers familiar with Buell's careful, wide-ranging discussion of ecocentrism will no doubt see that Costello's account is an oversimplification.

Nevertheless, Costello's challenging essay, vexing as it is in its opposition to what it views as an overly earnest, doctrinaire conservationism and in its (somewhat mischievous) construction of an equation between the natural and the "entrepreneurial," is a deft and subtly argued piece of work, particularly valuable for its inventive readings of poems by Frost, Stevens, Amy Clampitt, and A. R. Ammons. For Costello these poets represent an alternative to Snyder, Wendell Berry, and other writers whom she disparagingly classifies with those "latter-day Romanticists, primitivists, and 'poets of place' and mystical presence who are usually celebrated by ecologically oriented critics" (572). As such, they also represent "a line of American poetry"—she calls it "a poetry of superfluity," informed by Richard Poirier's notion of an Emersonian "ethos of extravagance"—that "has confronted the changes in the landscape brought about by the human will to enter, transform, abstract, and exploit the environment," and that, despite evidence of natural decline and despoliation, "has consistently refused the responses of mourning, nostalgia, and the restriction of the self to a receptive role," by which she means the pursuit of ecocentric awareness that Buell describes (571). Environmental entropy, for these writers, who take their cue from nature's own superfluity, is not an occasion for despair but a creative opportunity, Costello argues. Thus when Frost imagines his oven bird wondering "what to make of a diminished thing," he is not (or not only) withdrawing into sorrow over the loss of natural plenitude, but is considering his options for transforming, or making something out of, the new, albeit diminished, situation. As Costello sees it, Frost's speaker discovers "a new outlet for his superfluity," and so the poem is one not of grief or rage but of "entrepreneurial challenge" (579).

Except for the fact that she assumes a stance, if not antagonistic toward, then certainly critical of, ecocriticism, Costello here pursues an ecocriticism of her own, one that she promisingly defines as rhetorically oriented and interested not in thesis- or agenda-driven "statements about reality" but in texts that reveal, through their play with structure and language, "the entanglement of nature and culture; the interplay between our desires, our concepts, and our perceptions; and possibilities for renewal and vitality within that entanglement" (574). If her thinking is weighted more toward the text and language than the natural world, this in itself is not an unwelcome move in a field that can be overly involved with environmental ethics and politics and often inattentive to the mediated and motivated nature of representations of the environment, as if these representations were simply and transparently equal to the mute reality they portray. In distancing herself from environmentalism, however, and from what Buell calls "a spirit of commitment to environmentalist praxis" (430)—and in favoring Poirier's Emersonian superfluity against Buell's Thoreauvian relinquishment—Costello will not endear herself to environmentally concerned readers, particularly when she argues that an ethic of restraint will never satisfy "the fecund imagination" of our culture and "its entrepreneurial individuals, who want to go on creating not just works of the imagination but things of material substance as well, even if that productive energy performs a kind of violence on the existing world. What are humans to do," she wonders, "if not proliferate and even struggle to dominate?" (569–70).

Environmentalists and ecocritics of various stripes (who, for Costello, see humans "only as a threat to the wealth of nature" and naively yearn "after the lost wilderness" [569]), will have their own answers to her question. But even if we grant (as I do) that ecocriticism, as she suggests, can sometimes approach literature with insufficient sophistication, at the same time that it may harbor unrealistic expectations about what literature can accomplish environmentally—and even when she asserts that "Closeness to nature, the escape from the anthropocentric perspective, is a fiction" (594), a point that expresses reservations about relinquishment not unlike my own—it is still hard not to feel that Costello's ecocriticism is precisely an ecocriticism without the "eco," a study of texts undertaken largely at the expense of place and of place's implication in the text not simply as a referent or an abstraction but as a generative force, a force that Wallace Stevens, for example, famously acknowledges when he writes, in *Notes toward a Supreme Fiction* (and does so in lines that to my ear sound very much like a didactic statement about reality), "that we live in a place / That is not our own and, much more, not ourselves / And hard it is in spite of blazoned days" (210). Stevens addresses himself here not so much, perhaps, to place per se as to his modernist sense of our estrangement from place, his sense, as he puts it elsewhere, "that we live in the center of a physical poetry, a geography that would be intolerable except for the non-geography that exists there"—by which he means the world of our own thoughts and our own feelings (*Necessary* 65–66). But it is from this estrangement, or tension between ourselves and our place, that "the poem springs" for Stevens (*Palm* 210).

After taking her reader through some "nimble and courageous reckonings with modern landscape" in texts by both Frost and Stevens, Costello observes that, in contrast, "the protests against modernity formed in images of an idealized past and imposed on the present in various primitivist visions can be terribly unsatisfying. Gary Snyder," she continues,

> seems altogether embarrassed by active consciousness, including metaphor, asking us to settle instead for a combination of presentational and didactic modes. He would have us, paradoxically, become "native" again. Snyder's poems do much, admittedly, to awaken our admiration for the vast spaces of the Sierras, and Wendell Berry charms us with his sacramental marriage to enduring place, carried on through his subsistence farming in Kentucky. For them such places have essences that can provide identity and continuity to those who dwell in them. But these are not the places where most of us live or will live in the future. (586–87)

In response to this statement, however, with its doubly divisive rhetoric of "us" in our places and "them" in theirs, one might appeal to Aldo Leopold's remark that "The weeds in a city lot convey the same lesson as the redwoods" (292). For Snyder and Berry, surely, *all* places, urban, rural, or wilderness, have essences that can potentially provide identity and continuity to those who dwell in them. We are not being asked by these poets to move to the Sierras or to take up subsistence farming. But the important point is that we all live in places, of whatever kind and no matter where, and that what Snyder and Berry offer us, beyond awakening our admiration for *their* places, is a model of what authentic relationship to place, *any* place, might be and an example of how to achieve it. As it turns out, in fact, a project of just this sort, which represents the broadest aims of Snyder and Berry (defined entrepreneurially or otherwise), is not inconsistent with the "possibilities for renewal and vitality" that Costello sees within "the entanglement of nature and culture" portrayed in the texts of poets like Clampitt and Ammons. And in this sense the divide that she sets up between her poets and what is clearly an overly selective version of Snyder will not hold. Something there is that doesn't love *this* wall either. But to discredit Snyder as a poet whose interests lie only in "a remote or lost nature," as opposed to "a nature in our midst" (573)—or to see him as "ready to adopt an aesthetics of relinquishment in return for an abiding natural scene" (602)—is to view his work partially and inaccurately. More important, it is to misrepresent a writer who, revising Thoreau, has argued that "Wildness is not just 'the preservation of the world,' it *is* the world," so that what we need is not an escape from culture to nature (even if it were possible) but precisely a productive recognition of their entanglement—or, as Snyder himself puts it, "a civilization that can live fully and creatively together with wildness" (*Practice* 6).

NOTES

1. Karl Kroeber argues that "anything cultural must be understood as part of a natural ecosystem," a realization that should, in his view, "radically reorient *all* critical theorizing of the past 50 years." See "Ecology and American Literature: Thoreau and Un-Thoreau" (310).

2. For an account of Emerson's "language of nature," see the chapter on Emerson in Robert Kern, *Orientalism, Modernism, and the American Poem* (36–67).

3. Karl Kroeber insists, perhaps too categorically, on a difference between what he calls Thoreauvian and un-Thoreauvian ecological writing, arguing that Thoreau not only "adopts a stance antagonistic to science and sociability" but that in doing so he "opposes basic principles of environmentalism." (See "Ecology and American Literature: Thoreau and Un-Thoreau," [315].) One may wonder, however, about the availability of such principles to Thoreau, to whom, as Buell points out, " 'thinking like a mountain' did not come any more naturally . . . than it did to Aldo Leopold," one of Kroeber's chief examples of an un-Thoreauvian writer. Buell also suggests that although Thoreau was aware of an incipient environmentalism as early as the

1840s, and that he was familiar, for example, with George B. Emerson's 1846 *Report on the Trees and Shrubs Growing Naturally in the Forests of Massachusetts,* with its warnings about deforestation, he nevertheless avoided issuing such warnings himself "because the pastoralizing impulse to imagine Walden as an unspoiled place overrode his fears about its vulnerability to despoliation" (120). Although it may be just this "pastoralizing impulse" that is problematic for Kroeber, Buell's point here is an important one, to my mind, because it calls attention to a need, in ecocritical work, to maintain an awareness of the claims not only of ecology but of the literary imagination, whereas Kroeber seems all too ready to sacrifice the latter in favor of the former, or to invalidate what he sees (mistakenly, it seems to me) as Thoreau's overly transcendental and insufficiently ecological understanding of nature, and on this basis to downplay the importance of Thoreau for more recent nature writing, which he regards as more fully and rigorously scientific. Aside from the fact that this move makes for a rather narrow definition of nature writing, one which separates it from some of its most vital roots, I would also argue that the interests of ecocriticism are best served when it pursues a complex, indeed ecological, attentiveness not only to environmental processes seen as the basis of culture but to the whole range of circumstances—aesthetic, psychological, literary-historical, ideological, and so on—by which all texts (even scientific ones) are inescapably conditioned.

4. In her introduction to *The Ecocriticism Reader,* Cheryll Glotfelty asks a series of questions designed to illustrate the characteristic interests of ecocriticism. One of them is, "In what ways has literacy itself affected humankind's relationship to the natural world?" Abram's *The Spell of the Sensuous* may be regarded as the major answer to that question to date. See *The Ecocriticism Reader: Landmarks in Literary Ecology* (xix). See also Abram's chapter "Animism and the Alphabet" (93–135), in *The Spell of the Sensuous.*

5. In a note at the end of his edition of *Pride and Prejudice,* Tanner calls attention to the extent to which Austen's presentation of this episode is informed by "a main line of eighteenth-century thought," one that is best expressed in Pope's 1731 "Epistle to Richard Boyle, Earl of Burlington" (398).

6. On the relation between the eighteenth-century idea of the "picturesque" (set forth by the British travel writer William Gilpin [1724–1804]) and the continuing tendency in modern environmentalism to aestheticize nature, see Alison Byerly's fine essay "The Uses of Landscape," in *The Ecocriticism Reader* (52–68). For a good account of Gilpin and his influence, not only on Thoreau but on the nineteenth-century American articulation of landscape in general, see Robert D. Richardson Jr., *Henry Thoreau: A Life of the Mind* (260–66).

7. In *The Practice of the Wild,* Gary Snyder writes: "Thoreau set out to 'make the soil say beans' while living by his pond. To cause land to be productive according to our own notion is not evil. But we must also ask: what does mother nature do best when left to her own long strategies?" (90).

8. In an argument about the "potentially unlimited polysemy" of literary texts (25), Antony Easthope, in *Literary into Cultural Studies*, proposes that critical readings or interpretations are not determined by texts but that "they are constructed between the text and a context by a process or practice of reading." In this account, Easthope employs the term "context" to emphasize "the active participation of a reader in producing a reading . . . brought about by privileging certain features and meanings in the text" and bypassing others (33) . Such bypassing, however, may strike us as somewhat cavalier and arbitrary, an imposition of the reader's interests upon the text that amounts to a rewriting of it.

9. See, for example, Daniel R. Schwarz, *Narrative and Representation in the Poetry of Wallace Stevens* (26).

10. See William Kowinski, *The Malling of America: An Inside Look at the Great Consumer Paradise.*

11. In "The Poet" (1844), Emerson makes a roughly similar point when he writes: "Readers of poetry see the factory village and the railway, and fancy that the poetry of the landscape is broken up by these; for these works of art are not yet consecrated in their reading; but the poet sees them fall within the great Order not less than the beehive, or the spider's geometrical web. Nature adopts them very fast into her vital circles, and the gliding train of cars she loves like her own" (321).

12. In a brief statement called "The Wilderness" in the "Plain Talk" section of *Turtle Island*, Snyder writes that his aim is to "bring a voice from the wilderness, my constituency. I wish to be a spokesman for a realm that is not usually represented either in intellectual chambers or in the chambers of government" (106).

13. Relevant to my point here is Jonathan Bate's discussion of Wordsworth's "Poems on the Naming of Places," a series of texts in which, as Bate puts it (quoting Geoffrey Hartman), "the setting is understood to contain the writer in the act of writing," so that these poems become self-conscious performances of the poet's sense of place. See *Romantic Ecology: Wordsworth and the Environmental Tradition* (90).

REFERENCES

Abram, David. *The Spell of the Sensuous: Perception and Language in a More-than-Human World.* New York: Vintage, 1997.

Austen, Jane. *Pride and Prejudice.* Ed. Tony Tanner. Harmondsworth, Eng.: Penguin, 1972.

Bate, Jonathan. *Romantic Ecology: Wordsworth and the Environmental Tradition.* London: Routledge, 1991.

Berry, Wendell. *Recollected Essays.* San Francisco: North Point, 1981.

Buell, Lawrence. *The Environmental Imagination: Thoreau, Nature Writing, and the Formation of American Culture.* Cambridge: Harvard UP, 1995.

Byerly, Alison. "The Uses of Landscape: The Picturesque Aesthetic and the National Park System." *The Ecocriticism Reader.* Ed. Cheryll Glotfelty and Harold Fromm. Athens: U of Georgia P, 1996. 52–68.

Carroll, Peter N., and David W. Noble. *The Free and the Unfree: A New History of the United States*. Harmondsworth, Eng.: Penguin, 1977.

Costello, Bonnie. " 'What to Make of a Diminished Thing': Modern Nature and Poetic Response." *American Literary History* 10 (1998): 569–605.

Dillard, Annie. *Pilgrim at Tinker Creek*. New York: Harper, 1985.

Easthope, Antony. *Literary into Cultural Studies*. London: Routledge, 1991.

Emerson, Ralph Waldo. *Selected Writings of Ralph Waldo Emerson*. Ed. William H. Gilman. New York: Signet, 1965.

Glotfelty, Cheryll. "Introduction: Literary Studies in an Age of Environmental Crisis." *The Ecocriticism Reader*. Ed. Cheryll Glotfelty and Harold Fromm. Athens: U of Georgia P, 1996. xv–xxxvii.

Kern, Robert. *Orientalism, Modernism, and the American Poem*. New York: Cambridge UP, 1996.

Kowinski, William. *The Malling of America: An Inside Look at the Great Consumer Paradise*. New York: Morrow, 1985.

Kroeber, Karl. "Ecology and American Literature: Thoreau and Un-Thoreau." *American Literary History* 9 (1997): 309–28.

Lentricchia, Frank. *Modernist Quartet*. New York: Cambridge UP, 1994.

Leopold, Aldo. *A Sand County Almanac*. New York: Ballantine, 1970.

Richardson, Robert D., Jr. *Henry Thoreau: A Life of the Mind*. Berkeley: U of California P, 1986.

Schwarz, Daniel R. *Narrative and Representation in the Poetry of Wallace Stevens*. New York: St. Martin's, 1993.

Snyder, Gary. *Axe Handles*. San Francisco: North Point, 1983.

———. *The Back Country*. New York: New Directions, 1968.

———. *No Nature*. New York: Pantheon, 1992.

———. *The Practice of the Wild*. San Francisco: North Point, 1990.

———. *Turtle Island*. New York: New Directions, 1974.

Stevens, Wallace. *The Palm at the End of the Mind*. Ed. Holly Stevens. New York: Vintage, 1972.

———. *The Necessary Angel: Essays on Reality and the Imagination*. New York: Vintage, 1951.

Thoreau, Henry David. *Walden and Other Writings*. Ed. Joseph Wood Krutch. New York: Bantam, 1981.

Wright, James. *The Branch Will Not Break*. Middletown, Conn.: Wesleyan UP, 1963.

JOHN TALLMADGE

Toward a Natural History of Reading

Go out there.
BARRY LOPEZ, *Of Wolves and Men*

THOSE OF US interested in both literature and the outdoors have welcomed ecocriticism as a justification for our eccentric passions. But does it go far enough? The term has been used thematically, to denote ordinary analysis of writing concerned with environmental issues, and politically, to revisit classics or valorize neglected works by reading them ecocentrically. This sort of criticism has already produced impressive results by opening the canon, revitalizing the curriculum, and deepening our understanding of many great writers. But the underlying method has generally been that used by other schools, namely, close reading of a primary text, mediated by close readings of other, chiefly literary texts. In other words, the "eco" refers more often to the content of the work or the purpose of the critic than it does to the critical method itself.

Thoreau declared that great books should be read in the spirit in which they were written. What would it mean to actually follow this advice? In the case of nature writing and environmental literature in general, what would an ecological method of criticism look like? Scholars have recently begun to explore this question, with fascinating results. According to Lawrence Buell, to read ecocentrically ("under the sign of nature") means to have accepted a priori the value and worth of a referential world beyond the text itself. The stance of the critic mandates attention to extratextual realities: he or she has assumed a political position that affects reading and interpretation.[1] But attention to this referential world is also invited by the work itself. According to Buell, the salient feature of environmental literature is that nature is not merely a setting or backdrop for human action, but an actual factor in the plot, that is, a character and sometimes even a protagonist (7–8). This is particularly obvious in nature and wilderness writing, which originate in the narrator's transformative encounters with a landscape and its inhabitants. Such works often manifest plot structures of romance or conversion, in which the act of writing appears either as a rite of obsessive homage prefiguring an "eternal return," or as a demonstration of faith and loyalty, a gesture of thanks for gifts received from the land. Writing in this mode becomes part of the story, so that the text itself is an action to be evaluated in terms of the originary event and the world from which that event springs; such is the case with spiritual autobiography in the Augustinian or Dantean mode, a genre with which Romantic and post-Romantic nature writing is closely bound up.[2] By compelling the reader's attention to return to the referential world—bearing, of course, the more enlightened view conveyed by the story itself—such writing also manifests a social agenda. It wants to change the way we relate to nature. Philosopher David Abram in *The Spell of the Sensuous* (1996), a work that has aroused considerable interest among ecocritics, argues that our environmental problems have arisen because we have lost the habit of relating to other creatures in a manner consistent with how we actually perceive them; we regard beings in nature as inscrutable, mysterious, incomprehensible, or "other," but a close phenomenological analysis shows that we actually encounter them synesthetically as perceiving, expressive beings who interact with us in an "intersubjective field"(31–72). In short, although the world "speaks," we have grown deaf; we do not think of other beings in nature as ethical equals, possessing valued attributes such as language, feelings, or character; as a result, we recklessly consume and despoil. Abram blames "alphabetic literacy" for this sad state of affairs, arguing that it has displaced our synesthetic perceptions from nature to texts. He looks to nature writing as a redemptive mode of discourse that can redirect our attention toward an animate, "more-than-human" world.

Given arguments such as these, it is easy to see the prescience in Barry Lopez's famous statement to *Antaeus* in 1986 that nature writing would not only one day "produce a major and lasting body of American literature" but also "provide the foundation for a reorganization of American political thought" (297). It is also understandable that ecocritics might see themselves and their works as furthering such a process. But where are the methods to match our mountains? How can we read professionally in a manner that brings consideration of the referential world to bear on our interpretations and judgments in more than a casual way? Even Buell finds it hard to pursue the consequences of his vision beyond a text-based analysis. At one point in *The Environmental Imagination* he invokes the damp, gray winter scene outside his Massachusetts window to expose Thoreau's aesthetic and thematic agenda in editing Walden's winter to a uniform "chilly whiteness" (246). This brief, vivid moment endures long enough to suggest tantalizing possibilities, but it is soon eclipsed by the profoundly erudite, sophisticated, and relentlessly textual argument that has made Buell's work indispensable.

Nevertheless, promising approaches toward incorporating the "real world" have emerged on the expanding horizon of ecocriticism. As early as 1984, Michael Cohen drew on his own experience in the Sierra to interpret the writings of John Muir in *The Pathless Way*. John Elder's seminal study of poetry, *Imagining the Earth* (1985), argued that "natural scenes engender and inform meditations on literature as well as the other way around" (3), and his *Reading the Mountains of Home* (1998) "explore[s], in a direct and personal way, an ecosystem of meaning that includes both literature and the land" (4). In *For Love of the World* (1992), Sherman Paul presented readings of nature writers informed not just by his reading but also by his Leopoldian practice of inhabitation (which he called "worlding") at Wolf Lake in northern Minnesota. Don Scheese, in *Nature Writing* (1996), has argued for the central importance of field work in understanding "the dynamics that develop between author and locale," as well as checking the writer's accuracy and, not incidentally, giving the critic some fresh air (9–10). David Robertson, in *Real Matter* (1997) finds pilgrimage a valuable method, since both the writer and the scholar find the "real matter" of their life and work in both texts and landscapes. Ian Marshall's exciting *Story Line* (1998) presents a "literary geography" of the Appalachian Trail that blends conventional literary interpretation with poststructuralist theory and his own direct experience of the landscape, arguing that "narrative scholarship is a way of putting into practice the ecological principle of interconnectedness" (3–8).

This sample suggests the rich and varied possibilities for field-based reading that have begun to emerge in ecocritical practice.[3] In a step toward synthesis, and perhaps toward theory as well, I would like to offer natural history as a model for the disciplined integration of field work—that is, experience of the referential world—into interpretation and criticism. Because natural history is both a scientific practice and a literary genre, it can serve as a guide for both reading and writing, that is, for studying the primary material and communicating the results. Of course, it is perilous to trade in scientific analogies; they can be quite seductive for humanists who regard the prestige of science with a mixture of fear and envy. Northrop Frye once famously disparaged the ordinary reader by invoking the image of a scientist at work:

The critic has a subjective background of experience formed by his temperament and by every contact with words he has made, including newspapers,
advertisements, conversations, movies, and whatever he read at the age of
nine. He has a specific skill in responding to literature which is no more like
this subjective background, with all its private memories, associations, and
arbitrary prejudices, than reading a thermometer is like shivering. (28)

Though dated, Frye's analogy remains instructive for its blend of optimism
and condescension. It posits a clear and absolute line between the critic
and the ordinary reader, as if a person were always one thing or the other.
It then assumes that literary criticism can be objective and impersonal, and
that these supposed virtues can be achieved by cultivating skills that make
the critic as precisely responsive as an instrument. It celebrates a kind of
numerical precision, to the implicit detriment of narrative and, indeed, of
any kind of unquantifiable experience, as if equations were more valuable
than stories, or reading a thermometer more interesting than shivering. In
so doing, the analogy trades in a naive view of the humanities that I have
heard from more than one scientist, namely, that humanistic inquiry is a
touchy-feely matter of impressions and emotions, lacking true intellectual
rigor—as if there were no such thing as evidence, logic, or coherent arguments in our work. But Frye's hope is misplaced. Criticism can never be
objective in any scientific sense, for reading is an ineluctably subjective en-
deavor, and an objective report of a subjective event is a contradiction in
terms. What distinguishes the literary critic from the casual reader, I believe,
is the *disciplined* subjectivity of the latter.

Suppose, then, that we envision a literary critic whose subjectivity is disciplined in ways similar to that of the natural historian. We might take as
our model any of the great naturalists, Humboldt or Darwin, say, or to pick
from the twentieth century, someone like Rachel Carson or Aldo Leopold.
To the observation and interpretation of nature, such a naturalist brings,
first, extensive learning in the discourse and material of the natural sciences:
a developing body of thought that aspires to a coherent picture of the living world. To this is added a liberal education in culture, ethics, aesthetics,
philosophy, literature, and the arts. In sum, the classic naturalist is learned
in both technical science and humanistic traditions.

Second, the naturalist brings an array of skills for gathering information:
observation, photography, drawing, writing. Some of these translate, when
necessary, into powers of expression needed to communicate the results of
observation and analysis. Both knowledge and skills come into play in the

third area, which is the actual field work. Before all, natural history depends upon direct observation: the naturalist works outdoors, in situ not in vitro, and his or her reports have an eyewitness authority that has been acknowledged as a principal standard of value from the time of Gilbert White on down through Darwin, Burroughs, and the "nature faker" controversies at the turn of the twentieth century. The great entomologist E. O. Wilson memorably depicts the naturalist entering a state of altered consciousness at the threshold of observation:

> I walked into the forest, struck as always by the coolness of the shade beneath tropical vegetation, and continued until I came to a small glade that opened onto the sandy path. I narrowed the world down to the span of a few meters. Again I tried to compose the mental set—call it the naturalist's trance, the hunter's trance—by which biologists locate more elusive organisms. I imagined this place and all its treasures were mine alone and might be so forever in memory—if the bulldozer came.
>
> In a twist my mind came free and I was aware of the hard workings of the natural world beyond the periphery of ordinary attention, where passions lose their meaning and history is in another dimension, without people, and great events pass without record or judgment. I was a transient of no consequence in this familiar yet deeply alien world that I had come to love. The uncounted products of evolution were gathered there for purposes having nothing to do with me; their long Cenozoic history was enciphered into a genetic code I could not understand. The effect was strangely calming. Breathing and heartbeat diminished, concentration intensified. It seemed to me that something extraordinary in the forest was very close to where I stood, moving to the surface and discovery. (6–7)

Significantly, the naturalist here enters the forest fully informed and prepared for discovery, but as observation begins he centers and empties his mind, so as to be receptive to the unknown. He must hold his learning and its world of discourse in suspense in order to experience and recognize anything new. Following observation, the naturalist returns to reflect on the experience and synthesize it with other observations, sometimes from remote places, to discover meaningful patterns and connections. Such was the practice of Humboldt and Darwin, setting the standard for the great synthetic works of latter day naturalists such as Wilson and Carson.

The outcome of this process is, of course, a narrative—a *history*, what Darwin called a "journal of researches," though it was much more coherent than a mere diary. John Hildebidle, in his excellent study of Thoreau's debt to the natural history tradition, describes the genre succinctly as "informal, inclusive, intensely local, experiential, eccentric, nativist, and utilitarian, yet in the end concerned not only with fact but with fundamental spiritual and aesthetic truths" (61). This sort of history reports the witness and interpretation of direct observation along with the results of synthesizing reflection. It is a story of the learning and illumination that comes to a subject prepared by prior study and centered by the naturalist's trance. As a mode of discourse, natural history not only conveys information but also demonstrates a method of inquiry; in other words, it describes both the process and the results of a disciplined subjectivity. In this respect it fully embodies the literary ideal of expressive form.

Adapting the method of natural history to the study of literature requires the cultivation of two critical virtues that I will call erudition and engagement. Erudition means all the discursive knowledge we gain from systematic reading, not just of other literary works but of all relevant criticism, theory, biography, and scholarship in allied disciplines such as philosophy, psychology, history, science, or religion. It also includes, needless to say, the essential skills of close reading and exegesis—in short, everything now required in graduate school. Erudition fosters attentiveness and heightens perception, not only within the textual world but out in the referential world as well. That latter world is primarily addressed by the second virtue, engagement, which means the deliberate and systematic study of the referential world through direct encounter. In the case of nature writing, engagement requires going out and experiencing the landscape itself.

For the critic as natural historian, erudition is prerequisite to engagement. Erudition creates the informed sensibility that enables productive observation. It fosters attentiveness both to the work and to the referential landscape. Before going into the field, the critic gains discursive knowledge of the landscape through guidebooks, commentary, and, perhaps, other works of natural history besides the primary text (which has, of course, also been read in depth). Once in the field, however, all this knowledge must be held in suspense: the critic exits discursive thought in order to be "tutored by the land" (in Barry Lopez's evocative phrase). Only a disciplined subjectivity can subject itself attentively to this sort of experience, a multisensorial, whole-body encounter, inherently synesthetic and thus charged with the immediacy and vivid mutuality of Abram's intersubjective field, so that the more-than-human world becomes a matter of intense, incontrovertible certainty that qualifies and may even clarify the impressions gained from initial readings of the work in question. The discipline of erudition charges the observer's mind with all the possibilities for meaning in the ordinary sense (as Thomas Kuhn speaks of "ordinary science"). These do not evaporate but are held in suspense, are present in the background, as it were, to provide a dark field against which the new can appear in full clarity, can be *discovered*. For the new is always both unexpected and yet connected to the known. The observer may not know at first what it is, but must know at once that it is significant. And here is the crucial difference between the critic as naturalist and the tourist or casual reader: both can encounter a text or landscape subjectively, but the critic's discipline is required for discovery.

To illustrate how engagement can transform interpretation, let me briefly describe a field research project that I conducted during the early 1980s on Clarence King's *Mountaineering in the Sierra Nevada* (1872), a classic of scientific adventure and a formative specimen of western Americana. In the late 1860s King, a young geologist fresh out of Yale, joined the California Geological Survey and spent three years exploring and mapping the Sierra Nevada. His accounts of peril and discovery in high places appeared serially in the *Atlantic Monthly*, delighting audiences throughout the genteel East. Perhaps the most memorable of these stories recounts his ascent of Mt. Tyndall, a peak just north of Mt. Whitney that King and his party, camped high in what is now Kings Canyon National Park, mistakenly thought was the highest summit in California. The intervening country was unknown and looked impassable; it sparked King's ambition:

> Brewer and Hoffman were old climbers, and their verdict of impossible oppressed me as I lay awake thinking of it; but early next morning I had made up my mind, and, taking Cotter aside, I asked him in an easy manner whether he would like to penetrate the Terra Incognita with me at the risk of our necks, provided Brewer should consent. In a frank, courageous tone he answered after his usual mode, "Why not?" Stout of limb, stronger yet in heart, of iron endurance, and a quiet, unexcited temperament, and, better yet, deeply devoted to me, I felt that Cotter was the one comrade I would choose to face death with, for there was in his manhood no room for fear or shirk. (50–51)

King and Cotter set off alone with improvised packs and, after five days of hair-raising adventure, managed to scale the peak and return to base camp, only to find that their companions, fearing the worst, had already left for the lowlands.

The passage quoted gives a fair idea of the energy and machismo of King's narrative, which abounds in the topoi of classic adventure embellished with allusions to literature, arts, and other forms of high culture as

well as pervasive (but discreet) appeals to the classist prejudices of his readers. All this makes King a great target for political or new historicist critiques, which have seen the literature of exploration and discovery as abet-
ting Western imperialism and environmental destruction, but my concern
at the moment is solely with textual artifice. A few examples suggest the
richness and diversity of King's literary devices. The journey is conceived in
epic terms as a descent to the underworld, reinforced by allusions to Dante
and the Doré illustrations ("at my feet the basin of the lake, still, black,
and gemmed with reflected stars, like the void into which Dante looked
through the bottomless gulf of Dis" [91–92]). The landscape is depicted as
a theater for heroic action ("West of us stretched the Mount Brewer wall
with its succession of smooth precipices and amphitheater ridges. To the
north the great gorges of the King's River yawned down five thousand feet"
[64–65]). Landforms are described in terms of the Romantic sublime with a
distinctly Ruskinian flavor ("the Kern divide . . . battlemented and adorned
with innumerable rough-hewn spires and pinnacles, was a mass of glowing
orange intensely defined against the deep violet sky" [58]).[4] Such constructs
are reinforced by King's geological catastrophism, which governs his scientific digressions ("old glacier valleys, these imperishable tracks of unseen
engines . . . the ruins of some bygone geological period" [79]). As for the
narrator, he appears variously as a promethean warrior attempting a "campaign for the top of California" (51) in the face of a hostile landscape ("if
Nature had intended to secure the summit from all assailants, she could
not have planned her defences better" [74]); as a knight accompanied by a
faithful squire ("deeply devoted to me"), or as a young hero "oppressed" by
an elder who "felt a certain fatherly responsibility over our youth, a natural
desire that we should not deposit our triturated remains in some undiscov-
erable hole among the feldspathic granites" (51). The plot structure follows
that of a medieval quest romance, in which the hero departs from a center of
civilization and enters the wilderness where, after adventures of escalating
intensity, he survives an ultimate test and returns with the power to bestow
boons, in this case scientific knowledge and a powerful story that affirms
his culture's ideals.

    King's adroit use of such literary devices makes for an exciting read
but also creates the suspicion that he may be less interested in accuracy
than in dramatic effects. King's biographers, too, mention his professional
and social aspirations, his fondness for posh men's clubs, and his reputation as a raconteur. He was clearly writing to an elite eastern audience, of
whom few, if any, were likely to visit the places he described. My suspicions

were further aroused by impressions gained from informal backpack trips
to the southern High Sierra in the late 1970s. I had seen the pass from which
Brewer and Hoffman had glimpsed Mt. Tyndall, and it did not look particularly steep, nor did the canyon below, through which I was hiking, seem
much of an obstacle. As for Mt. Tyndall, I had seen it from the Kern River
uplands along the John Muir Trail, and it looked like nothing more than
a big rock pile with a walk-in approach and an easy scramble to the top.
All this led me to conclude that King had overdrawn the landscape and
exaggerated its dangers for the sake of drama and heroic effects. His Sierra
was a caricature, based on a real place, perhaps, but largely constructed out
of literary topoi and other cultural apparatus with no intrinsic relation to
the actual landscape. These conclusions were based on conventional textual
analysis and reinforced by the handful of extant critical and biographical
studies. I taught the book this way for years.

It was not until a colleague from the geology department took issue with
this reading that I decided to go back to the High Sierra. She had used
King's scientific works in her course on the exploration of the West, and
she averred that his account ought to be taken at face value, given the precision and accuracy of his geological reports. Debate resolved nothing. So
I enlisted four students from my nature-writing course, and we retraced
King's ascent of Mt. Tyndall, having prepared assiduously by studying both
his text and his route using topographic maps, guidebooks, and published
accounts of the area.

Space does not permit a detailed account of our journey, which began in
a snowstorm at nine thousand feet and, like King's, included cliffhangers,
feats of endurance, and narrow escapes. Here I wish merely to mention a
few of the ways in which this exercise of engagement altered and clarified
our interpretation of King's account. Because the route lies wholly within
the backcountry of two national parks, it is largely unchanged since King's
day; there are only a few miles of trail, and the only other "improvement" is
a park service footbridge. Psychologically, however, things are quite different. The landscape has been surveyed, named, and administered; our maps
gave a precise aerial view of the terrain, revealing alternative routes and
showing that we could have walked out to civilization in two or three days
from any point; we carried nylon tents, sleeping bags, down jackets, and
freeze-dried food. In short, the mountains were no longer terra incognita,
as they had been for King. We felt a good deal safer and more comfortable.

The landscape, however, proved much more rugged and challenging
than expected. I first began to suspect that King might not have exaggerated

when we reached the top of the Mt. Brewer pass and gazed down a precipice at a snow gully as steep as a ski jump; the view from below, distorted by foreshortening, had made the pass look easy. The Mt. Brewer wall, along which King and Cotter had climbed, was studded with giant, precarious blocks that eventually forced us to rock climb down six hundred feet into a snowy amphitheater, across which we pushed to rejoin King's route below Longley Pass, now blocked by a thirty-foot cornice of overhanging snow. These were the first of many episodes that made us appreciate the appropriateness of King's descriptions in terms of both detail and atmosphere. The Dantean allusions and gothic imagery no longer seemed like gratuitous set pieces; they seemed invited by the circumstances. We were now able to calibrate King's descriptions more accurately as combinations of physiographic fact and cultural artifact. Similarly, we gained a more balanced view of King's own persona. We had suspected him of bombast and posturing; now phrases such as "at the risk of our necks" carried the scent of truth. Insights like these allowed us to appreciate how the idea of the West, with its attendant myths, aspirations, and master metaphors, could have arisen from a potent reaction between European archetypes and North American landscapes in the alembic of personalities as learned, imaginative, and ambitious as King's. Without this process of engagement and its culminating field work, we would have remained content to interpret King's account as a mere construct, a deftly woven fabric of topos and allusion rather than a creative struggle between a powerful mind and an equally powerful place. In sum, engagement adds balance to interpretation by addressing landscape as well as culture, recognizing that texts like *Mountaineering* always grow from a combination of both.

The preceding discussion is not meant, of course, as an actual demonstration of the method, but only a sketch of its possibilities for enriching a criticism historically based on erudition alone.[5] A full-scale natural history of reading would combine erudition and engagement in a balanced manner and eventuate, like classic natural history itself, in a narrative of illumination and discovery. Narrative is the appropriate vehicle for dealing with complex realities, such as landscapes, ecosystems, and literary works (which ecocritics like Joseph Meeker and William Rueckert have sought to construe ecologically). But it is also the best mode of discourse for conveying the results of observation, that is, of disciplined subjectivity. Though concerned with fact and accuracy, natural history does not pretend to a wholly objective truth. The critic as natural historian is always present, not only in the primary encounter with landscape, but also in the subsequent processes of reflection, interpretive synthesis, and eventual narration. The critical essay in this mode brings the two types of learning experience—text and landscape—together in a single narrative, thus providing a stereoscopic view of the work in question.

The critical essay is also, perforce, an exemplary narrative: it not only conveys information but also demonstrates a way of reading. It therefore serves the work and its readers, as all worthy criticism should. By bearing witness to engagement with the landscape, it also parallels the narrative of natural history which is both its subject and its inspiration. For nature writing always exemplifies and envisions new possibilities for human relations with the rest of the living world and hence serves a prophetic political purpose. The critical essay participates in this politics of redemption by exemplifying relations to both art and landscape, thus bringing nature and culture together. It therefore has the potential to help counteract the alienating effects of Abram's alphabetic literacy and the notion, inherited from Descartes and his age, of culture as somehow apart from or opposed to nature.

These are large claims, to be sure. Objections to a natural history of reading might be raised on various grounds: that such criticism is mere self-indulgence; that the critic, by engaging in narrative, presumes to supersede the artist and blur the line between literature and criticism; that by endeavoring to speak for nature the critic is merely perpetuating the scandal of human domination; that engagement is just an excuse to avoid real, serious work in the library; and so forth. Of course, any method can be abused, and someone will always make a career out of doing so. There have always been bad critics, just as there have always been nature fakers and sentimental outdoor writers. But all these are judged, sooner or later, by their fruits. To what degree does an essay serve the work rather than the ego or personal needs of the critic? Does the critic adopt a confessing posture, in the Augustinian manner, toward both the work and the world to which it refers? For there is no place and no work, however humble it may appear, about which we cannot learn more.

As for the line between literature and criticism, it has never been very clearly drawn, and why should it be? Lately it has begun to appear as artificial as the line between fiction and nonfiction. One should get pleasure from any text worth reading. Moreover, other recent schools of criticism also use narrative and foreground the experience of the critic. Feminist criticism, to take an obvious example, maintains that personal witness in a climate of oppression constitutes primary evidence.[6] Another trend, "narrative criticism," foregrounds the experiences of the critic as literary pilgrim.[7] Here the danger is an understandable temptation to lapse into journalism or travelogue, to the neglect of erudition or systematic engagement and consequent diversion of attention from the work to the critic. Similar issues arise with what has been called "autobiographical criticism,"[8] which narrates the critic's own personal relation to the work: one can easily fall prey to the vice that C. S. Lewis, speaking of Milton's Satan, called "incessant autobiography." The critic's private issues take center stage, because his or her subjectivity has not been disciplined, has not actually been *subjected* to the work. But a true natural history of reading calls for subjectivity that is doubly disciplined: to land and library, nature and culture both. And because it eventuates in a narrative of learning, the method describes a path that others can follow, thus opening itself to verification and testing.

A natural history of reading offers exciting prospects for scholars and teachers in an era of postmodern ferment. It promises to revitalize critical practice by adding a research dimension that both draws on and transcends the virtues of existing method even as it returns, paradoxically, to the root meaning of method itself: a systematic journey or pathway toward a goal. In this respect the naturalist, the explorer, and the literary scholar have always been kindred spirits, aspiring to lofty and synthesizing views even as they delight in local, particular knowledge and the personal encounter with place. In elevating our vision, therefore, to encompass mountains as well as texts, we honor not only the natural world that sustains and inspires us, but organic tradition as well.

NOTES

This essay grew out of a presentation delivered at the Association for the Study of Literature and Environment (ASLE) roundtable on ecocriticism at the 1992 meeting of the College English Association.

1. This is hardly an unprecedented situation, of course. Consider the leftist agendas of Marxism (e.g., Terry Lovell, *Pictures of Reality*) or even deconstruction (e.g., Paul De Man, *The Resistance to Theory*). On politics in interpretation generally see Stanley Cavell, "The Politics of Interpretation."

2. For discussions of conversion paradigms in nature writing, see Schauffler, *Turning to Earth*, and Tallmadge, "John Muir and the Poetics of Natural Conversion."

3. Other works that incorporate narrative or field research into ecocritical practice include William Howarth, *Thoreau in the Mountains* (1982), John P. O'Grady, *Pilgrims to the Wild* (1993), Scott Slovic, *Seeking Awareness in American Nature Writing* (1992), John Tallmadge, *Meeting the Tree of Life* (1997).

4. For an excellent discussion of King's responses in light of prevailing scientific

and aesthetic norms, see Roger Stein, *John Ruskin and Aesthetic Thought in America* (169–83).

5. Two recent studies of *Mountaineering* also exemplify the fruits of engaged reading and fieldwork. See O'Grady, *Pilgrims to the Wild* (1993), and David Robertson, *Real Matter* (1997), 26–34.

6. Not surprisingly, a strong ecofeminist current within ecocriticism treats beings in nature as an oppressed class within the universe of patriarchal hegemony; see Gaard and Murphy.

7. Narrative criticism was the subject of a seminal roundtable at the 1995 conference of the Western Literature Association. Participants included Suellen Campbell, Michael P. Cohen, Gretchen Legler, Glen Love, Ian Marshall, Ann Ronald, Stephanie Sarver, Don Scheese, and Scott Slovic. Marshall's *Story Line* (1998) is a brilliant example of this approach.

8. For a definition and instructive example, see Diane P. Freedman, "A Whale of a Different Color."

REFERENCES

Abram, David. *The Spell of the Sensuous: Perception and Language in a More-than-Human World*. New York: Pantheon, 1996.

Buell, Lawrence. *The Environmental Imagination: Thoreau, Nature Writing, and the Formation of American Culture*. Cambridge: Harvard UP, 1995.

Cavell, Stanley. "The Politics of Interpretation (Politics as Opposed to What?)." *Themes out of School: Effects and Causes*. San Francisco: North Point, 1984. 27–59.

Cohen, Michael P. *The Pathless Way: John Muir and American Wilderness*. Madison: U of Wisconsin P, 1984.

De Man, Paul. *The Resistance to Theory*. Minneapolis: U of Minnesota P, 1986.

Elder, John. *Imagining the Earth: Poetry and the Vision of Nature*. 1985. 2nd. ed. Athens: U of Georgia P, 1996.

———. *Reading the Mountains of Home*. Cambridge: Harvard UP, 1998.

Freedman, Diane P. "A Whale of a Different Color; Melville and the Movies: The Great Whale and *Free Willy*." *ISLE* 4.2 (1997): 87–95.

Frye, Northrup. *Anatomy of Criticism*. Princeton: Princeton UP, 1957.

Gaard, Greta, and Patrick Murphy, eds. *Ecofeminist Literary Criticism*. Spec. issue of *ISLE* 3:1 (1996).

Howarth, William. *Thoreau in the Mountains*. New York: Farrar, 1982.

Hildebidle, John. *Thoreau: A Naturalist's Liberty*. Cambridge: Harvard UP, 1983.

King, Clarence. *Mountaineering in the Sierra Nevada*. Lincoln: U of Nebraska P, 1970.

Lopez, Barry. "On Nature." *Antaeus* 57 (1986): 295–97.

Lovell, Terry. *Pictures of Reality: Aesthetics, Politics, Pleasure*. London: British Film Institute, 1980.

Marshall, Ian. *Story Line: Exploring the Literature of the Appalachian Trail*. Charlottesville: UP of Virginia, 1998.

Meeker, Joseph. *The Comedy of Survival.* 2nd ed. Tucson: U of Arizona P, 1997.

O'Grady, John P. *Pilgrims to the Wild: Everett Ruess, Henry David Thoreau, John Muir, Clarence King, and Mary Austin.* Salt Lake City: U of Utah P, 1993.

Paul, Sherman. *For Love of the World: Essays on Nature Writers.* Iowa City: U of Iowa P, 1992.

Robertson, David. *Real Matter.* Salt Lake City: U of Utah P, 1997.

Rueckert, William, "Literature and Ecology: An Experiment in Ecocriticism." *Iowa Review* 9.1 (1978): 71–86.

Schauffler, Marina. "Turning to Earth: Paths to an Ecological Practice." Ph.D. diss., U of New Hampshire, 1998.

Scheese, Don. *Nature Writing: The Pastoral Impulse in America.* New York: Twayne, 1996.

Slovic, Scott. *Seeking Awareness in American Nature Writing: Henry Thoreau, Annie Dillard, Edward Abbey, Wendell Berry, Barry Lopez.* Salt Lake City: U of Utah P, 1992.

Stein, Roger. *John Ruskin and Aesthetic Thought in America.* Cambridge: Harvard UP, 1967.

Tallmadge, John. "John Muir and the Poetics of Natural Conversion." *North Dakota Quarterly* 59.2 (1991): 62–79.

———. *Meeting the Tree of Life: A Teacher's Path.* Salt Lake City: U of Utah P, 1997.

Wilson, E. O. *Biophilia.* Cambridge: Harvard UP, 1984.

MICHAEL BENNETT

From Wide Open Spaces to Metropolitan Places

The Urban Challenge to Ecocriticism

ECOCRITICISM, a field existing on the sometimes rocky terrain where culture and environment meet, has recently developed from a sparsely populated area of study into a busy intersection of scholarly work.[1] The number of journals, presses, and academic programs devoted to the field has mushroomed. There is perhaps no better evidence of the recent growth of interest in ecocriticism than the rapid expansion of the Association for the Study of Literature and Environment (ASLE) and its official journal, *ISLE: Interdisciplinary Studies in Literature and Environment*. But even as the community of ecocritics grows from a hamlet into a bustling metropolis, the movement itself has been slow to survey urban environments. Ecocriticism has instead developed in tandem with growing academic interest in nature writing, American pastoralism, and literary ecology. The resulting body of critical work claims rural environments and wild nature as its domain, meaning that most ecocritics in the United States have focused their attention on America's rural past or on the remaining wide open spaces of the Wild West.[2]

But what happens when ecocriticism crosses the Mississippi or heads for a night on the town? Once it's seen New York, how can you keep it down on the farm (or pine barren or desert ecosystem)? These are the questions which animate the following attempt to assess the urban challenge to ecocriticism. There is a growing body of cultural criticism engaged with urban ecology that tends to reject mainstream ecocriticism's focus on the genres of nature writing and pastoral, insisting on the incapacity of these genres to represent the complex interactions between political choices, socioeconomic structures, and the densely populated ecosystems that shape urban environments.[3] This essay attempts to bring this distaff branch of ecocriticism into dialogue with its more famous country cousin, exploring their different contributions to the philosophical grounds, cultural geography, and critical genealogy of ecocriticism.[4] I wish to maintain that the insights generated by this distaff branch, which I will call social ecocriticism, are needed if we are to successfully incorporate urban environments within the domain of ecological criticism.

The Grounds of Ecocriticism

THE BELIEFS that have been central for most practitioners of ecocriticism, whom I will call deep ecocritics, were laid out in the tremendously influential book *Deep Ecology,* in which Bill Devall and George Sessions describe the movement's "ultimate norms" as "self-realization and biocentric equality" (205). In Michael Tobias's volume of the same name, Arne Naess, the Norwegian philosopher usually credited with founding Deep Ecology, describes the movement through a series of oppositions with "Shallow Ecology," creating an opposition between the "shallow" focus on nature as a valuable resource for humans and the "deep" imperative to treat nature as valuable in its own right (257). The primary gospel of Deep Ecology is that we must abandon androcentric planning and develop a biocentric understanding of the environment, an understanding which is to be gained by existing in harmony with unspoiled nature.

In adopting this focus, the Deep Ecology movement has overlooked a variety of environmental concerns that are central to urban life. At one point, Devall and Sessions acknowledge the range of environmental issues, such as resource extraction and employment policy, that Deep Ecology dismisses by ignoring cities (158); while admitting that "these are vital issues" (159), Devall and Sessions insist that wild nature alone can provide the experience needed to foster "self-realization and biocentric equality" (111). They delineate four deep ecological principles that they believe can be developed only through interaction with wide open spaces: "1) developing a sense of place, 2) redefining the heroic person from conqueror of the land to the person fully experiencing the natural place, 3) cultivating the virtues of modesty and humility and 4) realizing how the mountains and rivers, fish and bears are continuing their own actualizing processes" (110). I would argue that these four qualities (minus the bears) can just as easily be found in urban environments. The failure to recognize this fact points to one of the major flaws with ecocriticism grounded in deep ecological theory: it tends to engage in a form of wilderness fetishism, analyzed in detail in the work of

William Cronon, that disables it from offering a useful analysis of urban environments.

In contrast with these deep ecological principles, the central tenets of social ecology, which have been so influential for the distaff branch of ecocriticism practiced by social ecocritics, are defined by the Institute for Social Ecology as a set of beliefs that "integrates the study of human and natural ecosystems through understanding the interrelationships of culture and nature" (Davis, *Ecophilosophy* 123). The man most centrally identified with the social ecology movement, Murray Bookchin, has described the movement's "most fundamental message" in stating that "our basic ecological problems stem from social problems" (*Philosophy* 35). This focus on how the social, political, and economic decisions made by humans affect our interaction with the environment has been particularly fruitful for analyzing urban areas.

Social ecologists have not, however, simply accepted cities as they are; they frequently offer a critique of the ways in which metropolitan culture transforms urban environments. In *Urbanization without Cities,* Murray Bookchin writes about cities as a necessary though flawed step toward human progress, much like the role of the bourgeoisie in Marxist historiography. Social ecologists like Bookchin offer a critique of urbanization at the same time as they note the progressive role played by cities in the ongoing social dialectic that weaves together humans and nonhuman nature. In Bookchin's effort to "redeem the city," he makes a series of connections between the ecology of wide open spaces and that of metropolitan places, noting that this argument "runs counter to the conventional wisdom that city and countryside, like society and nature, are necessarily in conflict with each other, a theme that pervades so much of the writing on urbanity of western society" (x)—including the writings of Devall and Sessions and other deep ecologists.

As can be seen from this thumbnail sketch, at the root of the difference between deep and social ecocritics is a profound philosophical disagreement about the role that humanity and our built environments play in global ecology. Most ecocriticism, following the lead of Deep Ecology, insists that we "must break through our preoccupation with mediating between only human issues" to realize that human domination of the environment, more than human domination of other humans, is "the overriding problem" (Love, "Revaluing" 203). For cultural critics influenced by social ecology this position has two theoretical flaws: first, it establishes an absolute dichotomy between domination of humans and domination of the environment, though social ecocritics would argue that they are linked by what Murray Bookchin calls the "epistemologies of rule" (*Ecology* 89); second, humans can only act on human values and make human choices, so it makes little sense to speak of moving beyond human issues and adopting a biocentric viewpoint.

Another problem with the appeal of deep ecocriticism to some primal experience of nature is that, as poststructuralist theory often reminds us, we can never definitively know something outside of the language we use to describe it. In applying this insight to ecocriticism, Alexander Wilson argues that "our experience of the natural world . . . is always mediated" (12). Wilson points out that whether we experience nature through a trip to the mountains, an animal show on TV, or working in our garden, this interaction is always shaped by "rhetorical constructs like photography, industry, advertising, and aesthetics, as well as by institutions like religion, tourism, and education" (12). For this reason, "there are many natures" (12), and not a seamless Mother Nature who dictates certain actions and policies. As Raymond Williams noted, "nature" is one of the most complex words in our language; it is intimately interconnected with words like "society" and "culture"—words which are all too often seen as its antonyms rather than as its co-conspirators. This insight is often downplayed or even dismissed by deep ecocritics, who tend to have a strong antipathy for poststructuralist theory.[5]

Deep and social ecocriticism are alike in their rejection of humanism, but the difference is that the former rejects the "human" part of the equation while the latter is more troubled by the "ism." Michael Branch argues that ecocriticism and poststructuralism are similar in their basic premise that meaning, and individuals, exist only in a series of contextual relationships which poststructuralists call "intertextuality" and which ecophilosophers see as the primary interconnection of humans and their environment. Thus both poststructuralists and ecocritics (and especially critics who are both) object to claims of ungrounded objectivity and authority, the former on the grounds of a resistance to theories of language which instantiate notions of "presence" and the latter as part of a program to undo anthropocentrism. In the end, however, Branch rejects poststructuralism for sneaking anthropocentrism in through the back door by attempting "to use the ubiquity of language to *keep* humans at the center of our cosmological paradigm" (50). In short, deep ecologists are troubled by humanism because they hope to replace androcentrism with a biocentric view that displaces the human, while social ecologists, influenced by poststructuralism, are more likely to be troubled by the raising of the human into an "ism"—a transcendent, ahistorical, and monological category of absolute value (as in the popular bromides which begin something like "The time-honored truths of Humanism tell us that . . .").

Like Branch, SueEllen Campbell attempts to reconcile poststructuralism and ecocriticism but is unable to do so because of the limitations imposed by a deep ecological perspective. She begins by positing an opposition between poststructuralism and ecocriticism that must then be breached. In the very act of applying a theory that breaks down binary oppositions, a distinction between "theorists" and "ecologists" is maintained. And the two are relegated to very different environments: "All those days in the wilderness had taken me about as far as I could be from the crowded cafes and academic closets of theory" (199). The province of the ecologists is the great outdoors and wide-open spaces of the West; theoryheads, cut off from the rejuvenating forces of nature in their dingy eastern enclaves, are corralled into the cramped spaces of smoky cafés and even closets. If ecocriticism is to speak for both environments, it is time to bring theory out of the closet and realize that it is a necessary presence, not just among café society but in confronting the open spaces patrolled by the ecological posse (their trusty .45s in hand, ready to shoot trespassing, beret-wearing theoreticians).

In other words, Campbell's attempt to find parallels between the opposed realms of theory and ecology is misguided because a truly effective ecocriticism is, to borrow popular poststructuralist phraseology, "always already" theorized. Wilderness areas, as much as cityscapes, are shaped by complex sociopolitical, economic, and philosophical discourses. A remote pond in the Rocky Mountains is affected by the decision *not* to build a resort on its shores just as the Manhattan landscape was affected by the decision *to* build the World Trade Center. Campbell's attempt to reconcile theory and ecology on the basis of a mutual "experience of lost unity and a desire to regain it" (209), which she argues is central to both Lacanian understandings of the self and ecological conceptions of the environment, ignores the poststructuralist insistence that such a desire for unity is illusory and not recoverable. Rather than search for a mythic Edenic past, a society can try to model itself after other societies which have been more beneficent toward their environment, but this requires complex social, political, and economic—that is, theoretical—decisions. There is no unmediated way of existing in harmony with nature, and there never has been. Once we make human decisions on how to exist in our surroundings, we are already involved in sociocultural (and again, theoretical) modes of thought. Campbell's desire for unity with the land can certainly motivate a kind of theory which will benefit our planet, but it will fail to move us "beyond the human" (210) and outside of "networks of language and culture" (211) because we are human, and our understanding of the land is visible only in our language and culture. We can attempt to harmonize with our surroundings, but these attempts will be meaningful only to the extent that they are manifested in our ways of speaking to one another and living together. The deep ecological perspective adopted by many ecocritics, bereft of the theoretical insights of social ecology, will always be incomplete; it will also be unpersuasive and unavailable for most city dwellers and ultimately inadequate for non-urbanites as well.

George Sessions presents an extreme version of deep ecological dogma which is clearly anathema to urban ecocritics: "To be fully human we must protect and nurture our wildness, which involves bioregional living, intimate contact with wild animals and plants in wild ecosystems, animistic perceptions, and primal nature rituals" (6). One hears an unfortunate echo of this thinking in Glen Love's insistence that the only way for urban writers to gain true ecological awareness is for them to "slough off their New York or L.A. skins when they confront western landscapes" ("Revaluing" 209). When the arrogance (a profoundly anthropocentric posture) of Sessions's statement that only those in contact with the wild can become fully evolved humans is transported into Love's version of ecocriticism, we are provided with a prime example of the danger of importing the postulates of Deep Ecology into an undertheorized ecocritical perspective. Gratuitous swipes at urbanites and claims that only wild nature can "humanize" our sorry lot are all too common in ecocentric thinking. Yet anyone who has spent some time in the great outdoors knows that there are plenty of unevolved, anthropocentric, close-minded folk residing in remote areas. Where I grew up, on the Washington/Idaho border, we had a saying: "this place is much too nice for the people who are moving here." As the neo-Nazis and members of the Aryan Nations and The Order built their compounds in northern Idaho, it was hard to see how the crystal-clear lakes and majestic mountains infused them with enlightenment. And do we really want to exclude from "essential humanness" (Sessions 5) the many people of color and the gays and lesbians who are primarily urban dwellers in part because they have been chased away by the enlightened inhabitants of rural America? I purposefully overstate the case to draw attention to the very real plight of those of us who have sought refuge in the city only to be told by our betters that unless, like them, we commune with wild nature we will always be less than human—part of the problem and never part of the solution.

To return to an argument promulgated by William Cronon, the "wilderness fixation" of many deep ecocritics can blind them to the existence of urban environments and the ways in which these metropolitan places challenge overly narrow conceptions of ecotheory. Cronon has pointed out flaws in the very concept of wilderness as it appears within certain forms of environmental thinking associated with Deep Ecology, arguing that "in its flight from history, in its siren song of escape, in its reproduction of the dangerous dualism that sets human beings somehow outside nature— in all these ways, wilderness poses a threat to responsible environmentalism at the end of the 20th century" (43). He makes a compelling case, noting the myopic view of the "frontier" as a supposedly simpler time and space and the ways in which the opposition between man and nature was written onto the wilderness through policies of Indian removal. But surely there are ways to celebrate the wilderness which do not inherently represent it as "a flight from history" based on a "romantic ideology" with "no place in which human beings can actually make their living from the land" (42–43). This point of view overlooks the aesthetic and spiritual components of diversity, not to mention its contribution to biodiversity. In short, the insights of Deep Ecology should work in tandem with the social ecological approach to ecocriticism. Despite the flaws in Cronon's analysis of the flaws in wilderness thinking, he reasonably concludes that we need to "see a natural landscape that is also cultural, in which city, suburb, countryside and wilderness each has its own place" (43). He is right to conclude that we need to find a middle ground between country and city—and he doesn't mean the suburbs—which might be called "home."

The Geography of Ecocriticism

THE DIFFERENT CONCEPTIONS of the human element manifested in deep and social ecocriticism are related to the very different cultural geography of the two modes—the two different homes in which they have resided. The predominance of deep ecocriticism is connected to the fact that ecocritics have been disproportionately located in the West or in rural areas. The schools where you find a higher than average concentration of scholars who might call themselves ecocritics are places like the University of Oregon, the University of Nevada, Reno, or rural colleges. Not surprisingly, then, a quick glance at ASLE's 1999 *Membership Directory* reveals that there are more members from Nevada (a state with roughly one and a half million residents, according to the 1990 census) than from New Jersey (population: eight million). Oregon and Ohio are equally represented in ASLE's membership though the latter contains almost four times more people than the former. The scholarly journals most likely to publish essays on ecocriticism tend to be in places like Utah (*Weber Studies, Western American Literature*), Nevada (*ISLE: Interdisciplinary Studies in Literature and Environment*), or other western states: *Arizona Quarterly, Iowa Review, North American Review, North Dakota Quarterly, Texas Studies in Language and Literature.* The cultural geography of ecocritics is not unrelated to the terrain that they study. Glen Love provides evidence of the ways in which these two are related when he argues that pastoralism is a natural outgrowth of the literature of the American West, in which "nature continues to occupy a much larger place than it appears to in the eastern and urban imagination" ("*Et*" 196).

Indeed, the pastoral looms large in deep ecocriticism. And Love is not alone in arguing that pastoralism will only become more significant as its chief concern, the interconnections between human beings and nature, comes to dominate a time "when the comfortably mythopoeic green world of pastoral is beset by profound threats of pollution, despoliation, and diminishment" ("*Et*" 196). But Love also sees a need to reconceptualize the pastoral to make it relevant for a contemporary world: "Pastoral's ancient and universal appeal—to come away—requires new examination in an age in which there is no away. Pastoral, rightly understood, has always been a serious criticism of life. Ecocriticism, I think, can give us a serious criticism of pastoral" (198). This is, however, a criticism from within the pastoral rather than a criticism of the pastoral from some other vantage point. According to Love, one of the markers of this "new pastoral" is that "wild nature has replaced the traditional middle state of the garden and the rural landscape as the locus of stability and value, the seat of instruction" (203). While in classic pastoral the city dwellers took a refreshing trip to the country in order to return to their home rejuvenated, this new pastoral sees the remaining American wilderness as offering a radical challenge to the eco-unfriendly ways of urbanites.

The challenge which social ecocriticism offers to this rural focus of deep ecocriticism is of a parcel with the environmental justice movement's effort to reconceptualize the notions of "habitat preservation" and "endangered species" to include the homes of inner-city people of color and their inhabitants, whose lives are threatened by the results of "environmental racism."[6]

Many within the environmental justice movement felt that the mainstream environmental agenda was captive to classist and racist interests in issues like the preservation of wilderness and wildlife for the leisure and recreation of those Americans from the same class as the leadership of the environmental movement, which was almost devoid of people of color—a fact which Dana Alston points out was viewed by some as "another form of 'environmental racism'" (3). As one Hispanic woman protesting the effects of a gasoline terminal in her neighborhood put it, "we are the real endangered species in America, people of color" (Suro A1). And many civil rights leaders were slow to see how lead paint and air pollution were indeed a "Black thing" or a concern for Native Americans, Hispanic Americans, and other people of color. The United Church of Christ's report on toxic waste and race made it hard to ignore the relevance of environmentalism to the civil rights movement when it revealed that three out of five Black and Hispanic Americans and about half of all Asian/Pacific Islanders and Native Americans live in communities with uncontrolled toxic waste sites (Marks 9).

It is important that the ecocritical movement not replicate the larger environmental movement's marginalization of the ecological plight of communities of color. Rather, we should learn from the more recent efforts to bring the civil rights and environmental movements together in theory and practice.[7] In the past, the environmental movement's emphasis on issues such as wilderness preservation and protecting endangered species often served to deny the relevance of incidents of environmental racism. Now groups exploring the connections between these different forms of ecological destruction can provide a basis for united action. Such connections can also be formed in the theory and pedagogy of ecocriticism if it is not held captive by an exclusively non-urban bias. At the same time, the focus on urban environments should not blind us to the insights of movements concerned about "wild nature" or to the fact that environmental racism is not solely an urban phenomenon. In fact, many of the case studies in Robert Bullard's classic collection *Confronting Environmental Racism* are devoted to the ecological concerns of rural communities of color.

Still, ecocriticism will continue to be a relatively pale and undertheorized field unless and until it more freely ventures into urban environments. Even some of the practitioners of the nature writing and new pastoralism beloved by deep ecocritics have cautioned that their works and the larger scope of environmentally concerned writing and culture are too constrained by the critical rubrics used to contain nature. The superlative tone of John A. Murray's celebration of the "rise of nature writing" as "America's next great genre" in a special nature-writing symposium published in *Manoa* was critiqued by some of the very writers celebrated by Murray. These writers responded to the elevation of their craft with suspicion. For instance, Barry Lopez and Christopher Merrill caution against fetishizing nature writing at the expense of more nuanced analysis of the interaction between humans and their environment in all kinds of writing and various settings. Merrill argues that the "strongest writers" recognize the ways in which environmental, cultural, aesthetic, spiritual, and political problems "intersect and overlap and shed light on one another" (93). Lopez cautions that "natural history writing takes as its proper subjects not solely things like polar bears or sunsets but the complex biological, social, economic, and ethical relationships among these things." He fears that nature writing will "come to be seen as a genre rather than a tendency in American literature toward justice." Harmonizing with the call of social ecocritics, he argues for a broad definition of "natural history writing," one which allows for exploring the relationship "not simply with all that composes the Earth but between conquering and conquered people, for example" (89). He indirectly chastises Murray and other celebrants of nature writing for overlooking the work of Louise Erdrich, Barbara Kingsolver, J. M. Coetzee, and other writers who, like Lopez, are "addressing issues of prejudice, of dignity, and of tolerance" (90).

These are the qualities of environmentally committed writing that is not solely the domain of celebrants of wild nature and inhabitants of rural environments. Contrary to the implicit assumption of many ecocritics that daily contact with the green world is more likely to develop ecoconsciousness than life in the city, studies which have compared the environmental consciousness of urban and rural dwellers have either found little difference or have discovered that rural residents tend to express lower levels of environmental concern than do urbanites. Some have theorized that this counterintuitive result—those living closest to the land having the least respect for it—is based on the dependence of many rural residents on the extraction or use of natural resources and their greater likelihood of favoring economic development at the expense of environmental protection.[8] Whatever the cause, this rural-urban gap reveals that it may be less than wise to counsel those entering our field to "go West, young ecocritic" if we want them to look for environmentally enlightened cultural practices.

And, of course, the West itself is not merely so monolithic as it some-times appears in the pages of ecocritical essays. Looking through the pages of *Western American Literature* or the other major journals of ecocriticism, one would never guess that much of the most interesting literature of the American West and some of the most astute readings of the western land-scape have been devoted to unearthing the culture of one of the largest urban environments in the world: Los Angeles. A diverse and interesting group of fiction writers have taken Los Angeles as their subject, ranging from Nathaniel West to Philip K. Dick, Walter Mosley, and Joan Didion. Yet these are not the names which appear in deep ecocritical analyses of the literature of the American West. And some of the best contemporary cul-tural criticism has also focused on Los Angeles. Mike Davis excavates the future of Los Angeles in his stunningly perceptive book *City of Quartz*. The final chapter of Edward Soja's *Postmodern Geographies* explains how "It All Comes Together in Los Angeles" (197). And for Fredric Jameson, Los Ange-les becomes the "concrete totalization" of postmodernity in his widely in-fluential study, *Postmodernism; or, The Cultural Logic of Late Capitalism*. These are not the usual suspects when one lines up nature writers and ecocritics, but their work speaks to an experience of urban environments more ger-mane to the lives of the majority of the inhabitants of the western states, who live in cities and suburbs, than the most eloquent testimonials to one man's or one woman's encounter with the wilderness.

With these exclusions and evasions in mind, let us revisit Glen Love's pronouncement that in the American West "nature continues to occupy a much larger place than it appears to in the eastern and urban imagination" ("*Et*" 196). Does this mean that the West is devoid of urban areas? Does it imply that nature and urban space are antithetical? Is there no such thing as urban nature? Do cities somehow exist separately from the ecosystems of which they are a part? Adopting the theoretical perspective of a Deep Ecology–inspired new pastoralism forces aspiring ecocritics to give unten-able answers to these questions. We would do well, instead, to adopt a the-oretical frame as spacious as the land about which we write—one which makes room for the urban, suburban, small-town, rural, and wild spaces that fill the physical and cultural landscape of the United States, West and East, and its literature. This inclusive mapping of the terrain explored by social ecology is necessary if ecocriticism is to deserve the accolades that it has only lately won in moving from the academic hinterlands to real estate bordering on the cultural mainstream.

The Genealogy of Ecocriticism

IT IS NOT SURPRISING that the distinct cultural geography of deep and social ecocriticism has given rise to a distinct critical genealogy as well. Just as the *ASLE Membership Directory* reveals a decided bias toward non-urban areas, so the *ASLE Bibliography* is dominated by contemporary nature writers; poets like Wendell Berry and Gary Snyder and their Romantic or neo-Romantic forbears, especially Henry Thoreau. Recently, references can be found to a more diverse group of writers, including Susan Fenimore Cooper, Annie Dillard, N. Scott Momaday, and Leslie Marmon Silko. But despite increasing gender and ethnic diversity, few ecocritical works have much to say about urban culture of any stripe. In this final section, I bring into dialogue one such work—Andrew Ross's *The Chicago Gangster Theory of Life*—with Lawrence Buell's *The Environmental Imagination*. Ross's work represents the distaff side of the genealogy of ecocriticism, providing a social ecology–inspired cultural study of urban life, while Buell's work is firmly within the main branch of ecocriticism, with its deep ecological literary analysis of nature writing.

The latter's work has been especially influential, as we might expect given the predominance of deep over social ecocriticism. Buell's book has, in a very real sense, become paradigmatic for literary analyses of the environment. In fact, Jay Parini argues that *The Environmental Imagination: Thoreau, Nature Writing, and the Formation of American Culture* has already become "the standard work on the subject" of ecocriticism (52). The title itself provides a mini-history of deep ecocriticism, with its implicit argument that our culture and our understating of the environment are shaped by a nature-writing tradition stemming from Thoreau. The book, which Buell describes as a "kind of pastoral project" (31), begins with his statement that despite his intention to write only about Thoreau and nature, he ended up with a "broad study of environmental perception, the place of nature in the history of western thought, and the consequences for literary scholarship and indeed for humanistic thought in general of attempting to imagine a more 'ecocentric' way of being" (1). In clarifying what he means by "ecocentrism," Buell accepts, with slight modifications, Timothy O'Riordan's definition: "Ecocentrism preaches the virtues of reverence, humility, responsibility and care; it argues for low impact technology (but is not antitechnological); it decries bigness and impersonality in all forms (but especially in the city); and demands a code of behaviour that seeks permanence and stability based upon ecological principles of diversity and homeostasis" (425). Buell's focus is exclusively on the green world; he has little to say about urban ecosystems since "bigness" is in and of itself the enemy. And he eschews the broadly sociopolitical provenance of social ecocriticism to focus exclusively on literary concerns.

In the central chapters of *The Environmental Imagination*, Buell reevaluates many of the fundamental concepts of literary criticism from an ecocentric perspective. He goes to the root terms of literary analysis—representation, reference, metaphor, setting, characterization, personae, and canonicity— to suggest that all these elements are dramatically transformed by an environmental perspective. Buell concentrates on literature because he sees it as only proper to focus on "the most searching works of environmental reflection that the world's biggest technological power has produced" (2). He narrows his focus even further by developing a fairly restrictive "checklist" of what counts as an "environmentally oriented work" (7).

In the process of outlining his ecocentric literary theory, Buell makes several jabs at the kind of green criticism engaged in by Andrew Ross and others influenced by social ecology. In defending "environmental mimesis," Buell argues that it is "far healthier for an individual, and for a society, than the arrogance of cyberspace" (114). Buell characterizes Foucauldian analysis as premised on "the inevitable dominance of constructedness," which he believes is less "productive" than the kind of criticism built on a "theoretical distinction between human constructedness and nonhuman reality" (113). Contrary to social ecologists' insistence that the Earth is mute and their warnings against attempts to imbue it with a personality which speaks for itself, Buell approvingly points to James Lovelock's Gaia hypothesis as a worthy attempt to "bond ecology to ethics" through "personification of the planet" (201). Buell even suggests that it might be necessary to have a "degree of what passes for misanthropy" in order to obtain some distance from anthropocentrism and make the inward turn needed to transform one's self-consciousness (388).

It is precisely this perspective which worries Andrew Ross and motivates the questions he raises in his also widely influential book *The Chicago Gangster Theory of Life*. Ross would ask Buell in what way cyberspace is "arrogant" and why it should exist in opposition to (rather than simply in addition to) representations of nature; what it means to "extricate art from homocentricism" (161) if art is a human creation; and whether a human-authored text ever really encounters natural phenomena "as the environment manifests itself" (219). Such questions trouble the genealogical dominance of deep ecocriticism.

Questioning the faith of Deep Ecology in the ability of nature to speak for itself, the dominant concern expressed in *Chicago Gangster Theory* is that nature will be used as an authority dictating certain social and cultural policies. This insight underlies much of Ross's analysis of the relationship between the natural and social sciences, technology, and politics. He warns, in particular, that "discourse about scarcity and limitation in the natural world" translates into "calls for a reduction in rights and freedom in our civil society" (12). In other words, Ross is attuned to the ways in which dubious natural science (e.g., sociobiology) generates theories of nature which can provide justification for repressive social arrangements on the false premise that such theories are objectively revealed rather than culturally determined. This social ecological perspective requires a shift from Buell's literary analysis of wide-open spaces to cultural studies of metropolitan places.

Ross critiques the means by which theories of nature are used to justify what are in fact sociopolitical decisions in the process of analyzing a stunning variety of cultural phenomena, from the movie *Ghostbusters* and the bombing of the World Trade Center to the Gulf War and the "Chicago Gangster Theory" referred to in the title of his book. This theory refers to Richard Dawkins's hypothesis that humankind has evolved a "selfish gene" much like a Chicago gangster would, over time, adapt a "ruthless selfishness" to survive in an amoral world. Ross sees this unwarranted transformation of a metaphorical construction loaded with social assumptions into a supposedly disinterested scientific theory as paradigmatic of the misuse of nature to justify retrograde social theory (Dawkins argued that labor unrest was a sign of the selfish gene). In the process of proving his thesis that images of nature are used to cover over or falsely explain complex social issues, he examines the role of urban renewal and its metaphors of the "urban frontier" in creating a new "global city of finance capital and its two-tier post-Fordist service sector/professional economy" (113), while critiquing urban ecosystems theory. Ross also finds support for his thesis while analyzing how the "rhetoric of scarcity" and its accompanying image monoculture were used to bestow the mantle of ecological sanctity on the military-media complex during the Gulf War.

Underlying these wide-ranging explorations is Ross's insistence that local cultural practices are intimately related to economic and political conditions of global proportions. This insight reveals the potential of social ecology–inspired cultural studies at its best. In demonstrating how "ideas that draw upon the authority of nature nearly always have their origins in ideas about society" (15), Ross shows the importance of sociocultural analysis in getting at the ways we use and abuse nature. This analysis is on display in Ross's brilliant study of Polynesia, "the birthplace of modern ecological romanticism" (28). He contrasts a knee-jerk environmentalism which sees any disruption of tradition as an assault on the last vestiges of unspoiled nature with a more nuanced analysis of the specific ways in which "tradition" and "nature" are deployed for different purposes. Sometimes, Ross argues, efforts to reclaim "native rights" are strategically useful for combating the corporate exploitation of Native environments and indigenous peoples. In other cases, tradition is manipulated by self-interested elites in order to justify their authority and their own exploitative schemes. Ross points out that "a society bound together by a nature philosophy holds no guarantee of ecological well-being if it is governed by a pyramidal social hierarchy that depends upon selective access to natural resources to maintain its power" (71). Ross deflates the Romantic notion that all native islanders live in close harmony with nature, noting that many Polynesian societies degraded and even exhausted their environments. But he also points to indigenous movements, such as Hawaiian groups appealing to *malama 'aina* (reciprocal care for the land), as offering one of the best hopes for socially and environmentally responsible principles of sustainability.

This is a goal which Ross and Buell could agree on. And both critics believe that this goal will only be realized through a fundamental transformation in our relationship to the environment. But there are fundamental differences in how the two authors, and the critical genealogies that they represent, reconceptualize our role in the natural world. Ross refers to the theories of nature in need of overhauling as ideologies which are manifest in various cultural productions and the global socioeconomic system in which these productions take part; Buell, on the other hand, speaks of philosophies which must be revised through ecocentric literary criticism *before* we can address environmental problems. These divergent perspectives provide two different versions of ecocriticism. While Ross provides a cultural studies approach to analyze the sociopolitical components of various cultural phenomena, Buell provides a more traditional critical approach to interpreting the "metaphysics and ethics" of literary representations of nature.

The problem with Buell's model of ecocriticism is that it fails to consider that a market-driven economy frames and shapes the ways in which we appropriate the environment and that raising individual consciousness cannot directly counteract these larger forces. At the same time, Buell points to the problem with the way in which Ross's perspective seems to reify Nature, making it just another tool for human decision-making. As though providing a cautionary tale for Ross's vision of ecotopia, Buell points out that there is a natural world which, whether or not we can know it in an unmediated form, does have certain features beyond our comprehension and control. In other words, a deep ecological perspective can act as a check on visions of radical social transformations which fail to take into account the possible abuse of nature not figured into some versions of social ecology.

For deep ecologists, the dominant androcentric worldview needs to be transformed at the level of individual consciousness in order to develop true ecological awareness. For social ecologists, it doesn't make sense to speak as though individual consciousness somehow precedes or escapes from social life. Reading *The Environmental Imagination* and *Chicago Gangster Theory* together, as different voices in the same cultural conversation, might provide a way of reconciling these apparently divergent genealogies. The awakening of an environmental consciousness which Buell argues can happen through literature is a necessary but not sufficient condition for the kind of sociopolitical analysis Ross insists is needed to guide ecological praxis. However, both perspectives are united in their vision of a society existing in a non-exploitative relationship with the Earth and its inhabitants. Perhaps this shared vision could allow deep social ecology to exist as a productive tension within a repoliticized ecocritical movement.

THIS IS MY HOPE: that the fissure between the terrain of deep and social ecocritics can be bridged if not entirely healed. I have been especially critical of the ways in which most ecocritics have ignored or failed to learn from the insights of social ecology because Deep Ecology has so dominated the development of ecocriticism that it has been incapacitated in its analysis of the urban environments in which most of us now live. More than two thirds of the inhabitants of the United States now live in cities and, as Patrick Markee reminds us, "the twenty-first century will dawn on a world in which, for the first time, more people live in urban areas than in the countryside." Social ecocriticism takes this fact into consideration in its efforts to encompass the terrain of urban environments, and it reminds us that all environments—wild, cultivated, and built—are only approachable through language, community, and culture—a lesson that is needed to counteract the anti-theoretical bias of deep ecocriticism and its fantasy of unmediated contact with Nature. Shifting to a more community and cultural based understanding would not only complete ecocriticism, it would end the fetishization of rural, western, and wilderness spaces that has dominated the field at the expense of urban, eastern, and communal places.

Uniting the dominant and distaff branches of ecocriticism would make the whole movement more capable of engaging in the political, aesthetic, and ethical actions needed not just to preserve but to transform the environments that we inhabit. By overemphasizing and romanticizing distant climes, the influence of Deep Ecology on ecocriticism has too often prevented us from seeing both the beauty and the decay in our own backyards. In a sense, social ecocriticism can help us recall the original mission of Deep Ecology, which was defined by Arne Naess as the effort to extend the ecological movement beyond such issues as "pollution and resource depletion" to "deeper concerns which touch upon principles of diversity, complexity, autonomy, decentralization, symbiosis, egalitarianism, and classlessness" (95). Particularly in the last two instances, these principles tend to dovetail with social ecologists' interests in transforming relations of domination inscribed in the current sociopolitical arena. In fact, the relation between the two ecologies could be seen as complimentary: Deep Ecology gives rise to the kind of internal moral transformation that social ecology hopes to harness for larger institutional change. Bringing together the two branches of ecocriticism that these movements have inspired—two branches which have been shaped by separate grounds, geography, and genealogy—offers the promise of strengthening the whole movement by allowing it to be responsive to Nature in all its manifestations, from the most remote outpost of our globe to Times Square on New Year's Eve.

NOTES

1. The expansion of ecological criticism might, without too much exaggeration, be termed a "population explosion" which challenges the "carrying capacity" of any one academic trying to haul the voluminous publications in the field from library to office. For a helpful bibliography of recent and classic ecological literary criticism, see Glotfelty and Fromm's *The Ecocriticism Reader*. The Association for the Study of Literature and the Environment (ASLE) publishes occasional bibliographies as well. And each issue of the ASLE journal *ISLE: Interdisciplinary Studies in Literature and Environment* has a large section devoted to book reviews of ecocritical works.

More generally, Donald Edward Davis's *Ecophilosophy* provides, as the subtitle states, a "field guide to the literature" from Rachel Carson's *Silent Spring* in the 1960s to efforts in the 1980s to create a "new culture of wholeness and harmony with Nature" (ix). *Teaching Environmental Literature: Materials, Methods, Resources,* edited by

Frederick O. Waage, was the first guide to appear which acknowledged the development of ecocriticism as a "field." The attempt to provide an updated account of "environmental teaching" was undertaken by the 1996 publication of Collett and Karakashian's *Greening the College Curriculum*.

Further evidence of the explosion of interest in issues of culture and environment is provided by the plethora of recently published environmental readers. In addition to *The Ecocriticism Reader*, other titles include *Being in the World* (Slovic and Dixon), *Constructing Nature* (Jensoth and Lott), *The Diversity of Life* (Wilson), *The Endangered Earth* (Morgan and Okerstrom), *The Environmental Predicament* (Verburg), *A Forest of Voices* (Anderson and Runciman), *This Incomperable Lande* (Lyon), *The Literature of Nature* (Begiebing and Grumbling), *The Norton Book of Nature Writing* (Finch and Elder), *Reading the Environment* (Walker), *Sisters of the Earth* (Anderson), and *Writing Nature* (Ross).

For contemporary references to ecocriticism in the popular press, see, for example, Erik Davis's "It Ain't Easy Being Green: Eco Meets Pomo" in the *Voice Literary Supplement*; Jay Parini's "The Greening of the Humanities" in the *New York Times Magazine*, which was attacked by Jonathan Yardley in the *Washington Post*; and Jonathan Collett and Stephen Karakashian's "Turning Curricula Green" in the *Chronicle of Higher Education*, which then published Karen J. Winkler's cover story "Inventing a Field: The Study of Literature about the Environment."

2. The "classic" works on American pastoralism are Henry Nash Smith's *Virgin Land* and Leo Marx's *The Machine in the Garden*. The development of "literary ecology" could be traced to Joseph Meeker's *The Comedy of Survival* and Yi-Fu Tuan's *Topophilia*. Building on this foundation, a "new pastoralism" has been constructed by such popular works of ecocriticism as Neil Evernden's *The Social Creation of Nature*, Jonathan Bate's *Romantic Ecology*, and a work that is discussed at length in the final section of this essay, Lawrence Buell's *The Environmental Imagination*.

3. In addition to Andrew Ross's work, which is explored in the final section of this essay, other examples of ecocriticism focused on urban environments can be found in Bennett, Bennett and Teague, Cronon, Lukes, and Wright. Special issues of *Orion*, *Terra Nova*, and *American Book Review* have also addressed what the latter calls "urban nature."

4. In genealogical terms, "distaff" refers to the "secondary" branch of the family descended from the female side as opposed to the "primary" father-to-son inheritance (the "spindle side" in contrast to the "spear side"). I use this term to express my belief that social ecology has not been the primary route through which ecocriticism has been transmitted and that (like a "distaff" branch in a patriarchal culture) it has thus been devalued.

5. Glen Love, for example, reveals this anti-theoretical bias when he claims that ecocriticism is separate from "that devaluing of the real and the consequential which has turned much of literary criticism into what Frederick Crews has called 'the queen of techniques for overturning common sense' " ("*Et*" 197).

6. The term "environmental racism" seems to have first been used in the 1987 United Church of Christ Commission for Racial Justice report, *Toxic Wastes and Race in the United States,* written under the supervision of Benjamin Chavis. The *concept* of environmental racism arose much earlier than the phrase itself. Robert Gottlieb notes that issues of environmental justice have been debated since the beginning of the Industrial Revolution. He points to Jane Addams and her associate Alice Hamilton (author of *Industrial Poison in the United States*) as precursors to contemporary efforts to analyze environmental racism. The beginning of the modern environmental justice movement is usually traced to the series of protests and demonstrations set off in 1982 by the selection of poor and mostly African American Warren County, North Carolina, as the site for a PCB landfill. This incident was closely followed by a 1983 General Accounting Office report which discovered that three out of four hazardous waste landfills in the southeastern United States were located in predominantly black communities.

7. In the words of Benjamin Chavis, who was then the head of the United Church of Christ Commission for Racial Justice, "the idea of civil rights is expanding to include freedom from pollution, and an emphasis on social justice is being added to the idea of environmental protection" (Suro B7). This reconciliation process resulted in part from a response to the complaints by a variety of civil rights groups which were formalized by a letter campaign in 1990 during which hundreds of organizations sent letters to the "Group of Ten" (the ten largest environmental organizations). These letters charged that the environmental movement had "shown little willingness to recognize the legitimacy of or provide support to the struggle to alleviate the poisoning of communities of color . . . [they] have only token involvement of people of color in their operations and policy-making bodies . . . [and] some national environmental groups have taken steps in local communities which have actually been detrimental to the interests of people of color" (Guerrero and Head 11). Over the last few years, the situation has improved as discussions between mainstream environmentalists and civil rights activists have brought the two movements closer together. Now it is not uncommon for a court case challenging an incident of environmental racism to draw upon the combined resources of the ACLU, NAACP, and Sierra Club.

8. See Freudenburg, though he questions the methodology and logic of some of the studies showing more positive environmental attitudes among urban dwellers.

REFERENCES

Alston, Dana, ed. *We Speak for Ourselves: Social Justice, Race and Environment.* Washington, D.C.: Panos Institute, 1990.

American Book Review 18.2 (1996–97).

Anderson, Chris, and Lex Runciman, eds. *A Forest of Voices: Reading and Writing the Environment.* Mountain View, Calif.: Mayfield, 1995.

Anderson, Lorraine, ed. *Sisters of the Earth: Women's Prose and Poetry about Nature.* New York: Vintage, 1991.

Bate, Jonathan. *Romantic Ecology: Wordsworth and the Environmental Tradition.* New York: Routledge, 1991.

Begiebing, Robert J., and Owen Grumbling, eds. *The Literature of Nature: The British and American Traditions.* Medford, N.J.: Plexus, 1990.

Bennett, Michael. "Urban Nature: Teaching *Tinker Creek* by the East River." *ISLE: Interdisciplinary Studies in Literature and Environment* 5.1 (1998): 49–59.

Bennett, Michael, and David Teague, eds. *The Nature of Cities: Ecocriticism and Urban Environments.* Tucson: U of Arizona P, 1999.

Bookchin, Murray. *The Ecology of Freedom: The Emergence and Dissolution of Hierarchy.* Palo Alto, Calif.: Cheshire, 1982.

———. *The Philosophy of Social Ecology: Essays on Dialectical Naturalism.* Montreal: Black Rose, 1995.

———. *Urbanization without Cities: The Rise and Decline of Citizenship.* New York: Black Rose, 1992.

Branch, Michael. "Ecocriticism: The Nature of Nature in Literary Theory and Practice." *Weber Studies* 11.1 (1994): 41–55.

Buell, Lawrence. *The Environmental Imagination: Thoreau, Nature Writing, and the Formation of American Culture.* Cambridge: Harvard UP, 1995.

Bullard, Robert D., ed. *Confronting Environmental Racism: Voices from the Grassroots.* Boston: South End, 1993.

———. *Dumping in Dixie: Race, Class, and Environmental Quality.* Boulder, Colo.: Westview, 1990.

———. *Invisible Houston: The Black Experience in Boom and Bust.* College Station: Texas A&M UP, 1987.

Campbell, SueEllen. "The Land and Language of Desire: Where Deep Ecology and Post-Structuralism Meet." *Western American Literature* 24.3 (1989): 199–211.

Collett, Jonathan, and Stephen Karakashian, eds. *Greening the College Curriculum: A Guide to Environmental Teaching in the Liberal Arts.* Washington, D.C.: Island, 1996.

———. "Turning Curricula Green." *Chronicle of Higher Education* 23 Feb. 1996: B1–B2.

Cronon, William. "The Trouble with Wilderness." *New York Times Magazine* 13 Aug. 1995: 42–43.

Davis, Donald Edward. *Ecophilosophy: A Field Guide to the Literature.* San Pedro, Calif.: R and E Miles, 1989.

Davis, Erik. "It Ain't Easy Being Green: Eco Meets Pomo." *Voice Literary Supplement* Feb. 1995: 16–18.

Davis, Mike. *City of Quartz: Excavating the Future of Los Angeles.* London: Verso, 1990.

Devall, Bill, and George Sessions. *Deep Ecology: Living as If Earth Really Mattered.* Layton, Utah: Gibbs Smith, 1985.

Evernden, Neil. *The Social Creation of Nature*. Baltimore: Johns Hopkins UP, 1992.

Finch, Robert, and John Elder, eds. *The Norton Book of Nature Writing*. New York: Norton, 1990.

Freudenburg, William R. "Rural-Urban Differences in Environmental Concern: A Closer Look." *Sociological Inquiry* 61.2 (1991): 167–98.

Glotfelty, Cheryll, and Harold Fromm, eds. *The Ecocriticism Reader: Landmarks in Literary Ecology*. Athens: U of Georgia P, 1996.

Gottlieb, Robert. *Forcing the Spring: The Transformation of the American Environmental Movement*. Washington, D.C.: Island, 1993.

Guerrero, Michael, and Louis Head. "The Environment—Redefining the Issue." Alston 11.

Jameson, Fredric. *Postmodernism; or, The Cultural Logic of Late Capitalism*. Durham: Duke UP, 1991.

Jensoth, Richard, and Edward E. Lott, eds. *Constructing Nature: Readings from the American Experience*. Upper Saddle, N.J.: Prentice Hall, 1996.

Love, Glen A. "*Et in Arcadia Ego*: Pastoral Theory Meets Ecocriticism." *Western American Literature* 27.3 (1992): 195–207.

———. "Revaluing Nature: Toward An Ecological Criticism." *Western American Literature* 25.3 (1990): 201–15.

Lukes, Timothy W. *Ecocritique: Contesting the Politics of Nature, Economics, and Culture*. Minneapolis: U of Minnesota P, 1997.

Lyon, Thomas J., ed. *This Incomperable Lande: A Book of American Nature Writing*. Boston: Houghton Mifflin, 1989.

Markee, Patrick. "Asia's Urban Landscape." *Nation* 27 May 1996: 27.

Marks, Donovan. "Toxic Wastes and Race in the United States." Alston 9.

Marx, Leo. *The Machine in the Garden: Technology and the Pastoral Ideal in America*. New York: Oxford UP, 1964.

Meeker, Joseph *The Comedy of Survival: Studies in Literary Ecology*. New York: Scribner's, 1972.

Morgan, Sarah, and Dennis Okerstrom, eds. *The Endangered Earth: Readings for Writers*. Needham Heights, Mass.: Allyn and Bacon, 1992.

Murray, John A., et al. "The Rise of Nature Writing: America's Next Great Genre?" *Manoa: A Pacific Journal of International Writing* 4.2 (1992): 73–97.

Naess, Arne. "Identification as a Source of Deep Ecological Attitudes." *Deep Ecology*. Ed. Michael Tobias. San Diego: Avant, 1985. 256–70.

———. "The Shallow and the Deep, Long-Range Ecology Movement: A Summary." *Inquiry* 16 (1973): 95–100.

Orion Magazine 13.4 (Autumn 1994).

Parini, Jay. "The Greening of the Humanities." *New York Times Magazine* 29 Oct. 1995: 52–53.

Ross, Andrew. *The Chicago Gangster Theory of Life: Nature's Debt to Society*. London: Verso, 1994.

Ross, Carolyn, ed. *Writing Nature: An Ecological Reader for Writers*. New York: St. Martin's, 1995.

Sessions, George. Introduction. *Deep Ecology for the Twenty-first Century*. Ed. George Sessions. Boston: Shambhala, 1995. 3–7.

Slovic, Scott, and Terrell Dixon, eds. *Being in the World: An Environmental Reader for Writers*. New York: Macmillan, 1993.

Smith, Henry Nash. *Virgin Land: The American West as Symbol and Myth*. New York: Vintage, 1950.

Soja, Edward W. *Postmodern Geographies: The Reassertion of Space in Critical Social Theory*. London: Verso, 1989.

Stone, Christopher. *Should Trees Have Standing? Toward Legal Rights for Natural Objects*. Los Altos, Calif.: William Kaufmann, 1974.

Suro, Roberto. "Pollution-Weary Minorities Try Civil Rights Tack." *New York Times* 11 Jan. 1993: A1, B7.

Terra Nova: Nature and Culture 1.4 (Fall 1996).

Tuan, Yi-Fu. *Topophilia: A Study of Environmental Perception, Attitudes, and Values*. 1974. New York: Columbia UP, 1990.

United Church of Christ Commission for Racial Justice. *Toxic Wastes and Race in the United States: A National Report on the Racial and Socio-Economic Characteristics of Communities with Hazardous Waste Sites*. New York: United Church of Christ, 1987.

United States. General Accounting Office. *Siting of Hazardous Waste Landfills and Their Correlation with Racial and Economic Status of Surrounding Communities*. Washington, D.C.: Government Printing Office, 1983.

Verburg, Carol J., ed. *The Environmental Predicament: Four Issues for Critical Analysis*. Boston: Bedford–St. Martin's, 1995.

Waage, Frederick O., ed. *Teaching Environmental Literature: Materials, Methods, Resources*. New York: Modern Language Association, 1985.

Walker, Melissa, ed. *Reading the Environment*. New York: Norton, 1994.

Wilson, Alexander. *The Culture of Nature: North American Landscape from Disney to the Exxon Valdez*. Cambridge: Blackwell, 1992.

Wilson, Edward O., ed. *The Diversity of Life*. New York: Norton, 1992.

Winkler, Karen J. "Inventing a Field: The Study of Literature about the Environment." *Chronicle of Higher Education* 9 Aug. 1996: A9–A15.

Wright, Will. *Wild Knowledge: Science, Language, and Social Life in a Fragile Environment*. Minneapolis: U of Minnesota P, 1992.

Yardley, Jonathan. " 'Ecocriticism,' Growing Like a Weed." *Washington Post* 13 Nov. 1995: B2.

Home on the Prairie?

A Feminist and Postcolonial Reading of
Sharon Butala, Di Brandt, and Joy Kogawa

"AMERICA'S OLDEST and most cherished fantasy," according to Annette Kolodny, is that of the land as a "maternal 'garden,' "a place of bountiful abundance, nurturance, and nonalienation (171–72). The promise of the "New World" was the promise of a return to Eden, a homecoming: a "regression from the cares of adult life and a return to the primal warmth of womb or breast in a feminine landscape" (173). Kolodny is more interested in the coding of nature as female rather than as home, centering her analysis on the translation of " 'America the Beautiful' into *America the Raped*" (178), but the Edenic trope of nature as a place to "come home to" is a prominent theme in Anglo-American culture and literature. More recently, this narrative has less to do with material progress than with ecological restoration: " 'sustainability' is a new vision of the recovered garden, one in which humanity will live in a relationship of balance and harmony with the natural world . . . [where] each earthly place would be a home" (Merchant 156, 158). For many contemporary nature writers, the solution to ecological crisis involves "coming home" to nature.

"Home" seems to be a salient metaphor for nature in women's writing in particular and has been claimed by ecofeminists as the "feminine" alternative to the "masculine" resourcist approach to the environment (Nesmith and Radcliffe 383). In *The Land before Her,* Kolodny suggests that women pioneer writers—primarily genteel, educated white women—differed from their male counterparts by writing nature as a domesticated garden rather than as bountiful mother or beckoning virgin. Other versions of domesticity also emerge in women's nature writing, such as early American writers Mary Austin and Willa Cather, who wrote of the land itself as a "home" for women which was less restricting than the physical and social confines of domesticity and femininity: Austin "enlarged the traditional concept of home into a 'house of earth' which included all outdoors" (Benay Blend qtd.

in Taylor 122). On a distinctly Canadian note, Andrea Pinto Lebowitz argues that the recurring theme of making and finding home in the nature writing of Canadian women disrupts Northrop Frye's infamous proclamation that Canadians suffered from a "garrison mentality," fearful of nature which appears beyond their control and indifferent to their needs and values (2).[1] "Nature may well be dangerous and awesome," she concedes, "but it is also a place of beauty, solace and home," and she uses "home" as an organizing theme for her collection of nature writing by women in Canada (2). Perhaps the strongest claim for nature as a "home" for women is ecofeminist science fiction writer Ursula Le Guin's assertion that "where I live as a woman is to men a wilderness. But to me it is home," specifying a distinctly female alternative to the androcentric wilderness adventure genre (qtd. in Gaard and Murphy 8).

But as Jennifer Browdy de Hernandez points out, "for the postcolonial [writer], man or woman, home is a particularly charged autobiographeme, a contested site on which the cultural conflicts of the larger society are played out in microcosm" (21), and the politics of the home—as a site of both oppression and resistance, as both safe place and exclusionary boundary, in the multiple experiences of women variously situated within relations and discourses of race, ethnicity, class, gender, ability, and sexuality—is central to feminist criticism. *Always Coming Home,* the title of Ursula Le Guin's ecotopian novel, may not be as "all-American" as it seems. Who has the privilege of a home to return to? For whom would returning home be a desirable experience? What escape routes are there from the home that is hell? What sacrifices and strategies are involved and for whom in making a place "home"? How does writing "nature" as "home" privilege particular experiences and cultural narratives? What is "nature" for those who are "homeless" or, in the words of postcolonial theorist Homi Bhabha, "unhomed"?

As ecological writing begins to be taken seriously by literary critics and other scholars, it becomes important to consider how particular sociocultural histories and geographies shape "nature writing" and how "writing nature" involves particular exclusions, historical erasures, and representations of Others, human and nonhuman. There has been little dialogue between postcolonial theory and ecocriticism to date, and this essay is an attempt to further such conversations by adding "nature" to the dimensions of "home"—body, domestic space, community, nation—unsettled by postcolonial and feminist theorists and by unsettling the "nature" too often unproblematically written as "home" by nature writers and ecocritics alike.

In this essay, I draw on postcolonial and feminist theorizing of "home" to consider the politics of writing nature, place, and identity in the quasi-autobiographical prairie writing of three Canadian women, Sharon Butala's *The Perfection of the Morning*, Di Brandt's "This Land That I Love, This Wide Wide Prairie," and Joy Kogawa's *Obasan*. These writers are positioned quite differently in relation to the natural and social landscape of their (shared?) "prairie home" on account of historical relations of race, ethnicity, class, religion, and gender; more significantly, they choose different strategies for writing this history into (or out of) their approaches to nature.

Home: Identity, Place, and Nature

IN HER ESSAY "A Place Called Home?" feminist geographer Doreen Massey questions the nostalgia for secure identities and stable places which surfaces in First World critiques of globalization. "Those who today worry about a sense of disorientation and a loss of control must once have felt they knew exactly where they were, and that they *had* control," a presumption Massey suggests does not hold for colonized peoples: "*from the point of view of* [the] colonial periphery that encounter has for centuries been 'immediate and intense'" (165). In a different way, this nostalgia for a place "to come home to" does not even accommodate the experiences of women—those Others within the center—for whom "home" is a site of work, conflict, and violence, not just repose. It is not insignificant, according to Massey, that "such views of place, which reverberate with nostalgia for something lost, are coded female," for "the identities of 'woman' and of the 'home-place' are intimately tied up with each other": both are essentialized into the role of a "stable, symbolic centre—functioning as an anchor for others" (180).[2] Massey suggests such constructions of home/place as a source of belonging, identity, and security are common to a range of discourses, including nationalism, tourist marketing, and gated communities: "all of these have been attempts to fix the meaning of places, to enclose and defend them: they construct singular, fixed and static identities for places, and they interpret places as bounded, enclosed spaces defined through counterposition against the Other who is outside" (168). To her list, I would add the discourse of environmentalism, particularly wilderness conservationism, which has similarly attempted to fix and contain the meaning of "nature" as an authentic, original essence/place untainted by human touch; an essence/place to which we may refer or go for ecologically, and possibly even spiritually, redeeming values and experiences.[3]

Massey argues that the essentializing of place is as dangerous and unfounded as the essentializing of identity, which has been extensively critiqued by feminist, anti-racist, and postcolonial theorists.[4] Space and place, as Edward Said so incisively demonstrated, are central to the construction of Self and Other: grounding identity in geographical referents, such as the Orient, naturalizes the traits attributed to the people of that place (i.e., Orientals) as essential differences which "they" all share and which differ from "us." Massey clarifies that the problem of associating identity with place lies in the conceptualization of place as "bounded space" which naturalizes boundaries and locates them within a site rather than as constituted by social relations and contestations:

> what is specific about a place, its identity, is always formed by the juxtaposition and co-presence there of particular sets of social interrelations, and by the effects which the juxtaposition and co-presence produce. Moreover, and this is the really important point, a proportion of the social interrelations will be wider than and go beyond the area being referred to in any particular context as a place. (168–69)

So a place is defined not by borders and enclosures but by the social relations at a particular location and the relations between that location and other locations at a particular moment in time. It follows that the identity of places, like the social relations which compose them, are dynamic and unfixed, and thus always open for contestation:

> Places cannot "really" be characterized by the recourse to some essential, internalized moment. Virtually all the examples cited above—from forms of nationalism, to heritage centres, to ascriptions of the "real Isle of Dogs"—seek the identity of a place by laying claim to some particular moment/location in time-space when the definition of the area and the social relations dominant within it were to the advantage of that particular claimant group. (169)

In sum, Massey's argument is an extension to place of the poststructural, postcolonial, and feminist undoing of an essential identity.

Although some would argue that there is a more urgent need to hold on to the idea of a concrete, bounded, knowable "nature" than there is for "place,"[5] Massey's re-theorization of place is particularly valuable for ecocriticism in two ways. First, her extension of the critique of essentialism to place can be further extended to a skepticism toward what we define as "nature" and codify as "nature writing." Indeed, poststructuralist critiques of environmentalism challenge notions of an authentic, knowable nature "out there" of which we may have direct experience, unmediated by culture, technology, or social relations of power and privilege.[6] Rather, the particular forms of "nature," whether climax forest ecosystems, a pristine Antarctica, or photogenic mega-fauna which conservationists wish to "save," represent the desires of particular social groups embedded in sociohistorical relations of power with other people and animals. As Massey qualifies, and Cronon echoes, "this does not mean that there is no justification for any notion of conservation, but it does mean that the debate should focus on . . . wider realms of social debate and politics rather than issues of the supposed authenticity of a particular locality" (Massey 9).

Second, and more pertinent to the subject of this paper, Massey's reconceptualization of "place" calls into question all those references to "place"—"sense of place," "living-in-place," etc.—and "home" within environmental thought and nature writing, which are often nothing more than thinly disguised references to a rural idyll as opposed to some universal, abstract "ecological wisdom." [7] Such constructions are always already social, cultural, and political, and it is the very role of literary criticism to tease out these various dimensions: "nature" need not be reduced to language and discourse for greater attention to be paid to the historical specificity of our literary constructions of particular places, whether those places be peopled or (supposedly) unpeopled.

Sharon Butala: *The Perfection of the Morning*

AUTHOR OF several novels and short story collections set in the prairies, Sharon Butala is best known for her nonfictional, largely autobiographical work *The Perfection of the Morning*, a Canadian best-seller nominated for the Governor General's Award in 1994. Significantly subtitled "An Apprenticeship in Nature," *Perfection* is the diary of an urban newcomer who, after years of trial and adjustment, makes the countryside "home." It is an eclectic text which jumps from nature observation and description to details about her rural neighbors, to the history of the First Nations who were dispossessed of the land, to her clumsy attempts to psychoanalyze herself; the one common theme is Butala's spiritual journey of homecoming, where "home" may be read as her body, her inner self, her community, and what

Butala refers to as capital-n Nature to give a sense of agency to the natural world.

At the time of writing the book, Butala had lived on her husband's ranch in southwestern Saskatchewan for almost twenty years, having moved out to the country as an abrupt shift in lifestyle at age thirty-six, leaving behind an unfinished master's degree, a feminist and independently minded single motherhood, and the city of Saskatoon, where she had lived since her teenage years. Her particular circumstances allowed her the freedom—and spiritual anguish—to wander at length in the unbroken grassland of the ranch. She writes:

> I walked every day. I was in a position few people, especially women, are ever fortunate enough to be in: alone, in no danger of meeting anyone, without a job or boss, no small children to look after, no family, no pressing personal problems, no commitments and no plans. It was the first time since childhood I had experienced such freedom. (140)

Through her walking and the experiences, visions, and dreams she has in the process, Butala begins to feel closer to and more in tune with "Nature" as well as more spiritually whole. The two are inextricably linked for Butala: "the only possible way to come to an understanding involving Nature is by being in Nature. And . . . coming to an understanding of and building a relationship with Nature is essential in order to understand oneself" (191). As she explains further,

> [I]f in the beginning I often found myself having a difficult, even painful time in finding a social footing and in feeling I could ever be a member of my new society of rural, agricultural people, in my awe at the beauty and openness of the landscape, I felt as if *my soul had at last found its home*. Slowly, through my joy in the beauty of this new landscape, I began to learn new things, to see my life differently. (xv; emphasis added)

The simple lesson she learned, and the message she hopes to deliver in *Perfection*, is this: "More and more I am coming to believe that our alienation from the natural world is at root of much that has gone wrong in the modern world, and that if Nature has anything to teach us at all, her first lesson is in humility" (105).

What Butala neglects to consider in describing and analyzing this crisis of belonging and identity is class and how this "position" of freedom she enjoys is a privileged position. While Butala discusses her own experiences

and histories extensively, she lacks any critical reflection on her own biases and "formative culture" except as an Edenic fall and return to grace.
Nor does Butala ever consider the power relations undergirding her relation to her rural community: her privilege to come into the community and
observe, free from any sense of responsibility and accountability to that
community, and the authority which her representations of the rural carry
due to her status as "writer." Instead, she presents herself as free from culture and politics as she walks in "Nature," "merely looking at the prairie
as a human being" (94). Such a humanist stance pervades nature writing
and the dominant academic traditions in literature and geography and,
more recently, ecocriticism. As Patrick Murphy points out, the combination of "personal voice with factual and accurate description" which typi-
fies Anglo-American nature writing and indeed defines it as a *genre* "justi-
fies the presentation of universalizing general philosophical statements that
are often based on an author's very specific and relatively minute experiences" (24). He goes on to note how "for the most part, such nonfiction has
been written by white males yet treated as if it were speaking for everyone"
(24). Butala, in her claim to read and re-present "Nature's lessons," similarly
cloaks her particular experiences in a universalizing narrative which privileges a white, androcentric, leisured enjoyment of the prairie land/scape.

To demonstrate these lessons that "Nature has to teach us," Butala emphasizes the differences between urban and rural ways of life, actively constructing the rural as Other in order to demonstrate that there are other ways
of knowing and living in nature than can be experienced in the city. Indeed,
she emphasizes this difference through reference to more commonly perceived Others: her new world was "as alien to me as if I'd married an Arab
or an Inuit and gone to live in his culture" (42). Like many writers of the
rural, Butala delights in the pastoral myth of a secure sense of place and
belonging, holding up her husband, Peter, as an example of ecological and
spiritual wholeness. Seeing how Peter was "at ease . . . on the prairie, how
completely at home" (148), how "he loved his life," how he was "secure
in his community" where he knew everyone, how he had a "calmness engendered by the deep sense of security stemming from a life lived all in
one place" (2), Butala sees her move to the countryside as an "escap[e] into
a simpler, more pure and more ethical life" (18). Her own observations of
the drought which caused the banks to foreclose many family farms and
seemed to signal the end of a three-generations-long lifestyle indicate the
temporariness of this way of life, and yet she writes: "a world was wash-
ing slowly over me, seeping in without my noticing, a slower world, and

a timeless one that resonated with a sense that it must always have been there in just this way and always would be" (5). Even more insidious, but predictable given Massey's critique of the desire for a bounded, stable sense of place, Butala conflates a secure sense of place with an essentialized "rural people" who "live close to Nature." She constructs the rural as a homogeneous Other and neglects, indeed actively excludes, the possibility of Others, such as gays and lesbians, people of color, and people with disabilities, within the rural as she creates her idyllic "home."

Based on her observations of her husband, a "true rural man" (87), Butala takes the geographical referent of "rural"—a category which itself is highly ambiguous, yet a long-established dualism in western thought and culture—and essentializes it into an identity with particular conditions and clear boundaries of who it would include and exclude:

> A *true* rural person must be somebody born and raised on the land, outside of towns, and far from most people. That being a *given*, then it follows that such life experience *must* result in an *intrinsic* understanding of the world different from that of someone raised in the cement, asphalt, glass and crowds of the city. (88, emphasis added)

Under these conditions, Butala states, "rural people" have maintained a relationship with nature lost by everyone else, except, Butala qualifies, "Native people." But in Butala's text, the First Nations are historicized into history books and artifacts on the landscape; it is the bankrupt and dying-out lifestyle of the family farm and cattle ranch which offer her a taste of what can be learned from recovering those "abilities we all once had, and which people who remain close to Nature have maintained" (140). Butala claims not only to be able to accurately know and depict these other lives but also to understand the underlying principle which shapes them: "the most basic ingredient of all in rural life [is] *that it took place in the midst of Nature,* that Nature permeated the lives of rural people, and that this was, more than anything else, the element which separated true rural people from urban people" (130).

Tellingly, Butala is particularly selective about which elements of rural life she accepts as "authentic." For example, she is not able to reconcile her experience or idea of a relationship with "Nature" with hunting, despite its popularity and prevalence in rural areas. While, in her mind, "Native people" hunting for food demonstrate a "legendary" respect for their prey (161), a neighbor who killed a coyote suffering from mange and hanging around the farmhouse was showing a "casualness, a carelessness and a lack of respect for the animals" in his "casual, unthinking shot" (162, 160). Similarly, in considering her female neighbors who, according to Butala, led lives "still close to those women [have] been leading for several thousand years" (181), Butala explains,

> Even while I deeply admired the women around me, I doubted that I would be happy in that traditional life which while it had a certain clear nobility to it, also had too much potential for making a virtue out of the inherent possibility of martyrdom, a way of life for women and an attitude for which I have no admiration at all. And it seemed plain it wouldn't give me the opportunity to try out all my gifts, all the things which I thought I had it in me to be or, at least, that I wanted to try out, whether I failed or I succeeded. For many of us, life is bigger than the round of gardening and diapering and cooking that takes up so much of the life of a traditional woman. (184)

How the "true rural life," now acknowledged to be androcentric and patriarchal, is to be pursued if this women's work is not done, or where exactly women and which women have been pursuing this "traditional life" for "several thousand years," Butala never explains. Southwestern Saskatchewan, at least, was settled by Europeans only in the last century. The arbitrariness of Butala's rigid characterization of "rural life" is further exposed by the subaltern characters which hover at the edge of Butala's prairie home. At the end of her novel *Luna*, the second book in a trilogy of rural life, there is mention of a woman with mental disabilities who returns to the family ranch only for Christmas, as she lives in the city in a group home "full of people like herself who couldn't manage on their own" (202). She is an object of pity for the rural women of the novel, clearly out of place— not "at home"—in the rural setting to which she was born, which leads one to ask whether she would qualify as a "true rural person" in Butala's classification system.

While no indigenous people appear in *Perfection* "in the flesh," Butala draws extensively on Native mythology to develop her ideas of "Nature" as a spiritual "home." Butala admits that "what I know of their traditional lives [comes] from 'as-told-to' writings," and yet she comfortably generalizes the cultures and practices of many different peoples into the statement that "Natives . . . have no difficulty accepting that dreamworld as as real as the flesh-and-blood world of every day" in order to substantiate and authorize the significance of her own dreams (168). Butala shies short of outright mimicry—although possibly more from embarrassment than concerns about cultural appropriation—but does believe that through her attentiveness to "Nature" she has access to Native cultures:

> For example, once I came upon a crescent of stones half-buried in the grass and almost completely covered by lichens, both circumstances suggesting, but not completely proving, that they had been placed there in very ancient times. The crescent was about seven feet from point to point, and I immediately thought of the moon and of lunar worship. That night I dreamt that I was to establish a place of worship for women at that site. This I certainly did not do; I thought, If I were Native, I would follow the dream's instructions, but I am not Native, and the very idea of even suggesting such a thing to women makes me feel like an utter fool.[8] (169)

Earlier in the text, she writes that "this land makes Crees of us all" (100): both statements show how Butala collapses indigenous cultures into nature and instinct and appropriates them for her own uses, denying indigenous people voice and agency in her universalized writing of "Nature." The corollary of Butala's ascription of agency to "Nature" is the dehumanizing reduction of rural people and Native peoples to be the objects of nature's teaching; she effaces culture by "naturalizing" their ways of life.

Di Brandt: "This Land That I Love, This Wide Wide Prairie"

DI BRANDT is a prairie writer and poet, born in a Mennonite farming community in south-central Manitoba. Brandt scandalized the Mennonite community when her first book of poetry, *Questions I Asked My Mother*, was published in 1987. Critical of the repression of women, domestic violence, and misogyny endemic in Mennonite culture, Brandt was ostracized from her community for breaking "centuries-old taboos against self-expression and art-making and public speech" (Brandt, *Dancing* 9). In her poetic essay "This Land That I Love, This Wide Wide Prairie," Brandt continues this critique and introspection, examining the colonial, patriarchal, and ecological underside of the Mennonite—and her own—relationship to the land. Like Butala, Brandt finds the prairie landscape dazzlingly beautiful, but as she writes in her first line, "it is impossible for [her] to write *the land*" (232). She refuses to reduce her experience, to reduce people, to reduce history to some essence of "the land" and instead fills that simple term with the weight of history, with the weight of experience, with the weight of contradiction and political implication until "the land" means too much to be taken lightly, or written naively.

Brandt's poetic, lyrical prose evokes her delight and pleasure remembered from a rural childhood:

> This land that I love, this wide wide prairie, this horizon, this sky, this great blue overhead, big enough to contain every dream, every longing, how it held me throughout childhood, this great blue, overhead, this wide wide prairie, how it kept me alive, its wild scent of milkweed, thistle, chamomile, lamb's quarters, pigweed, clover, yarrow, sage, yellow buttercup, purple aster, gold-enweed, shepherd's purse. . . . The bellows of cows, the cool wet nuzzle of calves' noses, the grunt and snuffle of huge pink sows wallowing in dirt, the squeal of newborn piglets, soft newborn kittens in the barn. How I loved you, how I love you, how I love you still. (232)

Despite the joy expressed here, Brandt disrupts the possibility of an idyllic rural childhood by exposing the child abuse hidden within the farmhouses: "we did it secretly, in our homes, we did it to our young children, so no one would see us, we did it to our adolescents, with ritual beatings and humiliations, so they would have no voice, no will, no say of their own" (234). Brandt does not reject the pleasurable aspects of her childhood on the land in the face of this horror; nor does she create a rural dystopia to contrast with the rural idyll. Rather she places both images side by side, bearing witness to both, living "in exile" while reaffirming her "ongoing love for the prairie" (238).

Brandt repeats this textual strategy of disruption and contradiction throughout the text, filling *the land* with more and more questions and more and more memories. "This stolen land, Rupert's land, Métis land, Indian land, Cree land," she accuses while simultaneously recognizing how this land was the promise of freedom from religious persecution for the Mennonites and how much hard work was required of the Mennonite farmers to make their livelihoods from it (232). She describes how "our many fields [were] patched together painstakingly, passionately, laboriously by our father, with devoted help from our mother, field by field, bank loan by bank loan, from a single field and two room shack in the 1940s, shortly after the war, into a large, modern farm," not to justify the dispossession of the land, nor to venerate the pioneer dream, but to show the layers of history which complicate any simplistic construction of heroes and enemies (232–33). The rural families are not innocent in Brandt's telling, unlike Butala's, nor do they have some more "authentic" claim to the land; indeed, she even points out how the land is actually "man's land" with ownership denied women despite their equal labor (234). She asks, "when did I first understand this, that the women had no place, no voice of their own," and finds that she must leave that home for the city in order to claim her voice (234). Together these histories make her both "lawful" and "unlawful" heir to the land: morally it is unlawful for her to possess this stolen land, and according to Mennonite customs, she as a woman has no claim to it; and yet legally, she has as much right to the land as her brother does, and morally, even though she has left, she is obliged to accept responsibility for this problematic inheritance.

Brandt concludes her piece by challenging the Mennonite stance of pacifism in the light of its "warlike" and military-technology–linked treatment of the land by use of pesticides, herbicides, and high-tech farming equipment. Brandt points out that "the weird, contradictory combination of warfare and husbandry . . . is a deadly accurate description of Mennonite farming practice in Manitoba as I knew it, growing up in Reinland" (235–36). She bears witness to the consequences of this other war:

> The rivers are being choked with reeds and fungi, because of fertilizer runoff into the water systems. Many, many people in south central Manitoba, in the heart of Mennonite farmland, are dying of cancer, MS, pneumonia, leukemia, all of them victims of damaged immune systems and, indisputably, environmental pollution. There are very few birds now, very few frogs, toads, gophers, foxes, deer, very few wildflowers and prairie grasses left. It is the same in other farming communities across the nation and elsewhere in this province, the forests and lakes are being ravaged by the pulp and paper and mining industries. It is the same in other provinces and countries across the globe. (237)

"In a little more than a hundred years, my fellow countrymen and women," Brandt announces, "we have managed to poison the land and our food sources and our own bodies so drastically as to jeopardize the future of all life in this country" (237). This general condemnation has deeply personal significance: Brandt describes her father's arrogance and denial when "he remembered spraying DDT all over his bare arms to ward off flies before it was banned. And look at me, he'd chortle, healthy as an ox" before dying of cancer at age sixty-one, and her brother's severe environmental illness at age forty-seven (236). Here again, Brandt is positioned as "lawful/unlawful heir" to the land, a poisoned inheritance which betrays the pioneer's dream and sadly mocks his sacrifices.

Despite this historical awareness, there is a sense of nostalgia in Brandt's liturgy for the death of the wild prairie and her desire for a time

> when it wasn't so, when this beautiful land was unconquered, unsubdued, unbroken, when the people of this land tried to live in harmony with its shifts and rhythms instead of in violent conquest over it, when the creeks and ditches were filled with frogs and meadow larks and red winged blackbirds and butterflies and wild clover and bees, instead of sprayed grass, when the fields were grazing grounds for wild herds of buffalo and antelope and deer, instead of straight hard rows of chemically altered grain. (238)

This binary opposition between harmony and violence, beauty and monoculture, life and destruction seems to reinvoke an authentic nature, pure and innocent before touched by white civilization. Does the difference between Butala and Brandt revolve around a question of optimism where Brandt mourns the Fall from the Garden of Eden and Butala proclaims the possibility of its recovery? Given Brandt's deliberate efforts at historicization, such a reading is too simplistic; I would like to offer a different one by drawing on bell hooks's theorizing of memory in her essay "Choosing the Margin." Here hooks labels the " 'struggle of memory against forgetting' a politicization of memory that distinguishes nostalgia, that longing for something to be as once it was, a kind of useless act, from that remembering that serves to illuminate and transform the present" (147). This is a memory which recognizes that the past, like the present, is continually being constructed and reconstructed, and a memory which does not settle into one home, one frozen moment of time, but is continually moving in its attempt to confront and resist oppression "within complex and ever shifting realms of power relations" (145). For hooks, "home is no longer just one place. It is locations. Home is that place which enables and promotes varied and everchanging perspectives, a place where one discovers new ways of seeing reality, frontiers of difference" (148). And one such "home" may be the "creation of spaces where one is able to reclaim and redeem the past, legacies of pain, suffering, and triumph in ways that transform the present reality" (145). I argue that Brandt's text is an example of an attempt to use memory not as *nostalgia* for time past but as a *political move* to open up a distance for critique and to create a space for new possibilities, although she might not fully achieve this effect in her revival of an idyllic nature peopled by noble savages. Wandering at the edges of her farm, Brandt finds in the "beckoning shadow" a wildness, a freedom, faint trace of thundering herds of buffalo and men on horses, whooping joyfully, dangerously, reining them in for the kill, unbroken prairie, sweet scented, rustling, chirping, singing, untamed, unsubdued, stretching to the wide horizon, women and children sitting around a campfire, the smell of woodsmoke in the air, the incessant beating of drums. (233)

In her search for a space outside of domination, Brandt conjures up the familiar trope of the "noble savage" by associating Native cultures with wildness and a harmonious existence with nature which ended with the advent of history, with white colonization. And yet she acknowledges that

there was no getting hold of this memory, this ghost, this whiff of another world, another way of life, no way to see it, or understand it, and yet it was there, in the wind, calling to us plaintive, grieving, just beyond the straight defined edges of our farms, just outside the firm rational orderliness of our disciplined lives. (233)

"Memory" here stands not for a frozen moment in the past, nor a completely recoverable history of oppression, but might be read as a political retelling where she insists that the land is not "empty," as wilderness is conventionally written in the Canadian colonization myth, but filled with the ghosts of previous times so that whatever history gets told, it cannot completely obliterate the past, the memory. The telling of history is called into question throughout Brandt's narrative as she successively tries to unravel the different histories she was told: "When did I first understand this, the dark underside of property, colonization, ownership? . . . Was it the time I read about our Canadian history, in grade Six . . . ? And later, in Mennonite history class, [when] I heard about our own arrival as a people" (233). Clearly, this "memory" is not offered as a more accurate, more truthful history, but indeed a "struggle of memory against forgetting," a struggle against those histories which erase and exclude stories of oppression.

In her critique of patriarchy in Mennonite culture, Brandt similarly creates a memory/space of women's freedom, one that she locates in her female body, rather than the wild prairie:

There was another memory, too, hidden in my blood, my bones, that sang out from me sometimes in that place of newly broken prairie, an older memory, of a time when the women of my culture had voices and power and freedom . . . before the persecutions, the Inquisition, the burning times, the

drowning times, the hanging times, before we became transients, exiles. . . .
The first time I participated in an Aboriginal ceremony near Winnipeg, a few
years ago, in the bush, under the full moon, I had such a strong sense of recognition coursing through me, I remember this, I remember this, my body sang.
I remember when we gathered, my women ancestors, around fires like this
one. (233–34)

This embodiment of memory does not erase the very particular markings of
history on women's bodies, as Brandt is careful to locate her bodily memory "across the sea . . . in the Flemish lowlands" (234), but it does imply
an ecofeminist alliance of a female-gendered nature with oppressed Native and Mennonite women, "her children" (232). The question becomes
whether this strategy creates a space of "radical possibility" or absolves the
women of their implication in history through their shared innocence with
nature (hooks 149). Given Brandt's insistence on her "implication in [the
land's] demise as lawful/unlawful heir" and her belief that "there is still
time to turn it around, to save the land, to undo its massive poisoning,"
she clearly intends her "remembering" as a site of resistance which could
change present practices (238). But, as hooks concedes, locating oneself on
the margin is a "risk": "it is not a 'safe' place," nor is it always emancipatory (149). What is important is continually repositioning oneself to "stand
in political resistance" (145).

In contrast to Butala's universalizing narrative, I argue that Brandt locates her particular desire for the wild prairie in its sociohistorical context.
Brandt fills up the empty prairie with the history of colonization, of dispossession, of hard labor, of childhood squeals; she makes no claim to be able
to wander freely without guilt or implication on the land or to be "merely
looking at the prairie as a human being" since each of us and the land itself
is marked by history. She self-consciously lives in exile, not trying to "come
home," but to remain alert to the violence embedded in attempts to claim
and secure a home. By locating her hope in a politics of memory, Brandt
risks reverting to essentialized characteristics of women, Natives, and nature, reinforcing old stereotypes rather than creating new possibilities. But
her attempt to use memory as a political tool in the "struggle against forgetting" can also be read as an act of resistance where she refuses to give
up her "lawful/unlawful" inheritance (238).

Joy Kogawa: *Obasan*

PUBLISHED IN 1981, Joy Kogawa's first novel, *Obasan*, has won numerous awards and international acclaim; its powerful retelling of the internment, relocation, and persecution of Japanese Canadians during World War II has found a secure place in the canon of Canadian literature. Told through the eyes of a child, Naomi, the novel shares much in common with Kogawa's own experiences as a young girl evacuated from Vancouver first to a ghost town in the British Columbia interior and then to the Alberta prairies. The novel opens with a date, August 9th, 1972, the anniversary of the atomic bombing of Nagasaki, and the stillness of the prairie grasses under an expansive sky of stars, interjecting a very different history into the prairie landscape desired and mourned by Butala and Brandt. I shape my reading of *Obasan* into a conversation with these other texts, recognizing how much of its many richly crafted themes I necessarily exclude by doing so. Indeed, literary critics have situated *Obasan* into a multitude of different themes and theoretical perspectives, including feminism, historical metafiction, postmodernism, ethnic minority writing in both the Canadian and North American context, and more rarely into Canadian women's wilderness writing and prairie writing.[9] Kogawa herself is both writer and community and environmental activist.

If Di Brandt writes out of a subject position of coming-to-awareness of how "home" as coherent, stable place is implicated in histories of oppression, the tension Naomi experiences as "both the enemy and not the enemy" (Kogawa 70) is best captured by Homi Bhabha's concept of "unhomeliness." Bhabha uses this term to describe the experience of colonized peoples, whose homes, like Naomi's, have been invaded, destroyed, or relocated, in either physical or cultural terms, such that identity is denaturalized from any reference to place, ethnicity, or language into an unstable, contradictory condition of liminality and hybridity. The rupture, unsettling, and reconfiguration of the home, and consequently of identity, take place in particular historical conditions: "The unhomely is the shock of recognition of the world-in-the-home, the home-in-the-world" (445). Naomi's identity in the hyphenated zone of "Japanese-Canadian" is formed in the movement between her homes of Vancouver, Slocan, and the beet farm near Granton; homes which can no longer represent family, community, or even nation, as the Orders-in-Council fragmented families, dispersed communities, and deported and deprived citizens of their rights and property in their "home

and native land." Against this intrusion of the "world into the home," Kogawa positions Naomi's two aunts: Obasan, who struggles to create a safe
space for the children through the construction of a home of silence and
forgiveness, and Aunt Emily, who struggles in the public realm to bring
the history of internment to light and redress and to restore the Japanese
Canadians' rightful claim to the land of Canada. Naomi's uncovering of the
story of their displacement and her mother's absence and disfigurement
represents her personal and political struggle to position herself within
these multiple tellings, strategies, identities, and locations. She searches for
voice and reconciliation in the rupture of home/land and the silence of her
mother.

The fabric for the entire story is the land itself, that "home and native
land" which opens the national anthem and which has long been intertwined with popular and official versions of "Canadian identity." Kogawa
evokes a mythical landscape in the poetic imagery which permeates *Obasan*
and grounds it in the historically and geographically specific landscapes of
the coast, mountains, and prairie in which the novel takes place. The significance of the landscape in the novel was first elaborated by Erika Gottlieb, who pointed out how it is "less through the people than through the
landscape that [Naomi] approaches the troubled question of her Canadian
identity" (42), but has been most extensively taken up by Karen Quimby,
who focuses on its political rather than spiritual meanings. While some
commentators have reduced the nature imagery of Obasan to a "yearning
for a return to 'natural' unity" and a correspondingly conciliatory gesture
toward multiculturalism (Davey 109),[10] Quimby reveals how the multiple
natures which occupy the text mirror the tension Naomi faces in "occupying
simultaneously multiple identities and positions" (268).

By making the landscape central to her narrative, Kogawa implicitly
writes back to and disrupts the nationalist, and Eurocentric, "nature thematic" in Canadian literature and the popular and literary coding of "rural"
and "prairie" as white. While Naomi may find that racist "thistles . . . grow
everywhere" in her new prairie home, Kogawa does not present the prairie
as an alien white space but establishes a continuous presence of families of
Japanese descent dating back to "the time of the coal mines and the construction of the railroad and the establishment of the North West Mounted
Police in Fort McLeod" (202). "We are those pioneers who cleared the brush
and the forest with our hands, the gardeners tending and attending the soil
with our tenderness, the fishermen who are flung from the sea to flounder
in the dust of the prairies," Kogawa writes in a reconstruction of history

from the perspective of the subaltern (112). The racist bias of conventional constructions of history and place is immediately exposed with these insertions of Japanese Canadians into the classic events in the "opening of the West" and the settlement of Canada.

The history which locates Naomi and her family on the prairie positions her in particular ways to that land, just as the hut they are to live in is positioned "at the far end of a large yard that has a white house in the middle" (191). On Naomi's arrival, the prairie is not the "homecoming" Butala describes, nor the "heaven on earth" Brandt remembers, but "the edge of the world . . . a place of angry air" where "the wind howls and guffaws at [her] eardrums," and "the whipping brown dust" makes her breathe in "short shallow gasps" (191–92). The symbols of death and violence—"a skeleton in the wind," "skull-shaped weeds," "fierce, almost leafless trees," "skeletons of farm machinery with awkward metal jaws angled upwards," "an army of Spartan plants"—which outline the landscape denote Naomi's "sleep-walk years" of hardship working on the beet farm, the racism of the unwelcoming white community, the destruction of the Japanese Canadian community through dispersal, and the deaths of her parents (191–92, 200). The horrific living conditions Naomi describes not only contradict the official telling of that experience, captured in a newspaper clipping encaptioned "Grinning and Happy," but also any universalized writing of the prairie as a landscape of beauty and "home."

> I mind everything. Even the flies. The flies and flies and flies from the cows in the barn and the manure pile—all the black flies that curtain the windows. . . . It's the chicken coop "house" we live in that I mind. The uninsulated unbelievable thin-as-a-cotton-dress hovel never before inhabited in winter by human beings. In summer it's a heat trap, an incubator, a dry sauna from which there is no relief. In winter the icicles drip down the inside of the windows. . . . It's the bedbugs and my having to sleep on the table to escape the nightly attack, and the welts over our bodies. . . . Or it's standing in the beet field under the maddening sun, standing with my black head a sun-trap even though it's covered and lying down in the ditch, faint, and the nausea in waves and the cold sweat, and getting up and tackling the next row. (194–95)

Nature here is not a new "home" for Naomi, unhomed from family and community, but a prison: "the clouds are the shape of our new prison walls—untouchable, impersonal, random" (196). " 'Grinning and Happy' and all smiles around a pile of beets?" she asks, "That is one telling. It's not how it was" (197).

Naomi, Obasan, and Uncle eventually do stay and make the prairie their home, although the social marker of race ensures Naomi is always perceived as Other. As an adult, she becomes a schoolteacher in the nearby town of Cecil, Alberta, where she is repeatedly asked, "where do you come from?" and presumed to be a foreigner, belonging somewhere else (7). And while it is true that Naomi's family comes from elsewhere—"perhaps some genealogist of the future will come across this patch of bones and wonder why so many fishermen died on the prairie"—they are able to reconcile themselves to this "strange" landscape which, as Uncle points out again and again, is "like the sea" (225, 1). Kogawa writes, "The hill surface, as if responding to a command from Uncle's out-stretched hand, undulates suddenly in a breeze, with ripple after ripple of grass shadows, rhythmical as ocean waves. We wade through the dry surf, the flecks of grass hitting us like spray" (1). These annual visits to the coulee which remind Uncle of his boat-building trade and fisherman heritage also commemorate Naomi's mother's tragedy in Nagasaki, as Naomi learns only later. As it is for Brandt, the land is holder of history and memory for Naomi, but the memories of which they speak are very different.

Kogawa does more than historically write the racialized Other into those white spaces; she naturalizes their presence:

> Where do any of us come from in this cold country? O Canada, whether it is admitted or not, we come from you, we come from you. From the same soil, the slugs and slime and bogs and twigs and roots. We come from the country that plucks its people out like weeds and flings them into the roadside. We grow in ditches and sloughs, untended and spindly. We erupt in the valleys and mountainsides, in small towns and back alleys, sprouting upside-down on the prairies, our hair wild as spiders' legs, our feet rooted nowhere. We grow where we are not seen, we flourish where we are not heard, the thick undergrowth of an unlikely planting. . . . We come from Canada, this land that is like every land, filled with the wise, the fearful, the compassionate, the corrupt. (226)

Rooting the Japanese Canadians in the very land of Canada undermines their construction as "exotic species" who must be weeded out and reveals how the racist policies do not leave Naomi and her family "homeless" but rather "unhomed": positioned in the contradictory place of alien and native. Indeed Kogawa uses the trope of the Native to further destabilize any simple conflation between national and ethnic identity and to underscore how "race" is socially constructed. Throughout the novel, there are frequent allusions to similarities between the First Nations and Japanese, such as how the Native children are as "alien" in the Granton school as the Japanese Canadians, how Slocan was first the site of a Native relocation, and how Japanese can "pass" for Natives. Kogawa writes:

> Uncle could be Chief Sitting Bull squatting here. He has the same prairie-baked skin, the deep brown furrows like dry river beds creasing his cheeks. All he needs is a feather headdress, and he would be perfect for a picture postcard—"Indian Chief from Canadian Prairie"—souvenir of Alberta, made in Japan. (2)

This passage simultaneously *naturalizes* the presence of the Japanese Canadian on the prairie by making him, quite literally, "native" and *denaturalizes* the category of "race" on which the historical dispossession and relocation of both the First Nations and Japanese Canadians was based.

Parallel to the rupture of home/land, and similarly symbolized through landscape, is Naomi's sense of loss and fragmentation from her mother due to her experiences of sexual abuse at the hands of her neighbor, Old Man Gower, as well as her geographical separation from her mother, who is unable to return from Japan as the war escalates.[11] The temporal coincidence of these events in Naomi's child mind reinforces the secrecy and shame she feels from the sexual abuse and creates a sense of guilt that she caused her mother's departure, so that while she first imagines herself as a limb of her mother's body, "a young branch attached by right of flesh and blood," she turns into "a parasite on her body . . . my arms are vines that strangle the limb to which I cling" (264). Quimby demonstrates how "Naomi figures herself into the landscape in multiple positions when remembering this abuse" and how "the landscape itself continually shifts significations" to demonstrate "the necessary complexity of an identity that forms through subjugation and abuse" (262–64). Her first response to Old Man Gower's approach is to seek safety from the male predator in the wilderness: "To be whole and safe I must hide in the foliage, odourless as a newborn fawn" (63). The vulnerability of the animal with which she identifies subverts the possibility of finding a safe home in nature, and the narrative shifts to gendering the forest "sanctuary" as male territory: "I am Snow White in the forest, unable to run. He is the forest full of eyes and arms. He is the tree root that trips Snow White. He is the lightening flash through the dark sky" (64). The tree appears again in the novel as the "dead tree" in the prairie to which Naomi goes for solitude, listening to and watching the frogs and insects in the swamp (205). Here the tree is not gendered but represents a barren landscape from which she finds no answers to her endless questions, nor any relief from her family tragedies. Indeed, Naomi rescues a frog with a broken leg from the swamp and "set[s] to work making and unmaking a home for the frog in [a] glass bowl," taking on herself the roles of mother and healer (207).

The most explicit example of Naomi's multiple positioning within violated space is her appropriation of the Goldilocks fairy tale.

> In one of Stephen's books, there is a story of child with long golden ringlets called Goldilocks who one day comes to a quaint house in the woods lived in by a family of bears. Clearly, we are that bear family in this strange house in the middle of the woods. I am Baby Bear, whose chair Goldilocks breaks, whose porridge Goldilocks eats, whose bed Goldilocks sleeps in. Or perhaps this is not true and I am really Goldilocks after all. In the morning, will I not find my way out of the forest and back to my room where the picture bird sings above my bed and the real bird sings in the real peach tree by my open bedroom window in Marpole? (126)

The "house in the woods" bears resemblance to Naomi's house in Slocan, which she describes as an earthlike hut hidden in the forest: "the colour of the house is that of sand and earth. It seems more like a giant toadstool than a building . . . [and] although it is not dark or cool, it feels underground" (121). But Naomi finds it difficult to identify this as her home and questions whether she is not Goldilocks, invading someone else's house in this move to the forest and able to recover her own—*her real*—house in the city. But the obvious coding, in both popular culture and Kogawa's re-presentation, of Goldilocks as white positions Naomi much more appropriately in the position of the bear family whose private space is violated by the white intruder. The difficulty of reading herself into either of these positions dramatizes the paradoxical condition of unhomeliness within which the exile lives.

Conclusions

WHILE THIS ESSAY has clustered a set of texts around the title "prairie," I hope to have disrupted any possibility of defining such a place, especially in terms of the prairie landscape or a particular "prairie identity," except in relation to various sociohistorical relations and discourses. Butala, Brandt, and Kogawa do not share similar historical experiences of the prairies, as land or as social community, nor do they view or write that landscape in similar ways—although "the prairies" as landscape, as home, and as imagined community plays a significant role in the writing of all three. In her humanist abstraction of rural life on the prairies to capital-n Nature, Butala may feel that her "soul had at last found its home," but that home is only hers to possess because of her privileges of class, race, and ability; social relations which she finds she must *write out* of her narrative in order to universalize nature into a spiritual experience of ecological enlightenment. Brandt, on the other hand, contemplates how the constructions of "home" and "community" on which her Mennonite childhood were based involved unacceptable denials of her voice, agency, and inheritance, as well as the exclusion of other histories of oppression and a legacy of ecologically damaging practices. Living in exile, she searches to rehabilitate both the land and her identity as a Mennonite woman through a politicization of memory, a strategy which risks reinscribing oppressive relations in her elaboration of an ecofeminist version of "home." Kogawa, as a final contrast, may suggest that Naomi is able to heal the wounds of her fragmented and violated female body, family, community, and nation through the symbolic associations of the sea with the prairie landscape; but the social marker of race ensures Naomi is always perceived as Other on the prairies. Significantly, the multiple natures which occupy the text and the difficulty Naomi experiences in locating herself within any one of these natures exemplifies the paradoxical condition of unhomeliness within which the exile lives, and exposes the privilege implicit in Butala's coherent sense of being "home on the prairie."

NOTES

1. The thematic of "nature," of course, enjoys a long tradition within Canadian literary criticism (see Frye; Atwood; Glickman), but from the outset it was intertwined with the search to define and construct a national identity. With the advent of a postcolonial and postmodern sensibility in Canadian literary criticism (see especially Hutcheon; Hutcheon and Richmond), the multicultural city has largely usurped the theme of nature, implicitly relegating the writing of nature to a colonialist past not an environmentalist present. Nature writing is currently undergoing a revival in North America, evidenced on both sides of the border by a proliferation of often best-selling new work, nature-writing anthologies, and coffee-table books, although this trend has been ignored north of the forty-ninth parallel. For this reason, I locate my essay more within the emerging conversation of "ecocriticism" than within Canadian literary criticism, although I hope my attention to Canadian writers and the Canadian multicultural/postcolonial context will offer one bridge between the two.

2. Massey is careful here to distinguish between the genderized discourse of home and the plurality of women's experiences, noting how the public/private distinction on which it is based is not only specific to white middle classes of Western societies but "has by no means been absolute nor held good for many women who did not live in heterosexual couples, with children, in suburbs" and so on (10).

3. For elaborations of this point, see Soper; Cronon; Quigley; Levy.

4. By "essentializing identity," I mean the ascription of a set of immutable characteristics to a group of people, such as women or Natives, a practice or discourse which has historically served as justification for their exclusion from particular social roles and places, as in the cases of sexism and racism.

5. The difference here is largely one of proponent as those currently engaged in struggles over nationalism are no doubt as earnest about the legitimacy of their claim and its importance to their survival as environmentalists are about the validity of their claims to an ecological crisis threatening the survival of the human race.

6. Soulé and Lease argue that such "postmodern deconstruction" posits an absurd denial of physical reality, thereby representing the ultimate appropriation of nature into the social and undermining the basis for an environmental politics. More sympathetic readings accept that while there might be an ontological category "nature," a physical reality outside our knowledge systems, we can only access and know this nature through social constructs, whether science or aesthetics, thus in practice there can be no separation of ontology from epistemology (i.e., what we know is shaped by how we know). The question of whether "nature is the one metanarrative which cannot be deconstructed" remains nonetheless and has been taken up most extensively by science studies scholars Katherine Hayles and Karen Barad.

7. I take the phrase "ecological wisdom" from Cheryll Glotfelty's definition of ecocriticism. In her introduction to *The Ecocriticism Reader,* Glotfelty suggests that ecocritics ask questions such as "Are the values expressed in this play consistent with ecological wisdom?" (xix).

8. Butala clearly draws the title of *Luna* from this dream, as the novel presents an ecofeminist "wise woman" character who roams the prairie at night and finds her authentic self in natural cycles of the moon and sun, and correspondingly menstruation, pregnancy, and menopause.

9. Indeed, *Obasan* is frequently taken up as an example of "Japanese American" literature by American literary critics, despite the historically specific significance Kogawa places on "Canada" as place, identity, and racist government within the novel (see Lim; Tharp). While Howells suggests *Obasan* "belongs to the capacious genre of prairie historical fiction which has documented the wilderness wanderings of numerous dispossessed ethnic groups," few surveys of prairie literature discuss the novel (107). Absent from Thacker's *The Great Prairie Fact and Literary Imagination,* it merits a paragraph in Fairbanks's extensive study of prairie women and prairie women's writing in American and Canadian fiction and two pages in Davidson's study of Canadian literary works which subvert the popular western genre.

10. Focusing on Kogawa's images of harmony and wholeness, Davey condemns the nature imagery which pervades *Obasan* as a "Wordsworthian refuge that compensates for social cruelties" and as a result "implicitly accepts the injustices done to Japanese Canadians" (105, 112). Not only is Davey blind to the multiple natures which Kogawa evokes, he is unable to read her nature imagery as a hybrid form which combines, challenges, and rewrites both Japanese and Anglo-Canadian aesthetics. Davey appropriates "nature writing" as a purely western trope, suggesting Kogawa's imagery consists of "organic signs familiar to readers of Western literature" as it represents "Japanese-Canadian participation in Wordsworthian nature" (105, 108). Kobayashi, by contrast, places *Obasan* in the role of generational bridge within the Japanese Canadian community, as Kogawa draws extensively on Japanese poetic traditions and archetypes which are rich in nature imagery, yet writes a "very un-Issei-like journey for a sense of belonging" (222).

11. The significance of the sexual abuse has been downplayed by some critics as secondary to the story of racial discrimination, but Kogawa repeatedly draws parallels between the sexual abuse and the "domestic war" against the Japanese Canadians, likening Naomi's response to the racial persecution to the silence and paralysis of a rape victim and sexualizing Naomi's nightmares about white soldiers who degrade and mutilate three Oriental women (Tharp 214).

REFERENCES

Atwood, Margaret. *Survival: A Thematic Guide to Canadian Literature.* Toronto: Anansi, 1972.

Bhabha, Homi K. "The World and the Home." *Dangerous Liaisons: Gender, Nation, and Postcolonial Perspectives.* Ed. Anne McClintock, Aamir Mufti, and Ella Shohat. Minneapolis: U of Minnesota P, 1997. 445–55.

Brandt, Di. *Dancing Naked: Narrative Strategies for Writing across Centuries.* Stratford, Ont.: Mercury, 1996.

———. "This Land That I Love, This Wide Wide Prairie." *Fresh Tracks: Writing the Western Landscape.* Ed. Pamela Banting. Victoria, B.C.: Polestar, 1998. 232–38.

Butala, Sharon. *Luna.* Toronto: Harper, 1994.

———. *The Perfection of the Morning: An Apprenticeship in Nature.* Toronto: Harper, 1994.

Cronon, William. "Introduction: In Search of Nature." *Uncommon Ground: Rethinking the Human Place in Nature.* Ed. William Cronon. New York: Norton, 1996. 23–56.

Davey, Frank. *Post-National Arguments: The Politics of the Anglophone-Canadian Novel since 1967.* Toronto: U of Toronto P, 1993.

Davidson, Arnold E. *Coyote Country: Fictions of the Canadian West.* Durham: Duke UP, 1994.

de Hernandez, Jennifer Browdy. "On Home Ground: Politics, Location, and the Construction of Identity in Four American Women's Autobiographies." *MELUS* 22.4 (1997): 21–38.

Fairbanks, Carol. *Prairie Women: Images in American and Canadian Fiction*. New Haven: Yale UP, 1986.

Frye, Northrop. *The Bush Garden: Essays on the Canadian Imagination*. Toronto: Anansi, 1971.

Gaard, Greta, and Patrick D. Murphy. Introduction. *Ecofeminist Literary Criticism: Theory, Interpretation, Pedagogy*. Ed. Greta Gaard and Patrick Murphy. Urbana: U of Illinois P, 1998. 1–14.

Glickman, Susan. *The Picturesque and the Sublime: A Poetics of the Canadian Landscape*. Montreal: McGill-Queen's UP, 1998.

Glotfelty, Cheryll. Introduction. *The Ecocriticism Reader: Landmarks in Literary Ecology*. Ed. Cheryll Glotfelty and Harold Fromm. Athens: U of Georgia P, 1996. xv–xxxvii.

Gottlieb, Erika. "The Riddle of Concentric Worlds in 'Obasan.'" *Canadian Literature* 109 (1986): 34–53.

hooks, bell. *Yearning: Race, Gender, and Cultural Politics*. Toronto: Between the Lines, 1990.

Howells, Coral Ann. *Private and Fictional Worlds: Canadian Women Novelists of the 1970s and 1980s*. New York: Methuen, 1987.

Hutcheon, Linda. *The Canadian Postmodern: A Study of Contemporary English-Canadian Fiction*. Toronto: Oxford UP, 1988.

Hutcheon, Linda, and Marion Richmond, eds. *Other Solitudes: Canadian Multicultural Fictions*. Toronto: Oxford UP, 1990.

Kobayashi, Audrey. "Birds of Passage or Squawking Ducks: Writing across Generations of Japanese-Canadian Literature." *Writing across Worlds: Literature and Migration*. Ed. Russell King, John Connell, and Paul White. London: Routledge, 1995. 216–28.

Kogawa, Joy. *Obasan*. Toronto: Penguin, 1981.

Kolodny, Annette. "Unearthing Herstory: An Introduction." *The Ecocriticism Reader: Landmarks in Literary Ecology*. Ed. Cheryll Glotfelty and Harold Fromm. Athens: U of Georgia P, 1996. 170–81.

Lebowitz, Andrea Pinto. Introduction. *Living in Harmony: Nature Writing by Women in Canada*. Ed. Andrea Lebowitz. Victoria, B.C.: Orca, 1996. 1–8.

Levy, Neil. "Foucault's Unnatural Ecology." *Discourses of the Environment*. Ed. Eric Darier. Oxford: Blackwell, 1999. 203–16.

Lim, Shirley Geok-lin. "Japanese American Women's Life Stories: Maternality in Monica Stone's *Nisei Daughter* and Joy Kogawa's *Obasan*." *Feminist Studies* 16.2 (1990): 289–312.

Massey, Doreen. *Space, Place, and Gender*. Minneapolis: U of Minnesota P, 1994.

Merchant, Carolyn. "Reinventing Eden: Western Culture as Recovery Narrative." *Uncommon Ground: Rethinking the Human Place in Nature*. Ed. William Cronon. New York: Norton, 1996. 132–59.

Murphy, Patrick D. " 'The Women Are Speaking': Contemporary Literature as Theoretical Critique." *Ecofeminist Literary Criticism: Theory, Interpretation, Pedagogy.* Ed. Greta Gaard and Patrick D. Murphy. Urbana: U of Illinois P, 1998. 23–48.

Nesmith, C., and S. A. Radcliffe. "(Re)mapping Mother Earth: A Geographical Perspective on Environmental Feminisms." *Society and Space* 11.4 (1993): 379–94.

Quigley, Peter. "Nature as Dangerous Space." *Discourses of the Environment.* Ed. Eric Darier. Oxford: Blackwell, 1999. 181–202.

Quimby, Karin. " 'This is my own, my native land': Constructions of Identity and Landscape in Joy Kogawa's *Obasan.*" *Cross-Addressing: Resistance Literature and Cultural Borders.* Ed. John C. Hawley. Albany: State U of New York P, 1996. 257–74.

Ricou, Laurence. *Vertical Man/Horizontal World: Man and Landscape in Canadian Prairie Fiction.* Vancouver: U of British Columbia P, 1973.

Said, Edward W. *Orientalism.* 1979. New York: Vintage, 1994.

Soper, Kate. *What Is Nature? Culture, Politics and the Non-Human.* Oxford: Blackwell, 1995.

Soulé, Michael E., and Gary Lease, eds. *Reinventing Nature? Responses to Postmodern Deconstruction.* Washington, D.C.: Island, 1995.

Taylor, Cynthia. "Claiming Female Space: Mary Austin's Western Landscape." In *The Big Empty: Essays on Western Landscapes as Narrative.* Ed. Leonard Engel. Albuquerque: U of New Mexico P, 1994. 119–32.

Thacker, Robert. *The Great Prairie Fact and Literary Imagination.* Albuquerque: U of New Mexico P, 1989.

Tharp, Julie. " 'In the Center of My Body Is a Rift': Trauma and Recovery in Joy Kogawa's *Obasan* and *Itsuka.*" *Creating Safe Space: Violence and Women's Writing.* Ed. Tomoko Kuribayashi and Julie Tharp. Albany: State U of New York P, 1988. 213–26.

Notes on Editors and Contributors

NANDITA BATRA was born in Bombay, India, and is currently professor of English at the University of Puerto Rico at Mayaguez. She is also English editor of *Atenea*, an interdisciplinary journal published by UPR-M. Her research interests lie mainly in nineteenth-century British literature, particularly in the area of animal motifs and symbols and the relationship between zoological and imperial discourse.

MICHAEL BENNETT is associate professor of English at Long Island University (Brooklyn). He is coeditor, with David Teague, of *The Nature of Cities: Ecocriticism and Urban Environments* and, with Vanessa Dickerson, of *Recovering the Black Female Body: Self-Representations by African American Women*. He is completing *Democratic Discourses: Antebellum American Literature and the Radical Abolition Movement* and beginning work on a project entitled *The Imprisonment of American Culture*. He is on the steering committee of the Radical Caucus of the Modern Language Association.

NIALL BINNS was educated in England, Chile, and Spain. He is currently associate professor of Spanish American literature at Madrid's Complutense University. His publications include *Un vals en un montón de escombros: Poesia hispanoamericana entre la modernidad y la postmodernidad*, *Nicanor Parra*, and *La poesía de Jorge Teillier: La tragedia de los lares*. He will soon publish *Ecopoesía en Hispanoamérica*, a series of ecocritical readings of Chilean and Spanish American poetry. He is also preparing a book on non-Spanish authors who have written about the Spanish Civil War. His two award-winning books of poetry are *5 Love Songs* and *Tratado sobre los buitres*.

MICHAEL P. BRANCH is professor of literature and environment at the University of Nevada, Reno. He is cofounder and past president of ASLE-US and has served as book review editor of *ISLE* since 1995. He is coeditor of *The Height of Our Mountains: Nature Writing from Virginia's Blue Ridge Mountains and Shenandoah Valley* and *Reading the Earth: New Directions in the Study of Literature and the Environment* and editor of *John Muir's Last Journey: South to the Amazon and East to Africa* and *Reading the Roots: American Nature Writing before Walden*. He also coedits the University of Virginia Press's book series "Under the Sign of Nature: Explorations in Ecocriticism."

CAROL H. CANTRELL is professor of English at Colorado State University. She teaches courses in modern literature and women's studies and serves as graduate coordinator for the English Department. Her research has increasingly focused on issues of culture and nature in the work of modernist writers, and she is completing a book on modernist literature and place. A high point of her career was coordinating the first ASLE conference, held in Fort Collins, Colorado, in 1995.

HAROLD FROMM is currently a visiting scholar at the University of Arizona. He is a frequent manuscript reader for *ISLE* and has recently been charmed into Darwinian literary studies as a result of Joseph Carroll's talk at the 2001 ASLE Conference in Flagstaff, Arizona. With Cheryll Glotfelty, he edited *The Ecocriticism Reader,* which appeared in 1996. He is involved in various writing projects at this time.

ANDREW FURMAN, the author of *Israel through the Jewish American Imagination* and *Jewish American Writers and the Multicultural Dilemma,* is associate professor of English at Florida Atlantic University, where he teaches American literature and creative writing. He has contributed essays, articles, and reviews to periodicals including the *Chronicle of Higher Education, MELUS, Contemporary Literature,* the *Miami Herald,* the *Forward,* and *Tikkun,* where he is a contributing editor. He is currently writing a novel, set in Florida's Everglades, condominium complexes, and strip malls. He lives in Boca Raton with his wife and two children.

R. EDWARD GRUMBINE directs the Sierra Institute, an undergraduate field program in wilderness studies, run through University of California Extension, Santa Cruz. He teaches field botany, ethnobotany, and wilderness history classes. He is active in wildlands protection in California, serving on the board of the California Wilderness Coalition. He has published two books—*Ghost Bears: Exploring the Biodiversity Crisis* and *Environmental Policy and Biodiversity.* He lives in a small cabin in the Santa Cruz Mountains.

URSULA K. HEISE is associate professor of English and comparative literature at Columbia University in New York, where she teaches contemporary literature and literary theory. Her interests, besides ecocriticism, include contemporary European and North and South American narrative and poetry, literature and science, literature and media, and science fiction. She is the author of *Chronoschisms: Time, Narrative, and Postmodernism* and is now completing a book entitled *World Wide Webs: Global Ecology and the Cultural Imagination.*

ROBERT KERN is associate professor of English at Boston College, where he teaches courses on the Whitman tradition, nineteenth- and twentieth-century poetry, and American nature writing, among others. His articles and reviews, mostly on modern American poetry, have appeared in a wide range of journals, and he is the author of *Orientalism, Modernism, and the American Poem.* His current project is an ecocritical study of the tension between anthropocentrism and ecocentrism in a variety of American literary texts, both poetry and prose.

LISA LEBDUSKA is director of College Writing at Wheaton College in Norton, Massachusetts, where she teaches various writing courses and assists colleagues in developing Writing Across the Curriculum pedagogies. A member of the Northeast Writing Centers Association Steering Committee, she is researching the environmental impact of the virtual world on teaching bodies, spaces, and places. Her most recent publication, "Peer Tutor Training in Visual Rhetoric," will appear in the CD ROM version of *The OWL Construction and Maintenance Guide*, edited by James Inman and Clinton Gardner.

GRETCHEN LEGLER is associate professor of creative writing at the University of Maine at Farmington. Her first collection of essays, *All the Powerful Invisible Things: A Sportswoman's Notebook*, won two Pushcart Prizes and has been excerpted and anthologized in *Orion* magazine, *Uncommon Waters, Another Wilderness, Gifts of the Wild, Minnesota Seasons, A Different Angle*, and other publications. Her ecocritical scholarship has appeared in such volumes as *Reading under the Sign of Nature* and *Writing the Environment*. She is currently at work on a book of essays about Antarctica, where she spent six months in 1997 as a fellow with the National Science Foundation's Artists and Writers Program. Her creative nonfiction about Antarctica has appeared most recently in *Orion* and *The Women's Review of Books*.

PAUL J. LINDHOLDT teaches courses in American literature, environmental studies, and nature writing at Eastern Washington University. He won an Academy of American Poets Award in 1984 and two Excellence in Journalism Awards in 2000 for energy and environmental reporting. He has published more than a hundred and fifty book chapters, journal articles, essays, columns, reviews, and poems—and has given more than a hundred invited lectures, conference papers, and readings—on the subjects of literature and culture in America. He is also a longtime leader of the Upper Columbia River Group of the Sierra Club.

CHERYL LOUSLEY is writing a doctoral dissertation on representations of rurality in contemporary Canadian literature in the Faculty of Environmental Studies at York University in Toronto, Canada. She serves as executive editor of *Alternatives Journal*, a quarterly magazine on Canadian environmental issues and ideas. Her research has been supported by the Social Sciences and Humanities Research Council of Canada.

SCOTT MACDONALD is author of the ongoing series *A Critical Cinema: Interviews with Independent Filmmakers*. Three volumes have been published by the University of California Press, and a fourth is in preparation. He has also published *Avant-Garde*

Film/Motion Studies and *Screen Writings: Scripts and Texts by Independent Filmmakers.* His newest books are *The Garden in the Machine: A Field Guide to Independent Films about Place* and *Cinema 16: Documents toward a History of Film Society.* He has programmed independent media at colleges and universities, art museums, and film festivals for twenty-five years and is committed to introducing teachers and scholars in fields other than film studies to the world of alternative cinema. He teaches film history at Bard College in Hudson Valley, New York.

IAN MARSHALL, professor of English and co-coordinator of environmental studies at Penn State-Altoona, is the current president of ASLE-US. He is the author of *Story Line: Exploring the Literature of the Appalachian Trail* and *Peak Experiences: Walking Meditations on Literature, Nature, and Need.*

PATRICK D. MURPHY, founding editor of *ISLE,* currently serves as chair of the English Department at the University of Central Florida. Author of *Literature, Nature, and Other, A Place for Wayfaring: The Poetry and Prose of Gary Snyder,* and *Farther Afield in the Study of Nature-Oriented Literature,* he has also edited and coedited numerous books, including *Ecofeminist Literary Criticism* and *The Literature of Nature: An International Sourcebook.* He maintains particular interests in ecological poetry, ecofiction, and the intersections of feminism, multiculturalism, and ecocriticism, while more recently exploring environmental awareness in genre fiction and young adult literature. He has also played a role in promoting ecocriticism in East Asia.

RANDALL ROORDA is associate professor of English at the University of Kentucky, where he teaches courses in environmental literature and discourse, nonfiction writing, and English pedagogy. He is the author of *Dramas of Solitude: Narratives of Retreat in American Nature Writing.* He is a former president of ASLE-US and was program chair for the 2001 ASLE Conference in Flagstaff, Arizona. In 1998 he founded ASLE-CCCC, a group for ecology and composition ("ecocomposition"). His research and teaching interests involve ecological English of all sorts: ecocriticism, ecocomposition, and ecologology. He is currently working on genres of participation in nature: wilderness wives, auto naturalists, deep maps, and others.

GORDON M. SAYRE is associate professor of English at the University of Oregon, where he is a specialist in colonial American literature. He was drawn into the field of ecocriticism by the opportunity to experience North American landscapes vicariously through the writings of European explorers and their encounters with native peoples. He has recently published ecocritical articles in Steven Rosendale's collection, *The Greening of Literary Scholarship,* and in *JEMCS: Journal of Early Modern Cultural Studies.*

SCOTT SLOVIC is professor of literature and environment at the University of Nevada, Reno, where he directed the Center for Environmental Arts and Humanities from 1995 to 2001. He currently chairs UNR's graduate program in literature and environment. The founding president of ASLE-US, he has served as editor of *ISLE* since 1995. He is the author of *Seeking Awareness in American Nature Writing* and dozens of articles in the field of environmental literature and ecocriticism and has edited or coedited seven books, including *Getting Over the Color Green: Contemporary Environmental Literature of the Southwest.* He also edits the University of Nevada Press's Environmental Arts and Humanities Series and Milkweed Editions' Credo Series.

JOHN TALLMADGE is an ecocritic specializing in American nature writers and outdoor education. He is the author of *Meeting the Tree of Life*, a memoir of teaching and wilderness travel, as well as numerous scholarly articles and personal essays. A director of the Orion Society, he served as president of ASLE-US in 1997 and is a founding editor of the series Under the Sign of Nature: Explorations in Ecocriticism for the University of Virginia Press. He lives in Cincinnati, endeavoring to learn from nature in the city while leading wilderness seminars for doctoral candidates at the Union Institute and University.

KATSUNORI YAMAZATO is professor of American literature and culture at the University of the Ryukyus in Okinawa, Japan. He has authored numerous articles on American writers. His books include *Great Earth Sangha* (dialogues between Gary Snyder and Sansei Yamao) and Japanese translations of Snyder's *A Place in Space* and *Mountains and Rivers without End.* He has also coedited *Post-War Okinawa and America: Fifty Years of Cross-Cultural Contact.* He currently serves as president of ASLE-Japan.

Credits

The articles contained in this book originally appeared in *ISLE: Interdisciplinary Studies in Literature and Environment* (ISSN #1076–0962), the journal of the Association for the Study of Literature and Environment (www.asle. umn.edu), and are reprinted here by permission of *ISLE* and the individual authors. Specific bibliographic information for each article (listed in the order in which they appear in this book) may be found below.

Fromm, Harold. "Aldo Leopold: Aesthetic 'Anthopocentrist.'" *ISLE* 1.1 (Spring 1993): 43–49.

Yamazato, Katsunori. "Kitkitdizze, Zendo, and Place: Gary Snyder as a Reinhabitory Poet." *ISLE* 1.1 (Spring 1993): 51–63.

Legler, Gretchen. "Toward a Postmodern Pastoral: The Erotic Landscape in the Work of Gretel Ehrlich." *ISLE* 1.2 (Fall 1993): 45–56.

Cantrell, Carol H. "'The Locus of Compossibility': Virginia Woolf, Modernism, and Place." *ISLE* 5.2 (Summer 1998): 25–40.

Furman, Andrew. "No Trees Please, We're Jewish." *ISLE* 7.2 (Summer 2000): 115–36.

Heise, Ursula K. "The Virtual Crowd: Overpopulation, Space, and Speciesism." *ISLE* 8.1 (Winter 2001): 1–29.

Sayre, Gordon M. "If Thomas Jefferson Had Visited Niagara Falls: The Sublime Wilderness Spectacle in America, 1775–1825." *ISLE* 8.2 (Summer 2001): 141–62.

Binns, Niall. "Landscapes of Hope and Destruction: Ecological Poetry in Spanish America." *ISLE* 9.1 (Winter 2002): 105–19.

Lebduska, Lisa. "How Green Was My Advertising: American Ecoconsumerism." *ISLE* 1.1 (Spring 1993): 5–17.

Batra, Nandita. "Dominion, Empathy, and Symbiosis: Gender and Anthropocentrism in Romanticism." *ISLE* 3.2 (Fall 1996): 101–20.

Roorda, Randall. "KB in Green: Ecology, Critical Theory, and Kenneth Burke." *ISLE* 4.2 (Fall 1997): 39–52.

Marshall, Ian. "Tales of the Wonderful Hunt." *ISLE* 6.2 (Summer 1999): 83–97.

Grumbine, R. Edward. "Going to Bashō's Pine: Wilderness Education for the Twenty-first Century." *ISLE* 6.2 (Summer 1999): 121–33.

MacDonald, Scott. "Ten+ (Alternative) Films about American Cities." *ISLE* 8.1 (Winter 2001): 53–72.

Lindholdt, Paul. "Literary Activism and the Bioregional Agenda." *ISLE* 3.2 (Fall 1996): 121–37.

Kern, Robert. "Ecocriticism: What Is It Good For?" *ISLE* 7.1 (Winter 2000): 9–32.

Tallmadge, John. "Toward a Natural History of Reading." *ISLE* 7.1 (Winter 2000): 33–45.

Bennett, Michael. "From Wide Open Spaces to Metropolitan Places: The Urban Challenge to Ecocriticism." *ISLE* 8.1 (Winter 2001): 31–52.

Lousley, Cheryl. "Home on the Prairie? A Feminist and Postcolonial Reading of Sharon Butala, Di Brant, and Joy Kogawa." *ISLE* 8.2 (Summer 2001): 71–95.

Index